Gail

with best wishes

Phiroshaw

Race, Repression and Resistance
A Brief History of
South African Civil Society to 1994

by

Phiroshaw Camay
and
Anne J. Gordon

CORE

Co-operative for Research and Education

Johannesburg

CORE

Published by:
The Co-operative for Research and Education
P.O. Box 42440
Fordsburg
Johannesburg
South Africa 2033

Tel: (27-11) 836-9942
Fax: (27-11) 836-9944
E-mail: corejhb@wn.apc.org

Race, Repression and Resistance: A Brief History of South African Civil Society to 1994

ISBN: 978-0-9802605-2-6

First published: January 2007

Authors: Phiroshaw Camay and Anne J. Gordon
Cover design by: HPGAdvertising

Acknowledgements:

The publication of this book was made possible by the Mott Foundation, Johannesburg, South Africa.

In memory of my mother
Jer Khorshed Camay
1924-2006

Table of Contents

Foreword

The history of civil society in South Africa is documented and analysed in a wide variety of sources, but many of these are either not widely available or each deal only with very specific segments of civil society. Until now, no publication existed that provided an overview of civil society as a whole from pre-colonial times to the advent of democracy in 1994. Furthermore, there has been little attempt to draw upon that past experience to analyse the main factors that have shaped South African civil society.

This history is both rich and diverse, and merits further study. Our effort offers an introduction to the emergence and development of a huge variety of civil society organisations. It is by no means comprehensive. One of our aims is to capture the interest of young historians, social scientists or civil society practitioners / researchers, in the hope that they will decide to pursue further research on one or more of the segments of civil society introduced in this volume. There are many gaps in existing research, and much to learn about the roots of South African civil society. As with the need to better understand the socio-political history of this country, it is essential to better grasp the meanings and influences of civil society as it evolved over the centuries so as to move modern society towards a less divisive and more mutually supportive future.

An earlier version of this study was prepared in 2000 as part of the Johns Hopkins University International Comparative Project on the non-profit sector. The local partner of Johns Hopkins, the Wits University School of Public and Development Management, commissioned the authors to write a contribution on the history of the South African non-profit sector as part of the broader project which also involved a study of the current legislative environment for non-profits and a quantitative study of the size and scope of the non-profit sector at the turn of the 21st century.

CORE's contribution on the history of the non-profit sector was, however, not included in the project publication of 2002 which focused primarily on the present size and scope of the sector. Since that time, CORE has tried to obtain further funding to broaden and deepen our historical study. We are grateful to the Mott Foundation in Johannesburg for providing the grant funds to permit us to do this and to publish it. We are also grateful to the Wits School of Public and Development Management for giving us permission to publish the material taken from our earlier study, but now much improved and augmented.

We sincerely hope that this initial effort will encourage many other researchers to delve further into this fascinating field of study and other grant-makers to support such research.

Phiroshaw Camay and Anne J. Gordon
Co-operative for Research and Education (CORE)
Johannesburg, South Africa

Introduction

The evolution of South African civil society over the centuries since before colonisation provides many insights into what is today a diverse, complex and divided civil society. Civil society at any point in time is inevitably a reflection of the prevailing social, political and economic context. Thus, it changes with time. However, some societal factors are so powerful that they continue to influence the organisational composition and essential nature of civil society over the long term.

In this brief study, the authors have traced the history of a wide range of civil society organisations and sectors with a view to improving our understanding of where we have come from and where we are today. Much has changed in South African civil society since the advent of a non-racial, democratic political system in 1994, but some of the historical factors that are identified here still affect the way that various civil society sectors and organisations interact with each other and with the state. We have probed these relationships in much more depth in our book, *Evolving Democratic Governance in South Africa (2004)*,[1] which studied in-depth the relations between citizens, civil society and government in the first decade of democracy.

For the purposes of our earlier book and this one, we have defined civil society as follows:

> *Those not-for-profit organisations and groups or formations of people operating in the space between family and the government, which are independent, voluntary, and established to protect or enhance the interests and values of their members.*

We take a broad view of civil society, ranging from small community groupings (e.g. burial societies) to non-governmental organisations to large formal associations (trade unions, professional associations, etc.). We include both faith-based and secular groups. We do not include political parties as their aim is essentially to contest elections and become the government.[2] We do, however, include many political organisations which were not permitted by law to contest democratic elections, but which had political aims such as the repeal of apartheid laws, the protection of certain group interests, or fundamental changes to the political system. In this regard, we do not accept the narrow view often taken by researchers and practitioners that "civil society" refers only to those organisations which are characterised by so-called "progressive" values and norms, i.e. those which are committed to political, social and economic equality for all, the eradication of poverty, and so on.[3] In fact, because of South Africa's divisive history, there were not many organisations that had the interests of "all" or the "common good" at heart. Rather they were divided by specific interests related to their race, ethnicity, religion, class and/or political views.

The first four chapters of this historical study are arranged chronologically, beginning in pre-colonial South Africa and ending in the early 1990s before the democratic transition:

- Chapter One looks at the Khoisan and Bantu-speaking indigenous peoples in the pre-colonial period. We provide a brief overview of their culture, traditions and the principles on which their societies were organised. This offers insights into the origins of practices

---

[1] See Camay and Gordon, 2004.
[2] We do mention some political parties by way of contextualising certain events or organisations.
[3] See Introduction to Camay and Gordon, 2004, for more on definitional issues.

such as ubuntu and collective responsibility which continue to play an important role in contemporary African communities.

- Chapter Two covers the period 1652-1910 during which the Europeans occupied and colonised first the Cape and then the rest of South Africa. It shows how the settler groups were divided by nationality, ethnicity, language, religion and class and how these were reflected in the organisations they established. It shows how the introduction and eventual abolition of slavery, the subjugation of the indigenous peoples by the settlers, and the arrival of various missionary groups affected the emergence of a diverse civil society. It also traces the beginnings of local religious organisations, of economic interest groups, and of African, Indian and Coloured organisations in the late 19th and early 20th centuries, including the birth of political resistance in these communities. The persistent divisions within civil society have their roots in this period.

- Chapter Three reviews the period 1910-1948, which began with the formation of the Union of South Africa and led to the consolidation of White rule. This was also a period of proliferation of civil society organisations in each and every South African community. Afrikaner nationalism had an increasing impact on the organisational life of that community, whilst resistance to racially-based oppression led to the establishment of many organisations – both political and other cultural or interest groups -- in the African, Coloured and Indian communities. Trade unions, womens' organisations and youth organisations also emerged as sites of solidarity and struggle. This period saw the entrenchment of racial segregation in all aspects of life.

- Chapter Four covers the period 1948 to 1994, beginning with the imposition of the legal instruments of apartheid and ending with the negotiated political settlement and the advent of democracy. Civil society in this period was hugely divided, by race, class, ethnicity, religion and politics. Its organisational forms and practice were fundamentally determined by the socio-economic and political context of inequality, discrimination and oppression. However, this is also the period during which the diversity and richness of civil society made itself felt through organisations in every aspect of life: family, religion, work, study, politics, and so on.

Each of these chapters begins by giving a brief outline of the political developments of the relevant period, highlighting some of the most significant events and trends, Each chapter then discusses the history of a variety of civil society organisations, arranged by type or sector (e.g. political, religious / faith-based, women, youth, trade unions, professional associations, etc.).

Chapter Five takes a somewhat different approach and reviews the experience of several important "social movements" at various historical moments. These are treated separately as examples of mass mobilisation and grassroots participation in political and economic struggles. The chapter deals with the following movements: rural community movements; Inkatha; the Black Consciousness Movement; civic associations; and associations in informal settlements. These movements tended to rely on the support of existing (or sometimes new) affiliated organisations, formed into networks, alliances, fronts, associations or committees. Some of the movements were formalised into umbrella organisations with democratic decision-making structures, whilst others were not. Some have evolved into political parties.

Overall, it is essential to note that several caveats apply to the entire study. Firstly, we make no claim to have treated all types or sectors of organisations comprehensively. Rather, we have tried to offer an introduction to a wide variety of groupings, providing brief introductions to different times and places and peoples and how they responded to their specific situations through their civil society organisations. We have certainly left out many types and sectors – without prejudice. We simply did not have enough time or resources to cover everything. Secondly, we have not given equal attention to each type or sector, in each period or in the study as a whole. We have not tried to attach a particular level of importance to them. Without doubt, some of our choices have been subjective. Others have depended on available literature and sources. Thirdly, this study inevitably includes a quantity of factual information. Analysis is largely limited to the concluding remarks in each chapter and to the Conclusion. Fourthly, in order to more vividly communicate the realities of some events or processes, we have in some instances told brief stories of people or organisations, or included quotes from those directly involved. We hope this will help to capture the imagination of the reader.

The Conclusion presents a brief summary of what we found to be the most important analytical themes reflected in the history of South African civil society. Pre-eminent amongst these is the theme of race – the discrimination, division, oppression which all occurred on the basis of race, and the resistance spawned amongst the Black communities as a result. The other themes include: class, the anti-apartheid struggle, colonialism and euro-centrism, and survival and solidarity in coping with poverty. Certainly these themes present ongoing challenges to the transformation of South African society and polity in the democratic dispensation. Though these divisions made it impossible for different communities to coexist and resulted in lasting damage to society as a whole and especially to those most subject to racial discrimination, it must also be said that the diversity of cultures and traditions reflected in organisational life have ultimately – in the new South Africa – enriched our society. This is especially so as the freedoms of expression, assembly and association in our democracy have permitted civil society organisations to flourish.

Chapter One

Indigenous Socio-cultural Roots of Civil Society

The conventional view of Africa even today is that the indigenous people have little to offer the Northern or Western world. Yet even a brief reading of the history, culture and traditions of the peoples of Africa will show an amazing and deep-rooted understanding of human behaviour and an even clearer perception of justice and fairness. Many of the essential characteristics of modern South African civil society have their roots in these indigenous societies.

This chapter reviews some of the basic principles on which these indigenous societies were organised, beginning with the Khoisan peoples and then dealing broadly with the Bantu-speaking peoples.

The Khoisan Peoples:
Indigenous Hunter-gatherer and Pastoralist Societies

The oldest of South Africa's peoples are the San hunter-gatherers. They were organised into small communities or bands, made up of not more than a few hundred members. Each band moved about within a large but defined area. In order to migrate onto the area of another band, they needed formal agreement. This type of social organisation stemmed from their primary need to adapt to their inhospitable natural environment.[4] Survival was their main concern.

Within the bands, principles of egalitarianism and sharing were stressed.[5] There was "little scope for specialisation" in terms of daily tasks, and a very limited sense of personal ownership. Instead, sharing of scarce resources was a crucial element of their social relations. They had no formal system of law and order, and had "leaders" rather than "rulers".[6] Internally, the bands were generally characterised by cordial relations.

"In relations with other bands, the band members seem to accept collective responsibility for the actions of all the members. But generally speaking, since bands keep within their own hunting territory and do not wander into the territory of other bands for trading, the members of one band will not normally have first-hand knowledge of members of other bands".[7] Thus, the bands were quite isolated and conscious of boundaries.

The San governed themselves in a simple but democratic manner: sometimes taking decisions by consensus amongst the adult men and sometimes by a leader recognised as chief in consultation and agreement with the others. The chief's authority was therefore highly circumscribed. Customs and traditions were the source of group cohesion. Infringements were dealt with through discussions amongst members of the band, and in the

---

[4] Stephen, 1982, p. 5.
[5] Kiernan, 1995, p. 16.
[6] Stephen, 1982, p. 5.
[7] Ibid., p. 7.

worst cases, guilty members might be ostracised by or expelled from the band. But, usually, the collective will prevailed and reconciliation was preferred to confrontation.[8]

Much of what is known about early San culture has been gleaned from present day surviving rock paintings -- evidence of a highly artistic culture linked to documentation of their daily lives. Myths and legends also constituted a means of maintaining and passing their culture from generation to generation. The San were "extremely attached to their way of life. The hunting band was a small, face-to-face community which produced strong feelings of loyalty and belonging".[9] Even today they value their sense of freedom and have little need or desire for material things.

The San did, however, interact with other peoples through trading, especially ivory and livestock. They also sometimes reached longer-term political arrangements with other peoples, e.g. becoming client communities of Bantu-speaking chiefdoms. "This meant that in return for tribute and other services, they would then enjoy protection and ... opportunities to barter for metallic and agricultural products."[10] Feinstein argues that the "San were no match for those with whom they shared the continent, and had been marginalised by the Khoi and by African farmers long before the appearance of the Europeans. They survived in remote mountain areas and semi-deserts, but as Europeans expanded their movement into the interior of the western Cape in search of pasture, they took over San hunting grounds, and there was a brutal and one-sided struggle in which large numbers of San people were viciously exterminated... Others were captured in raids, or kidnapped and indentured to farmers for the rest of their lives".[11] Such contact eventually led to most San becoming absorbed into other cultures, though a few small groups still survive today and continue to practice their traditional way of life.

Like the San, the Khoi engaged in hunting and gathering, but the Khoi enjoyed a somewhat higher standard of living. "Evidence from archaeological excavations indicates that in the beginning the only animals they kept were fat-tailed, wool-less sheep, but they later built up big herds of long-horned cattle, possibly obtained initially from contact with Africans in the eastern Cape, from whom they also acquired goats. The cattle needed large amounts of grazing land, and since the western Cape is not rich in grasslands the herders were forced to move seasonally within parts of the region to obtain sufficient grazing. Each of the constituent Khoi communities had land which it used, but their boundaries were not rigidly defined."[12]

The Khoi did not develop arable farming because their land was unsuitable for the indigenous grains (millet and sorghum). However, they did engage in other economic activities such as smelting iron and copper, wood-carving, basket-weaving and making clothing out of hides.[13]

The Khoi organised themselves into chiefdoms of roughly one or two thousand people. Each chiefdom usually consisted of several clans which recognised a senior clan, from which the chief was chosen. The chief ruled in consultation with the heads of each clan. The clans were based on descent from a common ancestor. As the chief had no power to enforce decisions, their implementation depended on strength of personality and loyalty. Membership of Khoi communities was fairly flexible -- sometimes clans would break away or

---

[8] Stephen, 1982, p. 7.
[9] Omer-Cooper, 1988, p. 4
[10] Ibid., p. 5
[11] Feinstein, 2005, p. 14. See also Dowson, in Hamilton, 1995, p. 63, who notes that San (or Bushmen), especially women and children, were taken by Europeans as slaves.
[12] Feinstein, 2005, p. 14.
[13] Ibid., p. 15.

communities would absorb San or Bantu-speaking groups.[14] The Khoi religion, unlike the San, made "separate provision for the individual and his or her circumstances and for the communal circumstances of a large-scale tribal unit".[15]

"There were no individual or family titles to land, but stock was owned by individual households, not communally, and there was considerable differentiation, with wealthy chiefs and headmen owning large herds while many others had no stock. The men of such poor households might, however, be engaged to care for part of the herd of wealthy stock-owners, and be rewarded for their labour by being allowed to take the milk."[16]

Virtually as soon as the settlers arrived, the Khoi were drawn into disputes over land and water. Jan van Riebeeck wrote in his diaries that the Khoi ironically asked whether, if they went to Holland, they would be allowed to take land from the Dutch in such a fashion? He said the Khoi "remained adamant in their claim of old-established natural ownership". The Dutch countered with the claim that they had won the land "justly... by the sword" and were therefore entitled to keep it! Despite their attempts at resistance, the Khoi quickly lost their land, livestock and independence to the "arrogant" and "aggressive" Europeans.[17]

Omer-Cooper argued that as their contact with Whites increased, the Khoi became more interested in other material goods. "They could thus be persuaded much more easily than the San to enter the services of white masters and alter their way of life for material rewards."[18] However, Feinstein wrote that Khoi engagement with Whites was largely a function of compulsion, not choice. When the slave trade was abolished after 1808, the Khoi "became an important source of labour for Cape farmers". However, they were treated little better than slaves, being paid only in food and clothing.[19] Over time, this situation of economic exploitation by Whites changed little.

By the end of the 18th century, "there were perhaps 10,000 white colonists, while the Khoisan population had declined from about 200,000 to around 50,000".[20] The Khoisan were basically caught between the white and Bantu population in a vicious circle. Their herds were depleted by the white colonialists, and the Khoisan were forced to resort to cattle-stealing from both Whites and Bantu in order to satisfy their own food and other essential needs.

The Bantu-speaking Peoples

The Bantu-speaking peoples comprised four main groups in what is now South Africa: Nguni, Sotho, Venda and Tsonga. They lived in communities which varied in size, partly depending on their access to water and other natural resources. For example, where water was plentiful and accessible throughout an area, communities were smaller; where it was found mainly in rivers, larger settlements emerged. Thus, the socio-political units also varied in nature from region to region. These peoples had a more settled life than the Khoisan. They practiced a mixed economy of both agriculture and cattle-keeping, and lived in more substantial dwellings.

---

[14] Omer-Cooper, 1988, p. 7.
[15] Kiernan, 1995, p. 18.
[16] Feinstein, 2005, p. 15.
[17] Van Riebeeck quoted in Ibid., pp. 15-16.
[18] Omer-Cooper, 1988, p. 7.
[19] Feinstein, 2005, pp. 51-52.
[20] Stephen, 1982, p. 5.

The Nguni and the Sotho were the largest groups. Hammond-Tooke argued that in terms of their main cultural characteristics, the Tsonga were similar to the Nguni and the Venda similar to the Sotho. He wrote that all the Bantu were, in fact, "innovative social engineers", adapting to their environments in very specific ways.[21]

The Bantu societies were patrilineal. Only the Lovedu – of the rain-making queens – consistently chose women leaders. In the Zulu culture, for example, the basic unit of social organisation was "the *kraal*, a patriarchal and polygamous colony consisting of a man, his wives, their children, and perhaps, a network of dependent relatives, along with their livestock... Similar homesteads of people from the same lineage would be found some distance up the valley, or on the other side of the river, and an informal hierarchy of clan heads, the *abanunzana*, would regulate matters affecting all members of the lineage, such as grazing rights. These elders were also the living representatives of the ancestors, and as such, high priests who would intercede with the spirit world to ward off disaster and celebrate the new harvest".[22]

The socio-economic significance of cattle

Cattle were the primary form of capital accumulation and social and economic value. Cattle were cared for by men, whereas the agricultural work was done by women. Marriage required the transfer of cattle in exchange for a woman -- known as *lobola*. Cattle figured prominently in how homesteads were laid out, in ritual sacrifices, and traditional stories and proverbs.[23] Cattle "were the focus of the entire social order... They were a source of conflict and the means of peacemaking". [24]

A widespread form of contract was *ukusisa* – this involved a wealthy person allowing some of his cattle to be kept by another. Similar to the Khoi system, the client could benefit from the milk but not slaughter or sell the cattle. Another important form of contract was the payment of a maintenance fee of cattle for looking after non-related children or paying a herbalist for doctoring during an illness. The possession of cattle also led to systems of clientelism -- poorer men would borrow cattle in return for loyalty, thus building up political communities or chiefdoms, beyond patrilineal clans.

Socialisation

The process of socialising the young was simple. Sons were appreciated to continue the descent group, to look after a parent in their old age, and to sacrifice to one's spirit after death. Boys also herded cattle and when older helped in the fields. Girls were special as they acted as nursemaids for the younger children but also added to the cattle herd of the family upon their marriage, through the practice of *ilobola*.

Social segregation between boys and girls occurred after the age of six. Boys were sent off to herd cattle often in far away areas. Fighting between boys of different groups fostered courage but also leadership and management of younger boys. The special rituals of puberty, e.g. initiation, also prepared both boys and girls for their future roles in society and led to a bond which often lasted a lifetime.

Worship of ancestors was another aspect of social life that brought people together in 'congregations'. This worship was generally led by an informal 'priest' (e.g. not officially

---

[21] Hammond-Tooke, 1993, p. 41.
[22] Taylor, 1995, p. 29.
[23] Omer Cooper, 1988, p. 11.
[24] Taylor, 1995, p. 30. See also Feinstein, 2005, p. 18.

consecrated as in other formal faiths) as a crucial part of the Southern Bantu religious life.[25] It was also an important element of socialisation which has retained its importance in the context of some of the African independent churches.

Kinship and neighbourliness

The concept of kinship relationships through both descent and marriage was a central force. For social purposes, kinship was linked to the paternal side. Several families living side-by-side acknowledging a common elder constituted a family group. Whilst kin lived close to one another, there was always close contact with neighbours. Neighbourliness was a much-lauded quality. In some circumstances, neighbours were even more important than kin, especially in emergencies.

In agriculture, neighbours assisted each other with the hoeing, weeding and reaping. Work parties were often organised and strengthened when additional help was needed. The reward was in the form of a feast or beer drink. Neighbourliness existed because it was the moral thing to do. This morality was guided by the anticipation of reciprocal assistance when required. However, the neighbourliness also had negative effects, giving rise to rivalries or envy of another's good fortune.

Ubuntu

> Ubuntu is goodness or humanity. It is a term used to express the qualities underlying the values and virtues of essential humanity and compassion.

The crucial concept of ubuntu is rooted in African tradition and has formed the basis for these communities' approach to community welfare as well as to voluntarism: "Ubuntu is a way of life that positively contributes to the sustenance of the well-being of a people/community/society. Ubuntu is a process that promotes the common good of a people/society."[26] It is a concept that is put into practice in various ways, through community self-help activities and sharing amongst the members of a community.

In Bantu societies, "man saw himself not as an individual but an element of a communal whole, a concept which embraced not just his society but the environment upon which he depended. An individual's interests were submerged in those of the community and the fate of both was in the hands of ancestral spirits... The broad effect of this creed was to make individual conduct selfless".[27]

The concept of ubuntu is reflected in the Bantu view of morality, e.g. what constituted a 'good' person. This included respect for seniors, loyalty to one's kinship group and to one's chief, being a good neighbour, being generous, observance of custom, avoidance of witchcraft and sorcery.[28]

"Common characteristics of ubuntu include 'awareness' of what is just and unjust; what is humane and inhumane; an awareness of the distinction between kindness and cruelty; between harmony and disharmony; appreciation of peace over war; love over violence and hatred; appreciation of life over death. Ubuntu therefore detests inhuman behaviour."[29] "The greatest strength of ubuntu is that it is indigenous, a purely African philosophy of life."[30]

---

[25] See Hammond-Tooke, 1993, pp. 149-158.
[26] Sindane, n.d., p. 9.
[27] Taylor, 1995, pp. 32-33.
[28] Hammond-Tooke, 1993, p. 99.
[29] Prof. Herbert Vilakazi, cited in Sindane, p. 12.
[30] Dr. Oscar Dhlomo quoted in Sindane, p. 10.

Ubuntu reflects what Jung later referred to as a "universality of the human spirit" or a "wholeness".[31] It is often cited today as a philosophy which, if adopted more generally in South African communities, would help to heal the divisions of the past and promote nation-building.

The rulers and the ruled

The homestead and the chieftainship were the "two essential pillars on which [Bantu] society was built".[32] However, homesteads could not be entirely self-sufficient. It was therefore aspects of life such as marriage, the need for labour-intensive tasks in the agricultural cycle, and the need for defence against attacks that brought the homesteads together in units led by various forms of "headmen". These social / political groupings each also had their own *kgotla* or group convened to discuss issues of mutual concern.

The Southern Bantu have had chiefs since around 800 AD. Chieftainship brought with it a differentiation between "royalty" and "commoners" – a new type of inequality and authority.[33] It also was strongly linked to territory, rather than being based on kin. The main difference in governance amongst the Bantu was that the Nguni/Tsonga in the east had a decentralised system of economic and political control, whilst the Sotho/Venda in the west operated a much more centralised chiefdom,[34] with concomitant advantages and disadvantages which manifested themselves in the colonial period.

The adoption of agriculture posed new issues for the Bantu societies. The new lifestyle posed issues of land distribution, division of labour between men and women, ownership of crops, inheritance and trespass and damage.[35] This required the creation of political authorities to take charge of these matters.

Different forms of government by chieftains prevailed amongst the Southern Bantu for 1500 years, based on a hierarchy of royals (chiefs and sub-chiefs) and *indunas* (officers chosen from commoner families and employed in various administrative functions). Government of chieftains had two main problems: (1) "the maintenance of the integrity of the state, and (2) the administration of areas lying outside the capital". It also had two main tasks: (1) "the making of decisions relating to public life, and (2) the settlement of disputes between its subjects".[36] "The chief regulated all use of the resources available to his people".[37]

An old Nguni proverb clearly reflects this dynamic: in Tswana, it says *Kgosi ke kgosi ka batho* [A chief is a chief because of the people]; in Zulu and Xhosa, it says *Inkosi yinkosi ngabantu* [A chief is not a chief without the people].

Despite their considerable powers, the authority of chiefs was not absolute. Chiefs could be selected from any close members of the royal family. This meant that a chief had to build consensus amongst the most powerful members of the community in order to maintain his authority. Amongst all the subjects there existed a clear understanding of acceptable and agreeable behaviours, as well as standards of fairness and justice. This was also

---

[31] Taylor, 1995, p. 33.
[32] Hammond-Tooke, 1993, p. 55.
[33] Aside from this distinction, however, Hammond-Tooke argues convincingly that "in the Marxist sense of an exploitative category of the population" classes were not discernible in the Bantu societies. 1993, p. 68.
[34] Hammond-Tooke, 1993, p. 50.
[35] Ibid., p. 51.
[36] Ibid., p. 66.
[37] Feinstein, 2005, p. 18.

underpinned by how a reasonable chief should behave. The ultimate sanction was rebellion or splitting off. The chief governed in association with a council of advisors and on important issues called meetings of all the subjects to discuss matters of interest to their chiefdom as a whole. The advisors were an informal body consisting of individuals who had won the trust of the chief and whom he consulted sometimes privately on matters of importance.[38]

The council was the main arm of government, except for the Sotho, and its decisions were binding. Amongst the Sotho (especially Tswana), however, all important "matters of public interest" were put to the *pitso* (an assembly which all adult men were expected to attend).[39] This is not to say that an idyllic democracy existed. Leadership varied in style from consultative and cautious to authoritarian and autocratic. Weak leaders generally did not stay in power for long, and were often challenged from within their clans. Many were killed by their opponents.

Whilst administration was widely in the hands of men, some Venda and Sotho-speaking groups also accorded women important roles. This was also common among the Swazi, the dominating figure usually being the Queen Mother -- the she-elephant (*Indlovukati*) to her son's lion (*Ingwanyama*). The Lovedu under the mysterious Rain Queen Modjadji have also fascinated many researchers and commentators.[40]

To translate decisions into actions, a hierarchy of *indunas*, chiefs, headmen and sub-headmen administered smaller areas as the chief's local representatives. Each had a court where local cases were heard with the right to appeal to the next layer of leadership.

Due to systems of tribute from commoners to the royals, chiefs and other royals were able to accumulate greater wealth. This allowed them to reinforce their power by marrying more wives and developing personal loyalties through the dispensation of patronage. Thus, economic and political power were – as always -- closely linked, leading to distinctions both within and between clans.

Certain economic circumstances led to the changing nature of chiefdoms. As population grew in certain areas and the grazing land became inadequate for the cattle, some clans -- after consultation and debate -- moved to new areas. Such movement increased with the encroachment of colonial settlers onto the land. In contrast, increased trade amongst communities as well as the forcible conquering of other chiefdoms led to the evolution of kingdoms. The Zulu kingdom under Shaka, the South Sotho kingdom, the Pedi confederacy and the Xhosa state were recorded in the 18th and 19th centuries.

Settlement of disputes

The settlement of disputes occurred through an understanding of clear distinctions between customs and laws. Custom referred to "a reservoir of rules and expectations that were *potentially* available for a court to apply". A custom became a law when it was used by a court in a particular case, and as such created a precedent which could be used in similar future cases. The task of the small panel of court advisors was to recall those precedents so as to "supply continuity of experience".[41] The formal handling of disputes occurred through the hierarchy of chiefs described previously.

---

[38] See Hammond-Tooke, 1993, p. 71, for more detail.
[39] Ibid., p. 73.
[40] Ibid., pp. 75-76.
[41] Ibid., p. 91.

Less formal disputes were handled first though a family court which essentially tried to resolve disputes through mediation. Only if this approach failed could cases be taken to the formal court.

Whilst the process of bringing a grievance to a hearing was simple, the process of judgement was sophisticated: "impassioned rhetoric and penetrating forensic questioning" were often used and responses sought.[42] Measures of "reasonableness" as noted above were sought. Eye-witness accounts were interrogated and other evidence formed the basis of the final decision. The aim was for the court's decision to reflect the views of the majority rather than the individual chief.

A distinction was also made between civil law and criminal law as it is understood in modern 'Western' terms. "Civil law concerned the private rights of people in regard to personal status, property and contracts, while criminal law defined various actions as offences against the society as a whole".[43] The principal remedies open to the victim of a civil hearing were restitution and compensation. The main offences under criminal law were "homicide, grievous assault, rape, crimes against the chiefdom's authority, and witchcraft/sorcery". "Incest was so heinous a crime that its punishment was either immediate death or to be left to the supernatural sanction of the wrath of ancestors". Often compensation to the victim's family in the case of murder was part of the sentence so that the victim's family would acquire a source of future capital.[44]

Disputes between the various Bantu peoples were often settled through violence. Probably the best known example is that of Shaka, the Zulu ruler who came to power in 1810. Soon thereafter, he began expanding his lands by defeating neighbouring tribes. His rule was despotic and characterised by the murder of many opponents. Successive Zulu leaders were murdered by their own tribesmen due to internal struggles.[45] In the mid-1820s, the Ndebele embarked upon "a period of state building" based partly on raiding of other local communities. "The Ndebele absorbed members of the conquered communities and their herds. They adopted many Zulu institutions, including the isolating of young men into regiments and the centralisation of cattle holdings under the king."[46] Though some of these communities were semi-autonomous and socially separate from the Ndebele, "they often accepted Ndebele representatives in their towns, the Ndebele supervising the political activities of the residents and local trade".[47] This ongoing process of territorial expansion and state-building resulted in "seemingly continuous low-intensity warfare".[48] Communities faced with a lack of economic resources due to this violence and displacement also suffered from social disintegration. However, they tried to re-establish their communities, traditions and hierarchies as quickly as possible.[49] Kinsman concluded that this process "unleashed a deep, slow and multi-directional social transformation which over the course of the nineteenth century would break existing social formations apart. The new emergent social groups – the peasant producers, the share-croppers, the migrant workers – would tie the African communities to the European-dominated capitalist structures surrounding them".[50]

As evidenced in other colonial situations, the Dutch and British settlers used various African tribes to attain their own expansionist objectives, often through a divide and rule approach

---

[42] Ibid., p. 93.
[43] Ibid., p. 94.
[44] Ibid., p. 97.
[45] Molema, 1920, pp. 80-82.
[46] Kinsman, 1995, p. 380.
[47] Ibid., p. 381.
[48] Ibid., p. 391.
[49] Ibid., p. 392.
[50] Ibid., p. 393.

(e.g. pitting two groups of Barolong against each other). The Xhosa led a series of campaigns extending over 100 years -- from the 1770s to the 1870s -- primarily over boundaries such as that of the Cape Colony at Fish River. In the 1870s and 1880s, the Zulu were caught between the Afrikaner trekkers and British annexation of land. Co-operation amongst the tribes, for example the Xhosa, Zulu or Sotho, was "rendered impossible by inter-tribal jealousies",[51] traditional antagonisms and territorial imperatives.

Concluding Remarks

Such a brief discussion cannot adequately communicate the profound impact of indigenous peoples' values and experience on the evolution of South African civil society. In this chapter, the following points have been highlighted:

- The emphasis amongst the Khoisan people on egalitarianism, sharing and collective responsibility;
- The use of customs and traditions to preserve group cohesion, both amongst the Khoisan and the Bantu people;
- The meaningful processes of socialisation of young people used to integrate them fully into society;
- The fundamental value of *ubuntu* amongst the Bantu peoples expressed through concepts and practice of neighbourliness, generosity, justice and harmony;
- The social stratification (e.g. between royalty and commoner) which allocated certain authority to chiefs and other leaders, but also provided mechanisms for accountability and settlement of disputes, thus circumscribing the authority of some over the others.

.

---

[51] Molema, 1920, p. 107.

Chapter Two

European Occupations and Colonisation, 1652-1910

The arrival of European colonialists changed the lives of the indigenous peoples forever. They brought quite specific ideas about what constituted "a civilised way of life", about acceptable cultural and religious beliefs and practice, and about the merits of a market economy, With very few exceptions, they had little interest in or respect for the established way of life of the indigenous people already living in South Africa.

The settler groups each came with their own seeds of division in society, grounded in their nationalities, languages, religions, and occupations. These too were to be reflected in the organisations they established and in the manner in which they interacted with each other.

This chapter deals first with the era when the Dutch East India Company ruled the Cape. During this period, the first White settlers arrived, slavery was introduced, indigenous peoples were subjugated by the settlers, and freedom of worship was severely limited. When the British took over as the colonial power in 1806, Christian missionaries of various denominations rapidly increased their presence in the Cape, beginning the battle for converts amongst the indigenous peoples as well as immigrants. The abolition of slavery, increasing immigration, the introduction of a free press, and the advent of religious freedom encouraged an increasing diversity in emerging civil society. Religious organisations and their offshoots proliferated, as did organisations linked to racial and ethnic groupings. This era also saw the beginnings of organisations created to promote particular economic interests.

The Era of the Dutch East India Company, 1652-1795

Initial settlements

The need for a way station on the route to the Far East led to the Portuguese arrival in the Cape in the late 15th century and its occupation by the Dutch East India Company ("the Company") one and a half centuries later in 1652. The occupation had only one purpose: to promote more effectively the profitability of trade between the colonial power and its commercial empire in the East Indies. This was clearly communicated in the instructions given to Jan van Riebeeck. By 1662, the Company had granted rights to a total of 130 men, women and children to reside in the Cape as free burghers with the intention that they would supply crops to the Company.

Initially, the white population of the Cape comprised mainly German and Dutch settlers who all used the Dutch language. The Dutch Reformed Church (DRC) was the established church in the colony. In 1688, 164 French and Belgian Huguenots (Calvinist Protestants) arrived. They had taken refuge in Holland from religious persecution in their home countries, and were sent by the Dutch to settle in the Cape. Their viticultural skills led to the establishment of the Cape wine industry. The Huguenots were absorbed into the community, joining the Dutch Reformed Church and were encouraged to speak Dutch.[52] The German Lutherans made more of an effort to retain their religious identity, but were only permitted to build their first church in 1779.

Simon van der Stel, the commander of the Cape, established systems of local government, including councillors, magistrates and a militia. The *veldkornet* – the officer responsible for local political and military organisation -- was often elected from amongst a group of local farmers, and was mandated to ensure that official policy was carried out in their area. This neighbourhood group became the centre of white settler political and judicial life.[53]

Whilst assisted immigration ended, the natural growth of the permanent settler community led to an increasing sense of community identity separate from that of the Company. This identity became known as the *Afrikaner,* which came to be applied to all White South Africans who were native speakers of Afrikaans, a language that evolved from Dutch. Also, a struggle between the Company and the free burghers emerged regarding contested economic rights to farming, the selling of produce in a restricted market, and access to labour. Though some Company servants continued to be provided as labour on the land, this was inadequate to meet the needs of growing agricultural production.

Slavery and the subjugation of indigenous peoples

Slaves were first introduced to the Cape in 1658. They came from the Dutch East Indies and later East Africa, and also included some royalty and political figures from Indonesia who were brought as state prisoners or hostages.[54] They formed the beginnings of the Cape Malay community. From the early 1700s, slaves constituted more than half of the Cape's population. This balance between Europeans and slaves remained fairly constant until 1797, even as the population of the Cape expanded considerably.

The following table dynamically reflects the growth and relative size of the European and slave populations in the Cape in the 18th century:

Year	Europeans	Slaves
1701	1,334	891
1713	1,699	1,794
1723	2,364	2,922
1743	4,096	5,361
1763	6,877	7,215
1783	11,064	11,950
1797	21,746	25,754

Source: van der Ross, 1979, p. 44.

The slaves were required to work on the expanding farmlands and in farm-related enterprises. Many of them were also skilled artisans. The table above clearly illustrates the inevitable dependence of European settlers on their access to slave labour. A key impact of the slave trade was the eventual economic exploitation of all non-White peoples, initially in the Cape and then in all other parts of the country. This, in turn, led to class distinctions closely corresponding to racial distinctions.

Colonisation and slavery also brought Islam to South Africa, beginning in the mid-1600s. Most of the Muslims brought to the Cape were either slaves or political exiles brought

---

[52] Omer-Cooper, 1988, pp. 19-20.
[53] Ibid., p. 20.
[54] Ibid., p. 22.

against their will. "Here they were stripped of their names as part of the dehumanising process of subjugation at the hands of their masters and denied the privilege of freedom of worship".[55]

In the late 17th and in the 18th centuries, Cape Town grew as a result of the expanded agricultural activity and trade links with Europe. It became the economic and cultural base of the White colony. However, business opportunities there were insufficient to provide employment for the increasing White population. Burghers began to move further into the interior and settle as cattle farmers. It was at this time that many Khoi were deprived of their land and cattle, and were absorbed as farm workers, herders, and servants, providing even cheaper labour than slaves.

In some areas, however, the settlers encountered resistance from Khoi and San peoples, though it was limited by their sparse population. Once the Khoi realised that the Whites wanted to push them off their land, they began to fight back, using guerrilla tactics. However, their division into chiefdoms meant that they did not act in concert with each other, and they were gradually weakened and their numbers depleted through fighting and smallpox epidemics. Though the San did not trade with the settlers, they too resisted occupation of their lands, were repeatedly attacked by burgher commandos (sometimes including Khoi servants armed by the settlers), and some were taken prisoner and forced to work in servitude. Nonetheless, some Khoi resistance did force the settlers to leave land they had already occupied.

Despite racist attitudes on the part even of the Company's servants, the fact that there were many fewer white women than men meant that sexual contact and marriage between races was commonplace. "Three quarters of the children born to slave women at the Cape up to 1671 were of mixed descent."[56] As the balance of the sexes amongst the white community equalised, and the belief in the inferiority of darker skinned people was perpetuated through religion and the justice sytem, racial discrimination and the denial of rights to people of mixed race became the norm. By the end of the 18th century, mixed marriages declined to 10% of White marriages and children of mixed marriages were excluded from white society. The Khoi who had adopted European culture also found their rights restricted.

The situation was rather different in the interior. In some cases the relationship between the farmer and his workers was that of employer and employees, whereas in others it was similar to that of a chief and his followers. In the most isolated areas, the farmers depended on co-operation with the indigenous people and their leaders.

The expansion of the eastern farming frontier deeper into the interior and the continuous search for more land and cattle led to contact and conflict between the White settlers and the Xhosa people. Despite their different socio-economic systems, their interaction with each other was shaped by the need to fulfil their respective societal status symbols. For the settlers, this meant expansion onto more land and employment of more African workers. For the Xhosa, this meant expansion to accommodate their growing numbers and more cattle to assure their social status. Thus competition for land was a crucial element of their relationship.

The decline of Company rule

In 1778, the burgher community in the Cape demanded greater representation in the structures of government and more open trading conditions. In April 1782, the burghers

---

[55] Davids, 1985, p. 33.
[56] Omer-Cooper, 1988, p. 30.

recommended a complete division of powers between the legislative and judicial bodies. Instability and lack of effective administration, as well as the settlers' desire to solidify their control over the Xhosa and Khoi in that area, led in 1795 to the Graaff-Reinet Rebellion and the Swellendam Rebellion by frontiersmen. The Company was unable to suppress these rebellions. In the same year, the British occupied the Cape to protect the sea route to the East.

The Era of British Colonialism, 1806-1910

Between 1795 and 1802, Britain's first occupation of the Cape was met with considerable resistance from various sources. Then for a brief period between 1803 and 1806, the Cape was handed to the Batavian Republic in Holland under the terms of the Treaty of Amiens. When the Treaty broke down, the British returned in force and again took over colonial rule of the Cape in 1806.

The occupation of the Cape by the British set the stage for the first interaction by British non-profit organisations in the South African context, interweaving South African political life inextricably with the developments in Britain and elsewhere in the world for centuries to come. This included the arrival of missionary organisations, as well as humanitarian groups such as the London Missionary Society and the Anti-Slavery Society aiming to abolish slavery.

Economic change under the British occupation favoured the new British merchant class which settled in the Cape to the detriment of their European counterparts. Whilst private business flourished, the inherited traditional loan farm system of extensive leaseholds severely disadvantaged the economy of the colony. Both urban and rural settlers continued to exploit indigenous Black labour.

In 1819, to escape the increasing unemployment situation in Britain after the Napoleonic Wars, the British Parliament voted 50,000 pounds sterling to transport families and individuals for an emigration scheme to the Cape. The 5,000 settlers arrived in 1820 and were placed by Lord Charles Somerset on small farms in the area of what is now Port Elizabeth as a buffer between the Xhosa and the Cape Colony. But rather than acting as a barrier to the contact between black and white, the settlers became the chief agents for opening up the hinterland and began a two-way traffic in people and commodities as well as ideas.

The increasing British economic and cultural control and the passage of colonial edicts in the Cape led the Afrikaners to feel that their separate identity and way of life was more and more threatened. The period from 1830 to 1910 was marked by tensions and conflict between the British and the Boers resulting in the Great Trek in which large numbers of Boers left the Cape and moved inland, the establishment of the Boer Republics in Natal, Free State and the Transvaal, and the Anglo-Boer Wars. Over this period, there were also numerous African rebellions and rural struggles, often unorganised or spontaneous, but all indicating a resistance to White racial hegemony and tyranny, whatever its origins -- British or Boer. It was therefore a period of considerable change and upheaval in the country.

The Trekboers were individuals or groups who left the Cape Colony as economic migrants, trekking into the hinterland in search of commercial or farming opportunities. The Voortrekkers were aggrieved collectivities of mainly Dutch descendants who left the Cape Colony to escape the British government and control for political reasons. These reasons were articulated in Piet Retief's *Manifesto* published in 1836. They wished to settle and govern themselves in a territory they could identify as their own.

This was also a period in which new waves of immigration brought a remarkable influx of religious, cultural and social influences which came to be reflected in all aspects of social and political life, notably civil society. A growing agricultural sector, the discovery of diamonds (1868) and gold (1886), and increasing industrialisation led to massive influxes of foreigners and a growing diversity in South African society.

Early Jewish settlers arrived from Holland as early as 1660 and later from England and Germany. Then, following the discovery of diamonds and gold, from the 1860s onwards, there was an increasing flow of East European Jews who were emigrating from their countries due to religious persecution. These Jews themselves were divided by different cultures and by class -- some were poor, and some very rich.[57] In the last decade of the 19th century, the "poor white problem" caused a backlash against the Jews, and anti-Semitic propaganda depicted them as a threat. The Jews were subjected to more discriminatory legislation than any other white group. However, over time, many Jews became acculturated into the English-speaking white group and highly urbanised.[58]

In 1860, 152,000 Indians were brought to South Africa as indentured labourers to work in the Natal sugar industry. These immigrants included three major religious groups: Hindus, Muslims and Christians. Towards the end of the 19th century, a small group of Parsees also arrived, but they came into South Africa as fare-paying migrants rather than as indentured workers. They and other paying passengers formed the commercial bourgeoisie among the Indian community in Natal, the Transvaal and the Cape. Both the Jews and the Asian immigrants were targets of the Immigration Restriction Act passed in 1902 in the Cape Colony.

Many of the Indians who came to South Africa in the 19th century came from very harsh living conditions in India resulting from economic depression, poor harvests and declining agricultural prices. A series of famines worsened these conditions and many were forced off their land. Their decision to immigrate to South Africa thus had more to do with push factors than pull factors. Ironically, however, some of them found life in South Africa even harder to bear. They came to do work that the settler population was not prepared to do. They were forced to live in poor conditions, were paid irregularly, had little or no access to medical care, education or welfare, received smaller rations than they had been promised, and in general, were badly treated. In 1871, the first migrants left to return to India when their contracts were completed. Whilst the numbers of returnees were not large, their decision demonstrates the level of exploitation to which they were subjected as indentured labourers.[59] The indentured labour system was ended after 1911.

The Indian immigrants were members of all castes and were used to living in a highly stratified society. Their Natal bosses, however, were oblivious to the caste origins of their new labourers, and treated them all with equal disdain.

In the late 19th and early 20th centuries, discrimination against people of colour became increasingly entrenched in the law. The Franchise and Ballot Bill of 1892 increased the income qualification for the vote and introduced an educational qualification which effectively eliminated the growing number of African peasant farmers who had previously qualified to vote. The Glen Grey Act of 1894 further restricted African access and introduced African representation on local councils with purely local powers. In 1903, steps were taken to prevent Africans from buying land and a poll tax was introduced.

---

[57] Hellig, 1995, p. 163.
[58] Ibid., p. 156. The "poor white problem" refers to the increasing unemployment amongst Afrikaner and English settlers, due not least to the employment of low-wage Black (African, Indian and Coloured) labour in unskilled occupations.
[59] See Brain, 1983.

Missionaries

The early efforts of Christian missionaries in the Cape to convert slaves and Khoi conflicted with the colonialists' economic agenda. The view that slaves who converted should be given their freedom caused the settlers to oppose active evangelism. Later, in the beginning of the 19th century, this situation changed somewhat, although there was still conflict between the missionaries and the White settlers who wanted to be able to exploit Black labour.

Missionaries began to move to indigenous communities outside of the towns with a view to both converting and "civilising" them -- encouraging them to adopt European norms and behaviour, develop a middle class and a way of life centred on the church. Much literature on these efforts is highly critical of the missionaries as essentially "agents of imperialism and capitalism". Many are criticised for having promoted (or at least accepted) racial segregation and undermined African culture and society. However, other studies have taken the view that the story of missionary activity is filled with ambiguities and contradictions.[60] Some have argued, for example, that "Africans accepted Christianity for their own reasons, and appropriated it and turned it to their own use".[61] Through the interaction of missionaries and indigenous peoples, Christianity was Africanised. Its adoption was also a function of the need for vulnerable societies, e.g. the Khoi with whom missionaries were initially more successful than with Bantu peoples, to look for a rationale for and spiritual understanding of their new conditions of life.[62]

Mission stations and missionaries

"In the last years of the 18th century the evangelical revival in western Europe had led to a mushrooming of religious and philanthropic organisations, not least of which were the Christian missionary societies. The 1790s became the most fruitful decade ever in the history of missionary endeavour in southern Africa. By the middle of the 19th century mission stations had been established both in and beyond the colony. Soon after 1800 work began in Little and Great Namaqualand among the Griqua. In 1820 John Brownlee established a Xhosa mission in the Tyhume Valley, and in 1825 he founded a station on the Buffalo River on the site of present-day King William's Town.

Among the most active missionaries were the Wesleyans who, under William Shaw, established a chain of six mission stations stretching from the colonial border to Natal. The Glasgow Society founded several stations among the Ngqika, including the famous Lovedale (1824), the Moravians established Shiloh north of the Tyhume mission, and to the east the Berlin Society opened a mission near Stutterheim. The American Board of Commissioners for Foreign Missions, following in the steps of Captain Allan Gardiner and Francis Owen, opened up the Zulu country to mission enterprise. All along the Orange and Caledon rivers missionaries commenced organised work: the LMS at Griquatown and Philippolis, the Berlin Society at Pniel, and the Wesleyans among the Rolong, among the Basotho at Thaba Nchu and among the Tlokwa at Mpharani. By 1850 the Paris Evangelical Missionary Society was preaching the gospel at some eleven stations in Lesotho and to the north of the Caledon River. From 1830 the Rhenish missionaries were active throughout the Western Cape and Namaqualand. The most successful London Missionary Society undertaking in southern Africa was that of Robert Moffat, who achieved great fame for his work among the Tswana, and his son-in-law, David Livingstone, who worked at Kuruman, from where he plunged ever further into the interior on his journeys of exploration and missionary enterprise."[63]

---

[60] Saunders, in de Gruchy, 1999, pp. 7-16.
[61] Referring to the work of Edward Said on culture and imperialism, see Saunders, 1999, p. 13.
[62] Ibid., p. 15.
[63] Cameron, 1987, p. 88.

The first missionary group to arrive in the Cape was the London Missionary Society (LMS) who came in 1799 and by 1816 had 20 active missionaries.[64] After the LMS came the Wesleyan Methodist Missionary Society, the Glasgow Missionary Society the Church Missionary Society, and many others. Essentially, the missionaries transplanted into South Africa the ecclesiastical situation found in their own European countries -- including the variety of denominations and the competition amongst them for adherents.[65] Whilst it is difficult to generalise about the huge variety of missionary groups who established themselves in South Africa, the discussion below can only cite a few examples to illustrate some broad trends of missionary behaviour and relations with indigenous communities.

The LMS is often remembered for the anti-slavery campaigning undertaken by some of its early leaders. It ran into trouble with settlers when it focused more on meeting the needs of indigenous and coloured people than those of the White settlers.[66] Despite this, research by the Comaroffs on LMS interaction with the Southern Tswana people demonstrates that the LMS was generally not unlike other missionary groups in its patronising attitude towards African culture and in its efforts to "civilise and convert" indigenous peoples. When discussing the Tswana, LMS missionaries engaged in a "discourse of absence" in African culture – the absence of money, markets, 'civilised' crops, technology, innovation and privately owned land. The missionaries disapproved of:

- The Tswana's politics of production, e.g. control exerted by chiefs;
- The role of superstition in their society as opposed to what Europeans considered 'rational' behaviour;
- The 'unnatural' division of labour between men and women, e.g. the fact that women did physical labour in the fields while men watched the herds (whereas the missionaries wanted to 'domesticate' the women and encourage them to work primarily in the home).

They also criticised the "socialistic" aspects of African culture, e.g. *ubuntu* (see above) and lack of competition.[67]

The result of this lack of understanding of African society and its benefits led the LMS and other missionary groups to insist that their African converts adopt "new means and relations of production" as were practiced in European commodity agriculture. The introduction of privately owned land led to many African people losing all access to productive land and to increasing indebtedness, poverty and dependency on wage labour. The new forms of wealth and status created class distinctions, e.g. between an 'upper peasantry' or petite bourgeoisie, and a lower peasantry. The upper group "became the prime conduit of Protestant values" whereas the lower group tended to maintain more of their traditions and their "collectivist ethos".[68] The men in the lower group were generally not orthodox Christians, and the women tended to join charismatic independent churches "which formed close-knit social communities".[69] Thus, the missionaries were not always successful in their efforts to undermine indigenous culture. They did, however, put in motion insidious processes which led to increasing inequalities and poverty.

Many early congregations were initially comfortably non-racial, e.g. the Union Chapel in Grahamstown.[70] Also, infant schools established in Cape Town by the LMS were quite

---

[64] A collection of essays written in honour of the bicentenary of the London Missionary Society (see de Gruchy, 1999) provides some fascinating perspectives on this particular organisation and its impact, both positive and negative.
[65] de Gruchy, 1995, p. 29.
[66] de Gruchy, 1979, p. 12.
[67] Comaroff and Comaroff, 1999, pp. 55-60.
[68] Ibid., pp. 69-79.
[69] Ibid., p. 76.
[70] Ross, 1999, p. 123.

inclusive both racially and culturally. In 1831, one school comprised children from the following groups: 24 free blacks, 37 English speakers, 17 Dutch speakers, and 75 slaves. Later, Malay Muslim children were added as well. In 1836-39, day school education was provided mainly for the poor and coloured communities. By 1844, there were 25 mission schools in and around Cape Town, including LMS schools. The 1830s were also characterised by the creation of several inter-denominational education-related bodies in Cape Town. These included the South African Infant School Institution (1830), the South African Christian Instruction Society (1831), and the South African Tract and Book Society (1831).[71]

As a missionary society, the LMS also encouraged other missionary groups to come to the Cape. So, for example, in 1824, the Glasgow Missionary Society established the well-known Lovedale Mission. As a result of the work done at Lovedale, the Bantu Presbyterian Church was founded early in the 20th century. Many important Xhosa scholars, professionals and politicians were ministered to and educated at Lovedale.

It did not take long for power struggles to manifest themselves within the church hierarchies and between the White and Black church officials. Early on, the LMS missionaries used African converts / agents to preach and proselytise in African communities. However, beginning around 1820, European missionaries became insecure and jealous of the African agents' access to communities and wanted to assure their own control over the church hierarchy. In contrast, African churches wanted more autonomy and felt that the White missionaries should concentrate their efforts on converting new African communities,[72] leaving them to manage their own affairs. The Khoi community in the Khat River Settlement outside Grahamstown was one of the first to "secede" from the church when they were not allowed to appoint their own minister. In 1850, one Khat River community leader said "We shall show the settlers that we too are men".[73] These conflicts over the autonomy of the African churches sowed the seeds of independence of the charismatic churches as well as political resistance.

Churches also promoted gender-specific roles in the congregations and related social life. Men took the leadership positions, heading committees and selecting pastoral staff. They also controlled financial matters and spoke on behalf of the church community. Women, in contrast, took more supportive and informal roles, teaching Bible classes, running the Ladies' Benevolent Society, and establishing industry schools for poorer girls and women.[74]

The missionary role was characterised by conflicts of interest as they sometimes allied themselves with the indigenous communities but often with the settlers. "The missionaries, being white, regarded themselves as the conscience of the settlers and the protectors of the 'natives'".[75] Missionaries also sometimes undermined the authority of the indigenous leadership and created divisions amongst their political units.

The amelioration and abolition of slavery

British entrepreneurs recognised that with increasing industrialisation a dependence on slave labour was not necessary as it had been in the plantation economy of the previous era. Thus their decision was not an altruistic one but based largely on pragmatic economics. The British Act of the Abolition of the Slave Trade came into effect in 1808, preventing any slave labour from being landed in any British port after the 1st of March of that year.

---

[71] Ludlow, 1999, p. 106.
[72] Elbourne, 1999, p. 133.
[73] Ibid., p. 154.
[74] Ludlow, 1999, p. 103.
[75] de Gruchy, 1979, p. 13.

Shortly thereafter, an investigation of charges of mistreatment of Khoi people by White farmers – known as the 'Black Circuit' of 1812 -- left such a bitter legacy of hatred and misunderstanding that a group of farmers led a rebellion but it was quickly suppressed. The Black Circuit had resulted from the protests in London by James Read relating to the ill treatment of the Khoi on the farms. This protest was later followed up by Dr. John Phillip, the superintendent of the London Missionary Society, who sought to ensure that the Khoi could sell their labour in a fair market.

This missionary advocacy finally bore some fruit. In 1828, Ordinance 50 was issued by Andries Stokenstroom, the commissioner for the eastern province, abolishing all discriminatory restrictions on the Khoi and other free non-Whites. Ordinance 50, in principle, removed all restrictions on their movement and granted them full legal equality with Whites. However, as van der Ross has rightly noted, in practice the social, economic and political status of non-Whites could not and did not change overnight. "People's lifestyles, their housing, clothing, food, education, leisure-time occupations, conversation, their occupations and skills, their access to medical treatment, their provision for old age, these and many other aspects of their lives did not become the same".[76] Ordinance 50 did not result in equal participation in access to political power or in decision-making – in fact, the non-Whites were still unable to exercise the rights accorded to them on paper.

As the anti-slavery movement shifted its focus from amelioration to outright emancipation, these objectives also found a resonance in the Cape Parliament which passed an Emancipation Act in 1834. At that time, it is estimated that there were approximately 39,000 slaves.[77] By 1841, the Masters and Servants Ordinance was passed, regulating the relationship and prescribing criminal sanctions for breach of contract.

Birth of a free press

Commercial publication started in the first quarter of the 19th century. In 1823, the Colonial Secretary agreed to the publication of *The South African Journal* edited by Thomas Pringle, a Scottish poet. In 1824, Pringle and his partners, John Fairburn and Robert Grieg, launched the *South African Commercial Advertiser* when they established that no state permission was needed. However, when they published an article that was considered critical of Governor Somerset, it was suspended. The recall of Somerset to Britain created new opportunities, and John Fairburn returned from Britain in triumph in 1828 with a guarantee of freedom of the press.

The Afrikaans press emerged partly as a means of countering the 1805 British takeover of the Cape. In 1830, a paper called *De Zuid-Afrikaan* was started to promote the Afrikaans language as well as Afrikaner nationalism.

Missionaries were also at the forefront of publishing in South Africa, though much of the early publications were evangelical texts. Lovedale Mission founded Lovedale Press in 1823, and began publishing translations by African writers of biblical readers or important English books. The first one was a Xhosa translation by Tiyo Soga of John Bunyan's *The Pilgrim's Progress* in 1867. The Marianhill Mission established a publisher in 1882, again with the intention of promoting Christianity. Mphe and Seeber[78] have criticised the missionary publishing ventures saying that they simultaneously supported Black writing and negated aspects of Black culture by heavily censoring much of the original work that they published. The missionaries were worried, *inter alia*, about offending the colonial state.

---

[76] van der Ross, 1979, p. 68.
[77] Ibid., p. 41.
[78] Mphe and Seeber, 2000, pp. 15-17.

The earliest African vernacular newspapers appeared as early as 1844. The first one under African editorship appeared in 1876: *Isigidimi Sama Xosa (the Xosa Messenger)* edited by Rev. Elijah Makiwane. He was succeeded by John Tengo Jabavu in 1881. Later, in 1884, Jabavu received financial support from liberal whites to establish his own Zulu language paper -- *Imvo Zabantsundu* – with a view to "opening the eyes of the Natives to their rights".[79] As editor, Jabavu ensured that the paper played an influential role and editorialised on a number of issues affecting African people. Then, in 1902, Sol Plaatje started *Koranta ea Becoana,* published in SeTswana and English. This was followed in 1903 by *Ilanga lase Natal (The Natal Sun),* another Zulu paper, founded by John Dube. These African initiatives in turn created more space for individual African writers. Unfortunately, due to financial constraints, only *Ilanga lase Natal* survived for long.[80]

Gandhi began running the Indian newspaper, *Indian Opinion,* in 1904 and continued to do so until his departure from South Africa in 1914. This gave him an excellent vehicle through which to influence the moral and political views of the Indian community.

The Emergence of Civil Society Organisations

Each of the cultural, ethnic and religious groups represented in South Africa developed organisations to serve their own interests and to protect and enhance their religious and cultural identities. Whilst in many ways this diversity of interests and organisations enriched South African civil society, it also meant that the various oppressed groups did not act jointly against their oppressor in the early stages of resistance. So, for example, the religious groups (Jews, Hindus and Muslims) and racial groups (Africans, Indians and Coloureds) each took action separately regarding protection of their rights -- making them each more vulnerable. This aided the government in its divide and rule approach.

Religious organisations

Christian organisations
There was considerable competition between the various Christian denominations. Further splintering of denominations resulted from splits which were transferred from Europe into South Africa. Due to Protestant antipathy to Catholicism, the Catholic Church was "reticent and hesitant to participate fully in the public and political arenas".[81] As British colonialism increased its dominance, Anglicans had "a strong sense of being the established church which served the needs of the colonial nation as a whole", but "it was impossible to be a national church without the NGK (Dutch Reformed Church) which had by far the largest membership, especially within the settler community".[82] Despite Anglican efforts to seek a union of these churches, there was in fact a growing alienation between them.

Parish churches became widespread, and with them local community welfare activities. As the English communities expanded and grew wealthier, they began to establish private church-linked schools of all denominations -- Anglican, Baptist, Congregational, Methodist, Presbyterian, etc.

Initial racial inclusiveness did not last and over time missionaries and their churches had a profound impact on increasing racial segregation. By the 1840s, there was a growing trend

---

[79] Ibid., p. 4.
[80] Oliphant, 2000, p. 115.
[81] de Gruchy, 1995, p. 37.
[82] Ibid., p. 38.

for white LMS missionaries to adopt a kind of "liberalism" which "defended black rights from a careful social distance, while assuming white superiority". At the same time, its churches began "to segment into white and black congregations which worshipped separately, even in different buildings".[83] The change coincided with a move from being purely a missionary society to being an institutional church. Slightly later, in 1857, despite some reservations and its initial refusal to allow race to determine church practice, the Dutch Reformed Church gave in to racial prejudice and took steps to segregate their congregations.[84] As with the LMS, separate parallel congregations were formed. It was ironically also at this same time that the DRC first began to conduct active missionary work amongst the Coloured population in the Cape. The first DRC mission church for coloured people -- Die Sendingkerk – was established in 1881. This was followed by the N.G. Kerk in Africa for Africans and the Indian Reformed Church.

The DRC disapproved of the Great Trek and did not allow any of its clergy to accompany the trekkers. In 1853, the trekkers founded their own church, the Nederduitsch Hervormde Kerk (NHK). Then, in 1859 another split occurred influenced by trends in Holland, resulting in the founding of the Gereformeerde Kerk. So, there were three white Afrikaner Reformed churches.

Other churches took somewhat different approaches to racial inclusion and exclusion. For example, the Coloured congregations of the LMS joined with the White congregations in the Evangelical Voluntary Union in 1864, which became the Congregational Union in 1883 and included some Africans. When they developed missions, the Presbyterians and Baptists created multi-racial unions, but with separate congregations. The Roman Catholics had "no separate autonomous church for black Catholics", but "this did not mean that there was no discrimination, nor that the problem of race was resolved".[85] Thus, the race problem arose in different ways in different churches.

As economic class differentiation and racial discrimination became more pronounced, the Christian missionary role became more complex. The discrepancy between what they preached and what their (White) congregations practiced grew. Missionaries were, to a large extent, gradually co-opted by colonial interests. "The attitude of white colonists also meant that mission came to be regarded as the work of white clergy and black evangelists, and not the task of the whole church".[86] The church structures that evolved were not characterised by equality, but rather by hierarchy. The prejudice of the White settlers quickly resulted in the racial separation of congregations. Furthermore, when the 1869 Synod set up a committee to consider representation for the 'native church', there were no Black delegates to play a role in the decision-making, and the church leadership essentially excluded them by default.[87]

The so-called 'liberalism' of the 19th century White Christian leadership ostensibly signified a belief in "the importance and dignity of the individual without regard to colour, culture, creed and sex; emphasis on equality of opportunity, freedom of thought, conscience, speech, movement and association; and the rule of law; and the conviction that society can achieve political stability, economic prosperity and social justice by human effort and at an evolutionary pace". Nonetheless, this 'liberalism' resulted in both socio-political and religious policies of "the maintenance of white power and the exercise of social control".[88] This was

---

[83] Elbourne, 1999, p. 146-147.
[84] de Gruchy, 1995, p. 32.
[85] Ibid., p. 16.
[86] Goedhals, 1989, p. 109.
[87] Ibid.
[88] Ibid., p. 111.

not least because the Christian leadership lacked their own vision of what they wanted their society to become.

Writing about the Church of the Province of South Africa (CPSA), Goedhals and Cochrane have argued that "conformity to the ways of the world has conditioned both the church's understanding and its practice of mission. Often, it is neither the inspiration of scripture, nor theological definition nor the needs of the society in which it is set that have shaped the church's definition of mission. Instead, the meaning of the Christian mission has been limited by the extent to which the church, consciously or not, is conditioned by secular ideology or by the structures of the surrounding society".[89] Thus, "Christian mission in the 19th century was shaped (and limited) by historical forces in which the extension of territorial control by the imperial powers, chauvinism and the pursuit of economic self-interest played no small part".[90]

The hypocrisy of most of the 19th century missionaries is obvious to present historians. Whilst they were on the one hand engaged in humanitarian efforts to alleviate the poverty of Black people which resulted from discrimination, urbanisation and industrialisation, on the other they played a major role in ensuring that those same people became essentially a docile and compliant working class. The White missionaries actively discouraged their African members from participating in more Africanised forms of Christianity, e.g. Ethiopianism, again because they wanted to retain control.[91]

There was, however, a growing solidarity amongst African church ministers across denominations. The formation, in 1915, of the Transvaal-based Interdenominational African Ministers' Association of South Africa (IDAMASA) was significant in this regard. In 1946, IDAMASA became a national movement. This was not least an effort to overcome the 'divide and rule' aspect of denominationalism in the Christian church, and instead to use Christianity as a unifying force for African nationalism.[92]

A related issue for the Christian denominations was the extent to which the South African-based branches had autonomy from the church hierarchies based in their European countries of origin. The CPSA – the local Anglican church – adopted its Constitution in 1870. The Constitution said that the CPSA was "legally a voluntary association of those who subscribe to the faith and practices which it exists to uphold and propagate". It also accorded the CPSA Ecclesiastical Tribunals the right to pronounce on "questions of faith and doctrine" "without being bound by decisions or interpretations of other tribunals",[93] e.g. those overseas. When in 1883, an attempt was made to limit this independence, the CPSA expressed a desire to be "indigenous". However, this aim was not truly achieved due to the continuing discrimination practiced within this Church.

The issue of separation between church and state emerged quite early on. In 1854, the Cape governor offered substantial grants to Anglican missionaries to establish schools "as part of a scheme to bring peace to the frontier through Christianity and civilisation".[94] The aim of the missionaries was, therefore, first to convert the Xhosa to Christianity, and second to ensure their submission to the British colonial government. Ironically, this arrangement occurred in the same year that the so-called "Voluntary Principle" arose in the course of an 1854 debate in the Cape Parliament. This led to the passage in 1875 of the Voluntary Act which made all denominations and religious faiths equal and ended the state funding of

---

[89] Goedhals, 1989, p. 104; Cochrane, 1987, pp. 150-162.
[90] Goedhals, 1989, p. 105-106.
[91] Ibid., pp. 112-113.
[92] de Gruchy, 1986a, pp. 50-51.
[93] Suggit, 1989, p. 81.
[94] Goedhals, 1989, p. 106.

churches. This did not entirely settle the matter, however, as governments and constitutions effectively upheld the pre-eminence of Christianity until 1994.[95]

African independent churches

Several factors led to the emergence of African independent churches. They were a manifestation of:

- Rejection of the control asserted by whites in both mission and 'multiracial' churches:
- Reaction against the denigration of African culture and the imposition of European culture:
- Reaction against discrimination and paternalism of Whites towards Africans.
- Reaction to black urbanisation, replacing rural tribal structures to provide a means of social cohesion in urban townships.[96]

By 1970, this movement included about 3,000 different groups with approximately 3.5 million members.

Pato has questioned why it took such a long time for "authentic" African churches to emerge. He argued that "the Christianity which is prevalent in Africa is not African in flavour. In the words of Ngindu Mushete, African Christians pray with borrowed words, think by proxy, and operate by way of Rome, Paris, London and other European capitals". He further suggests that "If the form and character taken by Christianity in Africa be alien to the people of Africa, that Christianity is most likely to be frail and superficial. The reason for this is that such Christianity is unlikely to penetrate the depths of African being, the results of which cannot be anything less than confusion as to self-identity". To have real meaning, a church must "reflect the totality of the experience of its members". [97]

Pato goes on to argue against "adaptation" of European models to fit the African context, saying that the "denigration and humiliation" that accompanied such adaptation, e.g. in the missionary era, has negated any legitimacy it might have had. "In the southern African context, adoption of African cultural forms and affirmation of blackness imply a rejection of the assumption that the cultures of Africa are inherently inferior to those of Europe or America".[98] Placing an "African blanket over Christian customs and values which are essentially western in form and character" means that Africans remain essentially strangers within the church. Africanisation of church leadership is also not an adequate solution.[99]

Despite the centuries of missionary challenge, African culture has remained remarkably intact. African independent churches emerged in the 19th century as "a reaction to the alienation that resulted from these foreign value systems".[100] It also reflected the fact that, historically, the churches have tended to better serve the needs of the rich than of the poor, not least because "the rich hold the ultimate power to determine resource allocation within the church".[101]

The harsh migrant worker experience elicited the evolution of the Zionist Church movement as a positive response to the needs of exploited Black workers displaced from rural to unfamiliar urban areas. Whilst Zionism was not a missionary church, it was (and still is)

---

[95] de Gruchy, 1995, p. 36.
[96] de Gruchy, 1986a, pp. 45-46.
[97] Pato, 1989, pp. 159-160.
[98] Ibid., p. 162.
[99] Ibid., p. 172.
[100] Ramphele, 1989, p. 179.
[101] Ibid., p. 186.

concerned with improving the conditions of workers and addressing the socio-economic needs of the poor and illiterate by overcoming their sense of deprivation and inadequacy.[102]

The Zionist churches "formed coping institutions which aimed at the delivery of benefits in the here and now". They did not attempt social reform of the entire system; rather they were concerned with the rescue of individuals on a voluntary basis through provision of economic, social and spiritual support. Thus, they addressed the symptoms rather than the causes of deprivation.[103]

Other separatist churches were formed as the more educated Christian Africans began to challenge the authority of Whites in the church and in society as a whole. These Africans became frustrated with the failure of the missionary churches to treat them as equals, e.g. by ordaining them as pastors / priests. The so-called "Ethiopian" churches emerged as a result of this protest against racial inequality, with similar denominational affiliations.[104] Thus, the first was a spin-off from the Wesleyan Church in 1892. These churches also received support from similar ones formed amongst Black Americans. The Ethiopian churches in particular provided leadership for African movements against the apartheid state and for African nationalism. Their members supported the Bambatha Rebellion in 1906, named after Chief Bambatha of the Zondi in Natal who led a violent rebellion against Natal government measures to force Africans off their land. The suppression of this effort led to the deaths of 3,000 to 4,000 Africans, the burning of many African settlements, seizure of their cattle, and the imprisonment of a further 7,000 Africans. This was effectively the last major armed resistance to settler attempts to deprive Africans of their economic independence, and resulted in large migrations of African workers to the Transvaal.[105] The Ethiopian churches also later endorsed the formation of the African National Congress.

Christian Indians of Natal

In her detailed study of Christian Indians in Natal, Brain[106] challenged the previously accepted estimates of Christians amongst the 152,000 indentured Indians. In describing the missions opened by the Anglican, Methodist, Roman Catholic, Lutheran and Baptist churches amongst Indian labourers, she clearly demonstrated that:

- Only 2,150 of the 152,184 indentured labourers who arrived between 1860 and 1911 -- 1.4% -- were Christian. This is close to Dr. Hilda Kuper's[107] estimate of 3%.
- Most of the indentured Indians came from North and South India, and very few if any from Calcutta;
- The Indian Christian churches were separate from those attended by other races;
- The schools established by these churches were only open to adherents of the Christian faith;
- Other missionary work done was also conditional on individuals adopting the Christian faith.

The first Christian denomination to work amongst Indian immigrants was the Roman Catholic Church. Brain argued that the missions of the other denominations were already over-extended in their existing mission activities, and also probably thought that the Indians would return home once their contracts expired.[108] The first schools for Indian children were

---

[102] Kiernan, 1995, p.118.
[103] Ibid., p. 124.
[104] Ibid.
[105] Omer-Cooper, 1987, pp. 153-154. By 1909, 80% of adult males in Zululand had become migrant workers, having been forced off their land.
[106] Brain, 1983.
[107] Kuper, 1960.
[108] Brain, 1983, p. 194.

opened by the Catholics in Durban in 1867 with 30 pupils and in Pietermaritzburg in 1885 with 40 pupils. In 1889, the first school for Indian girls was opened in Natal. In 1905, there were about 1,040 Indian Catholics in Natal. In the 1880s, the Catholics had begun appointing Indian catechists with a view to spreading the faith. By 1970, Catholicism was the largest denomination amongst Christian Indians in South Africa. In 1970, the census reflected 13,820 and in 1980, this had grown to 21,160.

In 1861, the Wesleyan Methodist Church became active amongst Indians in Natal. Their missionaries distributed religious tracts throughout the province, visiting immigrants in their homes. In 1879, their Reverend Stott tried to persuade the agricultural estate owners and large employers of Indian labour to establish schools for their workers' children. However, whilst a few had already set up small schools on their properties without government funding, most employers felt that education of labourers would harm their business. Only three employers agreed to provide facilities and teachers, on the assumption that they would receive government grants. Eventually, the Methodists succeeded in establishing a series of schools around Natal. They began using Indian evangelists in the early 20th century, but few Indian ministers were ordained and the numbers of Natal adherents grew slowly, to about 4,320 in 1980.

Anglican Bishop Colenso of Natal was primarily interested in conversion of the Zulu people and paid little attention to the Indian communities. Apparently the local White Anglicans also favoured the Zulu missions. Missionary activity with the Indians increased only in the early 1880s. The St. Aidan's Mission established by the Anglican Church in 1883 under the directorship of Dr. L.P. Booth was the first church medical mission in South Africa.[109] St. Aidan's also had a school and an orphanage. By 1894, there were 10 Anglican schools. It is worthy of note that in the early 20th century, Indian Anglicans were providing financial support to their churches and church schools as they became more financially secure. In 1980, approximately 8,900 Indians belonged to the Anglican Church in Natal.

Lutherans and Baptists also became involved in Indian communities. The Lutherans were the first to open a church in Chatsworth, but in 1980 only 1,140 adherents were recorded. American Baptist missionaries worked in the Telugu district but faced language problems in relating to the community. The first Telugu Baptist church was established in 1903 at Kearnsey. Internal disputes led to a rift in the Baptist community, with a formal split occurring in 1914. Two separate organisations were established – the Indian Baptist Mission and the Natal Telugu Baptist Association – both of which remained active at least until 1980 when their membership stood at about 2,960.

Brain concluded that although "no combined large-scale evangelisation of the Indian population of Natal took place between 1860 and 1911",[110] missions of the five churches noted above did play an important role in establishing schools, teacher training facilities, care for orphans, and medical treatment to the Indian immigrant communities. Others have suggested that conversion to Christianity became an attractive option for some Hindu Indians when they thought it might help to improve their socio-economic position by joining the faith of the ruling class / race, as well as to break away from their rigid caste systems.[111] This notion bore little if any fruit. Still others have noted that in the wake of the 1960s forced removals of Indians to completely new townships, e.g. Chatsworth, Christian evangelists (especially Pentecostals) may have taken advantage of the disorientation and disruption of pre-existing Indian communities to seek out more converts.[112] By 1980, Christians constituted 7-8% of the Indian population of Natal.

---

[109] Local Zulus and Indians attended the clinic at St. Aidan's. See Brain, 1983, p. 217.
[110] Ibid., p. 229.
[111] van Loon, 1995, p. 209.
[112] Maxwell, Diesel and Naidoo, 1995, p. 178.

Muslim organisations

In the late 18th century, under the leadership of the prince and religious scholar, Tuang Guru, efforts began to consolidate the teaching and practice of Islam in the Cape. As a political prisoner, he was taken immediately to prison on Robben Island upon his arrival in the Cape. Whilst there, in 1781, he wrote a book on Islamic jurisprudence which became the main reference for the Muslim community. Upon his release in 1793, he founded the first Muslim school which played a proactive role in the education and social advancement of slaves and freed Blacks.[113] Extensive education curricula and programmes were developed to prepare Muslim students as teachers, lawyers and imams.

Tuang Guru became the first Chief Imam of the Cape. Early petitions for a mosque site were rejected by the government, and prayers were held in the open air. Around the turn of the century, Tuang Guru established a mosque in a warehouse, despite the prohibition. This is today the Auwal Mosque in Dorp Street.[114]

The practice of Islam was forbidden until 1804 when religious freedom was granted to all. At this time, the Cape Muslims were also accorded the right to build the first mosque and were granted a burial site.[115] Despite this breakthrough, they continued to be second-class citizens, suffering from religious and political prejudice. They lived in conditions of extreme poverty and economic exploitation. Nonetheless, their faith and culture helped to sustain them. Davids writes that "their concern was to fulfil their economic needs and to pursue a life of social relevancy...They believed that their religion contained all the answers to their problems".[116]

Estimates put the Muslim population of the Cape at about 3,000 by the first quarter of the 19th century and 8,000 by the middle of that century. The religion attracted members of all races and classes.[117] About 7-10% of the Indian indentured workers who arrived in 1860 were Muslims. Islam spread as Muslim traders moved into rural Natal and to the Transvaal. Mosques proliferated in those provinces, with the first one being built in Durban in 1884 and another in Pretoria in 1887.[118] Muslim organisations grew considerably in number around the end of the 19th century, despite the prevailing religious prejudices amongst the colonialists.

Ulamas (jurists/teachers) played an important role in the Muslim communities early on. They educated the community regarding Islamic law and practice and dealt with religious offenders (sometimes with corporal punishment). It is not, however, known to what extent their activities were formally structured before the second half of the 19th century.[119]

In the late 19th century, there were several instances of collective Muslim resistance to White colonial authority. These involved making political statements through religious conviction. For example, at the time of the 1882 smallpox epidemic, Muslims refused to be vaccinated. Once infected, they objected to being quarantined or hospitalised. In part, this was due to their concerns about their people eating acceptable foods and receiving Muslim burial rites. Also, they "objected to what they saw as the opportunism of the white authorities, who were only concerned about poor sanitary conditions among the non-white community when white

---

[113] Ibid., p. 40.
[114] Ibid., p. 46.
[115] This action was not altruistic, but rather aimed at securing the loyalty of the Muslim community to the Cape government in the event of a British invasion. In fact, they formed two Muslim artillery units whose bravery was praised later by their British opponents. See Davids, 1985, p. 50.
[116] Ibid., p. 83.
[117] Moosa, 1995, p. 134.
[118] Ibid., p. 139.
[119] Ibid., p. 140.

health was at peril".[120] The health authorities "came to learn that they could not interfere in their religious practices with impunity".[121] Nonetheless, many Muslims died of smallpox as a result of their protest. Later in a small victory in 1901, during the outbreak of bubonic plague, Muslim nurses were employed to attend to their own sick.

Another example of resistance occurred when the Public Health Act of 1883 threatened to close the Tana Baru cemetery. The Muslim community's reaction to this measure "channelled the religious motivation of the community into positive political action". A Malay Cemetery Committee was formed initially; when it failed in its negotiations with the government, it was replaced by the Moslem Cemetery Board. They tried all sorts of advocacy approaches, including "persuasion, letter writing, and peaceful protests" but again failed. The violent uprising which followed illustrated the political dissatisfaction and frustration of the Muslim community. A government force of 1,200 men was called out to quell the uprising after policemen were stoned by the protesters. One community leader, Abdul Burns, and 12 other men were tried and sentenced to two months hard labour.[122] These events demonstrated both the patience of the community but also their devout beliefs and determination and their strong desire for access to the civil rights accorded to others.

Similar to the Hindu community, the Muslim community was not homogeneous. "Islam in Natal was clearly marked by class interests. ...There was a large group of Muslims from a working class background who were, in terms of ethnicity and language, very different from the merchant-class Muslims."[123] Due to their different origins, there were also differences in interests, attitudes and practice between the Malay Muslims on the Cape and the Indian Muslims in Natal. Within these different communities, religious, educational and welfare activity played an important role.

Jewish organisations
In the 1890s and early 1900s, a substantial influx of Jewish immigrants from Lithuania and Latvia arrived. There were quite substantial cultural differences between the Anglo-German Jews who had arrived earlier and had become somewhat assimilated, and the East European Jews. "The latter were Yiddish speaking, and their dress, mannerisms, speech and general way of life did not easily merge with their societal surroundings".[124] The transformation of what had been a relatively homogeneous religious community to a very culturally diverse one inevitably led to tensions. The newcomers formed their own synagogues, and had their own forms of religious practice. Thus, like Christians and Muslims, Judaism in South Africa was influenced by its various strains overseas.

In the late 19th century, Landsleit societies developed to bring together members who hailed from the same villages or *shtetls* in their home countries. Those who had come to South Africa first formed these societies as a means of offering financial (without interest or security) or other assistance to those who came later. The societies continued for many years, and a few even remain today. Some of the earliest were the Ponevez (1899), the Kaidaner Society (1900) and the Krakenowo Society.[125]

By the mid-19th century, every major settlement between Cape Town and Messina had some Jewish congregation, however small. The first synagogue, Tikvat Israel, was established in Cape Town in 1841. In 1887, the Witwatersrand Goldfields Jewish Association was formed. It purchased two plots in President Street in 1888 to erect the first synagogue in the

---

[120] Moosa, 1995, p. 141.
[121] Davids, 1985, p. 85.
[122] See Davids, 1985.
[123] Moosa, 1995, p. 145.
[124] Hellig, 1995, p. 162.
[125] See www.shemeyisrael.co.il/sa/sajbd/sajbd.htm

Transvaal. Somewhat later, the Park Synagogue was built. Services were also held in a variety of secular venues. The first Jewish School in the Transvaal started in Kerk Street in 1890.

In 1887, the Jewish Helping Hand and Burial Society (*Chevra Kadisha*) emerged in Johannesburg, initially to bury Jews, but soon it began to provide a variety of aid to the needy. During the Anglo-Boer War, this group started a soup kitchen to feed both Jews and non-Jews, and later formed the Jewish Ambulance Corps to distribute food rations to Jews in Johannesburg. Other charitable organisations were formed around this time, including the Society for Visiting the Sick (*Bikkur Cholim*) and the Ladies' Benevolent Society. A Jewish Hospital was founded in 1896 for Orthodox Jews requiring kosher food, and preferring Jewish doctors and nurses. This hospital was later incorporated into Johannesburg General Hospital, whilst still offering a kosher kitchen. Orphanages and old people's homes were also founded.

Social and cultural groups formed rapidly as the numbers of Jews increased. These included the South African Yiddish Cultural Federation, the Jewish Dramatic Society, the Jewish Literary Society, and the Jewish Museum Society. Study circles were formed to discuss issues and invite speakers; these were not exclusively Jewish. Fundraising concerts, exhibits and dances were held, along with many other less formalised cultural and social get-togethers. Sports groups were also quite common.

In 1898, the South African Zionist Federation was founded to deal with matters concerning Israel. In 1903, the South African Jewish Board of Deputies (SAJBD) was established in Johannesburg, and one was created the next year in Cape Town to promote the overall protection and well-being of the community, to safeguard their civil and political rights, and to act as their formal representative. The two Boards merged into one in 1912.

A fascinating series of studies on Jewish life has emerged in the last few years, sponsored and researched by the South African Friends of Beth Hatefutsoth.[126] They are part of a wider project to document the Jewish diaspora around the world. These studies have tried to recreate in considerable detail what Jewish life was like in country communities around South Africa, starting around the 1870s. Whilst the history of urban communities is better known, these studies of Jewish life in the dorps offer a real insight into how Jews in single and/or neighbouring communities came together to form a variety of mutual support organisations aimed largely at preserving their religious and social practice. Thus, even communities with only a few families managed to maintain a reasonable semblance of traditional Jewish life. "As communities declined, one by one, with the migration of Jews to the cities, remaining residents tended to join up with the nearest remaining viable congregation. Many would travel miles to attend a service, especially over the High Festivals".[127] They also formed Hebrew schools for the children. In more recent years, the SAJBD has formed regional bodies to ensure that Jews in small, isolated communities have access to some religious activity.

Other specific types of Jewish organisation emerged in many communities across the country. Often found were local branches of the Jewish Ladies Benevolent Society, the Union of Jewish Women, Jewish Ladies' Guild, the Jewish Women's Society, and/or the Women's Zionist Society. Local branches of the Chevra Kadisha were established from the early 20th century. Youth groups were also common, including the Zionist Youth Society, the Young Israel Society, the Jewish Youth Club, Youth Congregations, the Bnei Zion, and so on.

---

[126] See South African Friends of Beth Hatefutsoth, *Jewish Life in the South African Country Communities, Vol. 1* (2002) *and Vol. 2* (2004).
[127] South African Friends of Beth Hatefutsoth, *Vol. 1,* 2002, p. 13.

It is significant that throughout these communities, large and small, urban and rural, Jews were also active in civic and political life. Many became involved in local government, in secular organisations related either to their professional or commercial interests, or to their cultural and charitable pursuits. Thus, they did not restrict their organisational identities and activities to Jewish-related ones, but also became dispersed across the entire spectrum of South African political life, many supporting racial segregation whilst others were vigorously opposing it.

The beginnings of Black organisations

African organisations
In 1872, the Cape government established a non-racial franchise, permitting Africans and Coloured people to be part of the common voters' roll. This allowed political participation not present in the other provinces. The other provinces had already put in place significant barriers – legal and otherwise – to political participation by Africans, Coloureds and Indians.

In the Cape, an African elite had begun to emerge – "as teachers, ministers of religion, progressive farmers, craftsmen, clerks, interpreters, traders an editors".[128] Ten years later, African voters constituted around 10% of the common roll and had considerable political influence.[129] The first African political association was formed in the Cape in 1882. It was called *Imbumba Yama Afrika*, and aimed to "maintain African unity so that African interests could be forcefully articulated".[130] It held conferences from time to time when it was necessary to formulate positions and make representations on issues affecting Africans. Also in 1882, the Native Electoral Association (NEA) appeared, and in the 1884 election it attacked the pass laws as "unnecessary oppression".[131] Both were active with regard to electoral politics and with broader issues that affected the African population. The NEA helped to secure the election of a liberal white lawyer, James Rose-Innes, to the Cape Parliament. Other African organisations emerged somewhat later in the Cape, including the Native Vigilance Association in the Transkei and the South African Native Congress (1902) in the Western Cape.

In 1895, in Kimberley, elite Africans founded the South African Improvement Society to promote the use of the English language. It was another means for Africans to become, as they believed, more 'respectable' and 'civilised' in the hope of reinforcing their status within their own communities and being more widely accepted as equals by Whites. Proper use of English was considered to be evidence also of the adoption of certain moral codes and social attitudes. This was a sentiment found amongst people colonised by the British around the world. [132] This type of organisation and sentiment was symptomatic of the 'assimilationist' views and non-confrontational approach vis-à-vis government of many of the African elite at that time.

The Natal Native Congress was founded in 1901 with the aim of representing the entire African population in the province. However, its membership was largely confined to the Christian, educated Africans. Further African political associations emerged after the Anglo-Boer War to address the issue of the African franchise. These included the Orange River Colony Native Vigilance Association (later, the Orange River Colony Congress) which argued for the extension of Cape rights, local self-government and the abolition of women's passes. The Transvaal had the Transvaal Native Congress (1912), the Bapedi Union and

---

[128] Walshe, 1987, p. 2.
[129] Ibid., p. 3.
[130] Karis and Carter, eds., 1972, Vol. 1, p. 5.
[131] Ibid., p. 3.
[132] Nauright, 1997, pp. 60-61.

the Basuto Association. The TNC lobbied for "the education of the Natives and amelioration of their conditions". In 1908, it submitted a petition with 3,764 signatures requesting a common roll franchise for Africans throughout South Africa. Its membership was similar to the Natal Native Congress, and its tactics were similar – "official liaison with government for the representation of Native grievances".[133] They also petitioned directly to the British government or the King, illustrating their tendency to have a highly idealistic view of the beneficent British empire.

As editor of *Imvo Zabantsundu,* John Tengo Jabavu established himself as one of the most influential Africans in Cape politics and founded the Cape Native Convention (largely an Eastern Cape organisation) in 1908. In 1909, John Dube founded the Ohlange Institute modelled on the Tuskegee Institute in the United States, with a view to "training Zulus in a Christian environment for competence in the less demanding tasks of society, that is intelligent unskilled labour in the house store, workshop and on the farms". He later raised his expectations and added skilled craftsmen and university entrance to his list.[134] He also launched his own newspaper, *Ilanga Lase Natal (The Natal Sun).* In 1912 Dube became the president of the newly formed South African Native National Congress, and remained a leader in African political life for decades. His cautious approach to issues of African rights was strongly influenced by American "Negro" leaders such as Booker T. Washington and W.E.B. DuBois.

In 1909, in response to the drafting of a constitution for the soon to be declared Union of South Africa, Africans and Coloureds lobbied for the right to vote through several organisations. Provincial congresses of the organisations noted above were held early that year. Then, in March 1909, 60 elected delegates from these regional conferences held the South African Native Convention. Only Jabavu's Cape Native Convention did not attend – a reflection of the relative privilege enjoyed by Africans in the Cape. However, other Cape delegates did attend, led by Rev. Walter Rubusana, who was subsequently elected president of the Convention. The Convention resolutions endorsed the concept of Union, but rejected all the constitutional clauses providing for the colour bar. They argued for an extension of the Cape common roll tradition to the entire country.[135]

The Convention sent a high level delegation to England to lobby the government on these matters. They were backed locally in their lobbying by the Aborigine Protection Society and some church organisations, as well as the Independent Labour Party. They had little success aside from actually being offered the opportunity to put their case.

Coloured people's organisations
The Coloured people of the Cape enjoyed far more freedoms that any other Black groups in the provinces of South Africa. They were well aware of this and acted to protect their interests.

The press freedom enjoyed by all the residents in the Cape was exploited by writers and leaders such as Dr. Abdullah Abdurahman, who was a key figure in both the Muslim and coloured communities in the first four decades of the 20th century. His leadership of coloured organisations such as the African Political Organisation (APO) and the Non-European Conferences demonstrated that "at least within the coloured petty bourgeoisie, a sense of coloured solidarity transcended religious differences".[136] The APO was founded in 1902 to protect the rights of the Cape Coloured people. Dr. Abdurahman was elected as its President in 1904. Prior to the creation of the Union in 1910, he made numerous trips to

---

[133] Walshe, 1987, p. 17.
[134] Ibid., p. 13.
[135] Ibid., p. 21.
[136] Raynard, 2002, p.12.

England to plead the case of the Cape Coloured, fearing that the increasing implementation of colour bars in the other provinces would soon be applied in the Cape. Once the Union was a fact, the APO had increasing difficulty persuading White politicians to act on behalf of the Coloureds and other non-European people. The APO "dominated Coloured protest politics for nearly four decades. It became the main vehicle for expressing this community's assimilationist aspirations as well as its fears at the rising tide of segregationism until its demise in the 1940s".[137]

Adhikari described this "assimilationism" as "less an impulse for acculturation than a striving on the part of Coloured people for acknowledgement of their worth as individuals and citizens and acceptance as equals or partners by whites. Throughout the 20th century, gaining such affirmation was one of the strongest imperatives within the Coloured community, especially among the petit bourgeois elite". Essentially, they wanted to be accepted into the dominant society and to "share in the benefits of citizenship on the basis of individual merit".[138]

Those who disagreed with Dr. Abdurahman's approach and opposed the APO formed several alternate organisations. The first were the Coloured People's Vigilance Committees in 1906, then the United Afrikaner League in 1913, and the African National Bond and the Christian Coloured Vigilance Association. However, none of them was very successful and disappeared fairly rapidly.

Indian organisations
The historiography of South African Indians has been largely confined to two subjects. The first is a number of studies related to the indentured labourers and the indenture system in general.[139] The second is the repressed political position of Indians in South Africa.[140] By 1893, there were 16,051 indentured Indians and 24,459 "free" Indians in Natal. At that time, there were also about 15,000 Indians in the Transvaal, with many concentrated on the Witwatersrand. In the Cape there were only about 5,000 and in the Orange Free State none at all as they had been barred since the 1870s.[141]

The study by Brain[142] corroborates that the majority of the Indians who arrived in South Africa between 1860 and 1911 were Hindus, Moslems, Parsees and Buddhists. All of these freely practised their religion and established places of worship, schools and community centres. Many also established associations linked to their district of origin in India. An example is the Aligarh Old Boys Club, which among other things had established bursary schemes for scholars and university students. They also established trade, caste or religious groups such as the Kholvad Association, Darjee Mandal of the Transvaal, Transvaal Hindu Seva Samaj, or the Transvaal Parsee Association. All of these organisations helped them to reconstruct their Indian culture and to begin to feel at home in their new surroundings. The Indians were "very heterogeneous and this was reflected in the organisations that they created for themselves to fulfil basic needs of identity and sub-group cohesion".[143]

Despite their hardship, by 1872 it became clear that some Indians in Natal were contributing to the local economy through diversified farming as both owners and tenants. Over time, however, they moved increasingly into the growing of sugar cane which, in order to make

---

[137] Adhikari, 2005, p. 4.
[138] Ibid., p. 8.
[139] Thompson, 1938, p. 20; Choonoo, 1967, p. 131.
[140] See Pachai, 1979; Kuper, 1960; Polak, 1909; Meer, n.d., p. 213; Wilson and Thompson, 1969; Brookes and Webb, 1965, p. 85.
[141] Bhana, 1997, pp. 3-4.
[142] Brain, 1983.
[143] Bhana, 1997, p. 5.

ends meet, required larger-sized farms. Whereas the state made support funds available to White farmers early on, Indian farmers had no access to such funds nor to credit institutions. The state also began to restrict Indian access to land, through a series of discriminatory laws. It was not until 1972 that Indians had access to the Land Bank, and only in 1983 did Indian cane farmers begin to get loans through the South African Sugar Association. They formed their own Natal Indian Cane Growers' Association to protect their commercial interests.[144]

More and more Indians moved to the urban areas. In Durban, Indian communities were characterised by diversity. "Rarely were neighbourhoods comprised only of people speaking the same language. Indeed, predominantly Hindu neighbourhoods often contained Muslims and Christians. They also could not really be defined in class terms… Language and religion survived as important building blocks. Intermarriage… across these lines was rare… More difficult to explain, but more important from a general South African perspective, was the development of a sense of Indianness". The emergence of strong social networks within the Indian communities linked immigrants from different regions of India "in terms of common cultural discourse".[145] This was compounded by the segregation of the city and by the sense of racial superiority played out by the Natal Whites in all aspects of their lives.

Some of the indentured and fare-paying Indians who had been brought to Natal migrated to the Transvaal and to the Cape as permanent and free citizens. The Transvaal was problematic, however, as Indians were barred from citizenship, required to register and pass language and education tests, finger-printed, and prohibited from owning land. Indians were denied entry altogether to the Orange Free State. These conditions led to the formation of several organisations representing Indian socio-political interests.

Two important political organisations emerged from Gandhi's period in South Africa: the Natal Indian Congress and the Transvaal Indian Congress. Both were initially created to obtain rights for Indians in these two provinces. However, after the meeting of organisations in the late 1940s, both Congresses identified with the broad principles of the ANC and worked within the framework of the Freedom Charter (post-1955) towards wider freedoms for all South Africans. Youth congresses were also created. Present Indian leaders serving in the ANC governments since 1994 grew up in these traditions and were banned or exiled by the apartheid government.

The Natal Indian Congress (NIC), founded in 1894, began and remained a somewhat elitist organisation, led by members of the well-to-do commercial elite and limited in membership by a relatively steep subscription fee. By 1901, there were only 723 paid-up members.[146] In fact, whilst it gained support internationally due to the involvement of Gandhi, it did not have large support within the country. Gandhi was by no means the only significant leader in the early development of the NIC and other Indian associations. Others such as P.S. Aiyar, for example, were instrumental in founding the Natal Indian Patriotic Union (NIPU,1908), the Colonial Born Indian Association (1911) and the South African Indian Committee (1911). This community, however, was not always in agreement about positions or strategies to adopt in its efforts to counteract discriminatory legislation and policies.

Under the leadership of Mohandas Gandhi, these organisations pursued a path of passive resistance to racial discrimination, known as "satyagraha". This type of non-violent mass action influenced African nationalist leaders in later periods.

---

[144] Freund, 1995, pp. 25-27.
[145] Ibid., p. 37.
[146] Bhana, 1997, p. 13.

The Birth of Passive Resistance

Leading the protest against this violation of Indian's human rights was a young lawyer of Indian extraction trained in Britain -- Mohandas Gandhi. In 1894, he founded the Natal Indian Congress to protest against the Natal Franchise Bill which denied the vote to Indians. In 1903, when he moved to the Transvaal, Gandhi also helped in the formation of the British Indian Association.

Gandhi led several passive resistance campaigns for the equal treatment of all Indians. The Immigration Act passed in 1913 was a measure to discriminate against Indians. Gandhi led a march from Natal to the Transvaal. He was arrested and imprisoned but his actions led to the establishment of a commission to inquire into the Indian grievances. The result was that in 1914 Parliament passed the Indian Relief Act which somewhat ameliorated the conditions of the Indians.

Before leaving South Africa to return to India, Gandhi reached an agreement with Jan Smuts in which Smuts promised to apply the law in a just manner. But hardly had Gandhi landed in India when he heard that Smuts had perfidiously reneged on their pact.

The NIC sought assistance from the British government and the Indian National Congress (the political movement working for Indian national independence from Britain) to remove discriminatory laws in South Africa. Some of their appeals were successful, especially those related to Indian business interests. But on the issues related to the situation of indentured workers, the NIC was rather lame. The NIC at this time also did not seek alliances with other Black organisations. Gandhi and other Indian leaders felt their interests should be kept separate from those of the Coloured and African populations, partly out of racism and a misplaced sense of superiority. This position changed dramatically in later years.

Bhana[147] attributes the initial organisational success of the passive resistance campaign to "the nature of the Indian bodies at the time and their peculiar relationships with each other through overlapping memberships":

> "Thus, for example, the BIA's leaders were also the leaders of the HIS [Hamidia Islamic Society]; those who served NIPU could well have been members of the NIC, the Durban Indian Society (DIS) and the Young Men's Catholic Society (YMCS). Hindus could have been members of the NIC as well as the Hindu Young Men's Association (HYMA), or the Sanatan Ved Dharma Sabha. Many Muslims in the Anjuman Islam were also affiliated to the NIC. There were also Parsees who belonged to the Zoroastrian Anjuman, some of whose members were in the NIC as well. In February 1910, the Kathiawad Arya Society in Durban organised a meeting at which Gandhi explained the movement in the Transvaal. Some of the leading Muslim supporters were present at this meeting organised by a Hindu group."

This passage reflects the overlapping identities and interests expressed through the wide range of Indian organisations of that period. It also shows the breadth of participation in the passive resistance campaign in terms of class, religion and culture. It ignores, however, the religious teachings of the Indian community to mediate rather than violently confront the opposition.

---

[147] Ibid., pp. 26-27.

By 1913, after he had mobilised large numbers of Indians for the march to the Transvaal, Gandhi had lost some support of the commercial elite, but gained support from the indentured Indians. Gandhi's contribution to the Indian struggle for political and economic rights was in some ways a success. He helped to obtain certain concessions from the government. He developed the concept of passive resistance and ensured that the Indian campaigns acted according to its principles. Nonetheless, it must be said that his emphasis on "Indianness" actually strengthened racism within the Indian community vis-à-vis Africans and reinforced the Whites' efforts to establish clear distinctions between racial categories in social, economic and political life. This negatively affected South African politics for some time to come.

However, Gandhi must be judged in the context of the conditions of his times and his own upbringing. His loyalty at this time of his life was to the British Empire. His naivete at this point needs to be juxtaposed against his steadfast resistance to the Empire in his later years in the fight for Indian independence.

Early Afrikaner organisations

Early *Boertrekker* groups were highly organised, with each trekking party having a recognised leader, though they aimed to create a single unified society when they settled in the interior. Their first attempt to establish a government for trekker society occurred in 1836, with the formal creation of the *volksraad* or elected council. This included functions of both a council of war (*krygsraad*) and a judiciary (*landdrost*).[148] Provision was also made for military commandants and regiments or commandos. During the mid-19th century various attempts to join the various Afrikaner communities in the Transvaal, Natal and the Orange Free State were stymied by conflict and varying agendas within the Afrikaner fold. However, the Afrikaners were quite clear about their anti-British sentiments and the *volksraad* continued to play an important role in Afrikaner political life until the Anglo-Boer Wars.

With a view to cultural revival, in 1875, the *Genootskap van Regte Afrikaners* was started by S.J. du Toit in Paarl aimed at popularising the Afrikaans of the so-called "First Language Movement".[149] The first organised expression of Afrikaner nationalism was the foundation of the Afrikaner Bond in the 1870s by the same du Toit. It generally held enough seats in the Cape Parliament to make its support essential to any government, but unwilling to take direct political responsibility instead gave its support to a succession of English-speaking leaders up to the end of the 18th century.[150] Around 1880, Jan Hofmeyr founded the *Boeren Beschermings Vereenigingen* (Farmer's Protection Association) to represent Dutch-speaking Cape farmers. They argued for improved status for the Dutch language and for farmer's interests. Hofmeyr was also the editor of the *Zuid Afrikaan* which promoted the use of Dutch as a medium in Parliament.[151] Increasingly, the Afrikaner Bond and the *Vereenigingen* began to speak with one voice.

In the early 1900s, as High Commissioner for the Transvaal, Sir Alfred Milner demonstrated his distrust for the Afrikaners and introduced a policy of anglicisation through public education. In reaction the Afrikaners felt their culture even more threatened than before, resulting in the creation of an educational and cultural movement aimed at the establishment of schools with instruction in Dutch and based on the principles of *Christelike Nasionale Onderwys* (Christian National Education).[152]

---

[148] Omer-Cooper, 1988, p. 75.
[149] Cameron, 1987, p. 170.
[150] Omer-Cooper, 1988, pp. 134-135.
[151] Cameron, 1987, p. 170.
[152] Omer-Cooper, 1988, pp. 149-150.

Welfare organisations

The oldest charitable society in South Africa is said to be the Ladies' Benevolent Society at the Cape. Bradlow[153] examined its work and placed it within the framework of 19th century British philanthropic stimuli and practices. Many welfare organisations, as noted previously, emerged from religious groups. Some of the earliest references to local welfare organisations other than those of the various Christian churches are to Jewish women's organisations in Cape Town. These included the Jewish Ladies' Association and the Jewish Philanthropic Society.[154]

In 1895, the Present Help League was established with support from the Randlords' political organisation, the Reform Committee. It initially provided charity and shelter to semi-skilled English workers during the demobilisation following the Anglo-Boer War, and later also devoted resources to unskilled Afrikaner workers. The Reform Committee was also used to support the rebellion against Kruger government of the Transvaal simultaneous to the Jameson Raid in late 1985. Eventually, the government had to take on a greater role vis-à-vis the unemployment issue when the numbers of unemployed Afrikaners increased considerably in the next several years. The Johannesburg Relief Committee (JRC) was formed in 1897 by prominent Afrikaners to address the growing problem of Afrikaner poverty. The JRC assisted at least 500 unemployed Afrikaner workers to find jobs on the mines. [155] In 1903, a number of the mine owners joined together in Johannesburg to alleviate the plight of unemployed English workers after the Anglo-Boer Wars. They formed the Rand Aid Association, modelled after the Charity Organisation Society of London.[156] For the next two decades, it "virtually dominated Johannesburg's organised relief programmes".[157]

Despite these relief efforts, many of the unemployed felt the need to represent their own interests. In 1906, they formed the Unemployed Organisation (UO) to try to solve their own problems. They advocated with the government to establish a public works programme, but they also lobbied for Black (African and Coloured) workers to be fired so that they could take their jobs. They even asked the City for rent-free accommodation. When the government finally announced the launch of a public works programme through the Rand Aid Association, but at very low wages, the UO members were not thrilled. The UO became increasingly militant, invading the show ground and camping there, and later marching to Pretoria to make their views known. [158]

A wide variety of organisations became involved in the debates around prostitution and the possible legalisation thereof in the late 19th century. These included the Transvaal Medical Association, the Johannesburg Protestant Ministers' Association, the Young Men's Christian Association, the Transvaal White Cross Purity League (promoting chastity), and others.[159]

It was common for White households' to employ African men as domestic servants. The Transvaal Native Association, formed around 1903 with the sponsorship of several 'enlightened' white men, aimed to provide services to such Black 'houseboys' in Johannesburg. It established a meeting hall, library and night school and facilitated their efforts to educate and better themselves.[160] However, these 'houseboys' became problematic due to fears of increasing inappropriate relations between them and white

---

[153] Bradlow, 1991.
[154] Shrire, 1993.
[155] van Onselen, 1982, Vol. 2, p. 126 and p. 133.
[156] van Onselen, 1982, Vol. 1, p. 35.
[157] van Onselen, 1982, Vol. 2, p. 133.
[158] Ibid., pp. 135-138.
[159] Van Onselen, 1982, Vol. 1, pp. 116-117.
[160] Van Onselen, 1982, Vol. 2, p. 33.

women – both their mistresses and fellow servants. This became known as the "black peril" in the early 1900s. In 1907, it led the Associated Women's Organisations of the Transvaal to implement social segregation.[161]

The box below illustrates the involvement of international philanthropy in support of local non-profit organisations dealing with humanitarian and pacifist issues in the early 20th century. It is also an example of women's solidarity operating across borders and cultural / ethnic groups -- British women supporting Boer women and their families. Further, it is an early example of the promotion of small enterprise in order to alleviate poverty and rebuild post-conflict societies. The example of Emily Hobhouse also shows the roles played by both organisations and individuals.

Emily Hobhouse (1860-1926)[162]

Emily Hobhouse was a Cornish humanitarian and pacifist, the daughter of an Anglican clergyman. She came to prominence during the Anglo-Boer War of 1899-1902 as a champion of suffering Boer women and children who were interned in concentration camps by the British. In November 1899 Emily Hobhouse became secretary of the South African Conciliation Committee, which was opposed to the Salisbury government's policy towards the Boer republics. In June 1900 she organised a mass meeting of women in London to protest against the British army's actions in South Africa. Three months later, she launched the South African Women and Children Distress Fund to aid destitute Boer families.

In December 1900, she sailed for South Africa. During the first quarter of 1901 she visited camps in the Cape and Orange River colonies, distributing not only kindness and sympathy, but also supplies and clothing to the distressed inmates. She was, moreover, instrumental in instituting reforms in some camps. Her revelations on her return to Britain focused the attention of the Liberal opposition on the evils of the concentration camp system and contributed towards the government's decision to send a Commission of Ladies, headed by Dame Millicent Fawcett, to South Africa. Emily Hobhouse was not appointed to this commission, whose visit and recommendations in 1901 led to vastly improved conditions in the concentration camps. When Emily Hobhouse returned to South Africa in October 1901, she was arrested in Cape Town and immediately deported to Britain.

After the Anglo-Boer War, Emily Hobhouse established home industries in the Orange River Colony and Transvaal to help rehabilitate Boer families. She was invited to unveil the Women's Monument in Bloemfontein in 1913. Ill health prevented her attending the ceremony and her speech was read for her. After her death in June 1926, her ashes were brought to South Africa and buried at the Women's Monument.

Economic interest organisations

This period saw the creation of the first wave of economic interest organisations in South Africa. These included groups formed by owners / capitalists in emerging industries, smaller entrepreneurs, craft and trade unions, as well as groups of individuals engaged in particular occupations, both skilled and unskilled. Two of the most influential business organisations were formed in the late 19th and early 20th centuries: the Association of Chambers of Commerce (ASSOCOM) was formed in 1892 to represent retail commercial interests, and the Federated Chamber of Industries (FCI) was established in 1918 to represent organised industry in South Africa. These organisations remained key players in the economy and in politics until the 1980s.

---

[161] Ibid., p. 49.
[162] Cameron, 1987, p. 214.

Another of the earliest ones came about as small companies gave way to larger ones in the mining industry in the late 1880s. In 1887, the Transvaal Chamber of Mines was established as an employer organisation representing the interests of the various mining houses to government, to the Reserve Bank, to foreign institutional buyers of gold, coal, diamonds and other minerals, as well as with their workers. It was also intended to "regulate their common interests in such matters as labour recruitment and wage levels". [163] This organisation became one of the most powerful economic interest groups in the country.

Another powerful but totally different constituency was represented by the Witwatersrand Licensed Victuallers' Association (WLVA) – the liquor retailers. Their influence derived from the fact that workers on the mines were generally housed in compounds or hostels, and the liquor stores and bars were highly profitable, not least because they were also places where prostitution was rife. Charles van Onselen wrote that "A government anxious to protect a liquor industry that benefited its most powerful constituents, and a mining industry that sought to attract and stabilise a working class on the Witwatersrand, between them had good reason for condoning this conspicuous activity".[164] The members of the WLVA gradually constituted a significant element of the "petty bourgeoisie" and as such gained economic clout.[165] Groups such as the Transvaal Temperance Alliance were unable to have much effect on liquor policy when they came up against entrenched interests, that is at least until the Chamber of Mines thought better of its support for the liquor trade and became conscious of its detrimental impact on the mining labour force. Controls were finally imposed near the end of the century.

A more unusual grouping that appeared from 1890 was the *AmaWasha*. These were Zulu-speaking washermen who had copied the occupation of Indian washermen in Natal. They dominated the hand-laundry business in Johannesburg, and plied their trade on the banks of the Braamfontein spruit. The AmaWasha were essentially an ethnically-based craft guild. They were recognised by the Sanitary Board, and provided an essential service to the migrant miners who had no women family members living with them to undertake this task.[166] Each group of AmaWasha incorporated elements of Zulu social structure, including an induna who played a leadership and recruitment role. This brought some social stability to the lives of these migrant workers. They were also given the considerable privilege of being exempted from the pass system. Membership of the AmaWasha rose from about 500 in 1892 to more than 1,200 in 1895, but declined again to 500 by 1899. This decline was due in part to increasing concerns about public health and the removal of the washermen to a site much further from the population centre. Eventually, they also had to compete with new steam laundries and Asian laundrymen.[167] Their access to the occupation was virtually eliminated by around 1915, but a large number had managed to accumulate enough savings to create small businesses when they returned to their families in Natal.[168]

In early 1891, the Johannesburg Cab Owners' Association was established to represent the men who provided taxi services with carts and horses. Its 80 members were mostly Afrikaners who had used their small amounts of capital to enter this business. Other members included some Coloureds and immigrants from Europe.[169] As a group, they succeeded in petitioning the Sanitary Board to provide them with better roads and taxi

---

[163]Omer-Cooper, 1988, p. 128.
[164] van Onselen, 1982, Vol. 1, p. 7.
[165] Ibid., p. 57.
[166] van Onselen, 1982, Vol. 1, p. 8; and Vol. 2, pp. 74-102.
[167] van Onselen, 1982, Vol. 1, pp. 18-19.
[168] van Onselen, 1982, Vol. 2, pp. 100-101.
[169] van Onselen, 1982, Vol. 1, p. 9.

ranks.[170] During the 1890s, other racial and ethnic groups became involved in the cab trade, including a fair number of blacks (e.g. Africans and Cape Malays). As most of the owners kept their horses stabled in Fordsburg, when the organisation was renamed in 1896 it became the Fordsburg Vigilance and Cab Owners' Association. Through the Association, the cab owners' developed a real petty bourgeoisie class identity, and they actively protected their interests in coming years despite increasing regulation. The class solidarity was somewhat dented as a distinction developed between owners and drivers. A Cab Drivers' Union was formed in 1902. Race also became a factor as African cabbies were denied licenses, and Coloured ones were restricted to the 'second-class' trade. The business was forced into decline with the introduction of electric trams in the early 20th century.[171]

Other economic interest organisations on the Rand included the Witwatersrand Boarding-House Keepers' Protection Association (to lower wages in the sector by importing servants from London), the Witwatersrand Hotel Employees' Union (to protect the wages of existing employees), the Witwatersrand Native Labour Association (created by mine owners to eliminate competition for unskilled labour in the sector and keep African wages low), the Employers' Domestic Native Labour Association (created by employers to keep down the wages of African domestic servants), the Township Owners' Association (created by mine owners to facilitate the purchase of houses by white mine workers), the Waterfall Brickmakers' Association and the Braamfontein Brickmakers' Association (to protect predominantly Afrikaner brickmakers' jobs and leverage influence with government to assure land on which to conduct their occupation and to limit unfair trade practices).[172]

Criminal gangs

This period also saw the emergence of what are now sometimes referred to as "uncivil" society organisations – i.e. those that do not reflect the prevailing norms and values of society. Several of these groups were created as a means of bridging the gap between traditional rural societies and their new lives in a rapidly modernising urban economy. They allowed for some degree of transference of traditional kinship and customary linkages and thereby provided for some social cohesion in an unfamiliar environment.[173] In theory, one of their aims was to protect themselves against social injustices and to claim redress. However, they were non-political and became essentially criminal organisations preying on both other black workers and on white employers.[174]

One such group was the "Regiment of the Hills" which consisted of unemployed blacks and some criminal elements. The Regiment was organised along military lines, and their activities were largely anti-social, e.g. robbing migrant workers of their wages or robbing businesses in town. They became "a well-established feature of the Witwatersrand's criminal underworld".[175]

Amalaita gangs grew out of groups of various ethnicities of low-paid African 'houseboys', and were gradually taken over especially by young Pedi men who drifted into the urban areas of the Rand during the 1906-1908 depression. The members were both employed and unemployed youth, with each gang consisting of 50-100 members. To a large extent, the Amalaita "sought to give its members who laboured in alienated colonised isolation a sense

---

[170] Ibid., p. 172.
[171] Ibid., pp. 184-196.
[172] See van Onselen, 1982, Vols. 1 and 2.
[173] van Onselen, 1982, Vol. 2, pp. 193-194.
[174] Ibid., pp. 194-195.
[175] van Onselen, 1982, Vol. 1, p. 23.

of purpose and dignity".[176] However, whilst internally the groups may have provides some social cohesion, externally they were feared due to their criminal and violent behaviour.

The "Peruvians" were largely Russian and Polish Jewish immigrants who established an economic niche for themselves in the illicit liquor trade at the end of the 19th century. Their ethnic origins, combined with close kinship ties, resulted in the creation of a tight network of organised crime. Extensive publicity regarding the role of the "Peruvians" led to significant concern within the wider Jewish community that it might lead to an increase in anti-Semitism.[177]

Concluding Remarks

This chapter has highlighted the inevitable clashes between colonial societies and indigenous peoples, as well as the processes of assimilation resulting from the increasing contacts between them.

The importation of slaves and indentured labour was part and parcel of the oppressive and exploitative nature of the colonising process. However, in the long run, these peoples brought to the shores of South Africa either against their will or under the direst conditions have greatly enriched South African society with their religious and cultural practices. Despite the efforts of the colonists to destroy their identities and heritage, these communities have managed to preserve or to resuscitate essential aspects. They also succeeded in offering their beliefs to others and growing their religious community despite government persecution. Groups fleeing persecution elsewhere also added to the richness and diversity.

A wide variety of religious denominations, especially Christian, also succeeded in their proselytising and conversions through missions established around the country. However, as an integral part of the colonisation process, missionary activities largely reinforced the subjugation of indigenous and other non-White peoples, destroying or belittling their cultural and social practices and beliefs.

All of the religious groups spawned affiliated civil society organisations, especially in the welfare and education sectors. Most of these organisations, however, served only their own communities due to the increasing political and social pressures for separation of the races in all spheres of life. Initial attempts at racial inclusiveness did not last. The emergence of the African independent churches was a direct result.

Missionaries' role was often conflicted and hypocritical. They were caught between promoting the socio-economic advancement of their Black adherents whilst insistent on maintaining White control over church affairs. Church leadership was also plagued by competition between denominations and between the South African-based institutions and their European-based governance hierarchies.

Christian Africans soon emerged as leaders in their own communities. African ministers formed their own associations and gradually also became more influenced by African nationalism and resistance to oppressive colonial / state authority. This African elite formed political organisations aimed at contesting government attempts to deprive them of more and more rights. Similar trends occurred in the Cape Coloured community. Gandhi's passive resistance movement amongst the Natal and Transvaal Indians had a huge influence on the African and Coloured peoples' early approach to political contestation.

---

[176] van Onselen, 1982, Vol. 2, pp. 54-60.
[177] See van Onselen, 1982, Vol. 1, pp. 74-84.

Thus, the divisions in society – based on race, religion, ethnicity and capital – whilst reflected in huge differentials in access to political and economic opportunities, nonetheless provided a social and cultural richness. A limited amount of crossing of these barriers also helped leaders in each group to begin to push the boundaries of their own thinking and action.

Chapter Three

Formation of the Union of South Africa and Consolidation of White Rule, 1910-1948

This chapter considers the first half of the 20th century from the formation of the Union of South Africa in 1910 until the advent of the National Party government and its policies in 1948. This is the period in which White South Africans consolidated their power and their exploitation of the majority population, whether African, Coloured or Indian. It was a period in which civil society organisations multiplied amongst all South African communities.

After a brief overview to contextualise the socio-political environment of this period including the 'poor white' problem and the increasing urbanisation trends, the chapter focuses on the manner in which civil society responded. It examines the increasing impact of Afrikaner nationalism on their organisational life. The active opposition by African, Indian and Coloured people to racially-based government oppression is discussed, both in terms of overtly political organisations and other less direct means of creating community or interest group solidarity. As key examples, the emergence of trade unions, youth and women's organisations as sites of struggle and resistance during this period is reviewed.

The Socio-Political Environment

Following the Treaty of Vereeniging, the Union of South Africa was established when the two former self-governing British colonies of the Cape and Natal in the south joined with the Boer Republics of the Transvaal and Free State in the north. The Union came into being on 31 May 1910. Its population was racially heterogeneous, with White (1.28 m), Coloured (0.53 m), Indian (0.15 m) and African (4.02 m) people spread over the four provinces.

The franchise (vote) was then held as follows:
- Transvaal: White men over 21 years
- Free State: White men over 21 years
- Natal: All males over 21, but in practice only Whites qualified
- Cape: All males over 21, subject to qualification

According to Article 35, the franchise of the Africans and Coloureds in the Cape was entrenched, and a two-thirds majority was required in Parliament with a joint sitting to agree to any change in the franchise rights.

The advent of Union brought with it considerable fears amongst the African community that in creating national policy, the political rights they enjoyed in the Cape might be taken away. This feeling was exacerbated following the failure of the representatives of the 1909 South African Native Convention to gain a favourable response from the British.

The White electorate, in the main, supported social and political segregation. The South African Party advanced this segregation through the following legislation in the second decade of the 20th century:

Laws promoting social, economic and political segregation

Law	Content
Mines and Works Act 1911	Reserved categories of work for White workers
Native Labour Regulation Act 1911	Black victims of industrial accidents would receive less compensation; Black strikers could be charged under criminal law.
Defence Act 1912	Provided for a Whites-only citizen force
Industrial Conciliation Act 1924	Provided collective bargaining machinery only for unionised workers; Black workers were excluded from the Act
Native Land Act 1913	Imposed rural segregation
Native Affairs Act 1920	Made provision for Native Commissioners who were responsible for administration of African affairs
Natives Urban Area Act 1920	Similarly imposed urban segregation throughout South Africa; restricted influx of Africans into urban areas

Economic development between 1910 and 1924 was characterised by the post-war depression, strikes on the mines, the emergence of a secondary manufacturing sector, and the establishment of the Reserve Bank in 1920 and of Eskom as a power utility in 1923. This period was also characterised by large-scale labour disputes and new labour legislation which provided trade union rights to White, Coloured and Indian workers but not to African workers. The Riotous Assemblies Act was passed in 1924 curtailing demonstrations.

Previously subordinate to the British Parliament, South Africa established greater self-determination in foreign policy. South Africa had right of session at the Peace Conference, signed the Charter of the League of Nations, and assumed membership of the League separately from Britain.

As part of this growing international credibility, South Africa was brought into a hegemonic position vis-à-vis South-West Africa (SWA is present-day Namibia). As a former German colony, it had been placed in trusteeship to South Africa after World War I. However, South Africa acted in a repressive manner when, in 1921, the Smuts government became involved in the Bondelswarts revolt. Local inhabitants sought redress of grievances against the German authorities and restoration of their captain, Jacobus Christian. Abraham Morris led the revolt from South Africa with armed companions who refused to surrender their guns. The SWA Administrator launched a punitive expedition with South African troops and aircraft. Approximately 100 people were killed, including women and children. Thus, South Africa's role as a "colonial" power was similar to its internal repression of Black rights.

A referendum was held in Rhodesia in October 1922 to decide on self-government or amalgamation with the Union. By a narrow majority of 8,774 to 5,989, White voters in an 80% poll chose to remain a self-governing British colony. Some reasons advanced for this decision were: fear of the policies of Hertzog; the dependence of Rhodesian farmers on international markets; the desire to inhibit the southward flow of Rhodesian African workers; the suppression of the 1922 strike in South Africa; and the fact that White women enjoyed the franchise in Rhodesia but not in South Africa!

The Smuts government was plagued with difficulties related to establishing and maintaining a government with fractious smaller parties. The political differences between Smuts and Hertzog could not be resolved. Other problems included the economic Depression and a consequent rise in the cost of living, a severe drought in the early 1920s, the curbing of public service expenditure, and the handling of the strikes on the mines.

The 1920s and 1930s saw a series of coalition governments amongst the various White political parties, each with somewhat different composition and leadership, depending on the priority issues of the election. The successive governments largely managed to contain Black dissent during this period through a number of measures aimed at co-opting civil society organisations with minimalist concessions or promises thereof. White women were given the right to vote in 1928, but no political concessions were won by the non-White population in the face of increasing efforts to institutionalise White supremacy. Worse still, the government repeatedly failed to consult the African community before implementing more and more discriminatory and oppressive measures.

The Depression forced South Africa to re-examine how it dealt with the economic issues facing the country. But it also further entrenched the position of White workers and White civil society organisations. Following the collapse of Wall Street in 1929, the foreign market found it increasingly difficult to pay adequate prices for South Africa's main primary export products. South Africa abandoned the gold standard in December 1932 and within a month the country began to experience an economic boom period. The price of gold rose substantially, the South African pound achieved parity with the British pound, and foreign capital was invested on the Johannesburg Stock Exchange.

The more open attitudes of a small number of liberal Whites did lead to the creation of the Joint Councils of Europeans and Bantu / Natives. These multi-racial initiatives were found in the main urban centres around the country and provided opportunities for dialogue aimed at improving the situation of Africans. Related to this was the Conference of European and Bantu Christian Student Associations held in 1930. The informal Joint Council meetings spent much time discussing issues of African welfare rather than some of the more political issues. Annual National European-Bantu Conferences were held from 1929, and were eventually incorporated into the regular activities of the South African Institute of Race Relations. These conferences too were relatively non-political, but they did "argue for a sharp reversal of government policy away from the accelerating trend to segregation".[178]

Following Smut's resignation and the election in June 1924, Hertzog won 63 seats and Labour 18, giving him a total of 81 seats against 53 won by the South African Party and one by an independent. The PACT government had won an important propaganda victory but also united English- and Afrikaans-speaking Whites -- both in government and in opposition. The stage was set to establish White hegemony in South Africa.

As the only Cabinet member with experience in government, Hertzog was able to control the new Cabinet and the policies of the new government. In 1929 he fought the election on the question of Native policy -- *swartgevaar* or 'the Black Peril'. As a result of this fear factor, Hertzog won 78 seats, the South African Party 61 seats, the Cromwell Labourites 5, National Council Labourites 3 and independents 1.

In 1933, Hertzog and Smuts established an election coalition to address the impact of the deep worldwide Depression and to unite against Tielman Roos who had returned to active political life and advocated abandoning the gold standard. This coalition developed into Fusion -- the Foundation of the United South African National Party. The followers of Malan opposed to the Fusion formed the purified National Party. In 1938, the United South African Party won 111 seats to the National Party's 27, the Dominion Party's 8 and the Labour Party's 3.

---

[178] Karis and Carter, 1973, Vol. 1, pp. 150-151.

World War II broke out on 3 September 1939. Parliament, in special session, heard a motion from Hertzog to remain neutral. Smuts countered with an amendment to participate in the war against Germany and won by a majority of 80 votes against 67. Hertzog asked the Governor-General Duncan to dissolve Parliament and hold an election. He refused and asked Smuts to form a new cabinet which he did with support from the Dominion and Labour Parties.

The 'poor white' problem

Despite the political and economic hegemony of the Whites, the Dutch Reformed Church had in 1916 already identified a 'poor white' problem. A 'poor white' was described by J.F.W. Grosskopf as a White person who has become dependent to such an extent, whether from moral, mental, economic or physical causes, that he is unfit, without help of others, to find proper means of livelihood for himself or to provide it directly or indirectly for his children.

The causes of the "poor white" problem were many. Major factors were the trek movement into the interior of the country where conditions of life were harsh; the eviction of unskilled rural Afrikaners who had squatted on White-owned farms but were forced off the land into wage labour in the cities – known as *bywoners*; and the Anglo-Boer War and 'scorched earth' policy implemented by the British which resulted in the destruction of much of what the Afrikaners had built. The subdivision of farms made it more difficult to earn a sufficient living, and led to increased poverty in rural areas. This situation was compounded by a lack of education and skills, resulting in reduced access to employment in trades. Poor Whites began to gamble on the diamond and gold diggings to provide an income to sustain their families. In addition, their livelihoods were hit by natural disasters such as stock diseases, the influenza epidemics, periodic droughts. Other special political and economic events of the era such as the 1914 Rebellion, the 1922 strikes and the Depression worsened their situation.

In response to the plight of poor Whites, the Dutch Reformed Church (DRC) took action on several fronts. They started a labour colony for poor Whites at Kakamas in 1893, established the Goedemoed Irrigation Scheme in 1913, and helped in urban areas by finding work and teaching them to be independent. They also submitted a request to the Carnegie Foundation in the USA to launch an investigation and provide solutions to the problem.

In 1935 the volumes of the comprehensive Carnegie Report detailed the nature and extent of the 'poor white' problem. The Report dealt with rural impoverishment, the psychology of those affected, the educational, health and social aspects of the problem. Its suggestions led the government to offer employment opportunities to thousands of unemployed Whites.

The response of the Hertzog government to the Carnegie Report took several forms: they offered privileged employment for White workers through the Civil Labour Policy; they tried to entice people back onto the land by settling people along irrigation schemes at Koppies, Langersdrift, and Roos-Senekal and other means; they created public works programmes such as building railway lines, roads and irrigation schemes and laying out forest plantations; and they improved the education system for Whites so as to offer them wider employment opportunities.

The impact of growing urbanisation and industrialisation

Urbanisation of both the White and African populations through the post-World War II industrialisation process led to 62% of Whites and 24.3% of Africans living and working in urban areas by 1945. By 1951, the African total had increased to 27%. This urbanisation brought with it a new political, social and economic dynamic.

World War II resulted in major changes in the South African economy which, in turn, led to more proactive and concerted action by resistance organisations. The increase in industrialisation created a rise in demand for industrial labour. More Black workers -- men and women -- went to work in industry, especially due to the absence of White men in the army. The growing Black population in towns and cities exacerbated racial tensions with the 'poor white' communities. White workers began to feel more threatened as the Black labour force obtained more skills and was able to fill jobs previously held only by Whites. One example is that many Coloured women were employed in textile factories.

At the same time, African people came under increasing economic pressure. Bus boycotts occurred in the face of rising transport fares. Whereas the Chamber of Mines had moved to employ more African workers during World War II, they came under renewed pressure to retrench those workers and employ more Whites. Those who remained on the mines were paid much lower wages than the Whites. This situation came to a head when the African Mineworkers' Union went on strike with 70,000 workers in August 1946 demanding higher wages. The issue of the colour bar, preventing Africans from holding higher skilled and better paid jobs despite their proven capabilities, was an ongoing source of protests.

The racist legislation and the practice which accompanied it created the context for the ongoing struggle for and against White racial hegemony in South Africa. Socio-economic relations and therefore most organisational life were in some way a reflection of this societal division and conflict. Education was a cornerstone of these policies.

Education

Segregation of school education was the order of the day. The minority Coloured and Indian population attended each others' schools, and where no schools existed for them, they attended African schools. Those Africans who attended school went primarily to missionary schools. In 1920, Molema wrote that:

> "The Government gives a show of financial support to ... missionary schools for the Bantu [sic] throughout the length and breadth of South Africa, and in return expects these schools to maintain a prescribed standard of efficiency in their teaching and their staff, and, of course, the schools are examined by Government inspectors. The Government grants to the missionary schools for Bantu education are, however, extremely niggardly, and almost nominal when two factors are taken into consideration; namely -- first, the fat taxes which are paid by the Bantu into the Public Treasury; and second, when a comparison is made between the Government grants for European education on the one hand and for Bantu education on the other". [179]

The following table illustrates the completely skewed attendance and funding of European versus African schools in the Cape -- considered to be the most liberal province!

Cape Province, 1915

	Estimated population	School enrolment	Total State expenditure	Per student expenditure
European	592,000	105,742	863,000 pounds	8.16 pounds
African	2,000,000	137,238	140,000 pounds	1.02 pounds

Source: Molema, 1920, p. 228.

---

[179] Molema, 1920, p. 226.

These missionary schools largely trained Africans to become tradesmen, preachers, or teachers. Some of the types of jobs filled by these mission-educated Africans also included interpreters and clerks to magistrates/judges, postal clerks and letter carriers, railway employees, police, labour contractors, hotel proprietors and newspaper editors/journalists.

The Response of Civil Society

Political organisations

Afrikaner nationalism and organisations

The first half of the 20th century saw a rapid growth in the number and importance of Afrikaner organisations, especially those espousing Afrikaner nationalism. Shortly after World War I, an Afrikaner nationalist organisation called Jong Suid Africa (Young South Africa) was founded by young Afrikaner teachers and white collar workers reacting to what they saw as "the desperate plight of Afrikaners" and their domination by the English.[180] In 1918, this became the Broederbond, an exclusive and originally secret organisation promoting the cultural, political and economic interests of the Afrikaners.[181] Its membership was by invitation only. After 1926, it established secret cells in the major organisational and administrative institutions.

In December 1929, the Broederbond created the *Federasie van Afrikaanse Kulturverenigings* (FAK - Federation of Afrikaans Cultural Associations) to act as a public front and to give direction to Afrikaner cultural organisations. By 1937, 300 cultural organisations were affiliated to the FAK. They held large-scale people's congresses (*Volkskongres*), sponsored radio programmes, art and books, songs, and public festivals.[182] From the 1930s onward, the Broederbond played an active role in all aspects of life in the Afrikaner community and had a huge, if largely unseen, influence on the policies of future Afrikaner-led governments.

Other organisations were also formed to ensure the continuation of Afrikaner culture and society. For example, the Voortrekker Movement was started in 1929 to take the place of the Boy Scouts for Afrikaner boys. In 1933, the *Afrikaanse Nasionale Studentebond* (Afrikaner National Student Union) was formed as a breakaway from the National Union of South African Students (NUSAS).

The Afrikaans press expanded significantly in 1915 with the establishment of three Afrikaans newspapers: *Het Volksblad* in Potchefstroom (later moved to Bloemfontein); *Het Burger* in the Cape; and *Ous Vaderland* in Pretoria. These newspapers "laid the foundation for the extensive Afrikaans-based publishing interest, concentrated in Nationale Pers, that would develop in the latter part of the 20th century".[183] The major newspaper, *De Burger,* was Nationale Pers' primary means of providing support for the National Party. It also published a wide range of Afrikaans literature and text books.

Afrikaner nationalism became virtually a "civil religion" through its all-encompassing outreach into the Afrikaner community through the Dutch Reformed Churches, the FAK, and other related organisations.

---

[180] Omer-Cooper, 1987, p. 167.
[181] Smuts described the Broederbond in 1944 as "a dangerous, cunning political, fascist organisation". In 1990, *Newsweek* writer, Matthews, described it as "elite white Afrikaners pushing forcefully for reform".
[182] Omer-Cooper, 1987, p. 174.
[183] Oliphant, 2000, p. 116. Nationale Pers (Naspers) was founded in 1914, partly as a means to promote Afrikaner interests.

"The Broederbond had come to be led predominantly by Afrikaner theologians and other academics and had elaborated an ideology for Afrikaner nationalism which was to provide the theoretical basis of apartheid. This was the belief that the nation rather than the individual or the family is the basic unity of moral and cultural life... The Afrikaner nation had been specially created by God from members of several different European peoples brought together on the soil of South Africa. It was intended to fulfil a divinely ordained role in the continent."[184]

This theology also led to the development of an economic strategy to compete with the English-speaking capitalists. The strategy aimed to channel Afrikaner resources into Afrikaner business, banks, etc. A "salvation-deed fund" (reddingsdaadbond) was created to assist Afrikaner enterprises.

The Dutch Reformed Churches played an active role in promoting the colour bar in industry. In 1944, they joined with the National Party and the FAK in denouncing the employment of coloured women in factories alongside White women. They issued pamphlets calling for continuation of the colour bar. At the same time, the Broederbond founded yet another organisation -- the *Blanke Werkers Beskermingsbond* (White Workers' Protection Society).

Then, in the late 1940s, several anti-black unions split from the Trades and Labour Council to form *Die Ko-ordinerende Raad var Suid-Afrikaanse Vakvereniginge* (Co-ordinating Council of South African Unions) which pushed a militant pro-Afrikaner line.[185]

African political organisations

Both before and after unification, Africans attempted to unite their forces and improve their capacity to protest and to win a say in the country of their birth. In January 1912, Pixley ka Izaka Seme, who had studied law in the United States and Britain, organised a conference in Bloemfontein at which the South African Native National Congress (SANNC)[186] was founded. Dr. John L. Dube was elected the first president, Seme became the treasurer, and Solomon Plaatje became secretary-general of the SANNC. The SANNC resisted the Native Land Act, petitioned Cabinet ministers, protested to the Governor-General to withhold his assent, and sailed to London on a mission to petition the British Parliament. Their advocacy fell on deaf ears.

J.T. Jabavu opposed the creation of the SANNC because it was not based on his approach of continuing to work with "sympathetic Whites to exert pressure on the existing parliamentary system". He therefore established the South African Races Congress (SARC) in April 1912 to serve as his own political platform in the Cape.[187] However, in 1914, Jabavu and the SARC were discredited when his lack of support led to the defeat of the only African ever to run for the Cape Provincial Council.

The SANNC constitution was prepared over a period of six years. When finalised, it "outlined an organisation which was to formulate uniform policy upon African affairs for presentation to the Union government, while at the same time both educating White public opinion to African concerns and Africans to their rights and obligations. From an unequivocal platform of opposition to the colour bar, the organisation was to agitate and pressure government bodies for measures it judged favourable to African interests". The constitution was

---

[184] Omer-Cooper, 1987, p. 176.
[185] Walker, 1991, p. 114.
[186] The South African Native National Congress (SANNC) was renamed the African National Congress (ANC) in 1923.
[187] Karis and Carter, eds., 1973, Vol. 1, p. 62

influenced by Gandhi's emphasis on "passive resistance" and advocated using means such as petitions, deputations and propaganda campaigns.[188]

The SANNC did not have much initial success in challenging laws such as the Native Land Act of 1913. Their deputation to the British government had no more impact than their appeals to the Union government. They also had little impact in stopping government moves toward territorial segregation and the imposition of African administration.

During World War I, the SANNC restrained itself from protest action, its members proclaiming their loyalty to the British. But, when S.M. Makgatho succeeded Dube in 1917, he adopted a more aggressive tone sponsoring a passive resistance campaign (similar to Gandhi's efforts) against the pass laws on the Rand, followed by a spate of strikes. These efforts were also unsuccessful. These activities had begun, however, to involve Africans beyond the middle classes who had traditionally constituted the majority of members and protestors.

At the end of World War I, the SANNC sent a deputation to the Versailles Conference hoping to negotiate a better future, in the light of the United States and British leaders' statements in favour of a more equitable dispensation for colonial peoples. SANNC members, led by Sol Plaatje, undertook the mission, but returned without any success. Such failures caused dissension and disillusionment in the organisation, leading to divisions. The situation of Africans had not improved at all since the advent of the Union.

In 1918/19, due to the collapse of the South African Races Congress, and the limited impact of the SANNC, Meshach Pelem created and led a new African pressure group in the Cape called the Bantu Union. He had a less blindly loyal attitude to the British than that expressed repeatedly by the SANNC. His main rival was S.M. Makgatho who criticised the Cape politician for his exclusively Cape outlook.

The early 1920s brought new attention from Black South African leaders to the Pan African movement on the continent. Dube attended the Second Pan African Conference in 1921. This movement was to become a more and more important influence on African political organisations around the country.

As time passed, resistance by Blacks took many forms -- the formation of black trade unions, labour strikes on the mines and elsewhere against the colour bar (job reservation) and low wages, passive resistance against the pass laws, petitions, deputations and submissions of evidence to government commissions regarding the impact of various policies and laws, and so on. Some support came from liberal whites, e.g. in 1929 the leaders of the Joint Councils of Europeans and Africans decided to set up the South African Institute of Race Relations "to undertake research and pursue conciliation to lessen racial tensions".[189]

Despite its problems, the African National Congress (formerly the SANNC) maintained its predominant position in African politics. It brought members from all four provinces together regularly to address ongoing issues and to find more effective means of taking their grievances to the government. The ANC also had created a House of Chiefs to strengthen its links to traditional authorities and to engage them in protesting against government's efforts to limit African rights. However, its activities between annual conferences were limited and internal conflicts continued to plague its attempts to achieve unity. Its moderate approach also constrained its impact.

---

[188] Ibid.
[189] Omer-Cooper, 1988, p. 179.

Four "non-European" conferences were held in 1927, 1930, 1931 and 1934 on the initiative of Dr. Abdurahman of the African Peoples' Organisation (APO). Several other organisations participated, including the African National Congress (ANC), the Cape Native Voters Association (CNVA), and the South African Indian Congress (SAIC). Whilst all of these attempts failed to create a permanent organisation which could co-ordinate resistance political activity, they did represent "an important extension of the range of African political activity".[190] Nonetheless, their proceedings reflected the difficulty in achieving common positions across African, Indian and Coloured organisations. This was not least due to the reluctance of each organisation to cede any independence of action.

In 1935, the first All Africa Convention (AAC) was held in Bloemfontein, bringing together all the existing African political groups: the ANC, the CNVA, the Communist Party (CP) and the ICU. The Convention was led by Professor Jabavu and was attended by more than 400 delegates from around the country. Though the Convention called for "no one racial group to be dominated by another", it did accept the principle of a "civilization test" to qualify for the vote.[191] Its initial opposition to racially segregated representative institutions was dropped upon the passage of the Representation of Natives Bill, and members competed for seats in the new institutions. However, the AAC did continue to lobby government with regard to many issues prevalent in African communities such as land rights, taxation and social facilities,[192] using the same moderate tactics as the ANC of that period. Whilst those who attended the Convention represented a wide spectrum of political views, the leadership of that time was generally conservative and against militant action. There was as yet no mass movement, and once the AAC became a formal organisation, considerable competition arose between the AAC and the ANC for the allegiance of a small elite.

Extra-parliamentary activities amongst the African people were not dormant during the war years. The ANC resuscitated itself in the 1940s and re-seized the initiative from the All Africa Convention. Dr. A.B. Xuma became president of the ANC in December 1940. By 1942 it had set up a committee to study the Atlantic Charter and its implications for South Africa. The result was the document entitled "African Claims in South Africa", including a statement of their interpretation of the Atlantic Charter[193] as it should be applied to Africans in South Africa, and most significantly, a Bill of Rights calling for full citizenship rights and "the abolition of political discrimination based on race, such as the Cape Native franchise and the Native Representative Council under Representation of Natives Act, and the extension to all adults, regardless of race, of the right to vote and be elected to parliament, provincial councils and other representative institutions".[194] This was the ANC's strongest political statement to date on the issue of the vote.

In 1944, the ANC Youth League was formally authorised by its parent body, constituting a more radical constituency within the ANC. The Youth League emerged out of provincial or local student associations such as the Transvaal African Students' Association and the

---

[190] Karis and Carter, 1973, Vol. 1, p. 151.
[191] Karis and Carter, 1979, Vol. 2, p. 7.
[192] Ibid., p. 11.
[193] The Atlantic Charter was an agreement signed by US President Franklin Roosevelt and British Prime Minister Winston Churchill in 1941 with regard to the rights of citizenship of white people in the occupied countries of Europe. The Charter spoke of "the right of all peoples to choose the form of government under which they will live". The ANC felt that the principles of the Atlantic Charter should also apply to them and saw their statement as a means of "conveying to them our undisputed claim to full citizenship" in South Africa. The ANC said that: "We desire them to realise once and for all that a just and permanent peace will be possible only if the claims of all classes, colours and races for sharing and for full participation in the educational, political and economic activities are granted and recognised". See the full text of *African Claims in South Africa,* in Karis and Carter, 1979, Vol. 2, p. 209.
[194] Ibid., p. 217.

Social Studies Society at the University College of Fort Hare. The increasing activism of teachers also began to arouse the political consciousness of the youth, for example through the 1944 demonstration by 4,000 to 5,000 members of the Transvaal African Teachers' Association in Johannesburg. The "Congress Youth League Manifesto" issued in March 1944 said:

> "The formation of this League is an attempt on the part of Youth to impart to Congress a truly national character. It is also a protest against the lack of discipline and the absence of a clearly-defined goal in the movement as a whole. The Congress Youth League must be the brains-trust and power-station of the spirit of African nationalism; the spirit of African self-determination; the spirit that is so discernible in the thinking of our Youth. It must be an organisation where young African men and women will meet and exchange ideas in an atmosphere pervaded by a common hatred of oppression. As this power-station, the League will be a co-ordinating agency for all youthful forces employed in rousing popular political consciousness and fighting oppression and reaction. It will educate the people politically by concentrating its energies on the African homefront to make all sections of our people Congress-minded and nation-conscious. But the Youth League must not be allowed to detract Youth's attention from the organisation of Congress. In this regard, it is the first step to ensure that African Youth has direct connections with the leadership of Congress".[195]

The ANC Youth League therefore became the breeding ground for large numbers of anti-apartheid activists as well as the future leadership of the ANC itself.

By 1943, the AAC had been taken over by a more radical group of Coloureds and Africans in the Cape. In reaction to the creation of a Coloured Affairs Department (CAD) – implying more and more segregation of the Coloured community – they formed the Anti-CAD Movement. This, in turn, was linked to the Non-European Unity Movement (NEUM), formed in 1943, which "condemned all forms of participation in segregated forms of representation" such as the CAD and acknowledged the need for co-operation amongst all non-Europeans on specific issues. The NEUM initially brought together the Anti-CAD Movement and the AAC, with the intention that the South African Indian Congress (SAIC) would also join. However, the SAIC leadership was too conservative at that time and could not agree to the NEUM's Ten-Point Programme. Between 1944 and 1947, the NEUM tried to engage the ANC leadership but to no avail. The AAC remained concentrated in the Cape. When more radical Indian leaders had taken over the SAIC, they eventually joined an alliance with the ANC instead of the NEUM.

In 1943-45, an Anti-Pass Campaign was launched jointly by the ANC, the Communist Party and Indian Congresses. Following a conference of 540 delegates, and a march of 20,000 demonstrators in Johannesburg, 850,000 signatures were obtained on an anti-pass petition. The Campaign also received support from the Anti-CAD Campaign. This was an important step in multiracial political action. However, due to a lack of sufficiently dynamic leadership and organisation, the Anti-Pass Campaign fizzled out before its planned general strike and burning of passes took place.

Following the National Party election victory in 1948, the ANC and the AAC leadership maintained their unity negotiations, but these efforts came to naught. Progress was hindered, *inter alia*, by differences in organisational forms and cultures, as well as personality clashes. Also, their analyses of the political context, their priorities for action, and their respective willingness to undertake particular strategies, e.g. boycotts of

---

[195] See the full text of the Manifesto in Karis and Carter, 1979, Vol. 2, pp.300-308.

segregationist institutions, were too far apart. As the 1950s arrived, the ANC became ascendant and the AAC and NEUM lost profile and support.[196]

Early African rural resistance

Despite the absence of a mass movement in the rural areas, there were numerous instances of rural resistance to government policies which were causing the impoverishment of the people. The following are two examples of such resistance:

Zoutpansberg and Sekhukhuneland[197]

In the 1940s, these communities in what eventually became the homelands of Venda and Lebowa were increasingly overpopulated and impoverished. Only taxpayers were allowed to plough the land. Resistance was triggered by the influx of new tribes into the area, at which point the land allocation per family was reduced by half. This situation was exacerbated by a local natural disaster. Tactless enforcement of the regulations and heavy fines for tax defaulters resulted in an armed uprising by the communities. The government retaliated by bombing the allotted areas.

Witzieshoek

The original boundaries of this area in what later became the QwaQwa homeland were fixed in a treaty through land allocated to the Mopeli tribe by President Brand of the Orange Free State Republic. In 1937, grazing control was implemented through fencing. Residents in enclosed areas were forced to move. However, Sub-chief Mopeli refused. In 1940, their cattle were culled against the wishes of the tribe. In 1946, a second culling was proposed but ignored. As a result, Paulus Mopeli was convicted.

The leaders coalesced into the Lingangele movement which resisted further culling. The Paramount Chief Charles Mopeli asked for a Commission of Inquiry but was refused by the Secretary of Native Affairs. Native Senator Basner intervened with the Minister of Native Affairs, and the grazing fences were destroyed. A third cull was called in 1948. Ten convictions for refusal to cull were set aside on appeal.

The dispute escalated through the attempted enforcement of culling. Later, a commission was appointed. The Lingangele leaders initially refused to testify but relented later. On the day of their testimony, 1,300 tribesmen arrived and demanded an open sitting. However, public meetings were forbidden by a proclamation. The crowd ignored an order to disperse. Between police action and retaliatory action by the tribesmen, 14 tribesmen were killed, whilst police casualties were two dead and 16 wounded. The sequel to this event was mass searches and arrests. The court cases severely depleted the resources of the community. Organised political parties in the cities ignored this struggle.

These were largely localised struggles which showed the tenacity and courage of the people when their livelihoods were at stake, but failed for various reasons to bring about any major change in their condition.

Coloured people's organisations

Adhikari wrote that "because their primary objective was to assimilate into the dominant society, politicised Coloured people initially avoided forming separate political organisations. By the early twentieth century, however, intensifying segregation forced them to mobilise politically in defense of their rights".[198] We have noted in the previous chapter the 1902 formation of the African Political Organisation (APO) by Dr. Abdulurahman. This organisation was the primary vehicle for Coloured people's political activism until the 1940s.

---

[196] Ibid., pp. 117-119.
[197] See Delius, 1996, for a more detailed history of this region and its resistance.
[198] Adhikari, 2005, p. 4.

The APO's assimilationist strategy prior to 1910 had clearly failed, and the Coloured community found itself increasingly marginalised. The impact of Union had been to reduce the political clout they had in the former Cape colony, and the APO found it necessary to adopt a more pragmatic and cautious approach to political lobbying. In 1919, it changed its name to the African People's Organisation.[199] Adhikari argued that the APO and the Coloured community in general were caught between the Whites who rejected the Coloured attempts to assimilate, and the Africans, who felt the Coloureds had a more privileged status. They felt that identifying too closely with the Africans, with whom they sympathised, might compromise their own interests. As a result, he says that the APO, despite its purported non-racialism, actually promoted a separate Coloured identity.[200] Nonetheless, the APO did support some political initiatives of the African and Indian communities.[201]

However, other groups emerged as a result of growing dissent within the Coloured community as to how best to approach their political struggle. The late 1910s saw the emergence of the conservative groups such as United Afrikaner League and the late 1920s brought the establishment of the *Afrikaanse Nationale Bond* (ANB). Both of these groups were supported by Cape National Party leaders with the aim of winning Coloured electoral support, but neither had much impact.[202] In 1944, the Coloured People's National Union (CPNU) was founded in reaction to the radical takeover of the APO. These groups supported collaboration and participation in segregated political institutions as the best way to benefit the Coloured community.

In contrast, by the 1930s, many of the more educated members of the Coloured community were becoming frustrated with the lack of progress made by the APO. As with African activists, they were increasingly radicalised and influenced by Marxist ideology and formed new groups to promote their ideas. The most significant of the new groupings were the National Liberation League (NLL) established in 1935 and the Non-European Unity Movement (NEUM) in 1943 (see above for more on the NEUM). Their hope was to unify all the Black political movements in the fight against segregation and the abrogation of political rights. Once again, internal divisions within the NLL and NEUM, as well as the unwillingness of other Black political movements to transcend racial barriers, meant that these groups failed to achieve their goals.[203]

Other left-wing Coloured intellectuals in the Cape in the 1940s joined existing political groups such as the Fourth International Organisation of South Africa (FIOSA) and the Workers' Party of South Africa. Kenneth Jordaan, a teacher, formed an independent discussion group called the Forum Club in the early 1950s. These leftists took a non-racial approach and criticised the NEUM on the basis that "non-Europeanism" "was a form of 'voluntary segregation'".[204] Adhikari posits that It was only later in the 1960s that the NEUM adopted a consistently non-racial discourse.[205]

An important force within the Coloured community was the Teachers' League of South Africa (TLSA), founded in Cape Town in 1913. It was a professional association which represented the majority of Coloured teachers by the 1940s, and was the largest professional group in the community. It had its own journal, *Education Journal,* which "mirrored the values,

---

[199] Ibid., p. 72.
[200] Ibid., p. 73.
[201] Ibid., p. 74.
[202] Ibid., p. 5.
[203] Ibid., p. 5.
[204] Ibid., p. 104.
[205] Ibid., p. 129.

aspirations, and frustrations of the Coloured elite".[206] The TLSA also reflected the ambiguities of Coloured identity in the contractions between its pronouncements and its actions: by speaking out against racial discrimination but then actively distancing itself from African causes, refusing to admit African teachers as members, and endorsing relative Coloured privilege.[207] As a professional association, and as an elite class within their racial group, they felt they should be judged on merit rather than race. Yet they accepted government treatment of them as inferior to White teachers, apparently assuming that this inferiority would be temporary.

Indian organisations

The 1919 South African Indian Conference, which brought together representatives from all the provinces in Cape Town with a view to reviving Indian political activism following World War I, led to the revival of the Natal Indian Congress (NIC). The NIC had been created by Gandhi and a group of leading Indian merchants in 1894, but had become moribund by 1914. The 'new' NIC began to organise mass meetings and submit petitions to government as issues arose. Later, in 1923, the South African Indian Conference became an official organisation called the South African Indian Congress (SAIC). The SAIC was strongly influenced by Gandhi's use of the Indian National Congress in India to lobby internationally. Eventually, in 1926, a round table conference between the governments of India and South Africa was held in Cape Town. The Cape Town agreement provided for (1) subsidies for those Indians who wished to return to India and (2) a policy to uplift those Indians who chose to remain in South Africa. Both the NIC and the SAIC supported this agreement.[208]

New organisations began to emerge in opposition to the NIC and SAIC approach. The Natal Indian Vigilance Association (NIVA) was formed in 1926 and the South African Indian Federation (SAIF) in 1927. The SAIF did not last more than a couple of years, but still had an impact in helping to discredit the NIC and the SAIC. To its credit, the NIC created a Social Service Committee and the Indian Child Welfare Society in 1928. It also helped in the formation of the Indian Trade Union Congress.

Rifts also began to emerge between Indians of Hindu and Muslim faiths, of different economic classes, languages, and regions of origin. The Cape Town agreement also came back to haunt those who had acceded to it as the government was unhappy that so few Indians had opted to return to India and wanted to explore the possibility of shipping more Indians off to another colony. The SAIC was not averse to participating in such a study. In reaction to this, the Colonial Born and Settler Indian Association (CBSIA) was established particularly to represent the views of Indians descended from indentured workers. Having been born in South Africa, they considered it their home. Both the SAIC and the CBSIA rejected outright the recommendations of the Colonisation Committee when it recommended that a large portion of South Africa's Indians should be resettled in other countries. The agreement of the various Indian organisations on this issue led in 1939 to the disappearance of the CBSIA and the amalgamation of the NIC into the Natal Indian Association (NIA).

However, divisions remained. Younger members of the NIA were becoming impatient with the conciliatory tactics of the older members. In Durban, they formed a group called the Nationalist Bloc (NB), and in the Transvaal a similar group called itself the Nationalist Group (NG). These young people were involved in other activist organisations such as trade unions or youth organisations (e.g. the Natal Youth Council formed in 1937), and some were members of the SACP.

---

[206] Ibid., p. 79.
[207] Ibid., pp. 80-81.
[208] Bhana, 1997, p. 36.

There was finally some movement in the Indian community towards forming alliances with other groupings. The Non-European Unity Front (NEUF) which had been initiated by Dr. Abdul Abdurahman in 1927 was one such group. Despite some initial attempts towards unity, the divisions within the Indian community prevented any serious move towards such an alliance. The NEUF moved further to the left and in the early 1940s changed its name to the Non-European Unity Movement (NEUM) (see discussion above).

The NIC was revived yet again in the early 1940s, and in an about-turn, the NIA merged itself into the NIC in 1943. Shortly thereafter, there was what amounted to an internal coup when a militant group formed itself into the Anti-Segregation Council (ASC), developed a programme of action, and were elected onto the NIC executive. This programme was adopted in 1945 and included: "restoration of the franchise on the common roll; the removal of provincial barriers; the elimination of all forms of colour bar; the introduction of free and compulsory education; the redistribution of land; and the subsidisation of small market gardeners".[209] These goals were far more radical than those of earlier incarnations of the NIC / NIA.

Faith-based organisations

Christian churches
The missionaries and their churches did not confront the government regarding its unjust racial policies, but instead issued a series of mildly critical pronouncements. For example, the 1918 Provincial Missionary Conference (PMC) of the CPSA resolved that it was:

> "incumbent upon the white races to see to it that… the native races of South Africa… shall not be exploited for the benefit of the white races, nor forced into a position of servitude, but may have space in this country and opportunity for development and ample facilities to become useful and industrious citizens".[210]

In 1923, the PMC called for revision (not revocation) of the pass laws and criticised the 1913 Land Act for not making enough provision for land for the African population. But, their positions could hardly be called radical and they made few, if any, concrete alternative suggestions. They also tended to "separate mission work from issues of social justice" and to "ignore the race and class barriers in [their] own organisation".[211]

Despite the differences of approach and opinion between them, an attempt was made in 1936 to promote more cooperation between the DRC and the English-speaking churches through the creation of the Christian Council. However, this attempt was undermined by contestation over nationalism (Afrikaner vs. English), the 'native question', and language. These issues as well as internal conflict within the Afrikaner church led the DRC to leave the Council in 1941.[212]

It took quite a long time before the complete Bible, as the basic book of Christianity, was available to speakers of all official South African languages. The table below shows when and by whom the Bible was translated. Foreign missionary societies played a crucial role in in this process, with the assistance of local translators. Though the Bible Society of South Africa (BSSA) was created in Cape Town in 1820, it apparently did not play a significant role in the translation of the Bible into languages other than English until the late 20th century. The first translation by the BSSA was in Tswana in 1970. Its major activity has been the dissemination of affordable Bibles to all.

---

[209] Ibid., p. 52.
[210] Cited in Goedhals, 1989, p. 114.
[211] Ibid., p. 113.
[212] de Gruchy, 1986a, pp. 39-40.

First Translations of the complete Bible into South African languages

Language	Date of Translation*	Translated by:
English	1611	First edition of authorised / King James Version translated by six panels of translators consisting of 47 men
Tswana	1857	British and Foreign Bible Society, Kuruman
Xhosa	1859	Wesleyan Missionary Society and Berlin Missionary Society; printed at Mount Coke
Southern Sotho	1878	Paris Evangelical Missionary Society
Zulu	1883	American Board of Commissioners for Foreign Missions, Natal
Northern Sotho	1904	Berlin Missionary Society
Tsonga	1907	British and Foreign Bible Society, London; revised in 1929
Afrikaans	1933	British and Foreign Bible Society
Venda	1936	British and Foreign Bible Society
Swati	1997	Bible Society of South Africa
Southern Ndebele	Not complete**	Currently being translated by Bible Society of South Africa

Source: Bible Society of South Africa, www.biblesociety.co.za, 30 June 2006.
*In some cases, parts of the Bible were translated earlier, for example, the Gospel according to Mark or the New Testament or the Psalms.
**In 1977, the first Book of the Bible (Gospel according to Mark) was translated by the BSSA and in 1986 the First New Testament and selected psalms were translated also by the BSSA. Southern Ndebele is the only SA language into which the complete Bible has not yet been translated.

Even Afrikaans-speakers did not have a complete Bible translation until 1933. The translation coincided with growing Afrikaner nationalism, but was facilitated by the British and Foreign Bible Society, as with many of the other indigenous language translations.

Promotion of the Afrikaans language and Bible
Whilst a local Afrikaner civil society value system existed, it was also through the imperatives of Northern influence that it was maintained and supported. One such example is the advancement of the Afrikaans language and the production of an Afrikaans translation of the Bible. Afrikaans had been recognised as an official language in the Cape, the Transvaal and the Free State since 1914 in schools and universities. In 1925 Parliament enacted that the word "Dutch" in the Constitution would also be taken to include Afrikaans. A Select Committee of both Houses had agreed that the language was sufficiently developed to serve as an administrative and legislative instrument. In a joint session of both Houses, Dr. Malan made a strong oration. English-speaking members on both sides supported him and the measure was adopted unanimously. Afrikaans churches had since 1919 committed themselves to translating the Bible into Afrikaans and a joint committee of theologians was officially committed to the task. This work began in earnest in 1923, and by 1933 the task was completed. The British and Foreign Bible Society published the first complete edition. This intellectual and theological event was celebrated with great ceremony in Pretoria. British Christian support for this activity ironically reinforced the separate Afrikaner identity and values.

The close historical ties between Christianity and the ANC leadership and the re-emergence of the ANC as a political actor in the late 1930s and 1940s inevitably caused some reassessment within the churches of their policies of segregation and White control. Pressure increased for a greater African role in the church hierarchies and regular representation of African interests in decision-making. Proposals made by CPSA priests Calata and Maimane in the early 1940s to form a separate African branch of the church, *inter alia,* were rejected by the Bishops. The Bishops also failed to acknowledge the racism practiced by the church and instead defended their role as "champions of the natives".

Demonstrating the fallacy in this, in 1944 when Michael Scott founded the Campaign for Rights and Justice, he received no support from the church hierarchy. Scott, however, was asked by the liberal Council for Human Rights to go to Durban in June 1946 to observe the Passive Resistance Campaign of the South African Indian Congress. He was so inspired by the courage of the protesters that he joined them, and was subsequently arrested and sentenced to three months imprisonment. When he returned to Johannesburg, he and Miss Asvat and Dr. Dadoo (of the SAIC) were received by a rally of 10,000 people in a Johannesburg stadium. The CPSA hierarchy, however, received him and his notion of civic responsibility very coldly.[213] In the years to come, however, more and more dissenting voices began to emerge within the church.

Muslim organisations

The Muslim community is racially and ethnically heterogeneous, and has attracted adherents from all classes. Its religious practice is also diverse, depending on the tradition to which particular groups adhere and reflecting the divisions found amongst Muslims in other countries.

The Cape Malay Association (CMA), led by M.A. Gamiet, was established in 1923 as an essentially socio-religious body. It represented Cape Muslims, in opposition to the African Political Organisation (APO). It had a similar approach as the Afrikaanse Nationale Bond (ANB)[214] formed by Coloured leaders who identified with Afrikaner culture and who hoped that the 1924 "new deal" for Coloureds announced by Hertzog and the National Party would bring about advancement and greater rights for Coloured people. The CMA was not as closely allied to the National Party as the ANB, but it did draw on a "closely knit ethnic base".[215] By the 1930s, the CMA had lost influence to the "younger and more radical intelligentsia who espoused secular politics without any appeal to Islam". Some of its leadership were later (in the 1950s) convinced by the National Party's promises to accord Cape Malays higher status than Coloured people, and supported the party for some time. The NP later reneged on this promise.[216]

In Natal and the Transvaal, Muslim activists tended to work rather under the broader Indian civil rights campaigns (see above) rather than forming their own organisations. Some of the key figures who worked closely with Gandhi were the "Pretoria Group", including Moulana Mukhtar and Ahmad Muhammad Cachalia.[217]

In 1923, the Indian Muslim merchants formed an alliance with the *ulama,* and founded the Jamiat al-'Ulama (Council of Muslim Theologians) in the Transvaal. This organisation did not last long, but was revived in 1935 by Mufti Ebrahim Sanjalvi. It took another 20 years before a similar organisation was established in Natal: the Jamiat al-'Ulama Natal. In the 1950s, they opposed the government with regard to the Group Areas Act and its potential impact on

---

[213] See Clarke, 1989, pp. 131-133.
[214] See separate section above for more on Coloured peoples' organisations.
[215] Raynard, 2002, pp. 89-90.
[216] Moosa, 1995, p. 142.
[217] Ibid., p. 143.

mosques and other important Muslim facilities. In the 1970s and 1980s, they interacted with government on issues related to Muslim Personal Law and other Muslim affairs. The current mission of the Jamiatul Ulama is to "service the religious needs of the Muslims". This is carried out through branches around the country where Muslim communities exist.[218]

Since the mid-1940s, numerous Muslim organisations have emerged to play significant roles both within and outside their communities. Probably the most important organisation is the Muslim Judicial Council (MJC), formed in 1945, which stemmed from the Moslem [sic] Progressive Society which focused on social relief and welfare issues. The MJC arose out of a need for dispute resolution within the Muslim community. It aimed to preserve and strengthen Islam in all its dimensions, unite Muslims (especially the religious leadership), promote education by creating Muslim colleges for both religious and secular education, issue binding religious decrees, and secure legal recognition by the government of religious marriages. It also had broad political goals: "forging unity in the interest of all non-Europeans in order to combat oppressive forces that would hamper their progress".[219]

Hindu organisations

From their arrival in 1860 to the turn of the 20th century, Hindus in South Africa did not develop religious institutions aside from the many temples where they observed their traditional rituals. Rather, their religious life was centred on the joint family system which prevailed in their community. Priests inherited their function by studying under a Guru rather than being educated at theological colleges. This emphasis on ritual and dogma resulted in what was characterised as a "spiritual and religious degeneration" and what was perceived by an increasing number of Hindus as an urgent need for theological reform.[220]

Strong links existed between the Hindu faith as practiced in India and as it came to be practiced in South Africa. In 1875, the movement known as Arya Samaj (Society of Noble or Righteous People) was formed in India by Swami Dayananda. His intention was to "restructure Hindu society by eliminating social evils and re-introducing higher religious values among the people through numerous codes of behaviour". He advocated "the eradication of practices such as idolatry, the caste system, untouchability and child marriage". He believed that these practices deflected Hinduism from its basic objectives.[221] Amongst the ten basic principles of the Arya Samaj, two stand out in terms of their relevance to the development of civil society:

- "Doing good to the whole world is the primary objective of this Society, i.e. to ameliorate the physical, spiritual and social conditions of all men".
- "One should not be content with one's own welfare alone, but should look to the welfare of all".[222]

The influence of the Arya Samaj reached the Hindu population of South Africa slowly, but it eventually had a substantial impact. In the early years of the 20th century, increased interest in Arya Samaj developed due to a series of visits by prominent Hindu leaders from India. Gradually, localised groups began to form, e.g. the Ved Dharma Sabha in Pietermaritzburg formed by Swami Shankarananda, a Hindu monk from India, and the Arya Yuvak Sabha of Durban founded by Mr. D.G. Satyadeva. In 1912, Swami Shankarananda formed the South African Hindu Maha Sabha to "represent Hindu religio-cultural interests nationally".[223] The message about the Arja Samaj approach to the Hindu faith spread through community networks as described by Hilda Kuper:

---

[218] See www.islamsa.org.za/profile/history.htm
[219] See Muslim Judicial Council website www.mjc.org.za and Moosa, 1995, p. 147.
[220] Naidoo, 1992, pp. 55-56.
[221] Ibid., pp. 3-4.
[222] Ibid., p. 40.
[223] Ibid., p. 64.

"A house in an Indian area is never an isolated dwelling: it is integrated into the street, neighbourhood, and community. Kinsmen often live near each other, affairs of neighbours arouse the gossip that controls the moral standards of the whole area; temples and schools are subscribed by local donations and become local and public meeting places; shops give credit to the families in the area; the local community develops an in-group awareness expressed in a number of local institutions".[224]

The formation in 1925 of the Arya Pratinidhi Sabha of South Africa coincided with the centenary celebrations of the birth of Swami Dayananda. It was created in order to co-ordinate and unify the work of the 15 or so already existing organisations around Natal. In 1927, this umbrella body was affiliated to the Sarvadeshik Arya Pratinidhi Sabha of India. Subsequently, conferences bringing together the constituent organisations were held periodically to address common problems. In 1944, the Arya Pratinidhi Sabha organised a conference of priests to discuss the performance of ritual ceremonies. In 1948, the first Hindu youth conference in South Africa was held in Durban. Other meetings discussed children's education, the use of Hindi as the common language amongst all Hindus, and other issues.[225]

The Arya Pratinidhi Sabha was not welcomed by the entire Hindu community, however. Its proselytising tendency alienated especially those with a more conservative or orthodox view. In reaction, in 1941, those opposed to the Arya Samaj approach formed a national organisation called the Shree Sanatan Dharma Sabha of South Africa. The two groups engaged in serious theological debates on essential aspects of the Hindu faith, but the Shree Sanatan Dharma Sabha failed to have as great an influence as the Arya Samaj.[226] Seemingly, the Arya Samaj has been better able to adapt its values and faith to the changing environment.

A number of affiliated institutions were created by the Arya Samaj. In 1918, an Aryan Benevolent Home was established by the Arya Yuvak Sabha of Durban and became known as the Arya Anath Ashram in Mayville. This was subsequently divided into a Children's Home (Chatsworth, 1979) and the Dayananda Gardens Home for the Aged (1982). Social work services are also provided. In addition, an Aryan Youth League provides opportunities for cultural expression amongst Hindu youth, the Veda Niketan publishes books and other literature and offers examinations for students of Hinduism, and the Verdic Purhohit Mandal trains both young men and women to become priests. By 1992, Naidoo estimated that about 100,000 people from the four Indian language groups were members of the Arya Samaj movement or had been influenced by it. "This accounts for almost one-third of the Hindi-speaking people, 10% of the Gujarati-speaking people, 2% of the Telugus, and less than 1% of the Tamils".[227]

Little provision was made by the state for education of Indian children. This was confirmed by an Education Commission appointed in 1909. The first state school for Indians was founded in 1983, whereas 10 state-aided schools (built by the Indian community itself) already existed. To make matters worse, despite a strong desire for education, there was considerable conflict within the Indian community regarding "the choice between religiously oriented education and secular education". This fear was fuelled by a sentiment that Indian children would be 'westernised' by state-provided education, and their traditional customs undermined.[228]

---

[224] Kuper, 1960, p. XV.
[225] Naidoo, 1992, pp. 69-73.
[226] Ibid., p. 79.
[227] Ibid., p. 159.
[228] Ibid., p. 152.

The Arya Samaj was one of the first Hindu religious organisations to openly advocate the education of women and girls, e.g. in resolutions taken at the 1925 founding conference of the Arya Prathinidhi Sabha. Indian parents did not regard education as an asset for girls. In 1869, there were no Indian girls at school in Natal (as compared to 34 boys); by 1886, this number increased to only 274 girls, as compared to 1,428 boys. In 1947, there were only 47 girls attending secondary school in Natal, and by1955, there were only 781. The University of Natal only began admitting Indian women in 1936.[229]

Efforts to establish Hindi schools were limited until the Second Hindu Literary Conference in Pietermaritzburg in 1917. This was followed by the opening of a number of Hindi schools around Natal province from the 1920s to the 1940s. Nonetheless, pressures to accept secularisation continued, not least because Indians were persuaded that they would feel more welcome in South Africa if they adopted a more western outlook.[230]

Jewish organisations

As part of the White population, the Jewish community was relatively privileged, though many of its members came to South Africa as poor immigrants. It has always enjoyed full civil rights in the Whites-only political sphere, but it "has been subjected to more discriminatory legislation than any other White group in the country". The small size of the community (100,000 people or about 0.3% of the total population), its concentration in urban areas and its relatively homogeneous cultural origins, have resulted in it being "the most organised diaspora community in the world".[231] The vast majority of Jewish people in the country belong to conservative synagogues. These generally form the base from which individuals involve themselves in related social organisations.

The Federation of Synagogues was established in Johannesburg in 1933, and included a rabbinical court, Beth Din. This later became the Union of Orthodox Synagogues of South Africa in 1986. Also in 1933, the South African Union for Progressive Judaism was founded by people of German Jewish origin -- an indication of the ongoing split within the Jewish community (85% orthodox; 10-15% reform/progressive).

The first Jewish day school was the King David School, founded in 1948 in Johannesburg. This and other such schools provide both secular and religious education. In the 1950s, a more traditional Yeshiva College was established to provide more extensive study of the Torah and the Talmud. At present, there are 19 day schools, all of which are affiliated to the South African Board of Jewish Education. Since 1948, South Africa has had its own teacher training institution: the Rabbi Zlotnick Hebrew Teachers' Training Seminary in Johannesburg.

A large number of Jewish welfare organisations have emerged over the years in all the major urban areas. These include institutions for the aged, children and the disabled. The Union of Jewish Women also has branches throughout the country to provide welfare services to both Jewish and other people. The South African branch of ORT[232] has been operating since 1936 with a focus on skills training. Its ORT-STEP Institute provides technical education for both high school students and teachers. Other welfare groups include the Hebrew Order of David and B'nai Brith. Some synagogues run their own literacy

---

[229] Ibid., pp. 166-167.
[230] Ibid., p. 155.
[231] Hellig, 1995, p. 156.
[232] ORT is a Jewish-led, non profit organisation specialising in education, vocational skills and training, and community development. It was founded in Russia in 1880 by a small group of prominent Russian Jews with a view to uplifting five million Russian Jews from crushing poverty. Today, ORT is active in 60 countries, working in poor communities without regard to religion, race or ethnicity.

programmes or skills training for disadvantaged people locally. Several foundations have been established by Jewish entrepreneurs to assist disadvantaged communities.

The South African Zionist Federation established in 1898 and the Jewish Board of Deputies established in 1904 are still the two major bodies that "govern the general relations of the community with its surrounding world".[233] The Jewish Board of Deputies is the "central representative institution" to which most of the country's congregations, Jewish societies and institutions are affiliated. It holds biennial conferences to determine its policies and elect its president. In the 1930s it played an important role in intervening with the government to prevent discrimination against Jewish immigrants. It assisted the war effort by attending to problems facing Jewish soldiers and in providing comforts for the troops. It continues to act to protect the civil rights of Jewish people by developing relations with leaders, opinion makers and the media. It monitors anti-Semitism and offers a variety of services to the Jewish community. It has made representations to the democratic South African government on issues of civil rights, welfare, education, crime and violence, and on a range of constitutional matters.[234]

The South African Zionist Federation has a number of affiliated organisations, including Zionist youth movements and university youth represented by the South African Union of Jewish Students. Its departments deal with organisations and information, fundraising, youth activities, women's organisations and immigration to Israel.

Whilst the Jews generally lived in harmony with the other Whites regardless of language or culture, in the 1930s and throughout the period of World War II, anti-Semitism and Nazism (represented by the 'Greyshirts') did become a problem for Jews in some of these communities. The SAJBD sent representatives to educate communities, to advise Jews on how to deal with the threat, and to strengthen ties with local secular organisations. Where necessary, recourse was made to the courts to prevent anti-Jewish meetings or other actions against Jews (e.g. boycotts of businesses). This was also a time of discrimination imposed by the government, as Jews became "scapegoats" of negative sentiment from poor Whites. However, at the same time, Jewish religious life became more and more organised.[235]

Early trade unions

The discovery of diamonds and gold led to an influx of craftsmen from the UK, Australia and the US. These skilled workers brought with them the English tradition of unions organised by craft rather than by industry. As poorer Afrikaners drifted to the towns from the rural areas, they sought to protect their employment as they were unskilled in trade and craft, had little formal education, and had to counter the competition from the bulk of the unskilled African labour force. So, English and Afrikaner workers developed a common interest to protect their privileged economic existence. Black worker relationships were guided through the Transvaal Employment Bureau of Africa (TEBA). In later years, the Chamber of Mines was the most formidable opponent with which organised White labour and marginalised Black labour had to contend.

Coloured workers mainly from the western districts of the Cape Province were employed on the wine and fruit farms there or in the wheatlands. Some were employed as skilled artisans in the building industry as carpenters, bricklayers, or painters. As their language and custom

---

[233] Hellig, 1995, p. 156.
[234] See www.shemayisrael.co.il/sa/sajbd/sajbd.htm
[235] Hellig, 1995, p. 165.

was mainly Afrikaans, they were often viewed as a buffer between the African and White workers.

Kruger[236] observed that:

> "British skilled labour, first on the gold mines and then in other industries and trades, had organised itself in Trade Unions for protection against employers, and at the same time against competition from non-white labour. They closed their ranks against the entry of unskilled labour and established an exclusiveness akin to a racial colour bar. Their main aim was to defend their standardised wage against the lower scale of Bantu pay. At the same time they demanded a monopoly of skilled work and a fixed ratio between skilled and unskilled jobs. Employers tacitly recognised these principles and the Mines and Works Act of 1911 was considered by white labour as its Magna Carta. There thus existed side by side a conventional and a legal colour bar in industry, both designed to protect white skilled and semi-skilled labour against competition from outside.
>
> The protection of semi-skilled labour was a matter of life and death, especially to the landless poor Afrikaners who had flocked to the Witwatersrand. They hastened to join the Trade Unions established by British Labour, for their interests had become common. All of them had to withstand pressure on the part of their black fellow workers and possible attempts by employers to alter the ratio of skilled and unskilled labour in favour of the latter in order to reduce working costs. The English Trade Unions took the lead, but their Afrikaans poor relations stood solidly behind them. English labour naturally fortified the Afrikaners' social colour bar by their own industrial colour bar. Non-skilled labour could only penetrate the defence of skilled labour if the employers found it to their interest to lift the conventional bar which determined the proportion between the two."

In July 1913, five White underground workers at the new Kleinfontein mine were dismissed. Workers stopped working and a dispute arose across the mining industry. When workers were dismissed the White members' union demanded their reinstatement. The strike was followed by riots in Johannesburg which even the British garrison commander was not able to control. In a meeting at the plush Carlton Hotel, Generals Botha and Smuts conceded to the demands of the miners, led by J.T. Bain. It was agreed that the five dismissed workers would be reinstated, that the government would compensate workers who were not able to return to their duties, strikers would not be prosecuted, their grievances would be investigated, and the families of the victims of the riots would be looked after. The Mine Workers' Union would be recognised by the Chamber and the government.

After a few months, further disputes were flaring up in different parts of the country. Smuts took stern action, declared martial law, monitored essential services and trained guns on the Traders Hall in Johannesburg. The resistance collapsed but Smuts was not content. He took leaders of the miners' strike by train to Durban, and put them on a ship bound for Britain, before a court writ for *habeus corpus* could be heard. Smuts took his case to Parliament and appealed for an Act of Indemnity. He appealed that he had been forced to act against worker leaders who planned high treason. The Bill was passed by a large majority, but it unleashed a further reaction.

Many of the post-World War I economic troubles were ascribed to Smuts and his involvement with the mining magnates. Smuts attempted to test the country's mood by calling a general election but the results were a stalemate between the South Africa Party and the Labour Party. By 1920, membership of White trade unions had increased to 135,140

---

[236] Kruger, 1969, p. 121.

from just under 4,000 in 1900. This "represented a solid bloc of economic and political power committed to the protection of White interests and opposed to non-European advancement".[237]

Around this time, Indian workers began to organise into ethnically specific unions. The International Socialist League helped create the Indian Workers Union before 1917. A key leader, Rev. Bernard Sigamoney, saw the need for Indian unions as "a response to Indian exclusion and to the absolute preference of most white employers for white workers".[238] The Indian unions also received some support from the High Commission of the Government of India. The Indian unions struggled at a time when both White and African workers were also involved in major strike actions. Indians were regarded as "surplus" or redundant labour and were therefore at a distinct disadvantage in the job markets. Only a few of the Indian unions were able to obtain official recognition in the 1920s, e.g. the furniture workers and hotel employees.

In 1919, Clement Kadalie and others founded the Industrial and Commercial Workers Union (ICU) based in Cape Town. Kadalie submitted an application for affiliation to the South African Industrial Federation (SAIF) on the basis of the ICU's 20,000 members. Despite the fact that many members of the Internationalist Socialist League were present, the application was rejected on the grounds that the ICU would swamp the White unions.[239] In October 1919, the ICU led a strike of African and Coloured dock workers in Cape Town. Then, in February 1920, 42,000 African workers on the mines went on an 11-day strike against working conditions and practices. Despite its increasing strength, the ICU found it difficult to gain support from White unions. Kadalie, for example, lamented the fact that in April 1926, the South African Trades Union Congress refused even to send a "fraternal delegate" to the ICU Congress or to invite one from the ICU to its own Congress. The following year, the ICU Congress passed a resolution to push for the union of Black and White workers into one national Trade Union Movement. This time, The South African Trade Union Congress was somewhat more receptive and agreed to seek means of cooperation. However, Kadalie also noted that the government was making it increasingly difficult for the ICU to hold meetings and for its officials to travel around the country. The Native Administration Act was being used by employers to crack down on ICU members, e.g. on the farms.[240]

For a while, the ICU eclipsed the influence of the ANC due to the ICU's more militant and activist approach. It recognised that it could not separate labour issues from politics.[241] Kadalie criticised the "non-political" attitude of White trade unions, arguing that to neglect politics would be to render "a disservice to those tens of thousands of our members who are groaning under oppressive laws and who are looking to the ICU for a lead". Thus, he put forward an economic and political programme for 1928 so as to clarify the basis of ICU action.[242] This programme, however, never got off the ground.

However, personality divisions and differences in strategy and tactics between ICU leaders as well as accusations of corruption in the handling of ICU funds led eventually to its demise by 1930. "In its meteoric rise and fall can be seen the gropings of the new South African proletariat for an effective means to articulate their demands as workers and increasingly to link themselves with broader South African efforts to participate politically in South Africa on an equal and non-racial basis".[243]

---

[237] Walshe, 1987, p. 74.
[238] Freund, 1995, p. 48.
[239] Ibid., p. 280.
[240] Kadalie, in the *New Leader,* September 1927. See Karis and Carter, 1973, Vol. 1, pp. 328-330.
[241] Karis and Carter, 1973, Vol. 1, p. 157.
[242] See full document in Ibid., pp. 331-333.
[243] Ibid., p. 157.

In the post-war slump, marginal mines were finding it difficult to operate at a profit and made numerous suggestions to alter the work pattern, including the importation of migrant workers from the north of South Africa and the removal of the conventional colour bar to allow African labourers to perform semi-skilled work. The trade unions refused to accept these proposals. In January 1922, the wages of White miners were cut by five shillings a day. The workers threatened to strike and the government offered to mediate. Eight hundred workers went on strike and were summarily dismissed on 22 January. Other workers joined the strike and 20,000 White workers went on strike. As a result, 180,000 Black workers were left idle. Scabs and African workers were continuously attacked. Looting and arson shattered the peace.

Miners organised themselves into commandos and paraded through the streets of the towns in the Witwatersrand. Smuts attempted to negotiate with the strikers but failed as he was perceived to represent the Chamber of Mines. Following a number of skirmishes with strikers, the strikers were organised into an Action Committee which seized parts of Fordsburg and Boksburg. Fierce battles raged until the 15th March, ending with the suicide of the leaders of the Action Committee.

An Industrial Conciliation Act (modelled on the Australian Act) passed in 1924 allowed White, Coloured and Indian workers to form unions but prohibited African workers from doing so. Only 60 years later, after the Report of the Wiehahn Commission into labour matters, were African workers granted the legal right to establish unions.

This did not, however, mean that African workers did not organise or join unions. At the time of the ICU decline, the first new industrial union to be established was the Laundry Workers' Union in 1928. In the early 1940s, there was a spate of illegal strikes by African workers. A broader expansion of African unions was led by Max Gordon, a full-time organiser and Marxist, in the latter 1930s. By 1944, he had started seven unions claiming a membership of about 97,000.

By 1946, the Council of Non-European Trade Unions (CNETU, founded in November 1941) claimed a national membership of 119 unions, of which 59 were African unions on the Witwatersrand with 158,000 members.[244] However, in 1947, the Transvaal Council of Non-European Trade Unions estimated the membership of its 32 unions at only 48,000. The largest of these were the African Mineworkers' Union (10,000), the African Building and Allied Workers' Union (8,000), the Garment Workers' Union (5,000) and the Pretoria Non-European Municipal Workers' Union (2,500).[245] There was a discrepancy between the actual number of paid-up members and those who considered themselves members even if not paid-up. In 1947, the Council of African Trade Unions was formed in opposition to the Council of Non-European Trade Unions. As an all-African, anti-communist body, it obtained the support of more than 20 unions – about half of those in the Transvaal. It also distanced itself from the ANC's plans to establish a South African Trade and Labour Council.[246]

In 1941, the African Mineworkers' Union (AMWU) was founded under the auspices of the Transvaal Congress, led by J.B. Marks (a member of the Communist Party and the ANC). Having been restrained in its demands during the war, AMWU waited until 1946 to make further wage demands. The refusal of the government and the Chamber of Mines to recognise AMWU and to meet its demands led to a strike of about 70,000 miners in August 1946. The ANC Youth League said that the AMWU strikers had "risen in revolt against the most brutal, callous and inhuman exploitation of man by man in the history of mankind. Their

---

[244] Karis and Carter, 1979, Vol. 2, p. 81.
[245] Walshe, 1987, p. 309.
[246] Ibid., p. 364.

struggle is a challenge to the whole economic and political structure of South Africa".[247] As the government brutally repressed the strike, it was strongly criticised by both the Native Representative Council (NRC) and the ANC. The NRC decided to adjourn indefinitely. This mine workers' strike also led to further repression of the Communist Party, in the form of the 1950 Suppression of Communism Act.[248]

Indian workers and their unions went through a phase of increased militancy in the period from the mid-1930s to the end of the 1940s. This phase was accompanied by a rise in political radicalism and by increasing competition between Indian and African workers especially in the Durban area. "Indian militancy was powered by the pressure that this imposed on Indian workers, caught between white racism and African attempts to secure urban jobs and space".[249] Nonetheless, a series of strikes in the 1930s and 40s did on occasion bring Indian and African workers together, some in the context of non-racial unions. But employers such as Dunlop & Co. used race to divide workers, hiring migrant Africans as scab labour to replace fired Indians. The same happened in the case of a 1945 strike by the Laundry Workers' Union (also non-racial). The fact that the militant Indians were often led by Indian members of the Communist Party did little to help their cause, making the relatively conservative Natal Indian Congress nervous as well. Thus, political affiliation was also used to divide and rule the unions. Repeated failures of strike action and the negative effects of intervention by political forces in the early 1950s – e.g. the Passive Resistance campaign of the ANC and NIC in 1953 which led to 300 Indian workers being fired and thrown out of their homes – led disillusioned Indian workers to subside into passivity.[250] Race and class also came into stark conflict in the Durban race riot of 1949, creating further divisions and uncertainty amongst Indians about how best to proceed.

Women's organisations

Women, as individuals and through organisations, have been active in community welfare work and philanthropic endeavours for centuries. They have often been the conscience and strength behind key movements of social change. Many women were activists in the struggle against apartheid, and continue to play a key role in governmental and civil society structures.

The first White women's organisation to call for women's suffrage was the Women's Christian Temperance Union (WCTU), formed in 1889 to campaign against alcoholic beverages. In 1902, the Women's Enfranchisement League (WEL) was created specifically to campaign for their right to vote. Following the establishment of the Union, in 1911 all suffrage groups were merged into the Women's Enfranchisement Association of the Union (WEAU). These groups comprised mostly of middle-class, urban-based, English-speaking women who were both educated and salaried. Their attempts to recruit Afrikaans-speaking women were patronising and had little success. Inevitably, the suffrage movement was caught up in political conflict. In the 1920s, the National Party used the White women's campaign for the vote as a foil to abolish the Cape franchise for Black men. When in 1930 Parliament granted the vote to White women, they claimed that they would use their new right to fight for the disenfranchised Black majority, but they did not keep this promise. The White women's suffrage movement also did not take seriously the revolts by Black women around the country, thus "retard[ing] the struggle for women's liberation by [their] racist stance, and in fact widen[ing] the gulf between black and white women in South Africa".[251] It

---

[247] ANC Youth League, flyer, August 1946. Full text in Karis and Carter, 1979, Vol. 2, pp. 318-319.
[248] Ibid., pp. 70-71.
[249] Freund, 1995, p. 53.
[250] Ibid., pp. 56-57.
[251] Amanda Gouws and Rhoda Kadalie, in Liebenberg et al., 1994, pp. 214-216.

was only in the 1940s and 50s that multi- or non-racial women's organisations began to emerge.

Black women's struggles for basic human rights began early in the 20th century. In fact, women were probably more militant than men in their fight against influx control, passes, and price increases for rent, bus fares and food. In 1913, the Bantu Women's League led by Mrs. Charlotte Maxeke was formed to protest against the imposition of women's passes – a key symbol of inferior citizenship -- in the Free State. In various towns in the Free State, hundreds of women marched and handed over their passes to the authorities. Many were jailed. Eventually, the Free State government relaxed its policy on passes for women. The Transvaal province soon followed this example. Women remained largely exempt from influx control until the 1950s.

Urbanisation weighed most heavily on the women who shouldered the responsibility not only for themselves but also for their children, many living at or below the poverty line. The migration of men to the towns in search of work had left many women in charge of their rural households. Eventually they too began to migrate to cities. Little overtly political protest or resistance occurred against their condition, but they did revolt against controls on food supplies, on their right to brew beer and sell it in beer halls. They also began to be mobilised in their workplaces, e.g. in the clothing and industrial sectors, in the 1930s. For example, the Cape Town Women's Food Committee was linked to the trade unions and the SACP.

It must be said, though, that the SANNC was no more progressive than other political parties at the time in terms of the role of women in politics -- women were largely marginalised. Black women could not look to the Congress for help in fighting their struggles for survival. It was only in 1943 with the creation of the ANC Women's League that women were granted full membership and the right to vote within party structures.

Relief came largely from reformist organisations attempting to alleviate some of the stresses through welfare organisations. Black women at the higher end of the socio-economic spectrum spearheaded many small organisations and activities giving assistance to the needy, orphaned, crippled or the aged. The spirit of *ubuntu* survived with these women as they spread the values of their rural upbringing into urban townships.

> In an evocative study, Belinda Bozzoli (1991) traced the lives and experiences of 22 women from Phokeng, a small town in the North West Province. She showed how these women from a relatively well-to-do peasantry educated as Christians, with their experiences as domestic servants, showed an unusual rebelliousness of spirit. They married and settled in the historic Rand townships, built strong family structures, and supported them through illegal beer brewing. Their own respectability and resilience allowed them to withstand their experiences of police brutality. They turned their culture of subterfuge into a culture of opposition when the National Party attacked their very basis of survival.

The Orlando Mothers Welfare Organisation was started by Mabel Ngubane in 1937. The (White) Child Welfare Society of Johannesburg was asked to make a contribution. The Orlando organisation also influenced the authorities to provide a bus service to Orlando. The group had a membership fee of one shilling a month -- fairly expensive even at that time. This was a clear example of racially divided welfare organisations, rooted in British colonial practice.

Also in 1937, the National Council of African Women (NCAW) was started as an offshoot of the primarily male All Africa Convention which had met to resist Hertzog's Native Bills. The organisation received a great deal of support from White liberals. The NCAW was patterned on the all-white National Council of Women. The members were teachers and nurses and they concerned themselves with delinquent children, wayward husbands, new techniques for housework, and giving assistance to the sick and elderly.

> The example of the YWCA shows the way in which internationally-affiliated CSOs also condoned racial segregation, long before apartheid was formally introduced in 1948.
>
> "In 1941, a Young Women's Christian Association (YWCA) branch was started in Sophiatown by Madie Hall Xuma, the newly arrived black-American [sic] wife of Dr. A.B. Xuma, then President of the ANC. Meetings consisted of instruction on how to serve tea properly, how to give pleasant children's birthday parties or arrange flowers, giving it an elitist reputation. The group secured affiliation with the world organisation in Geneva, despite the fact that YWCA branches for whites had operated in the country since the late 1800s."[252]

Margaret Ballinger, the Native Representative in Parliament instituted the Association of European and African Women in 1936, based on the ideal of better co-operation between Black and White to promote better living conditions for Africans. The events were not very meaningful as they deteriorated into complaint sessions by Black women who saw no reason to work for their own welfare when White women could easily lend financial assistance! The Association did succeed in establishing the Bantu Children's Holiday Fund. However, Black participation ended altogether when in 1948 all White management committees took over the running of these programmes.[253]

The Johannesburg City Council also established a small women's programme through three clubs which operated in Orlando, Western Native Township, and Pimville. Less well documented are women's choir clubs and stokvels or burial societies which were collective savings clubs which often held all-night social parties or choir competitions. Most women, through church or other organisations, participated in a support group which served as a vehicle for their assimilation into urban life.

In the 1940s, the food crisis had a politicising effect on Black women who might otherwise have been uninvolved. Consumer protests were organised by various grassroots, working class women's organisations such as the People's Food Council in Johannesburg, the Women's Food Committee in Cape Town, and the Durban Housewives' League.[254]

White women lobbied for Parliament to appoint a commission of inquiry into the legal disadvantage faced by women under common law. Advocacy on this issue included the National Council of Women, Die Vroue Federasie, the University Women's Association and the Women's Christian Temperance Union. In 1946 such a commission was set up, but it totally excluded any consideration of African customary law and problems faced by African women.

---

[252] Wells, 1993, p. 96.
[253] The concept of this programme still exists today in the Star Seaside Fund which seeks to provide poor children of all races with an opportunity to have a seaside holiday.
[254] Walker, 1991, p. 81.

Sports organisations

Sport and recreation played an important part in the lives of many communities. Participation in team sports especially created a sense of camaraderie that helped to overcome the frustration and hopelessness that often resulted from apartheid repression of Black communities. As Bernard Magubane wrote of African's love of soccer in 1963, "The drudgery which their life imposes on them is temporarily forgotten... This preoccupation with football matches makes life worth living despite its frustrations".[255] In a similar vein, of rugby and other sport, Booley wrote that "these events served to cushion the effects of the socio-psychological onslaught of entrenched racism, discrimination and the toll of daily life under apartheid".[256] In many areas, sports were the centre around which social life revolved.

Imperial Britain was a major influence on the emergence of sport in English-speaking White schools beginning in the 1880s. Sport was an important identity that served to link imperial societies and to unify English settlers. Cricket was a prime example of this. The South African Cricket Association was formed in 1890. It offered participation to White cricket clubs from other colonies in Africa, but ignored Black communities within South Africa.[257] Afrikaners were not particularly eager to play cricket until around the 1960s, preferring rugby. This reflected the divisions within the White community.

Africans, Indians and Coloureds did, however, play cricket. In the late 19th century, they tended to "emulate the values and cultural practices of White cricket", but in the 20th century began to develop their own, due not least to the social and economic conditions in which they were forced to play. The first non-racial – e.g. including Coloured, Cape Malay and African clubs – sports organisation was the Griqualand West Colonial Rugby Football Union (GWCRFU), founded in 1894 in Kimberley.

There is evidence of early examples of non-racial sporting events. "Matches between whites and blacks were a feature of imperial public holidays, in particular in the late 19th century".[258] However, the competitiveness of Black clubs and the fact that they often defeated their White opponents eventually became just one of many reasons to reinforce segregation in sport as in all other aspects of life. By the early 1900s, inter-racial sporting events were abolished, and Blacks organised their own competitions. Blacks were also banned from Whites' sporting facilities.

Sports and sports clubs were used by missionaries and mine owners as a way of keeping Black workers busy during their leisure time. The Non-European Affairs Department (NEAD) in Johannesburg also implemented a recreation programme for workers in Johannesburg. The hope was that such activities would prevent workers from becoming involved in labour or political protest. However, the sports clubs and associations were run by Blacks themselves. Some well-off Black entrepreneurs also chose to support sports clubs / teams as a means of reinforcing their social status. Nonetheless, clubs were mechanisms of socialisation of Blacks into certain aspects of the colonial ethos.

The first White rugby clubs (Hamilton and Villagers) were formed in Cape Town in 1879, and the first Coloured clubs emerged in 1886. The South African Rugby Board (SARB) was founded in 1889. The national rugby team, the Springboks, went on tour in 1906/7 with players of both English and Afrikaner ethnicity. This tour was used as an instrument of reconciliation in the aftermath of the Anglo-Boer War. Despite ongoing divisions between

---

[255] Cited in Nauright, 1997, p. 101.
[256] Booley, 1998, p. 11.
[257] Nauright, 1997, pp. 25-26.
[258] Ibid., p. 62.

English and Afrikaner in the rugby arena, it does seem that they have been able to regularly unite behind the national team since that time.

Soccer was played by White clubs starting in the mid-1800s. The first recorded match took place in Pietermartizburg in 1866, where the first club was established in 1879, The Natal Football Association began in 1882, whilst the Football Association of South Africa started in the Cape in 1892.

Various other sport governing bodies were established in the 1890s and early 1900s, and "by 1910 most major sports were organised on a national basis".[259] These included the South African Cyclists' Union and the South African Amateur Athletic Association, as well as organisations for swimming, hockey, golf and tennis – all for Whites only. Lawn bowls was another popular sport with strong imperial linkages. Localised clubs in all these sports were also formed.

The involvement of non-White communities in sports such as soccer, rugby, boxing and others began in the latter part of the 19th century. Indian boys began playing soccer in the mid-1880s, and by 1886, the Indians in Durban had four soccer clubs. Boxing was another popular sport. "Sports clubs were very important organisations in which officiation and participation were as crucial as the events on the sporting field themselves".[260] The Transvaal Indian Football Association was founded in 1896. African soccer clubs began to appear at the end of the 19th century. The Orange Free State Bantu Soccer club started in 1898. This was followed by the Durban and District African Football Association (DDAFA) in 1916, the Witwatersrand District Native Football Association (WDNFA) formed in the early 1920s mainly for mine teams, the Johannesburg Bantu Football Association (JBFA) in 1929, the Natal Bantu Football Association in 1931, the Johannesburg African Football Association in 1932 (replacing the WDNFA), and the South African Bantu Football Association in 1933. The DDAFA had 21 affiliated clubs by 1923 and the JBFA had 153 senior clubs and 282 junior clubs by 1937. The South African African Football Association was established in 1930 as an umbrella organisation for all the provincial groups.[261] Coloured football leagues emerged in the 1920s. These examples show the huge support and enthusiasm for the sport of soccer throughout South Africa.

"The first African cricket club was founded in Port Elizabeth in 1869, and by 1887 *Imvo Zabantsundu* (the King William's Town African newspaper) had a sports edition that reported news of cricket and other sports in the Black elite community".[262] Nauright posited that "cricket became a crucial cultural activity that helped to define a 'civilised' man as the black middle class sought to achieve wider acceptance through tests of civilisation rather than of race". Serving as leaders and administrators of Black sports associations proved to be a crucial opportunity for Black advancement. "Although the prestige associated with sports administrative positions led to numerous political battles, and sometimes to splits within associations, the relative stability in administration allowed many black sporting organisations to survive the onslaught of apartheid and its many disruptive relocation policies and social restrictions".[263]

Booley wrote of the passion that Black people had for the game of rugby, and of the fact that the history of black rugby has largely been ignored.[264] In fact, Black involvement in rugby

---

[259] Ibid., p. 43.
[260] Freund, 1995, p. 39.
[261] See Nauright, 1997, Chapter 5.
[262] Ibid., p. 57.
[263] Ibid., p. 110.
[264] Booley, 1998, p. 13. Booley's study of the "forgotten heroes" of Black rugby is itself a passionately written volume with much fascinating detail and vivid reminiscences.

began more than a century ago. The South African Coloured Rugby Football Board (SACRFB) was created in 1896, based in Kimberley. It organised many competitions amongst the many Coloured rugby teams. Within the Coloured community, early rugby unions reflected religious divisions, The Cape had two Coloured rugby unions – the Western Province Coloured Rugby Union (WPCRU) established in 1886 and the City and Suburban Rugby Union (CSRU) founded in 1898. The WPCRU was largely Muslim with members coming from communities such as District Six and Bo-Kaap, whereas the CSRU members were based in District Six, Woodstock and other suburbs and it banned Muslim members until the 1960s.[265] Coloured rugby clubs were also the focus of male social activities in these communities. They were sometimes linked to gangs which supported particular rugby clubs.[266] Thus, an important civil society activity was in some cases tied to "uncivil" society.

The Bantu Men's Social Centre (BMSC) opened in Johannesburg in 1924. It was "crucial in the development of African sporting organisation as it was one of the few venues within the municipality of Johannsburg where African sporting competitions could be held outside of mining properties".[267] However, the BMSC was also seen by many Africans as an elitist organisation. White liberals, involved for example in the Joint Council movement and the South African Institute of Race Relations, lobbied the Johannesburg City Council and other municipalities to provide more and better recreational facilities for Africans.[268] Despite these efforts, facilities remained segregated and little government funding from local or national level was made available for Black sporting organisations.

In the 1930s and 1940s, soccer was hugely popular amongst working class Whites and in black townships especially in urban areas throughout the country. In the same period, rugby had become prevalent in the African townships of the Eastern and Western Cape, where missionaries had begun to teach it to the African elite. Of Black rugby's "forgotten heroes", Mluleki George wrote: "Forgetting their daily toil against an unjust and repressive regime, they could revitalise and regain their strength for days to come. It was through this communal and social interaction that communities grew closer, bonds were formed, new relations established and commitment intensified in the general struggle for freedom".[269]

Rugby was also increasingly prevalent amongst Afrikaners, who began to use the sport to promote their nationalist identity.[270] The numbers increased dramatically after World War II. Rugby was also used to "shore up beliefs of superiority" and masculinity within settler communities.[271] Nauright argued that "the links between the Broederbond, the government and Springbok rugby during the apartheid era cannot be over-emphasised... The cultural significance of rugby, overlaid with its political position in apartheid society, meant that rugby became the closest thing to a secular religion in white South African society".[272]

Women's sport was similarly divided. Nauright notes that the power structures of women's netball were, like those of men's rugby, tied to Afrikaner nationalism.[273] The first White women's hockey club was formed in 1901. Women in Coloured communities (especially non-Muslim ones) played netball and hockey. They occasionally even played charity rugby matches, and were strong supporters of men's rugby. Nauright cited the women's section of *Bantu World* in 1934 where African women said that "With all of us it is work, work, work.

---

[265] Nauright, 1997, p. 48. Similarly, within the Indian community in Durban there were separate sports groups for the Muslim, Tamil and Hindu communities.
[266] Ibid., p. 51.
[267] Ibid., p. 69.
[268] Ibid., p. 70.
[269] "Message", Booley, 1998, p. 7.
[270] Nauright, 1997, pp. 12-13.
[271] Ibid., p. 18.
[272] Ibid., pp. 89-90.
[273] Ibid., p. 19.

And when there is time for a rest we are only too glad of the chance for tennis, dancing or visiting our friends".[274] Clearly, women were interested and involved in sport, and the evolution of women's sport surely deserves more study.

Concluding Remarks

This period reflected the increasing entrenchment of racial segregation in all aspects of South African life. The socio-political environment led to exacerbated conflict and competition between Whites and Blacks. It was a difficult period in economic terms, encompassing two World Wars, the world-wide Depression, and a number of localised economic and natural challenges. In the face of these, each racial group formed organisations to protect and promote its own interests.

Even within the racial groups there were divisions. Amongst Whites, the English and Afrikaners had quite disparate perceptions of their needs and priorities. Afrikaners, seeing themselves as dominated by the English, formed a wide range of political, cultural and economic organisations to enhance their own identity and position within the broader society. Ethnic divisions aside, class consciousness also developed and Whites formed trade unions to protect their jobs and their predominance in certain trades and industries. Access to education, job reservation and wage levels favoured Whites over Blacks, increasing levels of racial inequality across the country.

In protest against these developments, Blacks formed political organisations aimed at resisting increased restrictions on their rights. Segregation was generally opposed, but because these organisations too were divided on racial lines, they were unable to achieve any real unity. Africans had the SANNC and later the ANC, Coloureds had the APO, and Indians had the SAIC. Within these racial communities, there were also political divisions – conservative vs radical, racial vs non-racial (willingness to work with sympathetic Whites), accommodation vs aggressive opposition. Attempts at unity such as the Non-European Movement (NEUM), had some impact in building relationships and co-operation across races, but had little effect on the bigger picture – the state oppression of all Blacks continued unabated.

Faith-based organisations continued to proliferate, also divided by race, theological tendencies, and political inclinations. The Muslim, Hindu and Jewish communities became more formalised during this period, creating more places of worship as well as organisations to promote community welfare, religious education and practice. During this period, these organisations did not engage publicly in political issues. Rather, individual adherents of each religion took personal decisions as to whether they should involve themselves in political affairs. There were, however, close ties between Christianity and the ANC leadership, and this caused some rethinking to take place within the various churches regarding their stance on segregation.

The emergence of a multiplicity of trade unions was a key feature of this period. White trade unions developed after the British tradition, and quite effectively protected their skilled and semi-skilled jobs from incursion by Black workers. Afrikaner workers who had migrated from the rural areas felt even more threatened by the possibility of Blacks taking their jobs due to their lack of skills. Black workers were by far the most exploited. Even though Black trade unions were not formally recognised by the government, many were established over this period. These too were often divided by race: African, Coloured and Indian, though there were exceptions such as the Industrial and Commercial Workers' Union (ICU) and later the

---

[274] Quoted in Ibid., p. 69.

union federation, the Council of Non-European Trade Unions. Labour unrest became a fairly constant feature of economic life. On several occasions, the Black mining unions challenged the power of the Chamber of Mines by significant strikes, but had little success in improving their wages or working conditions. White workers largely maintained their pre-eminence in the labour market.

Women's organisations provided various functions, but in the main helped communities deal with welfare issues. As always, amongst all groups, women were the main channels for transfer of community and family values from one generation to the other. As with other types of organisations, women's groups tended to be separated according to race. Whilst some attempts were made to promote more contact and co-operation, they did not have much success not least because of the differing lifestyles. In the political sphere, White women made common cause to protest disadvantage resulting from common law and to obtain the vote, and African women joined together in consumer protests to address the food crisis of the 1940s. Most women's groups, however, focused on helping each other adapt to urban life.

In all communities and racial groups, sport helped people deal with the stresses and challenges of life. Sports organisations also provided a means of developing leadership and gaining administrative experience, especially in Black communities. Sports such as rugby, football (soccer) and cricket were played by all races from the latter part of the 19th century if not earlier, despite mythologies perpetuated to the contrary. Local and national leagues emerged across the country, mostly divided by race. There is evidence, however, of early examples of non-racial sports competitions though these largely disappeared in the early 1900s. Blacks suffered the disadvantage of inferior sports facilities and training opportunities. They were also denied the opportunity to play on South African national teams in international competitions. Cynically, sports were used by employers, especially on the mines, to divert miners' attention from their poor working and living conditions. Sports played an important role in unifying communities, whilst at the same time dividing them.

The misconception that racial segregation only began in earnest with the advent of the National Party government and apartheid has been effectively dispelled in this chapter. Clearly, from the time the Union was created, laws and practices were put in place to keep the races separate and to suppress the political and economic development of all Black peoples in the country. Civil society organisations mirrored the prevailing dynamic, and though a variety of protest measures were taken by Black groups, little positive change resulted.

Chapter Four

The Role of Civil Society under Apartheid, 1948-1994

The system of apartheid was formally introduced in 1948, although the oppression of racial discrimination and segregation had been in place through law, policy and practice for more than a century already. The previous chapters have shown how civil society organisations tried in various ways to protest against these pre-1948 measures and to pressure government to treat all the people of South African equally. However, the protests, lobbying, delegations to colonial authorities, etc. had very little if any positive impact. Increasingly, the political system was entrenching the second-class status of Africans, Coloureds and Indians.

The post-1948 period saw increasing radicalism amongst apartheid's opponents. This, of course was countered by increasing repression by the government. This chapter briefly lays out the most egregious measures imposed by the National Party government in its attempts to create a system of separate development. The bulk of the chapter discusses a wide range of civil society organisations that operated during the period from 1948 to 1994, how they interacted with the apartheid system and in many but not all cases worked to end it, both by peaceful and ultimately violent means.

Consolidation of National Party Rule and the Statutory Basis of Apartheid

After 1948, racial segregation was legislated for in Act after Act by the apartheid regime, benefiting White people and implementing the National Party ideal of a segregated society. In addition to its severe violation of basic human rights, this ideology was flawed on several counts due to incorrect assumptions. It assumed that if segregated homelands were created, the urbanised African population would return to the 'traditional' land. It further assumed that the Coloured and Indian population would be a buffer and seek racial rights for themselves. However, any reading of the history of the struggle against White colonial rule and the resolute and principled fight for a franchise would alert the reader to the fact that the vast majority of the African, Indian and Coloured people would not be satisfied with anything less than a full franchise in a united sovereign nation, collectively guiding their destiny.

The apartheid system protected the interests of the Whites against the rest of the population. All aspects of life from birth to death favoured the White groups. Public hospitals were provided for them. Nurseries and primary schools catered for children near their places of residence. High schools were equipped with playing fields and laboratories and libraries, which other racial groups did not have. Technical or commercial colleges were easily accessible even to those with low school grades. University entrance was guaranteed to those who showed the slightest inclination. Jobs were secure and protected by the job reservation laws. Residences were in abundance. White property owners were able to build and own property. They could relocate between provinces, live in urban or rural areas, unhindered. They could bring up their children in safety and with cheap domestic help. They could open businesses anywhere and were not made to fulfil the obligations specified for other races.

Contrasted with this largesse for Whites were a number of laws and proclamations which sought to limit and prescribe the rights of all other South Africans in every aspect of their lives: where they could be born, live, be educated, work; who they could marry, and even where they could be buried. The table below lists some of the key pieces of legislation passed by the National Party government in the decade after their 1948 election victory to limit the rights of African, Coloured and Indian South Africans.

KEY APARTHEID LEGISLATION
Social
1949: Prohibition of Mixed Marriages Act
1950: The Immorality Act
1950: The Population Registration Act
Residential
1950: The Group Areas Act
1950: The National Resettlement Act
Cultural/ educational
1953: The Bantu Education Act
1954: The Extension of University Education Act
Political
1951: The Bantu Authorities Act
1959: The Promotion of Bantu Self-Government Act
Labour
1953: The Native Labour Act
1956: The Industrial Conciliation Act and The Wage Act

These provisions created a privileged racial group, but also a class of people who bought safety and security by voting for the apartheid system, election after election, from 1948 to 1994.

Contacts across the colour line

A figment of the apartheid regime was that no social or political contact across the colour line should take place. However, continuous economic contact between and amongst individuals of different races occurred every day in South Africa, e.g. between employer and employee, buyer and seller, professional and client, reader and writer, performer and audience. Contact took place on the farms, in the mines, in domestic service, in the shops, in doctors' rooms and legal offices, in the newspapers, in the (restricted) performing arts, in churches, etc.

These contacts provided individuals, families and groups with an appreciation of the brutality and stupidity of the apartheid legislation. But these contacts also built lasting friendships between employer and worker, dentists, doctors and lawyers, performing artists, teachers and students.

In the post-1976 era, many embassies and consulates often invited individuals across the colour line to speak to each other and encounter different viewpoints. Diplomats found these gatherings to be sources of information different from the official version of events.

Business leaders also often invited and spoke to political leaders of different racial groups on a range of political issues. Informal dialogue across racially divided churches, unions and other activist organisations occurred regularly or as occasions demanded. Contacts such as these gave rise to the establishment of organisations such as the Black Sash, the Detainees'

Parents Support Committee, the End Conscription Campaign, and the Consultative Business Movement, amongst others.

Resistance to Apartheid

African political resistance

The anti-apartheid movement brought racial groups together in some of their protest activities. The Defiance Campaign of 1952[275] is an excellent example of co-operation amongst organisations representing different racial groups. It was a coalition comprising the African National Congress, Indian Congresses and the Cape Franchise Action Council (Coloured) and resulted in more than 8,500 men and women going to prison. They were protesting against an array of new apartheid laws passed by the government led by Dr. D.F. Malan. "Batches of resisters deliberately infringed some minor apartheid law. On being brought to court, they pleaded guilty, made a statement from the dock and chose the option of a prison sentence".[276] Similar joint protests followed in later stages of the Defiance Campaign.

In his September 1952 "no easy walk to freedom" address to the Transvaal ANC, Nelson Mandela argued that the Defiance Campaign had created a "new spirit and new ideas" amongst the people. "Today the people speak the language of action: there is a mighty awakening among the men and women of our country and the year 1952 stands out as the year of the upsurge of national consciousness". He noted that it was no longer possible to have a strategy centred on "public meetings and printed circulars" but rather that it was time to "consolidate the Congress machinery", "to build up the local branches", and "to extend and strengthen the ties between Congress and the people", and "to consolidate Congress leadership". This new strategy of the ANC and the South African Indian Congress (SAIC)[277] was referred to as the "M" Plan.[278]

In addition to strengthening ties between the ANC and other Black political organisations, the ANC also attempted to engage with liberal Whites, e.g. those who belonged to political parties such as the United Party, the Labour Party and the Liberal Party. Oliver Tambo, acting secretary general of the ANC in 1955 said that these Whites should "face the central reality of South Africa politics: that democracy is indivisible".[279] However, in October 1953, a group of former communist[280] and left-wing Whites dissatisfied with the other political party options open to them formed the South African Congress of Democrats (COD).[281] Its policy was grounded in the Universal Declaration of Human Rights – equal political rights for all citizens regardless of race or colour. The COD did not take a position for or against socialism, though the government used the fact that some members were ex-communists to attack the group. Because it was so closely aligned to the ANC, had an exclusively White membership and was not constituted as a political party, it never grew beyond a membership of about 700. Nonetheless, Helen Joseph (a COD founding member) argued that the COD

---

[275] The full name was the Defiance of Unjust Laws Campaign.
[276] Clarke, 1989, p. 136.
[277] The South African Indian Congress should not be confused with the statutory body known as the South African Indian Council, a so-called representative body established by the NP government as part of their divide and rule strategy.
[278] Mandela, Presidential address to Transvaal ANC, 21 September 1953. The full text is available in Karis, Carter and Gerhart, 1977, Vol. 3, pp. 106-115.
[279] Karis, Carter and Gerhart, 1977, Vol. 3, p. 13.
[280] The Communist Party of South Africa (CPSA) had been dissolved in 1950 due to government repression, e.g. the Suppression of Communism Act which made the party illegal.
[281] At this time, membership of the ANC was still not open to Whites.

played a useful role in prodding Whites to think more seriously about the future direction of the country.[282] The COD continued to operate, despite the arrests of several members, until it was finally banned by the government in September 1962.

In 1955 the Cape leader of the ANC, Z.K. Matthews, called for a Congress of the People to further articulate demands for socio-political change. Grievances were collected from around the country. The Congress took place in Kliptown on 26 June 1955. Participating organisations included the ANC, the South African Indian Congress (SAIC), the COD, the South African Coloured People's Organisation (SACPO)[283] and the South African Congress of Trade Unions (SACTU).[284] The Congress of 3,000 delegates adopted the Freedom Charter which called for equal rights for all racial groups and said that South Africa belonged to all its inhabitants. It called for a democratic state based on universal suffrage. The government considered the Charter subversive, and many leaders were banned or arrested. Eventually, when the Treason Trials occurred in 1960, the charges against the accused were dropped. This experience, however, had the effect of bringing members of the ANC alliance closer together and reinforcing their resolve.[285]

Significant protests took place in 1956 against the government's intention to extend the pass system to African women. "When the government began systematically to issue reference books to all African women, opposition leaders had no difficulty in convincing them that passes were badges of subordinate status, symbols of humiliation and harassment, and instruments for the control and supply of cheap labour".[286] The Federation of South African Women (FEDSAW), led by Helen Joseph, Ray Alexander, Ida Mntwana, and Fatima Meer, played a major role in initiating and organising demonstrations against the passes, along with the ANC Women's League. A first major demonstration took place in October 1955, attended by 1,000 to 2,000 women from the Transvaal. They left petitions for the Minister of Native Affairs in Pretoria. The second was much larger, and attracted women from other provinces as well. About 20,000 women marched on the Union Buildings in Pretoria on 9 August 1956 and delivered a petition to the Prime Minister.[287] The women's petition said:

> "We want to tell you what the pass would mean to an African woman, and we want you to know that whether you call it a reference book, an identity book, or by any other disguising name, to us it is a PASS. And it means just this:
> - That homes will be broken up when women are arrested under pass laws;
> - That children will be left uncared for, helpless, and mothers will be torn from their babies for failure to produce a pass;
> - That women and girls will be exposed to humiliation and degradation at the hands of pass-searching policemen;
> - That women will lose the right to move freely from one place to another.
> In the name of women of South Africa, we say to you, each one of us, African, European, Indian, Coloured, that we are opposed to the pass system. We, voters and voteless, call upon your Government not to issue passes to African women. We shall not rest until ALL pass laws and all forms of permits restricting our freedom have been abolished. We shall not rest until we have won for our children their fundamental rights of freedom, justice and security."[288]

---

[282] Van der Westhuizen, in Liebenberg et al., 1994, pp. 72-80. Senior members of the COD included Jack Hodgson, Yettah Barenblatt, Piet Beyleveld, Joe Slovo, Ruth First, Helen Joseph, Rusty Bernstein, Ben and Mary Turok.
[283] See section on Coloured political organisations below.
[284] See section on trade unions below.
[285] See Cameron, 1987, pp. 282-283.
[286] Karis, Carter and Gerhart, 1977, Vol. 3, p. 74.
[287] This event is now commemorated as Women's Day annually on 9 August.
[288] The full text of the petition can be found in Karis, Carter and Gerhart, 1977, Vol. 3, pp. 250-251.

On 5 December 1956, 19 women including leaders of FEDSAW and the ANC Women's League, were arrested in treason raids as part of the total of 156 opposition leaders. Those arrested included leaders of all races. The Treason Trial went on for four years, and in 1961 the accused were all found not guilty. This trial had several significant effects:

- It placed major constraints on many ANC leaders, but also increased their prestige.
- It strengthened links between the Congress alliance and White Communists and liberals.
- It allowed younger leaders to emerge whilst many of the existing leadership were awaiting trial.
- It mobilised many supporters to assist in the defense of the accused and to provide for their families whilst they were in prison.[289]

This new solidarity provided a boost for the unity of the opposition forces.

The late 1950s saw the beginning of an era of economic boycotts in the townships. For example, the Johannesburg bus boycott in early 1957 involved more than 50,000 Africans protesting against crowded and uncomfortable buses. Local community organisations were instrumental in co-ordinating the boycott. Victory came when government passed a law requiring employers to subsidise transport for their workers. Government also made a contribution to the subsidy. Fares also were lowered to their pre-boycott levels. This was probably the first time that government had given in to pressure from African interest groups.[290] This signalled the start of many economic boycotts across the country – an instrument of opposition that became increasingly prevalent and effective.

The initial creation of the African homelands[291] by the government was the ultimate expression of apartheid. No real development was intended; rather the homelands were seen essentially as labour reserves with some amount of self-government along tribal lines but always under White trusteeship.[292] However, in 1959 the government of Dr. Verwoerd initiated a significant policy change which accepted that the homelands would eventually become "nation-states". "Instead of justifying discrimination against blacks in the heartland of South African openly on grounds of race, it would now be done on the grounds that they were citizens of separate states... Instead of a system of increased segregation and discrimination, apartheid was to be presented as a system of internal decolonisation".[293]

This insidious and cynical attempt to pull the wool over the eyes of the world did not succeed. It was quite clear that none of the homelands could support the populations that were being forced to live there. They were basically dormitories for African labour and dumping grounds for those Africans who were too young, old, infirm or unskilled to contribute to the growth of the South African economy. Any form of political independence for the homelands was to be a farce. Nonetheless, the process of granting independence began with the Transkei in 1963, which then created its own legislature. The homelands varied considerably in terms of their size, the level of political autonomy achieved, the extent to which they co-operated with (or were co-opted by) the apartheid government, the amount of political repression asserted by their leaders, and their potential for economic development.

Various statutory organs were established by the South African government ostensibly to assist with the economic development of the homelands, e.g. the Division of Economic and

---

[289] Karis, Carter and Gerhart, 1977, Vol. 3, p. 274.
[290] Ibid., p. 277.
[291] The homelands or Bantustans included: Transkei, Ciskei, KwaZulu, Bophuthatswana, KwaNdebele, KaNgwane, Gazankulu, Lebowa, QwaQwa, and Venda.
[292] Omer-Cooper, 1988, p. 212.
[293] Ibid., p. 212.

Development Co-operation in the Department of Foreign Affairs, the Economic Co-operation Promotion Loan Fund, the Corporation for Economic Development (CED) and the Development Bank of Southern Africa (DBSA). The homelands were almost completely dependent on resources provided by the South African government through these and other funding mechanisms (broadly categorised as 'aid' or 'development assistance')[294]. In fact, the resources provided to the homelands were wholly insufficient and most of the people there lived in poverty. The duplicity of this strategy was huge – on the one hand, Africans in the homelands were deprived of South African citizenship and dumped in the homelands, whilst on the other the South African economy could not survive without exploiting their labour.

The Pan Africanist Congress (PAC) was established in 1959 by a group who broke with the ANC. Many were members of the ANC Youth League, especially the Orlando branch led by Potlako K. Leballo, who held more strongly "nationalist" or "Africanist" views than the ANC leadership. Beginning in the early to mid-1950s, they were becoming uncomfortable with the ANC's increasingly close relations with Indian, Coloured and White political organisations. Their perspective was expressed *inter alia* through a mimeographed journal called *The Africanist*. The Youth League soon came to regard the Africanists as a disruptive and undisciplined faction. The involvement of Robert Sobukwe, then a language instructor at the University of the Witwatersrand, with the Orlando Africanists saw the further articulation of the Africanist position.[295] The Evaton ANC branch was heavily involved in organising the 1956 bus boycott which, after considerable violence, eventually succeeded in ensuring that the bus service to Johannesburg did not raise its fares. They organised in nearby Sharpeville as well. By 1958 other Transvaal ANC branches (known as "petitioners") joined Orlando in protesting against the provincial leadership elections. Eventually unable to influence the ANC policies from within, the actual breakaway occurred during the ANC Transvaal Conference in November 1958.

The PAC argued that co-operation in the liberation struggle was only possible "between equals". Thus, co-operation between the oppressed and their oppressors was unthinkable, especially as the PAC's goal was "the complete overthrow of white domination". They also argued however that they were not *a priori* anti-White, but rather hated Whites as the concrete, identifiable oppressor. Aside from race, the PAC also analysed the struggle in class terms, e.g. that Africans were highly exploited economically by Whites and other capitalists. They considered the Freedom Charter to be a "bluff" and specifically disagreed with the first clause of the Charter which stated that "South Africa belongs to all who live in it, Black and White".

Sobukwe's opening address at the PAC's Inaugural Convention in April 1959 set out their position on the historical role of Whites as "a foreign minority group which has exclusive control of political, economic, social and military power" and as the group "responsible for the pernicious doctrine of White Supremacy which has resulted in the humiliation and degradation of the indigenous African people. It is this group which has dispossessed the African people of their land and with arrogant conceit has set itself up as the 'guardians', the 'trustees' of the Africans". He argued that "true democracy can be established in South Africa and on the continent as a whole, only when the White supremacy has been destroyed". In order to accomplish this it was necessary, he stated, to "organise the African people under the banner of African nationalism... without interference from either so-called left wing or right-wing groups of the minorities who arrogantly appropriate to themselves the right to plan and think for the Africans". He further argued that "before full racial equality is achieved, no Whites could fully identify with the African cause".

---

[294] SAIRR, *Survey*, 1983, pp. 367-370.
[295] Karis, Carter and Gerhart, Vol. 3, 1977, p. 18.

Nonetheless, he asserted that "the freedom of the African means the freedom of all in South Africa, the European included, because only the African can guarantee the establishment of a genuine democracy in which all men will be citizens of a common state and will live and be governed as individuals and not as distinctive sectional groups". They sought "government of the Africans by the Africans, for the Africans, *with everybody who owes his only loyalty to Afrika and who is prepared to accept the democratic rule of an African majority being regarded as Africans* [italics added]. We guarantee no minority rights, because we think in terms of individuals, not groups".[296] Thus, Sobukwe's view was that Whites could eventually be included in the PAC's definition of Africans. Overall, the PAC insisted that they were "correctly interpreting the aspirations of the African people".

In early 1960, the PAC prepared to launch a non-violent mass campaign against the pass laws, e.g. by burning the passes. On the 21st March, a crowd of 5,000 peaceful protestors in Sharpeville was fired upon by the police, leaving 67 people dead and 186 wounded.[297] Most of the PAC leaders presented themselves at police stations and asked to be arrested, which they were.

In reaction to this massacre, the ANC launched its own campaign for pass burning and a stayaway, but the PAC had been largely silenced through arrests and the Transvaal campaign petered out. However, in Langa and Nyanga in the Cape Town area, a well-supported stayaway led to police firing on a crowd and killing two people. This in turn resulted in a three-week township rebellion, with angry residents burning government buildings and destroying the homes of African policemen. 95% of the work force went on strike, led by Phillip Kgosana. Whilst they succeeded in persuading the local police chief and eventually the Minister of Justice to suspend the pass laws, this was short-lived. On 30 March, the government declared a state of emergency and arrested thousands of political activists around the country. Police attempts to break the strike with violence backfired when Kgosana led a march of 30,000 people to Parliament. However, Kgosana was tricked by the perfidious police into turning the marchers around when he was told that he had been granted an interview with the Minister of Justice. He was subsequently arrested when he arrived for the meeting. This was followed by defeat of the strike and the government's banning of both the ANC and the PAC as unlawful organisations. Passes and influx control were reinstated.[298]

Early 1961 saw the ANC abandon their commitment to non-violent resistance. As Nelson Mandela said in court in 1964, "fifty years of non-violence had brought the African people nothing but more and more repressive legislation". He also noted that the government had closed what few channels of peaceful protest had been open to the African people.[299] However, the ANC wanted to avoid civil war and opted for a strategy of sabotage focused on economic targets, government buildings and other symbols of apartheid. This change in position led to the formation of Umkonto we Sizwe (known as MK), or the "Spear of the Nation" in 1961. Even Chief Luthuli had, by this time, come around to the view that "brave just men" could not be blamed "for seeking justice by the use of violent methods". He said that "they represent the highest in morality and ethics in the South African political struggle".[300] At about the same time, some young, radical White members of the Liberal Party also abandoned their policy of non-violence and formed the National Liberation Committee (NLC) which later became the African Resistance Movement (ARM). Both MK and ARM aimed initially to avoid loss of life and pressure the government to back down. This

---

[296] For the full text of Sobukwe's address to the Inaugural Convention of the PAC, see Karis, Carter and Gerhart, Vol. 3, 1997, pp. 510-517. See also pp. 307-325 on the formation of the PAC.
[297] The infamous Sharpeville massacre is now commemorated annually as Human Rights Day.
[298] See Tom Lodge in Liebenberg et al., 1994, pp. 104-110.
[299] Karis, Carter and Gerhart, 1977, Vol. 3, p. 647.
[300] Ibid., p. 651.

approach failed and simply resulted in a more repressive government response, one outcome of which was the Rivonia Trial and the 1964 imprisonment on Robben Island of Nelson Mandela, Walter Sisulu and Govan Mbeki, among others. ARM did not survive the aftermath of the 1964 bombing of the Whites-only concourse of the Johannesburg train station by John Harris. The bomb injured more than 20 people, one of whom died, despite a warning to the police to clear the area. Harris was caught and hanged, other members were arrested, and ARM ceased to exist.[301] After this, Whites who joined the armed resistance generally did so through MK, under Black leadership.

The banning of the ANC and PAC was a serious blow to the resistance movement. Under Clarence Makwetu, the remnants of the PAC began to form Poqo – forming underground cells of 10-100 men in the Cape which advocated violence to win the land back for Africans. Several attacks were mounted by Poqo in 1962, and upon the release from prison of Leballo and other PAC leaders, planning began for a wider rebellion. Orders emanated from exiled leaders in Maseru, and the nature of Poqo membership varied from region to region – from young well-educated men around Johannesburg to migrant labour in the Western Cape and Transkei. Leaders were mostly teachers, ministers and lay preachers. Plans for the national uprising were foiled once again by the police who arrested thousands of suspected Poqo members. The movement changed tactics and decided to focus on urban terrorism, but was reduced to only a few small cells, a few leaders in exile, and little access to funding. Its primary support came from the Organisation of African Unity's African Liberation Committee. The Azanian People's Liberation Army (APLA) was established under PAC control, began to train recruits outside the country, and established links with other Southern African liberation movements such as FRELIMO in Mozambique, UNITA in Angola and SWAPO.in Namibia. Nonetheless, leadership failures and squabbles limited the effectiveness of the PAC in exile, and it was only in the early 1980s during an upsurge in Africanist sentiment (e.g. amongst student organisations and trade unions) that the PAC regained some influence.[302]

The broader Black Consciousness Movement (BCM) emerged in the late 1960s and early 1970s not least due to the political vacuum resulting from the banning of the ANC and PAC. Signal events were the formation of the South African Students' Organisation (SASO) in 1969 and of the Black People's Convention (BPC) in 1972.[303] The radicalisation of university students, especially those at the so-called "bush colleges" or ethnically-based universities in the homelands, led to the emergence of Black students as a key political force in the resistance to apartheid and against NUSAS. SASO was itself a driving force behind the creation of the BPC which drew on "adult black religious, social, educational and cultural organisations" for its members. Even though both could be considered "elite" rather than "mass" organisations, and both had short life-spans, they still had a significant influence on Black public opinion due to their members' roles as teachers, preachers and journalists.[304] The death of Steve Biko in 1977 at the hands of the police was yet another blow to the BCM, especially to its intellectual base. Nonetheless, the banning by government of both SASO and the BPC in 1977 spurred adherents of "black consciousness" to form yet another organisation. Thus, in May 1979, the Azanian People's Organisation (AZAPO)[305] was established to take up the BC banner.

What did "Black Consciousness" organisations stand for? Essentially, they posited the need for Blacks to develop pride in themselves and reject the notion of their inferiority to Whites. As with the PAC, they said that Blacks needed "to stand on their own and direct their own

---

[301] Karis and Gerhart, 1997, Vol. 5, pp. 21-24.
[302] See Lodge, 1994, pp. 111-124.
[303] For more detail on SASO, see the section on University Student Organisations later in this chapter, and for more on the BPC, see the section on the BCM in the next chapter.
[304] Vincent Maphai, in Liebenberg et al., 1994, pp. 125-126.
[305] For more on AZAPO, see section on BCM in next chapter.

political struggle, instead of relying on white liberals to lead them to liberation". They also advocated the revival of Black culture and the rewriting of history to reflect the positive accomplishments of Black society. BC proponents argued that Whites should be excluded from BC organisations as part of the process of Blacks regaining their self-esteem. The latter position led to accusations of "reverse racism".[306] Pityana et al. cited the impact of Black Consciousness in replacing the "paralysing image of the victim" with that of "an active agent of history" amongst Blacks. This self-reliant approach therefore empowered people to do things for themselves rather than waiting for others to do things for them.[307] One of the results of BC was a proliferation of adult, youth, cultural and religious organisations aimed at building public awareness and creating a mass political philosophy amongst Black communities.

In 1972, a Parliamentary Commission of Inquiry was set up to investigate several high profile CSOs, including the University Christian Movement (UCM), The National Union of South African Students (NUSAS), the Christian Institute of Southern Africa, and the South African Institute of Race Relations. The Commission was led by a National Party (NP) MP, A.L. Schlebusch, with six members from the NP and four from the United Party. The Commission carried out its work in 1973. As just one significant example of government persecution of civil society, its terms of reference and its *modus operandi* were insidious. Broadly the terms of reference were to investigate and report on the objectives, structures, financing and activities of the four organisations as well as any related organisations, bodies, committees, groups of people or individuals. Particularly outrageous was the fact that the sittings of the Commission were held *in camera* and the full evidence was not published, so those who were called to give evidence or against whom evidence was given had no way to know what had been said or to defend themselves. As a direct result of the Schlebusch Commission's report, eight NUSAS leaders were banned. Shortly thereafter, even though their organisations had not been investigated by the Commission, eight leaders of the South African Students' Organisation (SASO) and the Black Sash were also banned. The Christian Institute and the SACC protested against the banning orders, and argued that any such investigations should be impartial judicial inquiries subject to due process of law, providing for the right of defence, the right to face their accusers, and should be held in full public view.[308] The SAIRR decided to withdraw its voluntary co-operation with the Commission and instructed its Director not to provide any documents without a subpoena. However, the Commission continued its investigations, and added the Wilgespruit Fellowship Centre – an affiliate of the SACC -- to its list of groups to be probed. Many people associated with these CSOs and others refused to testify and were charged in the courts.

As a result of the reports of the Schlebusch Commission, government felt that some foreign funders were having undue influence on local CSOs that were trying to achieve political ends. The Affected Organisations Bill in 1974 was put forward to give government wide powers to "enter premises, examine and seize documents and question persons". If, as a result of a "factual report" on the organisation, the Minister of Justice declared the CSO an "affected organisation", it became an offence to request foreign funds or use foreign funds on behalf of that organisation. Involvement in politics is, of course, a totally subjective criterion, and some members of Parliament spoke against the Bill due to its potential as a tool for repression. Many CSOs protested against the Bill. Nonetheless, the Bill passed and the first CSO to be declared an "affected organisation" was NUSAS, along with its three subsidiary bodies – Nused, Nuswel and Aquarius.[309]

---

[306] Maphai, in Liebenberg et al., 1994, p. 131.
[307] Pityana et al., 1991, pp. 9-11.
[308] SAIRR, *1973 Survey*, pp. 24-38.
[309] SAIRR, *1974 Survey,* pp. 25-35.

The Soweto uprising in 1976 was a signal event in the history of the anti-apartheid struggle. It "marked the transition from a period of conservative political culture in which the young played a distinctly subordinate role, to a new era of struggle energised by the participation and leadership of thousands of youthful activists for whom the student uprising had been a political baptism by fire".[310] The Soweto student uprising was probably second only to the 1960 Sharpeville massacre in causing a political crisis for government. It was particularly troubling due to the massive involvement of children in confrontation with the state. The emotive impact of these events was huge, and the reaction of parents, workers and other stakeholders changed the nature of the political struggle.[311]

The 1970s also saw the rapid growth of the Black trade union movement. The economic boom of the 1960s was accompanied by a growing demand for labour thus opening new opportunities for Black workers. But the government and employers continued their repression of worker organisations. By the mid-1970s, however, increased oil prices and world recession as well as technological issues and the inherent problems caused by apartheid (e.g. low productivity of labour, low skills levels due to poor education, low purchasing power of the African majority, etc.) resulted in a serious economic recession in South Africa. Unemployment increased. Government, faced with reduced resources, cut back its expenditure especially in Black townships causing the standard of living to decline further and Black anger to increase. Black trade unions became more militant and began to force employers to give them formal recognition. Major strikes occurred in Durban in 1973, causing many factories to close. This is considered a major turning point in South African labour history as well as in the history of the anti-apartheid resistance.[312]

The Broederbond, the "secret, opinion-forming cultural-political organisation" of the Afrikaner community, was extremely powerful in all aspects of Afrikaner life as well as in the political life of the country as a whole. However, in the beginning of the 1980s it came under attack both from the extreme right wing and a group of reformist Afrikaner theologians and academics. The secrecy of the Broederbond was particularly criticised, and even senior members such as Dr. Willem de Klerk suggested that public statements of its views should be made more often. Splits also occurred over the constitutional proposals. The right-wingers, especially members of the Herstigte Nasionale Party (HNP) who strongly supported separate development and no political rights for Africans, increased their political support in the 1981 general election from 30,000 to 200,000 votes.[313] In contrast, some of the reformists felt that the Broederbond was exerting undue influence within the Nederduitse Gereformeerde Kerk (NGK) and stifling open debate on key social and political issues.[314] Thus, political cracks were growing amongst Afrikaners.

These cracks were further demonstrated in 1982 with the split in the National Party (NP). Opposed to the concept of "power-sharing" proposed in the government's new constitutional plans, Dr. A. Treurnicht led a revolt against the NP. He created the Conservative Party (CP), and was followed out of the NP by 16 other MPs. Treurnicht and the CP took the view that the correct political solution for South Africa was a system of full political rights for each racial group – within its own group. They felt that people of different ethnic groups would not be able to work together in a "power-sharing" arrangement.[315] Thus, they argued that Africans, Indians and Coloured people should have no political rights in "White" South Africa.

---

[310] Karis and Gerhart, 1997, Vol. 5, p. 156.
[311] See section on Youth Organisations in this chapter for more on the Soweto uprising.
[312] See section on Trade Unions in this chapter for more on the emergence of Black trade unions, etc.
[313] SAIRR, *1981 Survey*, p. 9.
[314] Ibid., p. 6.
[315] SAIRR, *1982 Survey*, p. 9.

Just before the 1983 constitutional referendum for Whites, secret Broederbond documents were leaked to the press, showing how the new proposals would further entrench apartheid. The documents revealed a secret plan to secure Afrikaner domination, and to co-opt the Coloured population so that they would drop their demands for representation in the White parliament. These documents confirmed in graphic detail that the Afrikaner / NP government had no intention of divesting itself of any power. In 1984, a new Afrikaner "cultural" and ostensibly non-political organisation was formed by the right wing – the Afrikaner Volkswag (AV), led by Professor Carel Boshoff who had resigned earlier from the Broederbond. Its focus was on the maintenance of the "Afrikaner nation" and its Christian traditions. In 1985, the AV was refused membership of the Federasie van Afrikaanse Kultuurvereniginge (FAK), the cultural umbrella organisation, on the grounds that it was involved in political activities and opposed government. Even more militant was the Afrikaner Weerstandsbeweging (AWB) founded in 1974 and led by Eugene Terreblanche. The AWB was known for its paramilitary Blitzkomando, and it established an Afrikaner-only labour bureau and trade union.

The ANC was gaining popular support during this period, and government's attacks on it – both rhetorical and physical – grew. In a 1982 speech to the United Nations, Oliver Tambo, president of the ANC, called for an international year of sanctions against apartheid. Leaders of the front-line states declared their support for the ANC.

The Black Local Authorities (BLAs) Act of 1982 took effect in August 1983. Government's intention was to create a system of local government for Africans that resembled that of other race groups. The BLA powers were subject to ministerial discretion, and inherited the financial constraints of the previous system. They would never be self-sustainable in light of the limited financial resources to which they were entitled. When elections for the BLAs were scheduled for November and December 1983, a group of CSOs[316] formed an Anti-Community Councils' Election Committee[317] to persuade Africans not to participate in the elections as the BLAs were seen as yet another oppressive apartheid institution. The efforts of the Committee succeeded to the extent that the turnout of registered voters was only 21% (compared with 30% in 1978). In Soweto, the turnout was even less: 10.7%. The UDF argued that if non-registered voters were also counted, then the turnout was as little as 3% because such a large number of Africans had not even registered. Many Black councillors resigned during the 1980s in fear of attacks on themselves and their homes. The BLAs became a target for widespread resistance in African townships and never achieved any legitimacy with the people they were supposed to serve.

In June 1983, in response to an AZAPO call for a common front amongst Black organisations, a meeting was convened by a National Forum Committee. The Committee included Phiroshaw Camay, general secretary of the Council of Unions of South Africa (CUSA), Bishop Desmond Tutu, general secretary of the SACC, and Tom Manthata, a member of the Soweto Committee of Ten, and Mr. Saths Cooper of AZAPO. Speakers at the meeting urged Black organisations to overcome their ideological differences and join together. Dr. Neville Alexander of the South African Council for Higher Education (SACHED) argued that the class struggle against capitalist exploitation and the struggle against racial

---

[316] These included the Congress of South African Students (COSAS), the Azanian Students' Organisation (AZASO), the Soweto Civic Association (SCA), the Federation of South African Women (FEDSAW), the Municipal and General Workers' Union, the General Workers' Union of South Africa (GWUSA), and the General and Allied Workers' Union (GAWU). AZAPO also supported the boycott. See SAIRR, *Survey,* 1983, pp. 253-261.

[317] The Committee consisted of the Congress of South African Students (COSAS), the Azanian Students' Organisation (AZASO), the Soweto Civic Association (SCA), the Federation of South African Women (FEDSAW), the Municipal and General Workers' Union, the General Workers' Union of South Africa, and the General and Allied Workers' Union. It was supported by AZAPO. SAIRR, *1983 Survey,* p. 257.

oppression should be part of the same struggle. Principles adopted by the National Forum (NF) included "anti-racism and anti-imperialism, non-collaboration with the oppressor and his political instruments, independent working-class organisation, opposition to all alliance with ruling-class parties and the paramountcy of worker interests".[318]

The most significant political event of 1983 was the formation of the United Democratic Front (UDF), a non-racial coalition of many of the anti-apartheid organisations across the country. General councils of the UDF were formed in Natal, the Transvaal and the Cape by mid-year. On 20 August 1983, the UDF was launched nationally at a meeting of 1,000 delegates at Mitchell's Plain near Cape Town. Organisations represented included community / civic bodies, trade unions, sports bodies, women's and youth organisations. The UDF was formed as a front, rather than an organisation, and did not therefore make policy for its affiliates. The affiliates were free to take up UDF campaigns in appropriate ways related to their own activities and constituencies. Decisions were to be made by consensus. The conference declaration called for a "united democratic South Africa, free of Bantustans and group areas, and based on the will of the people". It recognised the need for "unity in struggle through which all democrats regardless of race, religion or colour shall take part together". It attacked the attempts by government to co-opt "false leaders" of the Black community with a view to controlling the people through the tricameral parliament and community councils.[319]

From 1984 onward, there were a series of township disturbances, some of which resulted in violent clashes with the authorities. School boycotts, expulsions and detention of pupils occurred due to unfulfilled demands regarding educational issues including the phasing out of the prefect system and the establishment of student representative councils (SRCs). Other clashes occurred during protests against the elections for Coloured and Indian representatives by a wide range of CSOs, including pupils and students, political, cultural, religious, sports and labour organisations. These groups – some of which were affiliated to the UDF and/or the National Forum -- urged Coloured and Indian voters to boycott the elections and align themselves with Africans who had been completely deprived of voting rights. The anti-election campaign claimed victory due to the high number of boycotters. In the vote for the Coloured House of Representatives, turnout of registered voters was 30.9%. Turnout as a percentage of all eligible voters was only 18.1%. For the Indian House of Delegates, turnout was 20.29% or registered voters and 16.2% of eligible voters.[320] Then, rent increases in the townships led to further protests, joined again by a variety of organisations including AZAPO, the UDF, the Soweto Civic Association, FEDSAW, COSAS, AZASO and Vaal civic associations. These protests led to violence between residents and police and residents and local councillors, leaving more than 60 people dead.[321]

Resistance against apartheid measures and authorities in general was escalating rapidly. The use of both the police and the army to quell township revolts was an increasing threat to human rights and race relations, and only provoked more protest. Dissatisfaction and anger had vastly increased in the townships and Africans had few channels to express their views. To further emphasise the seriousness of their specific demands and to show the government the power of the masses, a two-day stay-away on 5/6 November 1984 was called by groups including youth groups, trade unions, community groups, women's organisations and others. Demands covered:

- the introduction of democratically elected SRCs;
- the withdrawal of the army and police from the townships;
- the abolition of corporal punishment in schools;

---

[318] SAIRR, *1983 Survey*, pp. 54-55.
[319] Ibid., pp. 57-59. For more on the UDF, see Chapter Five. There was some overlap in the membership of the NF and the UDF, e.g. CUSA and the Soweto Committee of Ten.
[320] SAIRR, *1984 Survey*, pp. 127-128.
[321] Ibid., pp. 68-80.

- the scrapping of all increases in rents, service charges and bus fares;
- the withdrawal of the general sales tax;
- the release of all detaineed and political prisoners;
- an end to sexual harassment of female pupils;
- the resignation of community councillors; and
- the reinstatement of dismissed workers at Simba-Quix.[322]

The stay-away was a considerable success, with poor attendance at work and 400,000 pupils boycotting school. However, not all groups supported the stay-away. About 16 Black Consciousness organisations criticised the stay-away as "ill-timed" and as likely to cause harm to the people they were meant to help, especially if lives were lost. Buthelezi said that the organisers were intimidating fellow Africans and thereby dividing them. As a result of the stay-away, government detained about18 people including Chris Dlamini of FOSATU and Phiroshaw Camay, general secretary of CUSA. The detentions were condemned by civil society, including business organisations FCI, AHI and ASSOCOM as well as the Black Management Forum. All of the 18 were eventually released with only four actually being charged.[323]

Following the 1984 township disturbances, the Black Sash drew attention to the fact that violence was not only one-sided, that is the police and army against residents. They noted that there had also been "intimidation and retributive violence to sustain the boycotts and labour stoppages", e.g. petrol bombs used to stop people from going to work.[324] However, they also complained about the pass raids conducted on 23 October 1984 by 7,000 police and army operatives in Sebokeng, Sharpeville and Boipatong were an indication that government intended to use the army to enforce influx control as another means of repression.[325] In 1985, AZAPO leaders such as Ishmael Mkhabela cautioned against Black on Black violence, e.g. the burning of suspected informers at funerals, saying that members of the resistance movement would lose their moral integrity through such acts.[326] Ultimately, all sides were accused at one time or another of being party to violence against individuals and organisations, though the vast majority of people resisted apartheid by peaceful means.

In December 1985, the government imposed a six-month ban in 30 magisterial districts on gatherings of various political organisations, including the UDF and AZAPO. The countrywide ban on outdoor gatherings was extended in March 1986 for a year. Other specific bans were also put in place, e.g. on gatherings to mark the anniversary of the Freedom Charter. Then on 12 June 1986, another state of emergency was declared, accompanied by more detentions and individual and organisational bannings.

Political resistance in the Coloured community

Coloured leaders affiliated to the ANC saw the need to form an organisation that would provide stronger opposition to the removal of Coloured voters from the common voters' roll in the Cape. The South African Coloured People's Organisation (SACPO), formed in Cape Town on 12 September 1953, was led by Edgar Deane of the Cape Furniture Workers' Union, Dr. Richard van der Ross, a school principal, S. Rahim, Reginald September and John Gomas. Though membership of SACPO was open to other races, it was largely intended to speak for the Coloured community.[327].

---

[322] Ibid., p. 76.
[323] Ibid., pp. 77-78.
[324] Ibid., p. 79.
[325] Ibid., p. 351.
[326] SAIRR, *1985 Survey*, p. 12.
[327] Karis, Carter and Gerhart, 1977, Vol. 3, p. 12.

However, having been removed from the roll in 1956 despite their protests, SACPO decided to participate in the 1958 Coloured election for the new House of Assembly. This caused some members of SACPO to resign and boycott the election. Of the 130,000 Coloured males eligible to vote, and the 48,000 registered in 1953, only 14,451 actually voted in 1958,[328] indicating that the boycott and opposition to SACPO's decision was a considerable success. In December 1959, SACPO changed its name to the South African Coloured People's Congress (SACPC). As with other anti-apartheid political organisations, much of the SACPC's went into exile.

In 1966, its president, Barney Desai, and its chairman, Cardiff Marney, decided that the SACPC should be dissolved and merged with the PAC. They argued that the "sectional organisations representing exclusive group interests of the different 'races'" were no longer the best means of bringing together "all the oppressed masses into the liberatory fold". In their view, this historical approach had only increased racialism. They disagreed with the fact that the ANC leadership would not invite non-Africans (Coloureds and Indians) to join the ANC They decided to accept the invitation of the PAC to become members as "Africans and equals" and encouraged other Coloured and Indian people to do the same.[329] It was only in 1969 that the ANC changed its policy and instituted membership open to all races.

In 1968, Coloured representation in Parliament (by Whites) was ended. Instead, government instituted an advisory body, the Coloured Representative Council (CRC). "The CRC was composed of 20 nominated members and 40 members elected nationally by universal adult suffrage among Coloureds." Registration to vote was compulsory. In the first election of 1969, 76% of potential voters registered and the turnout of registered voters was 37%. In the second election of 1975, only 53% registered and the turnout declined to 28%.[330] The existence of the CRC encouraged the formation of exclusively Coloured political parties, and promoted the view that Coloureds should seek a superior status to that of Africans. However, those who participated in the CRC were increasingly considered to be opportunists and sell-outs as it became clear that the CRC had little or no power to advance Coloured interests. The Labour Party became more and more vocal in its protest against CRC and by 1979 had paralysed it from within.[331] The CRC was abolished in 1980.

Proposals for a tricameral parliament – one house each for Whites, Coloureds and Indians – were revealed by the National Party in 1981. The Labour Party, the most important Coloured political party, rejected this proposal as it was contrary to the principles of universal franchise within a unitary political system. It would also continue to deprive Africans of political rights and maintain the apartheid system, increasing racial polarisation.[332] The government's proposals were also rejected by a new Black political alliance of CSOs in the Western Cape, comprising civic and residents' associations, religious groups and student organisations. The Federation of Civic Associations (FRA) and the Cape Housing Action Committee (CAHAC) – a grouping of 32 civics – called the proposals racist and undemocratic and urged people to boycott any elections or referenda aimed at implementing them. They too continued to call for a unitary system based on one person – one vote.[333]

By 1983, the Labour Party had changed its position and decided to participate in the new constitution. Their leader, Rev. Hendrickse, said that they were opting for the "politics of persuasion" rather than protest. Other Black organisations were incensed and argued that

---

[328] Ibid., p. 285.
[329] "Statement of dissolution of the SACPC, by Barney Desai and Cardiff Marney, London, March 1966", in Karis and Gerhart, 1997, Vol. 5, pp. 370-372.
[330] Karis and Gerhart, 1997, Vol. 5, p. 239.
[331] Ibid., p. 243.
[332] SAIRR, *1981 Survey*, p. 13.
[333] SAIRR, *1982 Survey*, pp. 18-19.

the LP had joined the ranks of the oppressor. It was also felt that through this action Coloured people were looking out for their own interests rather than those of Blacks as a whole. The LP consequently lost considerable support to the UDF with the formation of new groups especially in rural areas. Also, CAHAC was a major affiliate of the UDF.

Other Cape Coloured organisations included the Cape Action League (the renamed Disorderly Movement and Settlement of Black Persons Bill Committee formed in 1982). Its affiliates included four civic organisations and the Cape Western Youth League. It was involved in setting up workers' clubs and in campaigning against the constitution. The Federation of Cape Civic Associations also joined the anti-constitution campaign. In the Transvaal, Coloured opponents of the constitution formed the Transvaal Anti-President's Council Committee, chaired by Professor Ismail Mohammed. This group was affiliated to the UDF. The United Committee of Concern pursued the same aims in Durban as did the Friends of the UDF in East London.

Political resistance in the Indian community

A new set of dynamic Indian leaders – both male and female – emerged in the 1940s and 1950s. These included Ismail Meer, Monty Naicker, J.N. Singh, Yusuf Dadoo, Dr. K. Goonam, Moulvi Cachalia, Ahmed Kathrada, and many others. Dadoo helped to found the Transvaal Indian Nationalist Youth Organisation in 1940; Kathrada was active in forming the Transvaal Indian Youth Volunteer Corps which later became the Transvaal Indian Youth Congress (TIYC).

A new passive resistance campaign was launched against the Asiatic Land Tenure and Indian Representation Act of 1946. They also targeted the Immigration Regulation Act that had been in effect since 1913. Records show that over the course of the campaign, 1,170 individuals, including 279 women, served jail sentences.[334] The campaign mobilised tens of thousands of protestors. The White backlash against the campaign (e.g. in terms of boycotts of Indian traders) also led to the realisation that a conciliatory or 'accommodationist' approach was never going to succeed.

Finally, in 1947, the NIC and the Transvaal Indian Congress (TIC) came together with the ANC to agree on future co-operation. In 1949, the South African Indian Congress (SAIC) joined with them. The Defiance Campaign against apartheid legislation was the first manifestation of real co-operation. The alliance expanded between 1952 and 1955 to include the South African Coloured People's Organisation (SACPO) and the South African Congress of Democrats (SACOD). The alliance came to be known as the Congress of the People (COP) and adopted the Freedom Charter in 1955.

The Natal and Transvaal Indian organisations, including the NIC, NIO and TIO, were heavily involved in protesting against the Group Areas Act of 1950. In May 1956, a conference was held, attended by 68 organisations, to determine a strategy for opposing the implementation of the law. Through the Cato Manor Indian Ratepayers' Association, they also opposed the planned expropriation of Indian land in Cato Manor, Durban, to build houses for Africans.

The Natal Indian community was also very active in the field of education. In 1953, the NIO established the Indian Education Committee (IEC) which mobilised resources to build schools with matching funds and to improve existing facilities. The NIC and the Natal Indian Teachers' Society took up the issue of state expenditure on Indian schools and especially teachers' salaries. They also pushed for more teacher training and access for Indians to technical and higher education. Despite a belief that education should be non-racial, these

---

[334] Bhana, 1997, p. 76.

organisations were forced by circumstance to work within the racially divided education system. [335]

Indian and other non-White organisations also had a difficult time gaining access to government officials at all levels to make their grievances heard. Whilst they took up a wide range of issues – with regard to education, agriculture, land, industry, welfare, etc. – it was always an uphill battle. The government tried to discredit various organisations and individual leaders, especially the more radical ones, whilst making small concessions to those that were more conservative. The end result was to limit the effectiveness of all of those groups.

It was also true that a portion of the Indian elite – professionals, entrepreneurs, skilled technicians, etc. – had benefited from the economic boom in the 1960s and were quite conservative in their political outlook. [336] By creating the South African Indian Council (SAIC) [337] as a 25-member appointed advisory body in 1961 (which became statutory in 1968), the government tried to supplant the South African Indian Congress and co-opt leadership. Partly as a result of this insidious situation, the NIC again was revived to oppose the Council. The NIC's goal, as stated in its revised 1972 constitution was "a unitary, non-racial South Africa, based on universal suffrage". [338] In its newly proactive form, the NIC was active on several fronts. It supported students at the University of Durban-Westville in their conflicts with university officials. It supported hawkers who were displaced in Durban. It formed the Durban Housing Action Committee (DHAC) which represented 20 organisations protesting against high rents and inadequate housing. It also encouraged non-racial sporting events.

In 1977, government decided to allow Indians to elect 40 members of the now 45-member statutory SAIC. Voter registration became compulsory for Indians, as it had earlier for Coloureds. The NIC campaigned for this move to be rejected. The NIC also successfully campaigned against elections in Natal for the Local Affairs Committees, boosting its anti-SAIC stance. Similarly, the Transvaal Anti-SAIC Committee (TASC) was formed representing 150 organisations to organise an election boycott. When the election finally occurred in November 1981, only 10% of the registered Indian voters actually voted nationally. The national election boycott was sponsored by the new Charter Movement – "a multi-racial coalition of more than 100 organisations that endorsed non-racialism and the ANC's Freedom Charter. [339] The boycott was a major civil society victory against the apartheid government and its political apparatus.

In 1983, the TASC decided to revive the Transvaal Indian Congress (TIC) which had existed in the 1950s as part of the Congress Alliance. Its revised constitution included objectives of working towards "a united, democratic, non-racial South Africa on the basis of universal adult suffrage" and "equal economic, political, social and educational freedoms for all its inhabitants". Whilst the new TIC was criticised by AZAPO being an "ethnic body", the TIC replied that it was a people's organisation with a history of participation in the broader anti-apartheid struggle and its composition was merely a reflection of the physical separation of communities due to apartheid. [340] Later that year, the TIC participated in a campaign against local authority elections in African townships, again demonstrating its resolve to support African struggles.

---

[335] See Bhana, 1997, pp. 107-110.
[336] See Dr. Frene Ginwala, ANC activist, cited in Karis and Gerhart, 1997, Vol. 4, p. 243.
[337] The South African Indian Council, advisory body created by government (equivalent to the CRC), should not be confused with the South African Indian Congress, the Indian political organisation.
[338] Bhana, 1997, p. 118.
[339] Karis and Gerhart, 1997, Vol. 5, p. 245.
[340] SAIRR, 1983 Survey, pp. 41-42.

The NIC, TIC and many other organisations campaigned vociferously against the government's proposed tricameral parliament and new constitution. The NIC was well represented on the executive of the United Democratic Front (UDF) which spearheaded the campaign. The NIC, as well as other organisational members of the UDF, tried to strengthen democratic grassroots groups in various constituencies such as workers, women, youth, students, etc.[341] Indians and coloureds were finally realising that if they did not work side by side with African organisations for political and economic rights, they would simply be assisting the apartheid government to achieve its aims.[342] In a joint statement, the NIC and the TIC said that "acceptance of the government's proposals would mean to participate in 'violence' against the African people".[343]

Despite the low voter turnout for the SAIC election, the SAIC remained a source of contention within the Indian community. Amichand Rajbansi, chairman of the SAIC, argued that it was necessary to give the new constitution a chance even though it was flawed and to work for change from inside. However, he was criticised by members of the UDF, the NIC and the TIC for making contradictory public statements on the issue so as to gain support from widely varying constituencies. This cynical effort was not successful. But, as a reward for his participation in the SAIC *inter alia*, Rajbansi was given a Cabinet post by State President P.W. Botha in 1984, becoming the first South African Indian to hold a cabinet office.

When government delegated powers to the SAIC over Indian education and social welfare, a major protest erupted on the part of social welfare organisations, teachers' organisations, and community and political groups. The Teachers' Association of South Africa, representing about 50,000 teachers, rejected any collaboration with the SAIC as it was a government-created body with no professional educational skills. Welfare organisations also rejected the proposed takeover of welfare services by the SAIC. They said "such a move would disrupt the prevailing partnership between the state and community volunteer movements and disunite the community, which had already rejected the SAIC".[344] The NIC also participated in the campaign against the SAIC takeover of these functions. In 1985, the NIC president, George Sewpersadh, argued that the tricameral parliament had been a total failure as it had no real power and could therefore not deal with the key issues.[345]

From the mid-1980s onwards, the Indian struggle against apartheid was largely aligned to that of the Mass Democratic Movement. Its leaders suffered alongside those of all the anti-apartheid organisations. The NIC and TIC leaders played a prominent role in the UDF structures, and suffered harassment, banning and arrest as a consequence.

The just struggle

As the levels of violence increased in the 1980s, various human rights organisations and religious leaders appealed for calm and a fundamental change of heart. Successive states of emergency were proclaimed by President P.W. Botha in 1984, 1985 and again in 1986.

In February 1988, the government reimposed restrictions on the activities of 17 civil society organisations and prohibited certain activities of the Congress of South African Trade Unions (COSATU). The politicised positions and activities undertaken by these banned

---

[341] Bhana, 1997, p. 126.
[342] Karis and Gerhart, 1997, Vol. 5, p. 46.
[343] SAIRR, *1983 Survey*, p. 40.
[344] Ibid., pp. 36-39.
[345] SAIRR, *1985 Survey*, p. 25.

organisations is evidence of the increasingly blurred lines between political and civil society in the context of the resistance movement against apartheid.

Banned organisations	Type of organisation
Azanian People's Organisation (AZAPO)	Political
Azanian Youth Organisation (AYO)	Youth
Cape Youth Congress (CYC)	Youth
Cradock Residents' Association (CRA)	Civic association
Detainees Parents' Support Committee (DPSC)	Human rights
Detainees Support Committee (DSC)	Human rights
National Education Crisis Committee (NECC)	Education
National Education Union of South Africa (NEUSA)	Teachers' union
Port Elizabeth Black Civic Organisation (PEBCO)	Civic association
Release Mandela Campaign	CSO aligned to ANC
Soweto Civic Association (SCA)	Civic association
Soweto Youth Congress (SYC)	Youth organisation
South African National Students Congress (SANSCO)	University students
South African Youth Congress (SAYCO)	Youth
United Democratic Front (UDF)	United front
Vaal Civic Association (VCA)	Civic association
Western Cape Civic Association (WCCA)	Civic association

In response, South African religious leaders issued a Call to Action at a meeting on 25 February 1988. Addressing "primarily the oppressed people of our land", the religious leaders:

1. Urged the intensification of the struggle for justice and peace;
2. Said to the White voters of South Africa that they were being deceived by the government, and that as apartheid was a heresy, nobody could reform it;
3. Warned the international community to wake up to the fact that this illegitimate government was threatening their interests as well, had nothing to offer but instability and bloodshed, and had to be isolated.

In a subsequent open letter to State President P.W. Botha, Archbishop Tutu affirmed that he rejected apartheid as abhorrent and evil. He appealed for a transfer of power to the people of South Africa and demanded that the President:

- Lift the state of emergency;
- Unban all political organisations;
- Release all detainees held under the state of emergency;
- Release all political prisoners; and
- Permit all exiles to return.

He asked Botha "to sit down with the authentic representatives and leaders of every section of our society to negotiate the dismantling of apartheid and drawing up of a new constitution".[346]

---

[346] Tutu, open letter, 8 April 1988.

These denunciations and challenges by leading religious figures, together with the marches and demonstrations which followed them, led to an intensification of the resistance to apartheid by both peaceful as well as violent means. Subsequent atrocities and township violence in KwaZulu/Natal, Thokoza and elsewhere created an irreversible momentum leading to the collapse of local government structures in many townships, no-go zones in many areas, a climate of ungovernability and an increasing reliance on the defence force and the security apparatus of the South African government to maintain control.

Each death led to the creation of another martyr, another funeral and an intensification of resistance by ever increasing numbers of individuals, young and old, White and Black, as well as their political and civil society organisations.

Within these communities, the absence of effective formal governance by the state also led to the creation of a variety of civil society organisations as alternative providers of services and other essential community roles. Such organisations were actively involved in the provision of social welfare, protection of human rights, monitoring of violence, police-community relations, and assisting with relocation. These organisations offered the only semblance of order.

The negotiated political settlement

In 1988/89, under enormous pressure from the mass democratic movement as well as international isolation applied through political and economic sanctions, the National Party government slowly began to reverse some of the racially discriminatory laws such as the Separate Amenities Act and the Group Areas Act. Political reforms were also instituted. However, whilst the White, Coloured and Indian populations went to the polls on the same day in September 1989, they were still electing representatives to the separate parts of the tricameral legislature, and Africans (the vast majority of the population) were still denied the vote. The trade unions and other organisations belonging to the mass democratic movement boycotted the election, and other forms of mass action such as consumer and rent/service boycotts continued. The trade union movement launched a major protest against the proposed Labour Relations Amendment Act. Religious organisations such as the South African Catholic Bishops' Conference and the South African Council of Churches mobilised opposition to apartheid inside and outside the country. In March 1989, the South African Law Commission issued a document calling for a negotiated bill of rights to protect individuals from arbitrary state action, and for repeal of all discriminatory laws. Detentions and trials continued under the apartheid security laws, and political violence continued to claim lives on all sides. [347]

In July 1988, the ANC released its vision for South Africa in a document called "Constitutional Guidelines for a Democratic South Africa", the result of intensive internal ANC debate. In August 1989, the Organisation of African Unity's special committee on Southern Africa adopted the ANC's document outlining guidelines for negotiation, in what became known as the Harare Declaration. The Conference for a Democratic Future (CDF) consisting of hundreds of internal organisations also endorsed the Declaration. This Declaration set the climate for a political settlement.

Just before he resigned in 1989, State President Mr. P.W. Botha held a meeting with the still imprisoned Nelson Mandela at which they agreed to promote peaceful solutions. Before the 1989 election, F.W. de Klerk, the new head of the National Party, adopted a five-year action plan aimed at creating a "new South Africa" based on equality before the law. [348] As State

---

[347] SAIRR, *1988/89 Survey.*
[348] Ibid.

President, de Klerk also began to hold talks with various leaders of the African front-line states to discuss the situation.

First steps began to be taken towards a negotiated settlement. Discussions were held between the government and various Black organisations with a view to preparing the ground for a new constitution and to bring Africans into Parliament. In February 1990, President de Klerk lifted the bans on the ANC, PAC and other organisations and released Nelson Mandela from prison. At that time, Chief Mangosuthu Buthelezi, leader of the Inkatha Freedom Party (IFP), also announced his willingness to enter negotiations with government. The government lifted the state of emergency everywhere except in Natal and KwaZulu. The ANC committed itself to ending the armed struggle, but did not yet disband its armed wing, Umkhonto we Sizwe (MK), or end mass action. Violence, however, escalated especially in Natal and the Vaal Reef.

On 14 September 1991, the National Peace Accord was signed by the government, the ANC, the IFP, the trade unions and several other organisations to establish mechanisms and structures to promote tolerance and reduce political violence. The Peace Accord was widely supported and to a large extent implemented by civil society, and its Secretariat was established as a non-profit organisation.[349]

The multi-racial, multi-party constitutional negotiations, the Convention for a Democratic South Africa (CODESA), began in December 1991 following the repeal of major apartheid laws.[350] On 17 March 1992, a referendum was held -- the last all-White poll -- to determine whether or not they supported the reform process. Sixty-nine percent voted in favour of reform. Negotiations in CODESA, however, broke down in June 1992. In September 1992, de Klerk said that in the next election, all South Africans would vote, regardless of colour, and in October 1992 he apologised for apartheid. The Goldstone Commission continued its investigation into political violence. Its work was assisted by several civil society organisations which monitored the changing political scene, human rights violations, violence, peacekeeping, etc. In November 1992, the ANC agreed to potential post-election power-sharing with other parties.

Negotiations resumed in March 1993, assisted again by several civil society organisations doing research and investigative work in the background. The negotiations became more inclusive of minority political parties, homeland administrations and traditional leaders.[351] In July 1993, the negotiating forum agreed on a date for the first democratic national elections -- 27 April 1994. Despite the absence of some parties, negotiators drew up legislation, including a constitution for the transitional period. In September 1993, the Negotiating Council adopted the Independent Media Commission Bill, the Independent Electoral Commission (IEC) Bill, the Independent Broadcasting Authority Bill and the Transitional Executive Council (TEC) Bill, and Parliament passed them the same month. By January 1994, amended versions of these Acts came into operation.

All citizens of "independent homelands" were reinstated as South African citizens from 1 January 1994 and the homelands themselves were reincorporated into South Africa as from the day of the 1994 elections. Many human rights and democracy education organisations began preparing voter information and education materials. The TEC was empowered to "facilitate, in conjunction with all legislative and executive governmental structures at national, regional and local levels, the transition to and preparation for the implementation of

---

[349] For more on the Peace Accord and the role of civil society, see Camay and Gordon, 2004, pp. 99-124.
[350] SAIRR, *1991/92 Survey*.
[351] SAIRR, *1993/94 Survey*.

a democratic order in South Africa".[352] It adopted the principle of "sufficient consensus" to permit it to make decisions in the absence of full participation and/or unanimity.[353]

The first democratic national and provincial elections took place on 27-28 April 1994. The people rewarded all of the efforts of the struggle with a huge voter turnout and elected the ANC to lead the new democratic government. Nelson Mandela became the first President of the newly democratic South Africa.

None of this political change would have been possible without the enormous contribution of civil society organisations which operated for decades under the difficult conditions imposed by the repressive and discriminatory apartheid system. The next section reveals their stories.

Apartheid's Impact on Civil Society Organisations

A number of civil society organisations (CSOs) launched at the turn of the 20th century continued to resist apartheid, but many were forced to restrict their activities to specific communities. Whilst the apartheid government after 1948 began its systematic and invasive plan to separate community welfare organisations by race, this policy and practice had already become well -- if less formalistically -- entrenched earlier in the century. After 1948, the government achieved its aims by withholding subsidies from organisations that would not amend their constitutions or beneficiaries. In the 1960s and 1970s, by further legislative control it prevented such CSOs from fundraising and receiving foreign funding, thus ensuring that segregated services were provided. The best example of these restrictions is the Fundraising Act of 1978 which was used to exercise control over CSOs that were perceived as opposing the state at that time. It sought to prevent them from being able to raise funds from the public by refusing them registration on the basis of a biased definition of the "public interest". The full might of the apartheid machinery was brought to bear on these organisations.

Few if any welfare organisations survived this onslaught. Religious schools, places of worship, clinics, universities, professional associations and welfare support organisations were all segregated and allowed to serve only specific racial groups. Some organisations formally or informally allied themselves with particular political persuasions (e.g. those who supported the United Democratic Front after the banning of the ANC). Alternatively, they were directly linked to particular cultures, religious groups or communities, and derived their financial and other resources from those groups and communities. Some supported the status quo as they represented communities which benefited from the apartheid system. Others began supporting the Freedom Charter for pragmatic reasons rather than due to a real political commitment -- the fact was that without such 'certification', many northern (mainly Nordic) country donors would not support them.

These racial restrictions, compounded by ethnic, cultural, religious and political divides within civil society, led to wasteful duplication of types of organisations. Thus, it was common to see replication of welfare, women or youth groups, private schools, etc. -- each serving a particular constituency. Many organisations within the White community followed euro-centric models, whereas those that emerged from other communities reflected their own particular heritage. This situation was further fostered by the discriminatory provision of services by the state on the basis of the apartheid racial hierarchy -- the best quality services provided to Whites, with Coloureds, Indians and Africans being provided with respectively lesser quality.

---

[352] SAIRR, *1993/94 Survey*, p. 504-505.
[353] Ibid., p. 549.

In response to economic deprivation and political repression, two main streams of Black civil society organisations emerged. Narsoo[354] referred to these as 'organisations of survival' and 'organisations of resistance'. He explained the differences as follows.

The 'organisations of survival' aimed to survive the rigours of apartheid and to provide for collective sustenance within communities. These included burial clubs, stokvels (informal savings clubs), hawkers' associations, and even football clubs. Those trade unions and professional associations which considered themselves non-political can also be included in this category.

As resistance and confrontation grew particularly in the 1980s, many of these organisations were forced to choose sides. Some organisations adopted the Freedom Charter because their constituencies had become increasingly militant or because donors preferred such an inclination. Others, such as those trying to achieve language rights in schools, entered into an alliance with groups in the tricameral Parliament. These organisations were caught between a state seeking legitimacy and liberation movements seeking hegemony in civil society. However, they remained primarily focused on survival strategies, and did not engage in active advocacy on behalf of their members.

The 'organisations of resistance', in contrast, were formed to fill the vacuum created by the repression of political organisations. While constituted as civics or trade unions, women or youth / student organisations, they were overtly political. It was sometimes difficult to reconcile their political agendas with the interests of their members. Most frequently, the national liberation struggle took precedence.

We have attempted to illustrate below the wide range of organisations which emerged in South Africa and the crucial role that they played in a society characterised by a state which served the interests of a small minority of its people. The Black majority were largely left to fend for themselves. The nature of civil society organisations which were established clearly reflects the divisions created by the policy of separate development and the resistance against both that policy and the state itself. The state inevitably became a target as it adopted a totalitarian approach to the political, social and economic life of the nation. Organisations adopted a wide range of approaches in relation to the state, from active support to tacit acceptance to reformist to total opposition and resistance.

The impact of forced removals on communities and civil society

One of the most significant impacts of apartheid on Black civil society resulted from the forced removals which were planned and implemented from the 1950s until the 1980s. Communities were torn apart, friends and families were separated, and religious and other civil society groups, including sports teams, essentially had to start from scratch.

The Group Areas Act of 1950 sought to bring about complete racial segregation. The process of forcing people of different races to live in separate residential areas had begun in many parts of the country in the early 20th century. However, the Group Areas Act made patently clear the intentions of the National Party government to follow its apartheid policy to its logical conclusion. The Act provided for "the proclamation of areas for occupation by members of a particular race group". The Population Registration Act of 1950 required every person to be classified into one of four racial groups, and "became a prime instrument of mass uprootal [sic] and dispossession of Coloured and Indian people, some Africans and a small number of Whties".[355] The Theron Commission Reports in 1976 showed that only one

---

[354] Narsoo, 1991, pp. 26-27.
[355] SACC and SACBC, 1984, p. 25.

in every 500 White families were affected by removals, whereas 100 of every 500 Coloured and 160 of every 500 Indian families were affected.[356] It was estimated that between 1960 and 1982, the following numbers of people were removed forcibly from their homes to new areas:

Numbers of people removed, 1960-1982

Province	Numbers removed
Eastern Cape	401,000
Western Cape	417,000
Orange Free State	514,000
Natal	745,500
Transvaal	1,295,400
Total	3,372,900

Source: SACC and SACBC, 1984, p. 14.

The Surplus People Project (SPP), a CSO, issued a report in June 1983 which confirmed the above figures. They estimated that 3.5 million people had been forcibly removed since 1960, excluding those within homelands, those resulting from betterment planning, and those resulting from pass law enforcement). "More than three-quarters of the people moved were Africans, the remainder being mostly Indian and Coloured people moved under the Group Areas Act." The SPP also noted that more than 1.5 million removals were still supposed to take place.[357] In August 1983, at the launch of the UDF, a motion was passed saying that "all people should have the right to live where they pleased in the land of their birth, and saluted all communities struggling against removals".[358] A civil society committee trying to stop evictions, Actstop, said that "the numbers of people removed in terms of the act, while horrifying, did not reflect the immense suffering of the affected people and the destruction of settled communities".[359]

The level of dislocation of communities caused by the removal of more than three million people was enormous. In general terms, when forcibly removed from their homes, individuals and families experience a sense of hopelessness and injured self-esteem. They also feel threatened and powerless, and find it difficult to cope with their situation and new surroundings. This experience was made worse by the absence of adequate infrastructure and housing in the areas to which they were moved, making even basic survival difficult. Traditions were disrupted if not destroyed, and organisations and other means of social cohesion torn apart. The absence of traditional authority figures and the lack of security created discipline problems and disputes. Schooling and religious worship were also disrupted. Opportunities for income generation were limited and poverty increased. Below, several examples are cited to offer more detailed evidence of the impact that these removals had on particular communities of Black South Africans, whether African, Coloured or Indian.

Numerous communities around the country where people of different races, ethnicities and religions had lived together in harmony for years were destroyed by the removals. These include areas such as Sophiatown and Fordsburg in the Transvaal, District Six in the Cape, South End in Port Elizabeth, Cato Manor in Durban, and many others. The removals, in turn, led to the creation of single race dormitory towns (essentially ghettos) such as Chatsworth, Newlands East and Phoenix in Durban, Lenasia, Eldorado Park and Ennerdale in the Transvaal, and Mitchell's Plain and Atlantis in the Western Cape.

---

[356] SACC and SACBC, 1984, p. 26.
[357] SAIRR, *1983 Survey,* p. 302.
[358] Ibid., p. 235.
[359] Ibid.

Removals of African people

The largest number and scale of removals affected African people. Several categories of removal were used, including black spot removals (black communities surrounded by white areas, usually farms), urban removals from townships or informal settlements to Bantustans, removals from white-owned farmland, and influx control measures limiting the rights of Africans to live or stay in White towns. Each Bantustan was created for a particular African ethnic group, and some people were even removed from one Bantustan to another to join people of their own ethnicity.

Some African communities did resist the removals, but only succeeded in delaying the inevitable in most cases. Their level of success depended on the extent to which the communities were organised. Some communities such as Driefontein managed to postpone removals for as long as ten years. But in the meantime, local authorities ceased providing services, maintaining infrastructure, etc. Where communities took it upon themselves to build schools or other facilities, these were lost when the removals finally occurred. The uncertainty and waiting also had a debilitating impact on the morale of affected people. Finally, when faced with concerted resistance, the authorities were quite willing to exercise force and violence against the resisters.[360]

The entire African population of Cape Town was removed to Khayelitsha, 43 kilometres from the city centre. Where townships already existed outside of urban areas, these were incorporated into the Bantustans by redrawing boundaries. These included, for example, KwaMashu, Umlazi and Ntuzuma in the Durban area, Mdantsane near East London, Madadeni and Osizweni near Newcastle, Esikhawini at Richard's Bay, and Ga-Rankuwa and Mabopane near Pretoria.[361]

Living conditions in the Bantustans compounded the tragedy of the removals. The government claim that they would be places where Africans could be self-sufficient was a total fabrication. The Bantustan governments were puppets of the Pretoria regime (despite their formal status as 'independent' or 'self-governing') and relied almost entirely on grants from Pretoria for their survival. These grants were, however, inadequate to provide for the desperately needed social services. The SACC and SACBC concluded that the Bantustans became "dumping grounds for the unemployed, the aged and the sick – in short, for all those people who are not useful to industry or other big concerns in urban areas".[362] They also served as a means of political control of the rural population, by distancing them even more from stronger resistance organisations largely based in urban areas. Bantustans were regarded as illegitimate by the majority of Africans, as immoral by the SACC and SACBC, and as illegal under international law. Organisations such as the SAIRR and the Black Sash added their voices to the protests and contributed useful data which undermined government's claims of voluntary removals. Contrary to the expectations and desires of the apartheid regime, the injustices of the forced removals and the Bantustans spurred the growth of a more united and radical opposition.

Removals of Coloured people

Cape Town: From the late 1960s onward, more than 30,000 Coloured people were forcibly removed from District Six, and the buildings they lived and worked in were destroyed. The trauma of their removal was compounded as the obliteration of District Six took away "their space at the foot of Table Mountain [which] was one true source of pride in themselves as a distinguishable ethnic identity". It was "a humiliation that leaves an aching lacuna in self-concept and self-esteem and a profound and bitter resentment".[363] Life in District Six has

---

[360] See Transvaal Rural Action Committee (TRAC), n.d.
[361] SACC and SACBC, 1984, p. 19.
[362] Ibid., p. 47.
[363] Western, 1981, quoted in SACC and SACBC, 1984, p. 26.

perhaps been romanticised in the wake of the removals. In contrast, it was described by Alex La Guma, who grew up there, as "a whirlpool world of poverty, petty crime and violence" resulting from apartheid oppression. Nonetheless, it was a vibrant Coloured working-class community.[364] This social vibrancy is clearly shown in the exhibits of the District Six Museum in Cape Town.

Port Elizabeth: Similarly, the community of South End in Port Elizabeth was devastated by removals. The origins of the community dated back to 1820 when the British settlers arrived. As it grew, South End was inhabited by Malays, Indians, Chinese, Europeans, Portuguese, Greeks, Khoikhoi, Fingoes and Xhosa.[365] It was characterised by a wide diversity of religions and worship, but they all co-existed in harmony. The religious centres also played a broader cultural role in the community, and were involved in social, educational, welfare and sports activities.

> "As the axe dangled over their heads, the people of South End became obsessed with the impending removals. In many instances, the eviction notice was a death notice. Many died of a broken heart long before the bulldozers and removal trucks arrived. The pain, anguish and worry took its toll long before the move was made. Most South Africans who did not undergo this experience will never even begin to understand the consternation in the earmarked communities, nor appreciate the mental and physical anguish that accompanied forced removals. To be thrown out of your home where you and your forefathers had lived all your life was an extremely traumatic experience... The Group Areas Act dealt people a crippling economic blow and caused the death of many of the old folk. This Act will go down in history as one of the most odious and devastating of the apartheid laws".[366]

Not just homes were destroyed. Churches had to be deconsecrated and most were then demolished. Congregations were scattered and had to start up their churches all over again in their new areas. Schools and sports clubs were closed. Booley wrote that "the dramatic upheaval [of District Six] destroyed many [rugby] clubs which by then had been in existence for over five decades".[367] Businesses and shops were shut down, and people had to buy homes all over again with heavy mortgages. Interestingly, quite a number of Indian and Coloured families from South End decided to emigrate rather than become casualties of the Group Areas Act. Thus, middle-class people, professionals, with much-needed skills were lost to the community and the country.

As part of the democratic transition in the early 1990s, organisations were founded to assist in the restoration of land to those dispossessed through removals in District Six and South End, or in the event that the land cannot be returned, to arrange for compensation from the government – four decades late.

Removals of Indians

Durban: The City Council of Durban had, of its own accord, imposed a policy of residential and commercial segregation long before the Group Areas Act. To a large extent, this was done in response to calls from the White population of Durban to prevent "infiltration" of Indians into the White areas. This effort was exemplified in the Provincial Ordinance No. 14 of 1922 – nearly 30 years prior to the 1950 law passed at national level. Prior to that, the issuance of trading licenses had been used by the Council to control where Indians were able to establish their businesses.[368]

---

[364] La Guma, *A Walk in the Night,* cited in Adhikari, 2005, p. 118.
[365] Agherdien, et al., 1997, p. 7.
[366] Ibid., 1997.
[367] Booley, 1998, p. 12.
[368] Schlemmer, 1967, p. 13.

"For the whole Indian population of Durban, the process was one that reminded them of their vulnerability to the power structure, defined in racial terms, of the city and the country, and the one that would alienate them further from that power structure. At the same time, the creation of legally constituted Indian group areas would have a major role to play in shaping economic structures in Durban, and in the development of consciousness, cultural, social and political."[369]

Chatsworth – a new Indian township – opened in 1964; it was followed by others, e.g. Phoenix. Tens of thousands of Indians were removed from their homes and forced to move to these new townships. Whilst some of the townships provided improvements in living standards, the removals had devastating effects on communities.

The social networks and economic connections that had been built up over decades were disrupted as families and neighbourhoods were split up and moved to different areas. Mosques, temples, schools and other institutions had to be abandoned. Traditional modes of family living were destroyed due to the new types of housing and other changes to the physical environment in which people lived. Extended family living was replaced by nuclear families. Young people formed gangs and crime increased, especially in Phoenix where unemployment was higher than in Chatsworth. Instead of very mixed class neighbourhoods, Chatsworth was clearly divided along class lines according to the clustered types of housing people could afford. Consumerism linked to a newly important material culture thrived. The use of Indian languages declined in favour of English.[370]

Despite the tragedy of the removals, people have rebounded. New cultural pursuits have emerged to bring people together, e.g. Indian film and music. Residents have also turned to new religions, e.g. Pentacostals, which offer them a new sense of belonging. In general, new forms of contact and new networks of neighbourhoods have developed, along with pride in their new homes and communities. New generations of Indians are afforded new opportunities which perhaps mitigate the trauma their parents experienced.

Despite the removals, a huge variety of religious, cultural and generally secular organisations existed within the Indian communities. These included, for example, the "Mayville Indian Youngmen's Society, Gyaan Prachar Natak Mudal, Gujarati Youngmen's Society, Natal Muslim Educational Committee, Crescent Debating Society, Karnatic Music Society, Clairwood Literary and Debating Club, and Durban Indian Women's Association". A range of clubs also played a major role in sports such as cricket and football.[371] Other secular organisations were: "the Natal Indian Blind Society, Natal Indian Boy Scouts Association, and the Merebank Literary and Debating Society".[372] Hindu organisations such as the "Ved Dharma Sabha, the Arya Pratinidhi Sabha, Andhra Maha Sabha, and the South African Hindu Maha Sabha, among others, are still actively promoting Hinduism through annual religious festivals".[373] The same holds for Muslims and Christians.

In many ways, the forced removals were amongst the worst abuses of the apartheid government. The destruction caused to communities was irreparable. Even government sponsored reports concluded that the Group Areas Act was the "burning point of bitterness and alienation in Coloured and Indian communities".[374]

---

[369] Freund, 1995, p. 64.
[370] Ibid., pp. 85-91.
[371] Bhana, 1997, pp. 138-139.
[372] Ibid., p. 141.
[373] Ibid., p. 140.
[374] Cited in SACC and SACBC, 1984, p. 26.

Faith-Based Organisations

The Muslim community

In the second half of the 20th century, forces originating in India created "fragmentation and schism" in the Muslim community between "puritanical scripturalist and charismatic folk tendencies".[375] For example, the introduction of the Tabligh Jama'ah (Evangelical Association) in the 1960s brought volunteer lay preachers to do evangelical work at mosques around the country in the tradition of Deoband seminary in India. Then, in 1978, the Sunni Jamiat al-'Ulama in the Barelwi tradition was founded in South Africa, bringing some internal conflict to the Muslim community.

The Central Islamic Trust was established in Johannesburg and acquired a property to provide accommodation and relief to the Muslim community. In recent decades, this relief activity has been extended to all persons needing help.

In the 1950s, the increasing politicisation of Muslim youth led to the formation of at least two organisations in the Cape. In 1957, the Muslim Youth Movement was founded in District Six, influenced by the trends of pan-Africanism and pan-Arabism. Similarly, in 1958, the Claremont Muslim Association started. Both organisations were active with regard to human rights and social issues. However, they gradually became inactive due to lack of leadership after the death of Imam Haron.

Also around that time, the younger generation began to express their disenchantment with the conservative leadership of the clergy. This led to the formation of small study groups and associations with a "modernising agenda in the service of faith".[376] One example was the Arabic Study Circle established in 1950 in Durban which published newsletters and pamphlets. Eventually these study circles emerged as a national movement drawn mainly from the middle class, influenced by similar movements in Egypt and Pakistan. In 1970, the Muslim Youth Movement of South Africa (MYMSA) was established.

In turn, MYMSA set up a number of national social organisations.[377] These included the South African National Zakaat Fund (SANZAF founded in 1983) which focuses on welfare; the Islamic Medical Association (IMA, formally established in 1980), a professional association of Muslim doctors which provides health services to disadvantaged black communities; and the Islamic Relief Agency (ISRA) which is an active disaster and relief agency. Also, MYMSA provided training and orientation schools for converts in the townships. The emphasis of these organisations was initially mainly socio-cultural-religious, aimed at preventing the westernisation of society. Later, in the mid-1980s MYMSA began to address political issues, in co-operation with the Muslim Students' Association (MSA).

In 1975, the Islamic Council of South Africa (ICSA) was launched. It was intended as an umbrella body speaking on behalf of the all Muslims in the country. However, its attempt to encompass the different strands of Islam encountered difficulties, and soon its leadership role reverted to the various affiliated organisations representing the 'ulama, professional associations, and others. However, in the mid-1980s, ICSA described apartheid as "mindless brutality and injustice" and welcomed the government's changing position on the political rights of Africans. A group called Muslims Against Oppression published a pamphlet,

---

[375] Moosa, 1995, p. 145.
[376] Ibid., p. 148.
[377] See Ibid., pp. 148-149.

"The Call of Islam" and rejected the new constitution, apartheid laws and collaboration with the state. It referred to apartheid as a "system of falsehood".[378]

The increased numbers of killings of Muslims by the security forces apparently also radicalised, politicised and Islamicised the Muslim community. Two important organisations emerged in the 1980s in response to these political realities. The Qibla Mass Movement, established in 1984, identified with Islamic Iran and supported the liberation struggle in South Africa. It allied itself with the Black Consciousness tradition and the Pan Africanist Congress. The Muslim Students' Association was also influenced by these new developments. The Call of Islam (COI) was created by a breakaway group from MYMSA which emerged as part of an internal conflict regarding whether to ally itself with the UDF. The COI emphasised the need for leadership by the clergy on crucial political issues, and pulled the MJC into the political arena. It supported the United Democratic Front (UDF).[379] A Muslim youth movement publication, Al Qualam, wrote in 1985 that "the present crisis in the country cannot be resolved within the present framework and only total change in all structures can bring freedom and justice for all sections of the population".[380]

In the second half of the 1980s, whilst some organisations privately acceded to the concept of the tricameral parliament, most of them (COI, MSA, MJC, MYMSA, and Qibla) participated alongside other religious and secular groups in protest marches, political rallies, and funeral services for victims of police brutality. Together they established a new ecumenism and a common moral foundation from which to oppose apartheid.[381]

The Jewish community

The consistency with which Jewish organisations have played their roles throughout the 20th century is notable. On the whole, the Jewish community has tended to be largely orthodox in its religious observance and pragmatic in its political positioning. The community has always taken a largely pro-Zionist stance, with public dissent being a fairly recent phenomenon.

The Jewish community was by no means monolithic in its racial attitudes. It was only in the 1950s that key figures in the Jewish community began to speak out against apartheid. Chief Rabbi Rabinowitz "denounced apartheid as alien to the authentic voice of prophetic Judaism...and he lashed out at the cowardice of his community".[382] However, individual Jews – such as Helen Suzman, Arthur Chaskalson, Franz Auerbach, Ronnie Kasrils -- have had high profile roles in the anti-apartheid struggle.[383]

In 1985, socially concerned Jews established a group called Jews for Social Justice in Johannesburg and Jews for Justice in Cape Town "in order to respond in an organised framework to the injustices which were part and parcel of South African society".[384] The members of these groups found the Board of Deputies to be too slow to act and therefore felt the need to create their own organisation. Though they no longer exist, these groups were an important means of Jewish involvement in the anti-apartheid struggle. In June the same year, the Jewish Board of Deputies issued a statement rejecting apartheid and "expressed its dismay at the violence in the country and called for the establishment of a

---

[378] SAIRR, 1985 Survey, p. 571.
[379] See Moosa, 1995, 147-150 for a more extensive discussion of the emergence of these organisations.
[380] SAIRR, 1985 Survey, p. 572.
[381] Moosa, 1995, pp. 147-151.
[382] Hellig, 1995, p. 168.
[383] Ibid., p. 156.
[384] See www.shemayisrael.co.il/sa/sajbd/sajbd.htm

climate of peace in which negotiations and the process of reform could be continued".[385] Shortly thereafter, the chairman of the South African Union of Progressive Judaism said that it was the "government's responsibility to ensure that no person in South Africa was discriminated against on the grounds of colour".[386]

The Christian churches

The leadership of some churches, such as the Anglican CPSA, continued to have close contact with 'liberal' trends of political thought. Some had close relationships with organisations such as the South African Institute for Race Relations. They did not, however, actively engage in political activity. Rather, they tended to limited themselves to making public statements of protest against the unjust measures imposed by the apartheid government. The Rosettenville Conference of 1948 was the first of a series of ecumenical conferences held by the English-speaking churches to address issues posed by apartheid laws and policies. A pastoral letter by Catholic Bishop Hennemann in 1948 called apartheid "noxious, unchristian and destructive" and denied the existence of 'civilisation' that could be construed as exclusively White.[387] The DRC Missionary Conference of 1950, on the other hand, concluded with a recommendation of "territorial apartheid" – thus providing further support for the government's ideology of separate development.[388] In 1953, when the CPSA bishops called racial discrimination "morally wrong", they still condoned separate schools for different races.[389] They could not seem to move away from their paternalistic attitudes. They were moved to act in a concerted fashion only in 1957 when the Natives Laws Amendment Bill aimed to regulate the worship of Africans in White areas. The churches' firm stance against this policy was, however, grounded in fear for religious liberty rather than in resistance to apartheid per se.[390]

A redefinition of the church struggle was sorely needed. In the 1950s, African leaders such as Chief Albert Luthuli, Robert Sobukwe and Z.K. Matthews highlighted this need. Earlier, many other leaders in the 19th century had challenged the churches. Despite this, there were only a few Christian leaders courageous enough to take strong, principled and public stands against the government. In 1952, Chief Albert Luthuli stated that:

> "Laws and conditions that tend to debase human personality – a God-given force – be they brought about by the State of other individuals, must be relentlessly opposed in the spirit of defiance shown by St. Peter when he said to the rulers of his day 'Shall we obey God or man?' I have embraced the non-violent Passive Resistance technique in fighting for freedom because I am convinced it is the only non-revolutionary, legitimate and human way that could be used by people denied, as we are, effective constitutional means to further aspirations."[391]

For his efforts, Luthuli won the Nobel Peace Prize – the first African to do so.

---

[385] SAIRR, *1985 Survey*, p. 571.
[386] Ibid..
[387] de Gruchy, 1986a, p. 98.
[388] Ibid., p. 71. De Gruchy wrote that initially it appeared that the DRC's interpretation of the Bible led them to reject racial discrimination whilst accepting separate development. However, it was not long before the DRC position was indistinguishable from that of the National Party government. This was probably largely due to a perceived need to preserve its Afrikaner identity. It is also interesting that, according to de Gruchy, the English-speaking churches whilst criticising apartheid tried not to be anti-Afrikaner, especially as they had Afrikaner church members. (p. 87)
[389] They did mention the possibility of "some children of all race groups to be educated together" – a vague and insignificant concession. *Eastern Province Herald,* 27 October 1953.
[390] Clarke, 1989, p. 155.
[391] Karis and Carter, 1973, Vol. 2, pp. 488-489.

In 1954, Father Trevor Huddleston criticised the 'liberal' stance taken by the church, which "occasionally talks in its sleep and expects (or does it?) the Government to listen".[392] He took the view that apartheid was a "blasphemy" against God, that racialism was an "attack on the Nature of Man" and on the nature of God himself. He argued that "when a government descends into tyranny its laws cease to be binding upon its subjects". He also took the struggle to the international arena through the publication of his book, *Naught for Your Comfort*, in 1956, and speaking tours in the US and UK. His efforts made a substantial contribution to increasing the international credibility of the ANC after it went into exile in 1960.

Moves toward church unity amongst the English-speaking Protestant churches began in 1960, with "official conversations" between the Anglican (CPSA) and Presbyterian churches, and somewhat later with the Methodist church. A Church Unity Commission was created in 1968, comprising the CPSA, Methodist, Presbyterian, Reformed Presbyterian and United Congregationalist churches. Some additional co-operation occurred between these churches. However, these efforts were overshadowed by the increasing prioritisation of calls for social justice and radical social change in South Africa, and little progress was made towards unity despite fairly detailed plans being drafted.[393] In 1966, all the Lutheran churches in South Africa and Namibia did join together in the Federation of Evangelical Lutheran Churches of Southern Africa (FELCSA) – a more manageable union than bringing together all the various denominations.

At the end of the 1960s, White Christian attitudes were severely shaken up. As a result of the Black Consciousness movement, Black Theology emerged as a concept and led to several Black confessing movements. The Institute of Contextual Theology emerged as a leading voice. A consequence was that Christians in every major church were being radically challenged and in turn then challenged their leadership and membership. This occurred both within the South African Catholic Bishops' Conference (SACBC)[394] as well as the South African Council of Churches (SACC).[395] In 1968, Alpheus Zulu became Bishop of Zululand -- the first African Anglican bishop. Also that year, the *Message to the People of South Africa* from religious leaders led by the SACC declared that apartheid was a false gospel. In 1969, the World Council of Churches (WCC) launched its Programme to Combat Racism.

A critical test for the churches occurred in September 1970 when the World Council of Churches (WCC) Programme to Combat Racism announced a grant to the ANC and PAC, and ZANU and ZAPU (the Zimbabwean liberation movements). The South African Council of Churches (SACC) distanced itself from the WCC action when Prime Minister Vorster threatened the SACC, demanding that it withdraw its membership of the WCC. This led to the churches agonising for several years through the SACC's Committee on Violence and Non-violence on the nature and context of their struggle.

In 1972, the SACBC issued *A Call to Conscience Addressed to Catholics by their Bishops*, which contextualised its criticisms of apartheid in relation to the economy and labour issues[396] – something not done by many other church commentaries. The 1974 SACC conference in Hammanskraal decided to make representations to government against

---

[392] Cited in Geodhals, 1989, p. 119.
[393] Suggit, 1989, pp. 84-85.
[394] The South African Catholic Bishops' Conference was founded in 1947.
[395] In 1968, the Christian Council was renamed the South African Council of Churches (SACC).
[396] de Gruchy, 1986a, p. 99.

classification under the Group Areas Act and against the removals of Africans as part of the consolidation of the homelands. It also passed a resolution saying that Christians should have the option of conscientious objection to serving in the military in an unjust war in "defence of a basically unjust and discriminatory society".[397] In 1975, the Lutherans (FELCSA) adopted *An Appeal to Lutheran Christians in Southern Africa* which stated that the prevailing discriminatory political system and the concentration of power in the hands of whites "cannot be reconciled with the gospel".[398] In late 1980, the Church of the Province of South Africa (Anglicans) issued a statement saying that "racial discrimination has no rightful place in church or society" and was the "fruit of our fallen state". Apartheid was characterised as "unjust and evil" and the CPSA committed itself to struggle against it.[399] In 1981, a conference of the Methodist Church of Southern Africa took a strong stand against apartheid and racial barriers in the church and committed itself to making a "concerted effort to eliminate all traces of racism". Perhaps most importantly, it recognised the need to get its own house in order, to set an example for the state.[400]

By the late 1970s, more and more Blacks were being appointed to high positions in various Christian churches: Father D. Khumalo became Natal's first African Catholic bishop; Reverend Peter Buthelezi was made Catholic Archbishop of Bloemfontein; Reverend W. Ndwandwe was the first bishop-suffragen of Johannesburg; and Reverend A.M. Loshaba became the president of the Methodist Church.[401] In 1978, Desmond Tutu took the post of Secretary-general of the SACC and presided over increasing internal SACC debates regarding the role of foreign investment and the issue of a "just revolution". By 1984, one third of the Catholic Church's bishops were Black.

The Christian Institute
The foundation of the Christian Institute (CI) of Southern Africa by Dr. Beyers Naude and some English-speaking church leaders in 1963 was an important milestone. Dr. Naude was a minister in the Transvaal Synod of the DRC and a member of the Afrikaner Broederbond. In its early years, the CI's emphasis was "one of changing the awareness and understanding of white Christians who had never questioned the status quo, through a rediscovery of the biblical message".[402] However, the DRC regarded the CI as a direct challenge to itself and to Afrikaner society. It called for its members to resign from the CI. By refusing to do so, Naude essentially cut himself off from the DRC. Even the English-speaking churches were hesitant to support the work of the CI. It did eventually receive considerable support from international sources and was able to develop significant programmes which had a major impact. Its achievements included:

- Bringing the African independent churches into greater contact with each other, and with other South African and international churches;
- Successfully developing the Study Project on Christianity in Apartheid Society which, with the SACC, worked to conceptualise alternatives to apartheid;[403]
- Becoming directly involved in the anti-apartheid struggle and the support of Black initiatives for social change (e.g. the Black Consciousness Movement (BCM)).

The government soon began to look more closely at the CI. In 1975 it was categorised as an "affected organisation", making it impossible to continue receiving foreign funding. Then, on

---

[397] SAIRR, *1974 Survey*, pp. 46-47.
[398] de Gruchy, 1986a, p. 101.
[399] SAIRR, *1981 Survey*, pp. 37-38.
[400] Ibid., p. 39.
[401] SAIRR, *1978 Survey*, p. 39.
[402] de Gruchy, 1986a, p. 104.
[403] Their report on *Apartheid and the Church*, 1972, had a significant influence on the changing attitudes of the churches due to its uncompromising challenges to almost every aspect of church life. It also provided a major boost to the profile and role of the SACC.

19 October 1977, as part of the mass bannings, the CI was declared illegal and its senior staff members were all served with individual banning orders.[404] After much soul-searching, in 1982 the Dutch Reformed Mission Church (DRMC), under the leadership of Dr. Alan Boesak, declared apartheid a heresy in the *Belhar Draft Confession of Faith*. The *Confession* was formally adopted in 1986. Despite the fact that the DRMC was only one branch of the DRC, the *Belhar Confession* forced the White hierarchy and members of the parent DRC to take notice and to finally move away from its support of apartheid in 1990.

In June 1985, at prayer services held throughout South Africa to commemorate the ninth anniversary of the Soweto uprising of 1976, the campaign for "an end to unjust rule" was launched. This paradigm shift led to the Harare Declaration which called upon churches inside and outside South Africa "to support South African movements for the liberation of their country".

It was only in 1987 that the international Anglican Church decided to call a moratorium on European missionaries in Africa. At the same time, the Russell Commission Report on the Theology and Practice of Mission clearly laid out a major change in the church's approach: that because most of their work takes place "in the world", the role of mission must begin to include a responsibility to fight against injustice. It was finally understood that the church must engage with the state on issues of social justice in a far more committed way.[405]

Black theology

Black theology began as a theological companion to the Black Consciousness Movement. Goba described the link as "that of soul mates walking together in the ongoing struggle of black liberation".[406] Black theology can be described as "the theological response (protest) of Black theologians in the established churches, as part of their growing consciousness of their ability to reflect on the Bible and on its relevance to society from the underside, the side of the poor and the oppressed". In turn, the black theology of liberation evolved in South Africa (and elsewhere) to address the injustices and dehumanisation of the prevailing socio-political system.[407] It was a reaction against a White theological interpretation of the Bible which could and did not resonate with the experience of oppressed Black people. In particular, Black theology emphasised the need to relate Christianity to local indigenous culture and customs. Whilst its origins may be found in the nineteenth century, Black theology took root in South Africa the 1960s and 1970s, and its proponents were situated firmly in the resistance / anti-apartheid camp.

The United Christian Movement (UCM), formed in 1967 in protest against the White-dominated Students Christian Association (SCA), provided a platform for the introduction of Black theology as an academic discipline. The UCM was also a forum for debate and a catalyst for the creation of SASO. However, UCM membership was both Black (about 70%) and White. The two most important leaders of the UCM were White: Basil Moore and Colin Collins. The first conference on Black theology was held at the Wilgespruit Fellowship Centre in 1972 and the second in 1975, the latter organised by Father Smangaliso Mkhatshwa. It did not take long, however, for government to react in repressive mode to the increasing profile of Black theology and theologians. Due to political pressure, the third conference only took place in 1983.[408]

---

[404] de Gruchy, 1986a, pp. 104-115.
[405] Goedhals, 1989, pp. 122-123.
[406] Goba, 1986, p. 63. For more on Black Theology see Goba, 1988; Maimela, 1987 and 1991; Moore, 1974; Motlhabi, 1985; and Setilonae, 1986.
[407] Bobby Nel, in Liebenberg et al., 1994, pp. 138-140.
[408] Ibid., pp. 139-142.

Dr. Mamphela Ramphele argued that "the framework within which Blacks do theology will of necessity be different from that of Whites, who are exposed to an entirely different way of experiencing the world". She also noted that the entry of women theologians into the mix added another set of challenges.[409] She quoted the BCM leader, Steve Biko, who said that:

"Black theology is therefore a situational interpretation of Christianity. It seeks to relate the present-day black man to God within the given context of the black man's suffering and his attempts to get out of it. It shifts the emphasis of man's moral obligations from avoiding wronging false authorities by not losing his Reference Book, not stealing food when hungry and not cheating police when caught, to being committed to eradicating all cause for suffering as represented in the death of children from starvation, outbreaks of epidemics in poor areas, or the existence of thuggery and vandalism in townships. In other words, it shifts the emphasis from petty sins to major sins in a society, thereby ceasing to teach the people to 'suffer peacefully'".[410]

The SACC evolved in the 1970s to become an important force representing the views and needs of Black Christians. The appointment of Bishop Desmond Tutu as General Secretary in 1978 and the role of other Black church leaders in the organisation enhanced its credibility with Black Christians generally. This also meant that the government regarded it with increasing suspicion. As with many umbrella bodies, the SACC walked a difficult path in trying to balance its member churches' needs and views with its own role. It began to play an increasingly militant role in the anti-apartheid movement. In 1984, Bishop Tutu was awarded the Nobel Peace Prize for his leadership role in the anti-apartheid movement. The Nobel Committee said the award to Tutu should also be seen as a gesture of support for "all individuals and groups in South Africa, who, with their concern for human dignity, fraternity and democracy, incite the admiration of the world".[411]

Other organisations for Black priests and preachers were used as forums for the expression of solidarity in the struggle for justice and to determine how best to realign and indigenise churches and their gospel. In the mid-1970s, the St. Peter's Old Boys Association (SPOBA) was formed in the Roman Catholic Church, and in 1976 the Permanent Black Priests' Solidarity Group (PBPSG) was founded to include priests throughout Southern Africa. Similarly, in the Methodist Church, the Black Methodist Consultation (BMC) aimed to get the church to take a stronger stand against apartheid. In the DRC, the Belydende Kring (BK) was formed in 1975 as a follow-up to the Black Renaissance Convention to make clear the opposition of ministers from the DRC in Africa (DRCA) and the Dutch Reformed Missionary Church (DRMC) to the positions being taken by the DRC hierarchy. The BK fought against the racial divisions in their church and the dependence of the Black DRC churches on their White counterparts. [412]

The Alliance of Black Reformed Christians in South Africa (ABRESCA) was established in 1981 for those who aligned themselves to the liberation struggle and who wanted to work under Black leadership. ABRESCA was chaired by Dr. Allan Boesak. The members resolved to "extend the hand of friendship, reconciliation, and forgiveness to the White people of South Africa" but would not enter into dialogue with the White Dutch Reformed churches until they "ceased to give a moral and theological justification for the apartheid policy, declared apartheid sinful, and confessed complicity in the suffering and oppression of our people".[413] At the same time, the Institute for Contextual Theology (ICT) was founded to give

---

[409] Ramphele, 1989, p. 180.
[410] Ibid., p. 181, citing Biko, 1978, p. 59.
[411] SAIRR, *1984 Survey,* p. 917.
[412] Bobby Nel, in Liebenberg et al., 1994, pp. 142-143.
[413] SAIRR, *1981 Survey,* p. 46.

more attention to Black and liberation theology under Rev. Frank Chikane. In 1984, the fourth conference on Black theology was entitled "Black theology and the Black struggle", leaving little doubt about the trends in thought. Nonetheless, amongst Black theologians some of the divisions between the ANC and PAC approaches to the liberation struggle were also apparent.[414]

The Kairos Document of 1985 was produced mainly by Black theologians during the height of the social crisis in South Africa and called for "all the necessary steps towards the elimination of all forms of legislated discrimination". It called for the release of all detainees and political prisoners and for immediate talks with the authentic leadership of the people. The document spoke of "a moment of truth not only for apartheid but also for the church".[415] The Kairos Document "shifted the whole terrain of the debate... [by criticising] both what it calls 'state theology', with its use of Scripture to legitimate itself, and 'church theology', based on stock traditional ideas of reconciliation, justice and non-violence. The Kairos theologians claimed to be restoring biblical theology against the misuse of the Bible by the Church."[416] As a result, it called for "a biblical theology of direct confrontation with the forces of evil rather than a theology of reconciliation with sin and the devil". Criticizing church theology for lacking "clear social and political analysis", they aimed to interpret the Bible in a manner that "is relevant to what we are experiencing in South Africa today".[417] Various church leaders who signed the Kairos Document were detained by the government or attacked by the government-aligned press and the SABC.

By the mid-1980s, it was estimated that there were about 3,000 independent Black churches in South Africa, most of them quite small. Overall, however, they were thought to have about five million members. There were broadly two types: the Zionist or Apostolic churches, which combined Christianity with indigenous beliefs and catered mainly to poorer and less well-educated people in both rural and urban areas, and the Ethiopian churches, which were usually spawned by Methodist, Presbyterian and Congregational mission churches but had come under Black control. Some of the smaller independent churches joined together in associations such as the Council of African Independent Churches and the Reformed Independent Churches Association. The largest separatist church was (and continues to be) the Zion Christian Church (ZCC) which had about four million members in 1984. Ironically, these independent churches were not particularly engaged politically, and in fact on some key issues, they opposed the anti-apartheid movement's positions.[418] The ZCC caused a major furor in 1985 when it invited the state president, P.W. Botha, to attend its annual gathering in Moria. The UDF, ANC and AZAPO all criticised the ZCC for allowing itself to be used opportunistically by Botha. They said that the ZCC leadership should align itself more with the feelings of the Black community.[419]

Advocating non-violent resistance
In a seminal article, de Gruchy[420] described four elements of non-violent social transformation which elaborate upon this changed approach:

1. In the struggle for a just society, the church cannot be neutral, but there are different complementary struggles.
2. The church must be the church, but this does not mean that it has its own political programme alongside that of the struggle for liberation. It must participate in critical solidarity.

---

[414] Nel in Liebenberg, 1994, pp. 143-145.
[415] Kairos, 1986.
[416] Draper and West, 1989, pp. 36-37.
[417] Kairos, 1986; Cochrane, 1987, p. 33.
[418] See SAIRR, *1984 Survey*, pp. 900-901.
[419] SAIRR, *1985 Survey*, p. 566.
[420] de Gruchy, 1986b.

3. The gospels of reconciliation and liberation as well as the political strategies of negotiation and confrontation are not antithetical but two sides of the same coin.
4. Non-violent redemptive action remains the paradigm for the Christian, even though there is an honoured Christian tradition which supports the idea of a just revolution.

It was this last element of a non-violent just struggle that encouraged many Christians like Archbishop Tutu and others to condone strategic economic sanctions in the struggle against apartheid, e.g. measures which could be carefully thought out, properly maintained and adjusted to observed effects. The SACC's 1974 Resolution on Conscientious Objection was another example of this approach by providing young men with a religious underpinning for their refusal to accept mandatory military service. By 1982, more religious organisations had joined the call for an alternative form of non-military service to be made available to conscientious objectors. In October that year, the South African Defence Force (SADF) had established a committee to investigate the issue.

The Methodist Church of Southern Africa joined the World Alliance of Reformed Churches and the NG Sendingkerk in denouncing apartheid. A1982 statement said that apartheid "is not simply a socio-political policy but a sinful contradiction of the Gospel which cannot be justified on biblical or theological grounds and is therefore an ideology which the Methodist Congress rejects as heresy". It urged Christians to become more involved in addressing social issues.[421] The Church of the Province of South Africa (Anglican) supported this move with its own statement condemning apartheid as "unchristian, evil and a heresy".[422]

The SACBC issued a report in 1984 on police conduct during township protests. The research team comprised SACBC field workers, priests and an attorney. The report "made it easier to understand why Black people have responded so indignantly during this tragic period". The report concluded that most of those who had been attacked by the police were innocent of any crime or provocation, but that a few had engaged in illegal or violent activities. It led the bishops to call for an inquiry into police conduct.[423]

IDAMASA, representing a wide cross-section of African Christian ministers, issued a statement in 1985 urging Black people in the townships to stop acts of violence. They felt that violence was not a constructive means to show their justifiable anger, was causing losses of life in their own communities, and would delay the liberation struggle rather than help it. They also called for the scrapping of Bantu education and urged township youth to return to school so that they would be better prepared for their future.[424]

The SACC and its member churches continued to advocate non-violence, but by 1985 it had also decided not to condemn those individuals who had joined the violent liberation struggle due to their strong convictions. This represented a major shift in approach and was an acknowledgement that people could participate in the struggle in different ways.

Justifying violent resistance
Others, more radical than those described above, argued that there was room for a just revolution theory and that violent resistance to a tyrannical system can be justified on the basis of the following criteria, *inter alia*:
1. All other possibilities of non-violent change must have been truly exhausted.
2. The cause fought for must be just.

---

[421] SAIRR, *1982 Survey*, pp. 572-573.
[422] Ibid., p. 575.
[423] SAIRR, *1984 Survey*, p. 909.
[424] SAIRR, *1985 Survey*, p. 570.

3. The methods used must be just and minimally inhumane; no unnecessary, excessive, uncontrolled violence should be used.
4. There must be reasonable prospects that the violent resistance will attain the ends desired.
5. There must be popular understanding and acceptance of the order which will be established after the violence succeeds.
6. The violent overthrow of the existing power structures must be an act of obedience to God and love toward men.[425]

Whilst the concept of the just struggle was widely adopted, resort to violent resistance was not.

Expanding religious support for the struggle

Support within the churches for the just struggle found resonance in the teachings of other religions. Hence, a body of non-violent religious reaction against apartheid emerged in the 1980s. The Jewish, Hindu and Muslim communities often joined the Christian community in its protest at the excesses of the apartheid regime -- initially against the bannings and detentions, then later against the deaths in detention and later still after the massacres in Thokoza, Boipathong, and Shobashubane.

This support also prompted leaders and members of various religious groups to provide spiritual and moral as well as financial and material support to individuals and their families who were directly affected by apartheid repression. This assistance is better documented for organisations such as the SACC and the SACBC, but such support was also provided by Jewish, Hindu and Muslim groups for their own members so affected. Substantial funding from foreign religious organisations was channelled through local counterpart organisations, and was sometimes distributed to secular organisations playing a key support role in communities, e.g. advice centres, community development organisations, etc.

Bridging the gap between religion and development

All of the religious denominations have also assisted other communities within South Africa, especially in the health and education sectors. Literacy classes have been conducted, and health clinics or ambulances sponsored in rural or urban African communities. Funding is collected from within the community, and/or members of the community contribute their time and skills. So, for example, the Islamic Medical Association has sponsored ambulances in rural districts or conducts eye examinations for the aged poor – without regard to religious affiliation.

Religious-based professional associations conduct seminars or roundtables on ethical, religious and professional issues. For example, Jewish lawyers debated the death penalty or secular divorce/maintenance laws, and the Muslim/Hindu community debated organ transplants and genetic research. Other religious professional associations such as the Interdenominational African Ministers' Association of South Africa (IDAMASA) became directly involved in community issues such as the 1984 phasing out of commuter buses between Soshanguve and Mabopane (both dormitory townships in or near Bophuthatswana) and Pretoria. This transportation issue was crucial to residents' ability to earn a living. IDAMASA worked closely with the residents' associations to have the bus services restored.[426] Increasingly, religious professionals realised the need to engage in key social and economic issues on behalf of their communities.

---

[425] Lamola, 1986.
[426] SAIRR, *1984 Survey*, pp. 422-423.

Religious organisations have played a significant role in establishing welfare, education and charitable functions. Their buildings have provided meeting places for communities and often their residential facilities have accommodated participants from many parts of the country without fear of police harassment or arrest under the ubiquitous pass laws of the apartheid era. Funds from religious organisations have helped communities, families and individuals to establish programmes/projects to assist with a wide range of socio-economic development issues / priorities::

• Pre-schools	• Hunger
• Nursery schools	• Nutrition
• Creches	• Flood disasters
• Self-help projects	• Evictions
• Agricultural projects	• Removals
• Disabled persons	• Welfare
• Water supply	• Research
• Family assistance:	• Documentation
• during detention	• Legal aid
• after deaths	• Housing
• Education	• Youth
• literacy	• Women
• schools	• Health education
• tertiary	• Environmental protection
• technical	• Economic understanding
• Teacher development	• Industrial mission
• Dispute resolution	• International campaigns

Religious organisations have been directly involved in the provision of educational services across the country, in both rural and urban aresa. As a significant example, the following table illustrates the extensive involvement of various religious organisations in education within the Coloured community in the 1950s and 1960s.

Aquiescence to apartheid

The fact that each of these religious organisations established schools exclusively on racial grounds indicates that they had acquiesced to the apartheid-legislated separation of educational facilities. This pattern was replicated in all racial communities -- White, Coloured, Indian and African. In each case, these educational institutions were complementary rather than a result of competition with each other and/or the state school system. Families chose specific schools for a variety of reasons -- tradition, religion, quality of education, etc. -- but it is not possible to draw generalisations. Despite their opposition to apartheid in certain arenas, religious organisations did not take this struggle into their approach to education. Schools remained segregated until 1988, when the progress of the political transition gradually began to be reflected in the emergence of multi-racial schools.

Illustration of the number of schools and pupils under the control of various religious organisations in 1953 and 1963, in the Coloured community

Religions and schools	Number of schools: 1953	Number of schools: 1963	Number of pupils: 1953	Number of pupils: 1963
Dutch Reformed Church	376	613	42 541	67 105
Anglican Church	186	169	30 087	32 134
Congregational Church	144	153	18 058	20 261
Methodist Church	96	88	14 409	12 835
Roman Catholic Church	80	93	17 324	23 585
Moravian Church	43	53	6 216	9 007
Berlin Missionary Society	29	35	3 698	5 695
United Church	28	26	4 832	6 186
African Methodist Episcopal Church	15	14	4 884	3 687
Malay	15	16	4 544	5 437
Interdenominational	14	26	1 350	2 146
Rhenish Missionary Society	14	13	2 674	2 565
Independent Church	13	13	1 526	1 593
Committee Schools (1953) Mission Schools (1963)	7	3	1 580	573
Volkskerk	7	7	2 153	2 388
Farm schools	4		75	
Presbyterian Church	4	3	51	231
London Missionary Society	4	9	390	537
German Lutheran Church	2		183	
Presbyterian Bantu Church	2		198	
United Congregational Church (1953); Salvation Army (1963)	1	1	150	29
City Mission (1953); People's Mission (1963)	1	1	312	393
Evangelical Church	1	1	167	264
Baptist Church	1	1	65	50
Methodist - Congregational Church (1953); Holy Pilgrim (1963)	1	1	67	75
Hindu	1	1	250	212
TOTAL	**1 089**	**1 340**	**157 784**	**196 988**

Source: Van der Ross, 1979, p. 60.

A major test for religious education arose with the adoption of Bantu education by the Verwoerd government in the mid-1950s. Government wanted to take over mission schools and impose Bantu education – instead of the relatively high quality education provided by the religious bodies. The CPSA Bishop of Johannesburg, Ambrose Reeves, declared that Bantu education was "designed to ensure the perpetual domination of one racial group by the intellectual starvation of another". Rather than submit to government's demand, he announced the closure of all mission schools in his diocese in April 1955. Six months later, the SACBC led by Archbishop Denis Hurley, met with Dr. Verwoerd and established that whilst the government was going to withdraw subsidies from mission schools unwilling to submit to Bantu education policy, those missions could keep their schools open as private entities. However, the financial burden of this option was too severe for many religious bodies. Whilst disapproving of the government's intentions, Archbishop Clayton and the Episcopal Synod took a decision to lease their school buildings to the state, based on the rationale that to close them entirely would deprive many children of any opportunity to attend school. Father Trevor Huddleston took the view that if the church had been more steadfast and united in its refusal to co-operate, the government would have been forced to back down.[427]

By 1982, there was heightened feeling amongst a large number of NGK ministers and theologians that the NGK should be "much more active in giving a Christian witness to the South African situation". A letter signed by 123 of them urged that the four racially-divided NGK churches should be unified into one church and that until this could be accomplished, "the doors of all four churches should be open to the NGK members of other racial groups". They also argued that government policies such as race classification, group areas, forced resettlement, migratory labour and inadequate provision of services to Black people could not be justified by the scripture or by "biblical demands for justice and human dignity". This letter was followed by another in support from 33 lay members of the NGK. Furthermore, the Coloured NG Sendingkerk called on the (White) NGK to confess its guilt in supporting the apartheid ideology with moral and theological foundations. Around this time also, the White NGK was being shunned by related churches in foreign countries due to its previous support for apartheid – an additional incentive for the NGK to change its position.[428] Despite all of this public pressure, the General Synod of the (White) NGK later that year rejected the open letter by a huge majority. It also rejected any contact with the SACC. Some progress was made in that the Synod did reject the notion that some races are superior to others and encouraged members to listen more carefully to the Black NGK churches. It maintained the policy of separate churches for the different races, but made a minor concession in allowing individual White churches to admit Blacks to worship on special occasions. Overall, the NGK made only very limited concessions.[429]

Without rancour, it must also be recognised that there were opinions in all religious organisations both to the right as well as the left of the mainstream of the struggle against apartheid. Many individuals, many religious adherents -- some organised and some charismatic churches -- sided with apartheid and separate development. Despite the admirable tradition and analysis of justice and equality, the Christian churches and schools accepted the advent of a number of Acts passed by the apartheid government. The churches did not defy these Acts by blessing mixed marriages, nor did they open their churches to communal worship. They condoned the racial separation of communities through the Group Areas Act, the separation of education and other pieces of apartheid legislation passed during the first 10 years of National Party rule.

---

[427] Clarke, 1989, pp. 143-147.
[428] SAIRR, *1982 Survey*, pp. 562-565.
[429] Ibid., pp. 566-569.

In 1994, Father Smangaliso Mkhatshwa wrote:

"The churches, especially in South Africa, are riddled with contradictions. All the contradictions of the society are reproduced in the structures, practices and ideologies of the churches. There are also the religious contradictions, specific to the Christian churches. Thus all the contradictions associated with rich and poor, black and white, men and women are mirrored in the church, as well as the political and ideological contradictions or conflicts between left, right and centre. On the religious level, we have the contradictions between faith and practice, the Bible and the dominant theology, the laity and the clergy, authoritarianism and love, appearance and reality. Perhaps the most serious contradiction in the churches is that between the promise of salvation or liberation and the reality of complete passivity or blind obedience".[430]

He also noted that, because of their heterogeneity and "multi-class character", the churches' had difficulty in making "decisive and unambiguous decisions" – unlike trade unions or political organisations. However, he stressed that the churches could only succeed in their interventionist role if they "are in true solidarity with the people". Thus, their roles in the late 1980s in the "Standing for the Truth" campaign to promote human rights and in the early 1990s against the township violence are more consistent with the credibility sought by the churches.[431]

Challenges for religious organisations

Stemming from the above experiences, an important "challenge facing the church is that of becoming a genuine alternative community. Religious belief is a many-sided social phenomenon, and not merely an expression of personal conviction, and devout religious views can also be the expression of social forces in a struggle for political power and domination."[432] This study has shown that all religious groups in South Africa have fallen prey to this weakness. It is therefore necessary for them to be more aware of the societal forces affecting their communities and their churches, to listen more carefully to the needs of those to whom they minister, and to engage with those forces (e.g. government) whose actions they contest. This contestation may stem from their theology, from their purpose of mission, or from their simple humanity.

Clarke wrote:

"If the evils against which the church feels called to protest are such as to merit the term heresy, then no Christian of social conscience, still less a church leader, can afford to stand back and adopt a merely reactive stance to the government. Surely the church and its leaders are obliged to take the initiative and to respond proactively. The church's methods of resistance towards a government whose policies are perceived to be heresy cannot be left at the level of polite requests or even peaceful protests. Resistance, if it is to be Christian, cannot contemplate any implicit, still less explicit, legitimation of the status quo. The will to say 'No! We must obey God rather than men!' surely means the adoption of methods of resistance appropriate to the evil that has to be denied. In this respect, the Gandhian way of Satyagraha, fidelity to the truth, should lead Christians to recognise that what has come to be called non-violent direct action is probably the only appropriate response to apartheid."[433]

---

[430] Mkhatshwa, in Liebenberg et al., 1994, p. 155.
[431] Ibid., pp. 161-162.
[432] Goedhals, 1989, p. 124. She cites Hastings, 1979, p. 263 and Guy, 1983, p. 253.
[433] Clarke, 1989, p. 156.

Dr. Mamphela Ramphele cited three major issues that need to be addressed "in relation to the wider ministry of the Anglican Church". They are almost certainly equally applicable to many other religious organisations. The issues are:

- "First, the capacity and ability of ordinary people to have a concrete and visible influence on the direction and quality of ministry [have] to be examined.
- Second, the use of 'tradition' as a resource to legitimate existing power relations has to be confronted.
- Thirdly, the issue of sexism within the church and its manifestations in both the understanding and practice of mission" must be addressed.[434]

Certainly the role of the various South African religious bodies and communities in such arenas has vastly increased under the democratic dispensation since 1994. However, the positions taken by their spokespersons / leadership are not always entirely consistent with their theologies. Over time, it is essential to reinterpret religious thought so that it becomes relevant to the changing world. This is another aspect of mission and social advocacy that religious organisations should genuinely confront.

Secular Civil Society Organisations

Welfare and service organisations

In response to the inadequate service provision by the state, secular organisations also developed to provide welfare services.

Given the skewness with which the legislators enacted legislation and allocated resources, it was inevitable that the White communities and their organisations would be advantaged. Black organisations and causes -- no matter how deserving or needy -- were ignored or received small percentages of the grants made by the government Welfare Department. In all aspects of life, apartheid played a role: welfare grants or other assistance to organisations were similarly allocated in a discriminatory manner.

Some organisations provided help across the races; others deliberately chose not to. When the apartheid government imposed its welfare legislation, it demanded that only specific population groups be serviced through the grants it provided. This led to a division of service, disparate levels of care and professionalism, as well as varying degrees of state aid. It was only in the late 1970s that middle-class charity groups such as Rotary, Round Table and Lions were permitted to admit Black members.

Around the same time, the Council of Child and Family Welfare noted the growing need for child welfare services and the consequent proliferation of community-based welfare societies especially in African communities. "Apparently in these cases the need for a crèche often resulted in the establishment of a committee which expanded into a child welfare society which maintained the creche as one of its objectives". Despite the increasing interest, these societies faced a serious financial crisis. Even the long-established Johannesburg Child Welfare Society (JCWS) found it increasingly difficult to respond adequately, for example, to the increasing abandonment of children in urban areas. Similarly, provision for the care of African elderly people was totally insufficient.[435] Access to government funding was difficult because of the severe restrictions placed on its distribution, including thorough investigations of recipient organisations before funding could be given.

---

[434] Ramphele, 1989, p. 188.
[435] SAIRR, *1978 Survey,* pp. 483-484.

In the mid-1980s, the JCWS and representatives of the legal, medical, paediatric, psychiatric, psychology and education professions, as well as from welfare and church organisations, came together to call for an end to the harassment and detention of children by the security forces. They noted that these children would suffer long-term damage from their trauma. The police claimed that to the extent that children were directly involved in perpetrating violence, they would be subject to arrest. They claimed that they would separate children from adults in prisons and release them as quickly as possible into the care of their parents, but Cape Town lawyer, Dullah Omar, and others insisted that this was often not done. Some children as young as eight or nine were being held.[436] This issue continued to be a priority for human rights and welfare groups. At the end of 1986, the South African Paediatric Association issued a code for the treatment of children in custody.

Worker service organisations

During the expansion of the trade union movement in the early 1970s and 1980s, a number of service organisations were formed to provide specific kinds of assistance to the movement. Some of the areas in which assistance was provided included legal training, health and safety, women's issues, international trade unionism. Subsequent to the formation of the major federations, a number of these organisations became absorbed within the federation structures. Some however continue to exist and provide an ongoing service.

Capacity building amongst non-profit organisations

Similarly, service organisations were formed to provide training and capacity building to the non-profit sector as a whole on issues such as organisational development, governance and management. The Human Awareness Programme of the SAIRR, established in 1977, provided consultation and training services to change-oriented organisations in project management, organisational development, strategic planning and promotion of attitudinal change.[437]

Community chests and trusts

Certain metropolitan areas have well-established *community chests* which provide funds for various civil society activities. Some have been operating since 1928. One community chest made grants of R2.5m to 158 welfare organisations in 1986. By 1995, there were a total of 21 community chests around the country. "Their competent and professional volunteers have years of experience, and through allocation committees, carefully scrutinise every application for financial support... All welfare organisations supported by the Chest become members and have all aspects of their work monitored on an ongoing basis. [They] obtain their funding from bequests, corporate and individual donations, competitions, scratch cards, and special events that encourage members of the public to roll up their sleeves and give of their time".[438] *Community development trusts* have also been set up in some communities, sometimes as joint ventures between community organisations and private companies, or with foreign donors, with a view to creating a source of sustainable resources. In South Africa, this is an activity which has been driven primarily by foreign donors.

Organisations for people with disabilities

One important sector of welfare organisations is that serving people with disabilities. The South African Development Directory, 2000 Edition, listed 158 organisations working in the area of people with disabilities.[439] The older of these tended to be organisations providing services in traditional areas of disability such as the organisations of the blind or the deaf,

---

[436] SAIRR, *1985 Survey*, pp. 443-444.

[437] Ibid., pp. 579-580.

[438] Ritchie, 1995.

[439] This list also encompasses organisations which may only tangentially be involved with people with disabilities.

often separated into quite distinct categories of disability. However, as in all other welfare sectors, African people with disabilities had far less access to education, training and accommodation facilities than those of other races. In 1984, for example, there was only one government-subsidised institution for cerebral palsied and severely physically handicapped Africans in the entire country, and it was run by the Dutch Reformed Church.[440]

In the mid-1980s a new cohesion emerged amongst a number of these organisations and new advocacy or networking groups began to emerge. Their key task was to provide inputs into the constitution-making process, to eliminate discrimination in all sectors against people with disabilities of any kind. Many of these organisations have come together to establish an organisation in the disability sector to oversee advocacy, donor relations and co-ordination locally and internationally.

Disabled People of South Africa (DPSA) was launched in March 1985, with a donation from South African Breweries. It aimed to draw attention to the needs of disabled people, to encourage a more positive approach to their situation, and to lobby government to make better provision for services. It called for equal pension, education and hospital facilities for disabled people of all races. The DPSA also launched a self-help initiative for disabled people in townships and rural areas, establishing 15 self-help groups within the first year with a view to providing employment.[441] When the government pronounced 1986 the Year of the Disabled, 35 research teams were appointed and reported on all aspects of the disabled. Their 37-volume report formed the basis for an inter-sectoral group to advise on the plight of the disabled. The Inter-sectoral Council for the Care of the Disabled, made up of a number of organisations, established five main committees with sectoral sub-committees to advise on the implementation of the recommendations. Two years later, with no material progress being achieved, the DPSA backed a majority of the Council in calling a halt and disbanding the committees.[442]

In this period, a national organisation which has operated for 60 years reaffirmed itself -- the National Council for Persons with Disabilities in South Africa. It has offices in all the provinces of the country. Each province determines its own position and works within the framework of an agenda set at the national level. Its mission is to serve the advancement of persons with disabilities so as to enable them to attain their maximum level of independence and integration into the community, and to prevent the occurrence of physical disablement. It provides the following services: social, medical information, vocational, educational, and equal opportunity advocacy. The Council is famous in South Africa for its Easter stamps campaign which year after year has raised funds to sustain the organisation.

Education organisations

Due to the limited access to adequate public education, many individuals and organisations founded night schools to assist in the education and upliftment of African working people in the urban areas. These night schools also became centres for political education. Many

---

[440] SAIRR, *1984 Survey,* p. 735.

[441] SAIRR, *1986 Survey,* pp. 591-592.

[442] Postscript: When the Government of National Unity was established in 1994, an Office on the Status of Disabled Persons was created in the Deputy President's Office. When Thabo Mbeki assumed the Presidency in 1999, this office was moved to the Office of the Presidency. On the 3rd December 1997, the then Deputy President Mbeki launched the Integrated National Disability Strategy. The White Paper provides guidelines for government to ensure effective delivery of services, implementation of policies, and promulgation of legislation which will protect and serve the interests of people with disabilities. This White Paper was achieved only with hard work and dedication of organisations representing people with disabilities. It is a remarkable achievement for a new government beset with so many diverse and immediate needs to satisfy.

CSOs provided basic literacy training, e.g. Operation Upgrade, the Bureau for Literacy and Literature, the Domestic Workers' and Employers' Programme of the SAIRR, as well as church groups. Other organisations focused on provision of adult basic education, vocational skills and career guidance for Black people.

In 1968, a group of prominent Soweto citizens formed the Association for Educational and Cultural Advancement of Africans (ASSECA) with a view to improving matriculation results in Soweto schools. ASSECA managed to collect considerable funding from large corporations such as Polariod, General Motors, Chase Manhattan and others, as well as from local citizens. The organisation established about 23 offices around the country, conducted seminars on problems confronting Black people, and made representations to government on education-related issues. However, there was some controversy when ASSECA wanted to raise funds from parents due to its lack of transparency about its financial accounts and seemingly little actual positive impact on African children.[443]

A number of educational organisations and bursary schemes provided for primary, secondary, and tertiary education of African, Coloured and Indian children. Various bursary funds were created, sponsored for example by the Anglo-American and De Beers Chairman's Fund, the South African Sugar Industry Trust Fund for Education, the South African Council of Churches, the American – South African Study Educational Trust (ASSET) funded by Polaroid, Pepsi-Cola, and American Express. Some smaller bursary funds were supported by the South African Association of University Women, the Transvaal Coloured Teachers' Association, Nused (affiliated to NUSAS), and by several newspapers. The South African Institute for Race Relations administered a number of these smaller bursary programmes.[444] Other for-profit and non-profit organisations joined the bursary efforts over the years.

In the aftermath of the 1976 Soweto riots, African parents from various other CSOs (YMCA, YWCA, Housewives' League, etc.) formed an umbrella organisation called the Black Parents' Association. Their aim was to assist the victims of rioting and their families as well as to persuade pupils to return to school. Student leaders also asked the parents to negotiate on their behalf with the authorities but because the student demonstrations and violence continued, government refused to meet with them.[445] Schools increasingly became a key arena of the struggle against apartheid. Students boycotted classes and demonstrated in protest against the imposition of inferior Bantu education and against the required teaching of Afrikaans.

At a meeting sponsored by the Soweto Civic Association, the Soweto Parents' Crisis Committee (SPCC) was formed in October 1985 to address education issues, initially in their own community. Later they began to play a national role in convening education groups throughout the country to discuss solutions to the education crisis. In December 1985, representatives from 160 organisations met in Johannesburg. They took a strong stand against apartheid education, calling it "totally unacceptable to oppressed people as it divided people into classes and ethnic groups". They said it was a "means of control to produce subservient, docile people, and entrenched apartheid and capitalism". Instead, they advocated the urgent introduction of "peoples' education" to enable "the oppressed to understand the evils of the apartheid system" and "to prepare them for participation in a non-racial, democratic system". Peoples' education would also "encourage collective input and active participation by all". The conference also called for:
- The formation of progressive parent/teacher/student associations at all schools;
- The formation of a single, progressive teachers' association;

[443] SAIRR, *1973 Survey*, p. 299.
[444] Ibid., pp. 347-349.
[445] SAIRR, *1976 Survey*, pp. 25-26.

- Parents to refuse to pay school fees in the next year;
- Free text books and other educational materials to be provided to all students in all schools;
- The unbanning of COSAS;
- The release of all pupils and teachers in detention;
- The reinstatement of dismissed or suspended teachers;
- The withdrawal of security forces from the townships and schools;
- The lifting of the state of emergency;
- The introduction of democratic SRCs at all schools and tertiary institutions;
- The formation of a national parents' crisis committee to work with local and regional organisations in the implementation of the above decisions.

At the same time, they called for students to return to school in 1986 and for the "struggle for a non-racial, democratic South Africa to be taken into every school and every home".[446]

In an attempt to give leadership and co-ordination to the education struggle, the National Education Crisis Committee (NECC) was created in March 1986. It also aimed to unify the students with the wider struggle. It promoted and tried to implement the concept of People's Education -- for all ages, and campaigned to get students to return to school. The NECC had problems communicating with students at the local level due to the banning of COSAS in 1985 and the consequent absence of formal structures. In 1986 a number of NECC leaders were detained. Nonetheless, the emergence of parent/teacher/student associations (PTSAs) at most African township schools and the role of the NECC posed a major challenge to official control of education by proposing the introduction of "peoples' education" and peoples' control of both curriculum and administration of schools. In 1985, in Coloured areas of the Cape, PTSAs also emerged in an attempt to set up an alternative educational authority. The NECC planned to redraft the English and history curricula as a first step towards "people's education for peoples' power". Such alternative education began to take hold in many areas, and students were introduced to topics that were left out of the apartheid textbooks.

When schools reopened in 1986, attendance was uneven around the country. Students were still not satisfied as many of their demands had not been met. The NECC met again in late March 1986 to assess government's response to the SPCC's demands of late 1985. More than 1,500 delegates from around the country attended the conference. Many of the demands were repeated, and some added. Boycotts of schools continued in some areas. In July, the government introduced new measures to try to reintroduce discipline in schools, but the NECC argued that these would simply lead to confrontation between teachers and students, and ultimately cause the total collapse of education in the townships. They also criticised the government's lack of consultation with parents and students. The NECC made a court application to have the new regulations withdrawn, but failed. Further boycotts and disturbances followed, attendance in many areas was low, and some schools were closed.

It was hardly surprising that the situation did not improve markedly. As noted by a leader of the Soweto Parents' Crisis Committee, Rev. Molefe Tsele, African children had been "hardened by a decade of violence, school boycotts, and the banning of COSAS" and they "could not be dictated to". He said that "it is necessary to show them why the resolution to go back to school was taken [by the SPCC]. If we can't explain to students that we are taking their grievances seriously, they could respond by saying that the reasons they went on boycott in the first place have not changed".[447]

---

[446] SAIRR, *1985 Survey,* pp. 394-395.
[447] SAIRR, *1986 Survey,* p. 446.

In January 1987, an order was gazetted banning any NECC gatherings from discussing "people's education" at any Department of Education school or hostel. On 24 February 1988, the NECC was completely banned and the entire executive was detained shortly beforehand. Later that year, action was taken against schools which had incorporated "people's education" into their curriculum. Nonetheless, many politicians and teachers' associations concurred that making school curricula more relevant to student's lives was a positive and necessary step. Huge controversy erupted over the content of textbooks, especially history.[448]

In 1990, an NECC offshoot, the National Education Co-ordinating Committee (also NECC)[449] launched a back-to-school campaign and encouraged all parents to register their children at the schools of their choice. The NECC general secretary, Ihron Rensberg, said that the education crisis was "created by the corruption within the departments of education, expulsion of students from schools, exclusion of large numbers of students from admission, the retrenchment of teachers in all departments, and the destruction of student representative councils and of parent-teacher-student associations".[450] These organisations had been the most representative organisations in the education sector. Their demise was a further blow to constructive communication between the government and the school system.

Nonetheless, the NECC monitored school registrations and informed the Department of Education and Training (DET) about waiting lists of students turned away from schools. The NECC lobbied for the unification of the education system and engaged in a campaign to occupy underutilised schools. This campaign led to a few White schools opening as fully non-racial schools in 1992, a small beginning in the lead-up to the complete deracialisation of the education system in 1994. The commitment of organisations such as the NECC, the SPCC and others and their inputs into educational reform were crucial in the transition to a democratic educational system, though many challenges remain.

Human rights organisations

The violation of human rights by the apartheid government gave rise to a number of human rights organisations spread throughout the country. At the local level, Advice Centres were established to provide basic legal services to communities. In the larger metropolitan areas, organisations such as the Legal Resources Centre (LRC), Lawyers for Human Rights (LHR), Socio-Legal Centre, etc. were created. Some of these were associated with universities, others were independent organisations. The association with universities was deliberate to protect them from attack and closure by the government. The LRC and LHR advocated the need to revise the definitions of "citizens" and "aliens" or "foreigners" posed by the homelands and to reduce the constraints posed by influx control so as to give Africans rights to live nearer their work. The South African Institute of Race Relations (SAIRR) cited a growing gap between Africans allowed to live in White-designated areas and those restricted to the homelands. The LRC established community advice offices in Black townships to provide legal aid and advice. These advice centres provided information on rights including housing, labour, unemployment insurance and pensions. Geoff Budlender, director of the LRC, said that the advice offices "played a major role in making people aware of and helping them to enforce their rights".[451] The Black Lawyers' Association (BLA) also founded a legal clinic in 1985 -- the BLA Legal Education Centre – to train articled clerks, establish law clinics, and conduct research.

---

[448] SAIRR, *1988/89 Survey,* pp. 255-259.
[449] This slight name change was clearly an effort to circumvent the banning order so that the organisation could continue its important work.
[450] SAIRR, *1989/90 Survey,* pp. 771-772.
[451] SAIRR, *1985 Survey,* p. 469.

A wide range of groups emerged in the 1970s and 1980s to support political prisoners and to campaign for their release. In addition to those mentioned above, such groups included the Democratic Lawyers' Association (DLA) which was affiliated to the International Commission of Jurists, the Vaal Youth Detainees' Committee, the Federation of African Women, the Black Priests' Solidarity Group, and others. The Detainees' Parents Support Committee (DPSC), supported by various other organisations, also continued in the 1980s to force the government to allow independent doctors to examine political detainees. The DPSC presented detailed evidence to the government showing that "systematic and widespread torture" of detainees was occurring at police stations around the country. They appealed to the 50 foreign medical associations for support in this campaign.[452] The DPSC also monitored political trials and reported on their outcomes to the public – information which would not otherwise have been readily available. The DPSC further accused the authorities of racial bias in the visiting privileges accorded to detainees. The Release Mandela Committee also campaigned for the unconditional release of political prisoners around the country. The SACC established the Asingeni Fund to pay the legal costs of people accused under the security laws, to provide bail and to represent families at inquests regarding those who died in detention. It also assisted with funeral costs and with the expenses of dependants left without any source of income, and it helped families to arrange visits to prisoners on Robben Island. Even an establishment group – the Association of Law Societies of South Africa -- spoke out against detentions in 1984, "saying that it believed that the very high number of people detained at the time might lead people to believe that there was a tendency on the part of the authorities to regard detention without trial as the first resort rather than the exception, which, at the most, was what it should be".[453]

Many groups emerged to deal with racial discrimination, as a key aspect of human rights violations under apartheid. The Centre for Intergroup Studies was established at the University of Cape Town in 1968 to promote "greater knowledge, keener appreciation and better understanding among all race groups". Its major activity was research, but it also was involved in the collection and dissemination of information on diverse forms of racial discrimination. In 1981 it launched a community conflict studies programme in co-operation with the Western Province Council of Churches, comprising both academic research and practical efforts in mediating conflict and developing related skills in local Black communities. The Mowbray Inter-Race Group, formed in 1976, also aimed to promote greater communication amongst persons of different racial groups. They organised "contact evenings" with about 12-20 Blacks and 40-100 Whites discussing key issues. This was a useful means of bridging the societal gap between people of similar education and professions but different races.[454]

Other organisations operated in the rural areas with the aim of protecting farm workers from exploitation. They played an important role in making known the plight of such workers, with regard to their working conditions, the use and abuse of child labour, the expulsion of workers from farms, and so on. The Surplus Peoples' Project (SPP) disseminated information and analysis. In 1983 it issued a comprehensive report on forced removals and documented the poor conditions in relocation areas. The Farm Workers' Union addressed issues of wages and child exploitation, and the Institute for Rural Community Development focused on improving living and working conditions through provision of housing, recreational facilities, clubs and training.[455]

The Association for Rural Advancement (AFRA) in Natal monitored removals and highlighted the difficult position of people living on land held by the South African Development Trust

---

[452] SAIRR, *1982 Survey,* pp. 252-253.
[453] SAIRR, *1984 Survey,* p. 760.
[454] SAIRR, *1978 Survey,* p. 47.
[455] SAIRR, *1983 Survey,* pp. 158-159.

(SADT) – land being held "in trust" with a view to transferring it eventually to the homelands. These people were living in poor conditions because neither the central government nor the homelands was willing to take responsibility for them.[456] AFRA also publicised the fact that some removals of African freeholders were conducted due to pressure from White farmers who wanted access to particular land which had non-farming economic value, e.g. coal deposits. They also tried to assist tenants who were being evicted from land on which they and their ancestors had lived for more than one hundred years. The land had formerly belonged to a missionary society who sold it to a commercial farming operation without making provision for the future of the tenants. These are only a few examples of the self-interested duplicity of various landowners in their mistreatment of long-term African tenants or neighbouring African freeholders.

The National Committee Against Removals (NCAR), an umbrella grouping of affiliates including the Association for Rural Advancement (AFRA), the Grahamstown Rural Committee (GRC), the Surplus Peoples' Project (SPP) and the Transvaal Rural Action Committee (TRAC), was established in late 1984 to monitor government's removals policy and actions, and to lobby for the cessation of removals. The NCAR argued that government's removals policy had become increasingly incoherent and inconsistent. Various other CSOs joined the NCAR in 1985 in calling for an end to all removals and forced resettlement. These included the SAIRR and Lawyers for Human Rights amongst others.[457] Into the late 1980s and early 1990s, the NCAR and its affiliates continued to monitor removals and other abuses of land rights and played a major role in publicising government's overt and covert policies and actions.

The Black Sash

In 1955, a group of predominantly English-speaking middle class White women created an organisation called the Women's Defence of the Constitution League. It began as a spontaneous process to protest against the Senate Bill introduced by government. The Bill proposed *inter alia* to restructure the manner in which members of the Senate would be elected (essentially ensuring that the minority government could remain in place) and to remove Coloured voters from the voters' roll in the Cape. Whilst White men stayed silent, thousands of women across the country were mobilised to protect democracy (as they saw it) and to ensure that the Nationalist government did not destroy the last remnants of trust placed in it by the electorate. Membership of the League was initially open to women who were citizens of South Africa (thus entirely White), but from any political party as long as they supported the aims of the League. "For the [White] women of the Union of South Africa , independent action such as this had never been known before".[458] An initial cell system rapidly developed into a huge network of branches around the country. Within ten days, the League obtained 100,000 signatures on its petition (counted by a chartered accountant live on a BBC broadcast)! Many of the League members had never been politically active before, but they moved more quickly than the opposition parties in Parliament. One press article wrote: "They rightly judged this [government] attack on democratic institutions and constitutional safeguards to be something transcending political alignments and party attitudes, and they went directly to the women of the country with what amounted to a declaration of rights to which all could subscribe. The result was spectacular…"[459]

Although they did not succeed in stopping the Bill, the League continued their protests. In particular, they marched, they maintained rotational vigils at government buildings and other relevant sites and they "sashed" senior government ministers when they arrived or departed. Groups of women would stand in two lines on either side of the ministers' path – essentially

---

[456] SAIRR, *1984 Survey*, p. 440.
[457] SAIRR, *1985 Survey*, pp. 329-330.
[458] Rogers, 1956, p. 25.
[459] Rogers, 1956, p. 30.

forcing them to walk a gauntlet of silent, sash-wearing women. This tactic was so effective that the targets took to leaving by back exits so as to avoid their humiliation! The government also arranged for the Jeugbonders (young party members) to jostle and push the League members against the walls as they stood in their lines. This pathetic attempt to intimidate the women had no impact. The League soon came to be known as the Black Sash due to its characteristic style of demonstration: "silent orderly stands and all-night vigils outside public buildings in the main urban centres, [wearing] black mourning sashes draped over one shoulder".[460] A poem written by a Black Sash member reinforced their resolve and attracted many younger members. It repeated the line, "For the female of the species is more deadly than the male…"![461]

The Black Sash was formed primarily to protect the constitution -- a conservative function. Its members were initially not pro-majority rule nor were they seeking radical change. They did advocate for "non-Europeans" to be "gradually brought into the councils of the nation". After 1956 and a split in the organisation, they refocused their attention on legislative and government action that infringed the rule of law and individual rights, e.g. bannings, detentions, abuses of press freedom, etc. However, they distanced themselves from the ANC Alliance despite their growing links with the FSAW. By the early 1970s, the Black Sash had become directly involved in providing legal advice to Africans regarding their rights, especially in relation to influx control legislation. By 1974 it had advice offices in Johannesburg, Cape Town, Durban, Grahamstown and East London.[462] It also made submissions to government advocating policy changes to simplify the lives of urban Africans and protested against many laws that violated human rights. They published several editions of their *Memorandum on the Pass Laws and Influx Control,* describing the body of law that controlled the movement of African workers, and the impact on migrant workers and their families.[463] In 1976, following the Soweto riots, the Black Sash tried to help locate missing children who had either been arrested or had gone underground to avoid police raids or had gone into exile.

In 1982, Sheena Duncan of the Black Sash outlined the impact on Africans who lost their citizenship. Nearly nine million Africans found themselves in this position by the end of 1981, and were consequently deprived of all rights to political participation in South Africa. Their access to employment, fair wages and free movement was severely curtailed, thus making it very difficult for them to provide for their families. The Black Sash also advocated on behalf of pensioners in the homelands whose pensions were in arrears. This was partly due to homeland leaders misspending their funding allocations – e.g. on lavish government building complexes instead of health and education.[464] The Black Sash's Transvaal Rural Action Committee (TRAC) publicised government's increasing use of force in dealing with communities under threat of removal. The role of the Black Sash in publicising these travesties was very important in making South African Whites aware of the plight of African people.

The 1983 conference of the Black Sash passed a motion to call for an end to compulsory conscription. A support group for conscientious objectors then launched the End Conscription Campaign (ECC). The campaign was formalised in mid-1984 and supported by

---

[460] Walker, 1991, p. 174.
[461] Mary Wright, quoted in Rogers, 1956, pp. 81-82.
[462] SAIRR, *1974 Survey*, p. 174. In 1972/3, the Johannesburg Advice Office assisted 4,505 people. They estimated that their success rate at that time was more than 20-25%. SAIRR, *1973 Survey*, p. 138.
[463] SAIRR, *1974 Survey*, p. 245.
[464] In 1984, the KwaZulu government spent R43 million on a new legislative assembly and office complex when it was facing deficits in its social expenditure for essentials such as pensions and health services. See SAIRR, *1984 Survey*, p. 533.

more than 40 church, student and civil rights groups. Conscientious objection had become a prominent issue as the SADF became more involved in direct repression in the townships as well as what was regarded by anti-apartheid groups as the unjust war against freedom fighters in South West Africa (now Namibia) and elsewhere.

The Black Sash played a crucial role throughout the 1980s and 1990s in monitoring a wide range of human rights abuses. It continues to operate today assisting people whose basic rights have been violated and lobbying government on key social issues.

Anti-crime groups

Organisations were also established to deal with the prevention of crime. The National Institute for Crime Prevention and the Rehabilitation of Offenders (NICRO) was, by the early 1970s, running hostels or 'halfway houses' in three major cities to help young men to make the transition between jail and total independence.[465] NICRO also became involved in studies to determine the underlying causes of high crime rates and to assist communities in finding solutions.

Some more informal groups emerged in township communities with the aim of fighting crime – called *magotla*, but they promoted what was essentially vigilantism. Sometimes their form of punishment clearly exceeded the bounds of justice. NICRO supported the *magotla* as long as their actions fell within the bounds of the law. There was in the mid-1970s some talk of giving official recognition to the *magotla*.[466] The *magotla* also became involved in local political issues and members even contested local elections. By the early 1980s, communities were expressing serious reservations about the role of the *magotla*. The "courts" were accused of being arbitrary and non-procedural. Sentences were not necessarily related to the specific crime, and corporal punishment was used indiscriminately. The *magotla* were also said to be serving the interests of a few people for personal aggrandisement instead of the wider good of the communities.[467] A 1983 research study of the *magotla* concluded that "practically every articulate segment of society was opposed to *magotla*, but that there were plenty of law-abiding township dwellers who were firmly in favour of them, even though... *magotla* activity all too easily became violent and lawless".[468] Though they had started out with seemingly good intentions, their role was being perverted in practice.

In the Western Cape, the People Against Gangsterism and Drugs (PAGAD) was established. It too saw its mission perverted when members took the law into their own hands. PAGAD disintegrated when it was infiltrated by police and destroyed from within.

Women's organisations

Social historians have paid little attention to the struggle of Black women against the pass laws and the inequities of racism in South Africa. Gouws and Kadalie noted that "the history (herstory) of women's struggles is probably the most invisible of all".[469] Walker wrote similarly that "in the case of the great mass of women, documentary silence may be erroneously equated with historical passivity or, even worse, with historical insignificance, so that women simply disappear from our view of the past".[470]

---

[465] SAIRR, *1974 Survey*, p. 93.
[466] SAIRR, *1976 Survey*, p. 98.
[467] SAIRR, *1982 Survey*, p. 208.
[468] SAIRR, *1984 Survey*, pp. 779-780.
[469] Gouws and Kadalie, in Liebenberg et al., 1994, p. 213..
[470] Walker, 1991.

Gouws and Kadalie cite several ways in which African women were affected by industrialisation, different from the impact on men:

- "The migration of males out of rural areas into wage labour left the women solely responsible for the maintenance of the household and subsistence cultivation in the rural areas.
- As the rural areas became increasingly impoverished due to a shortage of capital, land and labour, and with the growing requirements of industry, women began to migrate to the cities more and more in search of work.
- Initially only a small percentage of these women were required in industry, so the others moved into domestic and agricultural labour, and the informal sector.
- Traditional patriarchal households experienced a disruption in the sexual division of labour, so that the role of women in the rural areas became completely transformed.
- This disruption caused marital instability, the emergence of female-headed households and the break-up of the household as the traditional economic unit in which children were jointly cared for by both men and women."[471]

Women's increasing role in the formal economy heralded new organisations. In 1950, Amina Cachalia set up the Progessive Women's Union, a self-help society for Indian women in Johannesburg. It aimed to teach young Indian women marketable skills.[472] Also, women's increasing participation in trade unions such as the Food and Canning Workers Union (FCWU) was a politicising factor for women workers. It became clear that a national organisation was needed to co-ordinate women's political activity. In April 1954, the first national conference of women was called in Port Elizabeth and resulted in the formation of the Federation of South African Women (FSAW) and the adoption of the "Women's Charter". The majority of participants were Black women from urban townships.[473] FSAW affiliates included trade unions, the ANC Women's League, the Congress of Democrats, the Indian Congresses and SACPO.

Protest by women in South Africa, whether by Cissie Gool amongst the Coloureds, Ellen Khuzwayo amongst the Africans, Margaret Ballinger in the White community or Phyllis Naidoo in the Indian community, depicts a strikingly forceful, energetic and popular support which exploded against the apartheid regime. Up to the 1950s, women were exempt from the pass laws and other types of influx control. However, it became increasingly clear that government meant to change that. In 1952, the first major anti-pass campaign was organised by the SACP, the ANC Women's League and the trade unions. The campaign was successful and encouraged women in their political activism.

A key date in the role of women in the anti-apartheid struggle is 9 August 1956 when an estimated 6,000 to 20,000 women engaged in a massive anti-pass protest outside the Union Buildings through the ANC Women's League, supported by other women's organisations as well as political organisations. A protest song of the time said: "You have tampered with the women. You have struck a rock".[474]

Over the period 1956-58, the women's anti-pass campaign generated an enormous response. The movement did not have an effective network of local branches through which to obtain signatures on petitions outside of the main urban centres. For this, it relied on the outreach afforded by its affiliated membership organisations such as the ANC Women's League and the Food and Canning Workers Union (FCWU). The campaigns lasted until the banning of the ANC and the FSAW. It is shameful that most men did not participate in this

---

[471] Gouws and Kadalie, in Liebenberg et al., 1994, p. 217.
[472] Walker, 1991, p. 111.
[473] Ibid., p. 145.
[474] Ibid., pp. 190-191.

campaign with the women, or provide them with material or moral support. Even male members and the leadership of the ANC left women to their own devices.

The FSAW did not long survive the radicalisation in the early 1960s after Sharpeville. They remained committed to non-violence. Lilian Ngoyi attacked White women's pistol clubs which emerged after Sharpeville as a "disgrace to womanhood". As with other politically active groups, members of FSAW were subjected to police harassment and arrest. They received only minimal support from their male allies in the ANC.[475] When the ANC was forced to go underground after its banning in 1960, FSAW leaders were banned or detained (e.g. Helen Joseph and Lilian Ngoyi), effectively making it impossible for the organisation to operate.

The National Council of Women of South Africa (NCWSA), a White women's organisation, focused its activities in the early 1970s largely on family life, education and recreation for children in places of safety, as well as the supply of books to African pupils. They were also involved in welfare work, in assisting in the promotion of home industries in informal settlements, and holding adult literacy classes.[476] In 1974, its leadership acknowledged the absence of freedom of association and decided to make a greater effort to build relationships with Black women's organisations.[477] Around the same time, the Council made a representation to the Minister of Labour arguing that a minimum wage should be introduced for farm workers, that wages in kind should only constitute a limited portion of their total pay, and that their working conditions should include limited hours of work, payment for overtime, and annual leave – similar to those applicable to other types of labour.[478] The 48th conference of the NCWSA in 1982 redrafted the organisation's aims and objectives. These focused more on the promotion of "equal rights for men and women of all races, in particular to work for the removal of the legal, economic and social disabilities of women". They also emphasised the continuing importance of community work, the need to take action to remedy identified problems, and the need to foster understanding amongst all peoples of South Africa. They also held a conference on rural areas and as a result undertook to study rural issues and propose solutions. Various submissions were made to government on a range of social issues.[479]

In 1976, motivated by the crisis stemming from the Soweto riots a group of women led by Mrs. Bridget Oppenheimer created a "non-political, multi-racial organisation" called Women for Peace. It was supported, amongst others, by the Black Women's Federation and the National Council of Women of South Africa. Its first public meeting was attended by more than 1,000 women of all races. Broadly, the group aimed to promote mutual understanding and communication between different races and cultures, to work towards equal opportunity for all, and to make representations to government on important issues. Branches were formed in urban centres around the country.[480]

Another similar organisation called Women for Peaceful Change Now (WPCN) by 1981 had a non-racial membership of over 1,000 women. It had committees that dealt with education, social contact, local amenities, housing, labour and awareness. It published booklets on the rights of Black urban workers, wrote a report on "Fatherless Children of Migrant Workers" and collected 7,000 signatures on a petition to open Durban libraries to all races. It also investigated the accommodation of domestic workers and made recommendations for improvements. In 1981, WPCN collaborated in a conference on Black education with other CSOs, including Women for Peace (Johannesburg), Women's Movement for Peace (Cape

---

[475] Gouws and Kadalie, in Liebenberg, 1994, pp. 216-218.
[476] SAIRR, *1973 Survey*, p. 46.
[477] SAIRR, *1974 Survey*, p. 51.
[478] Ibid., p. 280.
[479] SAIRR, *1982 Survey*, pp. 581-582.
[480] SAIRR, *1976 Survey*, p. 30.

Town), and People for Peace (Port Elizabeth). It also joined with the Black Sash, Diakonia, and the Human Awareness Programme to create the Durban Housing Co-ordination Committee which organised opposition to removals. A booklet on career guidance for Blacks was so successful that it led to the opening of a career guidance counselling office to serve Black students, which in turn became the Careers Information Centre in Durban.[481]

The Women's Legal Status Committee (WLSC) focused attention on the issue of Black marriage in the context of the Matrimonial Property Bill in 1982. The argued for the inclusion of Black marriages in the proposed legislation, submitted a memorandum to the Parliamentary select committee, circulated a petition which was signed by many women, and endorsed the Law Commission's suggestion to set up a commission to study related issues.[482]

Ellen Kuzwayo, in her enlightening autobiography, *Call Me Woman,* cited numerous examples of organisations formed by Black women to meet crucial community or family needs. She wrote of her work as General Secretary of the Transvaal YWCA from 1963, and of the work they did with women in rural areas whose husbands were migrant workers and were therefore away from home most of the year. These women therefore needed additional sources of income generation for their families. She noted the formation of the Black Consumer Union in 1984 "to utilise the great economic buying power of Black people".[483] It was founded at a meeting of 250 Black women representing more than 50,000 members of various organisations.

Kuzwayo also wrote about the formation of the Soweto Women's Self-help Co-ordinating Council in 1978. This initiative emerged out of a meeting held in response to the passage of the Fundraising Act of 1978 which threatened the ability of many CSOs to sustain themselves. This group met "to formulate a way of working together so as to receive maximum benefit from their common resources of funding, expertise, person power, accommodation if necessary, and relevant equipment".[484] The Council included a wide range of women's clubs and other organisations in Soweto, including such groups as the Entokogweni Women's Club.

In 1980, the Council changed its name to the Zamani Soweto Sisters Council. It was funded through the Maggie Magaba Trust, established in South Africa by a British woman in honour of a South African Black woman who had cared for her as a child. Prior to the formation of the Trust, the Soweto women were trained in management and bookkeeping skills. The Council was also supported through the Black Women's Charitable Trust in London.[485] Kuzwayo wrote: "For more than forty years, our women have worked collectively, through small and large organisations, to improve educational and social facilities, for deprived urban communities in particular."[486]

In an attempt to move FEDSAW towards a more federal structure, 200 women's groups in the Transvaal launched the Federation of Transvaal Women (FEDTRAW) in 1984. Its president was Sister Bernard Ncube, and other patrons included Albertina Sisulu and Winne Mandela. Its intention was to address "practical issues faced by women such as unemployment, work conditions, removals, education and housing", with the 1955 Women's Charter as its reference point.[487]

---

[481] SAIRR, *1981 Survey,* p. 49-51.
[482] SAIRR, *1982 Survey,* p. 580.
[483] Kuzwayo, 1995.
[484] Ibid.
[485] Ibid., pp. 230-239.
[486] Ibid., p. 262.
[487] SAIRR, *1994 Survey,* p. 23.

A survey of Black women workers in the mid-1980s by Meer et al. found that "working women had few interests outside of their work and family routines and the vast majority (68.15%) had no organisational affiliation". The survey revealed that African women (45.2%) were more likely to belong to community organisations than Indian women (18.3%) or Coloured women (30.6%). Of those who did belong, the vast majority were religious (70.4%). A considerable number of African women belonged to burial societies (17.9%) whereas Indian and Coloured women did not. Small percentages of all Black women interviewed belonged to child welfare, ratepayers or residents associations, school committees, stokvels, or political organisations (all under 5%). However, 47.4% were aware of organisations other than those to which they belonged, and 38.3% indicated a desire to join them. A much larger 72.5% were in favour of women involving themselves in community work and 84.7% felt that women needed to organise. 65% said they would join a women's group.[488]

In the intervening years of the struggle, many other women's organisations emerged, performing a variety of functions. However, the struggle for women's rights and equality tended to be subordinated to the struggle for liberation. In the context of resistance organisations, women were generally subjected to patriarchal leadership structures.[489]

In the early 1990s, this began to change. The Women's Alliance in the Western Cape and the Women's Charter Alliance in Southern Natal as well as a women's coalition in the Transvaal were formed in 1991 to take up women's issues. The National Women's Coalition emerged in 1992 to co-ordinate the development of a women's charter. The Women's Charter Campaign, which began in the Cape in August 1992 significantly focused on rights demanded by both middle-class and grassroots women. This was the beginning of a broad-based movement for greater women's participation in the political process as well as for more policy attention to issues primarily affecting women.

Post-1994, the scenario has changed dramatically with entrenched constitutional rights and a strong commitment by political parties to equal women's participation in the political and economic spheres. Today a number of groups are focusing their attention on the empowerment of women in government -- elected and appointed officials. Others continue to deal with protecting women's rights, building women's capacity to provide for themselves through micro-enterprises, preventing women and child abuse, providing counselling, and so on.

Gouws and Kadalie offered a number of lessons from the history of women's organisations and struggles. Some of the most important are:
- Ongoing consciousness-raising activities regarding grassroots issues are essential, especially so that women's CSOs do not feel marginalised by national issues.
- Political organisations must recognise the importance of women as participants in policy debates as well as grassroots mobilisation.
- Women's issues should not be relegated to "women-only" organisations, but must be legitimated through being taken up also by student and youth groups, trade unions, professional associations, and political organisations.
- Broad-based coalitions amongst women can also help to put their issues on the table at local and national level simultaneously.[490]

Hassim has also noted that women's organisations are often a result of "women organising on the basis of their identities of women, in exclusively female organisations, taking up issues that they consider important". However, some of these organisations may be

---

[488] Meer et al., 1990, p. 178.
[489] Gouws and Kadalie, in Liebenberg, 1994, p. 218.
[490] Ibid., p. 224.

conservative, i.e. they will not question or challenge the existing power relations within their particular social base or within the society as a whole. Others will take a much stronger stance against the oppression of women both by patriarchal structures and by political structures.[491] It was primarily the latter that the women of today have to thank for their increasing opportunities and freedoms.

Youth organisations

In contemporary South Africa, youth have been generally defined as young people up to the age of 35. This is partly a function of the particular characteristics and needs of a generation of Black youth who sacrificed their childhood and their education for the liberation struggle, consistent with the slogan "liberation before education" which became prevalent in the 1970s and 1980s when township schools and school boycotts became a major site of the anti-apartheid struggle. That generation now makes up a large proportion of the roughly 40% of unemployed Black people in South Africa.

One of the older and better known organisations established to serve the needs of young people was the South African Association of Youth Clubs (SAAYC), established in 1939. It served all young people within its area of operation without discrimination on grounds of race, religion, class or age. It operated primarily in the Transvaal -- East Rand, West Rand, Vaal, and the Pretoria/Johannesburg areas.

Ellen Kuzwayo worked with the SAAYC from 1956 to 1963. She commented on the importance of voluntarism, especially that of women and girls, in this organisation. "Nearly all the people who initiated the clubs and ran them were women and girls in the different communities. They did this on a voluntary basis... [they] only received what were known as out-of-pocket expenses to cover lunch and travel costs". She added that this provides "a true testimony to the unselfish, devoted contribution of Black women towards the personal growth and development of the youth in their community".[492]

There were many other "conventional" youth organisations encouraging youth participation in sport, cultural activities, community welfare, and so on. The YMCA and YWCA were amongst these. Inevitably, many of these groups were racially exclusive. Some of them were affiliated to particular religious groups. The broad-based participation in the SAAYC was an exception. Our emphasis here, however, is on those organisations that drew the youth into politics, particularly the anti-apartheid struggle.

Youth in politics

In terms of youth involvement in politics, the ANC Youth League played a significant role between the 1940s and 1950s. During the 1960s and early 1970s, however, youth were less involved in political activity. It was during and after the 1976/77 Soweto student uprising that the youth re-emerged as a vibrant political force. SASO (see below) tried to organise young people in the schools – especially secondary schools -- with a view to developing future activists, whether in the context of tertiary education or in the workplace. Thus, various provincial-based youth organisations were formed. The Natal Youth Organisation was launched in 1972, followed by the Transvaal Youth Organisation (TRAYO), the Eastern Cape Border Youth Union, and the Western Cape Youth Organisation. The next year, these four groups created the National Youth Organisation (NAYO). Initially, SASO used cultural activities, literacy projects and other activities to build political awareness in these youth groups. But they soon became increasingly politicised. NAYO became a source of ANC recruitment, and in 1975 a number of its members were arrested and tried for terrorism.

---

[491] Hassim, 1991.
[492] Kuzwayo, 1995, pp. 148-149.

Some parents sent their children to boarding schools in the rural areas in an attempt to protect them from the risks of political involvement, but it was not possible to insulate them altogether.

At many schools, political clubs were formed. The most important was the Soweto-based African Students' Movement (ASM) which emerged in the late 1960s. ASM was converted with help from SASO into the South African Students' Movement (SASM) in 1972 with a view to creating a national organisation. This proved difficult as students did not have the resources to travel around the country and parents were able to instil a degree of fear of the authorities in their children. After a hiatus in activity in 1973/74 due to the banning of SASO leaders, SASM re-emerged. By 1976, SASM "was fully fledged as a national school student movement... [with] a well-organised structure, [and] a vigorous program of activities".[493]

The events of 16 June 1976 resulted from the intransigence of government with regard to the use of Afrikaans as a medium of instruction in Black secondary schools and the strong objections to this policy voiced by parents, students and teachers in townships. It also stemmed from SASM's efforts to grow its national support base. Strikes against the Afrikaans issue began in May 1976 at Orlando West Junior Secondary School in Soweto. This was followed by other student strikes at other township secondary schools, culminating in the protest march in Soweto on 16 June. A local SASM leader, Tsietsi Mashinini, played an important role in organising the protest. About 10,000 students marched to Orlando West High School, in a largely peaceful fashion. However, police were unprepared, and as the tension heightened they fired tear gas at the students. The children retaliated by throwing stones at the police. The police then fired real bullets into a crowd of children, killing 12-year old Hector Pietersen and wounding others. The peaceful march turned into rioting which spread through Soweto. Several other deaths occurred. Over the next few days as rioting continued, students were sent home from school. University students demonstrated in support of the school pupils and riots broke out in other townships, in some cases fuelled by tsotsis and gangs. By the end of June the death toll was 176, with many arrests and much damage to property.[494] Dozens of children were detained and kept in John Vorster Square police station, despite the protests of many civil society groups and individuals.

The students' demands regarding the medium of instruction were also supported by the "Committee of 30" urban African leaders and by the African Teachers' Association (ATASA). When schools reopened in late July, few students attended. By early August, the Black Parents' Association and SASM were encouraging children to return to school. The Soweto students' action committee was reconstituted as the Soweto Students' Representative Council (SSRC) on 2 August. They submitted a memorandum to government demanding the abolition of Bantu education and the release of all students held by police. Another march of about 15,000 students to John Vorster Square was met by police violence and ineffective riot control, leaving more demonstrators dead and sparking further rioting.[495]

Students sought support from their parents and other workers through stay-aways in an attempt to show their power, especially with regard to the economy. Three quite successful stay-aways were held in August and September in Johannesburg, and others were held in Tembisa and Cape Town. Some success was due to student intimidation of workers at train and bus stations who intended to go to work. Public support for the students grew by the second stay-away and less intimidation occurred. However, some Zulu hostel dwellers in Meadowlands were incited by police to attack residents, resulting in deaths and retaliation by the residents. Further tensions and police provocation, as well as class tensions between students and migrant workers in hostels, caused further conflict. Students took the initiative

---

[493] Karis and Gerhart, 1997, Vol. 5, pp. 156-163.
[494] SAIRR, *1976 Survey*, pp. 52-58.
[495] Karis and Gerhart, 1997, Vol. 5, pp. 171-172.

and went into the hostels to explain the reasons behind the stay-aways, eventually gaining more worker support for the third stay-away, with more than 80% absent from work. By this time, the school unrest had spread to many townships around the country, reflecting the increasing anger at apartheid policies and at police and army heavy-handed repression. SRCs were formed in many communities. The uprising lasted nearly a year, and affected more than 100 urban areas. It also spread to rural boarding schools and universities. "Student courage during the days of violence had inspired an awed respect from Black adults, but there were also critics who questioned whether the hundreds of dead and wounded was not too high a price for the meagre achievement of a government climb-down on the Afrikaans issue".[496] Nonetheless, the stay-aways were an impressive show of joint resistance by students and workers.

Police responded to the stay-aways and other actions across the country with massive arrests, raids on schools, and other forms of intimidation. Many youth fled the country to join the ANC, but maintained contact with activists who stayed behind and worked with them to build up organisations allied (overtly or covertly) to the ANC and/or the Freedom Charter (known as Charterist groups). Despite the repression, many SRCs remained intact. Many leaders of the 1976 uprising later became prominent as leaders of youth organisations, civic associations and trade unions in the 1980s. These so-called "graduates" of the 1976 protests were far less intimidated by state authority and more inclined to open defiance. As a result they gained the respect of the ANC in exile and other resistance groups.

The impact of the Soweto student uprisings reached far into some of the more remote rural areas and homelands. Some boarding schools in the Northern Transvaal experienced strikes and boycotts. Mathabatha's study of Catholic schools in the region cites the influence of tertiary students at the University of the North (Turfloop) despite the best efforts of the Catholic clergy and teachers to contain the discontent. In the homelands such as Lebowa, Afrikaans as a medium of instruction was not the issue, and localised issues took precedence. Another influence was the influx of pupils from the urban townships sent to boarding schools in rural areas by their parents to keep them out of trouble. The Lebowa government tried unsuccessfully to keep these children out of their schools and "urban youth became the key conduits for political information to the schools in Lebowa…They also carried word about the struggle and political organisation back to the rural areas like Sekhukhuneland".[497]

Further student revolts took place in Sekhukhuneland in the mid-1980s as more media had become available by then and stronger connections had been created with urban students and political organisations. Poor quality education in homeland schools, added to unprofessional conduct of teachers (e.g. sexual harassment and abuse of female students and excessive corporal punishment for minor offences), led to high rates of absenteeism and drop-outs. This led in turn to unemployment and anti-social or criminal activities. COSAS began to make inroads into schools in rural areas and in towns and villages outside major urban centres. Students began to call for more resources for Black schools and for SRCs as they became more aware of the discrepancies between their schools and those for Whites. Catholic schools, though, were largely spared these protests. They were better resourced and had better trained teachers who were more adept at maintaining discipline. Trade unions (e.g. the Metal and Allied Workers' Union (MAWU)) also played a role in raising consciousness amongst students in more rural areas, leading to the formation of a number of youth congresses in Steelport (STEYCO), Shiluvane, Apel-GaNkoana, Sekhukhuneland (SEYO) and other places. The congresses campaigned against poor infrastructure as well

---

[496] Ibid.. p. 170.
[497] Mathabatha, 2005, p. 57.

as the deficiencies of the education system. In March 1986, police action against student leaders led to a large student protest and state school closings.[498]

Various Black politically-oriented youth organisations emerged in the mid-1970s and the 1980s. Some youth clubs formed in township communities played a key role in exposing young people to political ideas, e.g. the Esukhayeni Youth Club in Soweto, the Young African Christian Movement in Kagiso on the West Rand, and the Parys African Students Organisation.[499] Such groups also included the Young Christian Workers (YCW) and the Young Christian Students (YCS). The YCW helped to form the local civic association in 1981. Reverend Frank Chikane, later secretary-general of the SACC, helped to form the Inter-denominational Youth Christian Club (IYCC) which engaged in social and religious activity. They ran welfare projects, assisted in the local advice office and conducted a household survey in the Kagiso township to identify residents' priority issues. Both the IYCC and the YCW were active in the local branch of COSAS.

The African areas of KwaZulu and Natal were not as well organised, as attempts at student protest action there had been forcefully put down by the homeland government. There were, however, a few relatively strong groups such as the Masibosane Lamontville Youth Organisation (Malayo) in Durban, and the DCO Matiwane Youth League and the Sobantu Youth League in Pietermaritzburg, The KwaMashu-based African Youth Congress did not survive long as it was highly politicised and subject to police harassment. It and some other groups were actively involved in recruiting for MK (the armed wing of the ANC).[500]

The Congress of South African Students (COSAS) was formed in 1979. It actually included in its ranks many non-student youth. It was established by ex-SASM leaders and student leaders interested in keeping up the political momentum started in 1976-77. However, it only really began to deal specifically with school-related issues in the early 1980s. The need to distinguish organisationally between school students and their grievances and non-student youth was recognised at the 1982 COSAS conference where membership was finally restricted to school students. Those youth who were no longer in school were encouraged to join either tertiary-level student groups or trade unions or other Charterist / ANC allied groups.

By 1983, COSAS claimed 44 branches nationally, with the largest number in the Western Cape. By 1984, it had grown further, with its Transvaal branches increasing from 17 to 25 and its Eastern Cape branches from 8 to 15. COSAS participated in the Transvaal stay-away on 5/6 November 1984. About 400,000 African pupils participated in the stay-away. It made various educational demands, including "the recognition of democratically elected student representative councils (SRCs), the scrapping of the age-limit restrictions, an end to excessive corporal punishment, an end to sexual harassment of female students, and free textbooks and qualified teachers".[501] These were key issues in schools across the country, but they were also signs of a deeper dissatisfaction with the education system to which they were being subjected.

Widespread school boycotts and other unrest occurred in schools during 1984. They initially centred on the above issues, but later encompassed wider societal protests around the general sales tax increase, elections for the tricameral parliament, and increases in rent and service charges.

---

[498] Ibid., pp. 61-78.
[499] Seekings, 1993, p. 23.
[500] Ibid., p. 41.
[501] SAIRR, *1984 Survey*, p. 671.

The Black Consciousness groupings established the Azanian Student Movement (AZASM) in 1983, and later the PAC established the Pan African Students Organisation (PASO) when working relationships with AZASM broke down. A pattern emerged whereby organisations were created around most political organisations and/or ideological orientations. Whilst they worked together in some instances, e.g. in rejecting the government's proposed constitution for SRCs in 1984, there were also tensions amongst them. There was also ongoing confusion about which groups represented school students and which represented tertiary students. The term "student" lacked clarity.[502]

Race was also a major factor in the formation of youth organisations. Because of the separate group areas and the segregated educational system, organisations were also largely divided by race. Thus, COSAS was relatively weak in Coloured and Indian areas, but this was compensated for by the strength of local organisations which emerged in these areas.

Coloured and Indian areas had their own school student organisations. School boycotts in Coloured areas of the Western Cape in 1980 spawned groups such as the Mitchells Plain Youth Movement, the Lansdowne Youth Movement, and the Hanover Park Youth Wing (part of the local civic).[503] These groups joined to form the Cape Youth Congress (CAYCO) in 1984. CAYCO had about 36 affiliates, including the Inter Church Group, which itself had 235 branches in the Cape. CAYCO had some African members and leaders, but was primarily a Coloured organisation until 1985/86. Also after the 1980 school boycotts, in Durban Indian students formed Helping Hands. It was involved in both social and charitable activities, and helped to politicise many Indian youth. In Lenasia, the Time to Learn project also performed community work. Both affiliated to the UDF in 1983.[504]

Between 1976 and 1984, few White youth were organised into overtly youth organisations outside of the established White-led bodies, churches and other religious groups such as the Boy Scouts, Girl Guides, Afrikaner cultural groups, or political wings of White political parties.

COSAS' decision to limit membership to school students led ex-COSAS activists to join with recently released political prisoners in forming political youth congresses such as those in Soweto (SOYCO), Alexandra (AYCO),[505] Saulsville / Atteridgeville (SAYO), Mamelodi (MAYO) and Port Elizabeth (PEYCO). More were formed in smaller townships. Most of them affiliated to the UDF when it was created in 1983. However, the youth congresses also suffered from factional divisions. Some split over issues such as whether to adopt the Freedom Charter, and others were able to compromise.

Most of the youth organisations engaged in some kind of community charity work, alongside their political education and recruitment activities. This helped them to build relationships with adult township residents and their organisations. It also helped to reduce the widespread fear of political activity and to reduce police harassment.

After 1984, the situation changed rapidly. Efforts to form a national youth organisation and campaign around the International Youth Year (1985) were not very successful. The South African Youth Congress (SAYCO) came into being in 1987, claiming a membership of half a million youth and the support of another two million.[506] Its president was Peter Mokaba, who later became an influential ANC politician until his premature death. Its federal structure comprised ten regional youth congresses, which in turn had local congress affiliates. Most of

---

[502] See next section on University student organizations.
[503] Seekings, 1993, p. 40.
[504] Ibid., p. 46.
[505] For a detailed anaylsis of AYCO and Alexandra politics generally, see Bozzoli, 2004.
[506] Seekings, 1993, p. 54.

these were launched in secret to avoid repression under the state of emergency. SAYCO was involved in several campaigns, including a focus on youth on death row, popularising the Freedom Charter, organising unemployed youth, etc. SAYCO was also allied to COSATU and generally supported the working class struggle. Along with many of its allies, SAYCO was banned by government in February 1988, and its leaders were detained under the state of emergency. By this time, it claimed a membership of one million – thus doubling its size in less than a year. SAYCO's key functions appear to have been to give political direction to the youth, to harness and sustain their militancy, and to escalate resistance.[507]

From 1976 to the mid-1980s, women participated actively in the civic struggles and youth organisations. Young women comprised about one-third of the active members of the Alexandra Youth Congress prior to the violence in 1986, and about one-half of the active members of the Tumahole Youth Congress in 1985.[508] However, even though they made up a considerable proportion of active membership of youth organisations, the leadership was almost entirely male. From the mid-1980s onwards, young women became even more marginalised from youth structures. Women members rarely participated in the violent protests. The reasons for this are not entirely clear, though some argue that the male youth considered themselves to be the fighters and protectors, and relegated the women to their home-based roles as 'nurterers'.[509]

A report of the Joint Enrichment Project (JEP) noted that "The category of youth in the mid- to late 1980s included a wider range of people as well as larger numbers. But broadening participation in youth organisations brought about tension, both within the youth and between them and other people. The youth of the mid-1980s included:

- Politicised youth, although the concept was broadened to embrace anyone defying the state, rather than the former understanding in terms of ideological clarity;
- Street fighters, gang members and more strategic exponents of violence;
- Conformists who enjoyed the camaraderie and fun of toyi-toying with the comrades, which gave them a sense of social affirmation; and
- A wide range of people who were briefly drawn into incidents of violence against the enemies of the community.

Most of these youth were male, as women withdrew or were forced out due to increasing violence in the townships.[510] Characteristics such as machismo, aggression and militaristic camaraderie emerged to counteract what some called a "crisis of masculinity" or "powerlessness" resulting partly from unemployment as well as the overall impact of apartheid repression and impatience with non-violent struggle tactics. Police violence elicited more violence. Factional fights between groups with different political allegiances also fomented violence.[511]

The organisational growth occurred as large numbers of youth were politicised through their experience of political conflict in the townships. Many were drawn into forms of direct action including protest, disobedience and violent acts. Such mobilisation also had some negative effects. Escalating violence opened new opportunities for formal criminal gangs who joined the youth and under the guise of political action committed criminal acts of violence. No control could be exercised over these actions by anybody including the leaders of political organisations, the police or the army -- creating a kind of "uncivil society".

---

[507] Ibid., p. 57.
[508] Ibid., p. 82.
[509] Ibid., p. 84.
[510] JEP, 1993, p. 22.
[511] Seekings, 1993, pp. 66-67.

In 1989-90, SAYCO began to re-emerge. At its national congress in April 1990, about 2,000 delegates decided to form a unitary instead of the earlier federal structure. Local youth congresses were reconstituted as branches. This was done partly with a view to an eventual merger with the ANC Youth section (in exile) and partly to make communication easier and to co-ordinate action within the organisation. The relaunch of the ANC Youth League and its incorporation of SAYCO occurred in October 1990, with Peter Mokaba as president. Regional Youth Leagues were soon launched. There was concern, however, that many youth might have developed such militant tendencies that they would be reluctant to accept the ANC's chosen path of negotiation (following the release of Nelson Mandela in early 1990). Youth-initiated violence continued to be a serious problem in the townships.[512]

As with many other types of resistance / anti-apartheid organisations, these youth groups found it difficult to continuously adapt to the changing political context. Their organisational development was hampered by consistent state repression, and many of their leaders were detained or jailed. They also suffered from ideological divisions. Nonetheless, youth organisations were quite effective in their mobilisation campaigns and in a wide range of struggle activities. Many of the leaders who joined UDF regional structures are still active in ANC politics or in civil society.

Mobilising on the part of the ANC was but another way of intensifying the people's war against the state in which the youth became the cannon fodder. Many tensions surfaced over the degree of militancy and the campaigns. Some revolved around educational differences, between tertiary students and secondary students, and around tactical or campaign particulars. The ideological and organisational conflicts were paramount, and a number of acts of violence took place amongst dissenting groups.

The period of the 1980s and early 1990s was characterised by severe social disintegration in Black – especially African – communities. The worst effects of this disintegration were suffered by the youth. Due to the repeated school boycotts and other disturbances, children were deprived of their education. The roles of the children on the frontlines of the struggle destroyed traditional relationships between adults and children. "Children became used to power and control, and refused to yield to the authority of adults whom they despised – their parents and teachers. Conflict became inevitable". The "politics of making South Africa ungovernable" -- the constant political protests and upheavals -- further destabilised children's lives. Indiscipline and blurred morality led the youth to become involved in intimidation of their opponents, often violent.

This socio-political environment also led to the emergence of gangs, warlords, vigilantes, comrades and so-called "com-tsotsis", all fighting for control of political terrain. The "com-tsotsis" were involved in criminal activities that were "legitimated in the name of the political struggle" – hijacking, looting, and even murder. In the absence of jobs, gangs provided access to material resources and were a source of emotional support for marginalised youngsters. Much violence was also directed against young women – they suffered sexual harassment, rape, gang-rape ("jackrolling") and other manifestations of men asserting their power over women, with or without their consent. In the Natal region, warlords and tribal headmen used the youth to fight their battles with ANC supporters, and vice versa, resulting in thousands of deaths.[513] This situation created a crisis for Black youth, and raised issues which are still being felt in South African society more than a decade after the democratic transition.

In 1986, Percy Qoboza, editor of *The World* newspaper, wrote emotionally of the country's youth:

---

[512] Ibid., pp. 87-90.
[513] Mamphela Ramphele, pp. 17-19, and Steve Mokwena, pp. 39-45, in Everatt and Sisulu, 1992.

"If it is true that a people's wealth is its children, then South Africa is bitterly, tragically poor. If it is true that a nation's future is its children, we have no future, and deserve none… (We) are a nation at war with its future… For we have turned our children into a generation of fighters, battle-hardened soldiers who will never know the carefree joy of childhood. What we are witnessing is the growth of a generation which has the courage to reject the cowardice of its parents… There is a dark, terrible beauty in that courage. It is also a source of great pride – pride that we, who have lived under apartheid, can produce children who refuse to do so. But it is also a source of great shame… that (this) is our heritage to our children: the knowledge of how to die, and how to kill."[514]

Some of these issues have been dealt with through the creation of a vast array of civil society groups. In 1993, the JEP commissioned the preparation of a directory of youth organisations. It revealed a total of more than 350 organisations of youth or for the benefit of youth in South Africa.[515] The 1993 JEP directory reflects youth organisations involved in a wide range of activities -- education (bursaries, science and maths, business, leadership, etc.), culture (arts, theatre, dance, choirs, etc.), religion, vocational skills, career information, child protection and welfare, human rights, resource centres, environment, youth clubs, community development, and so on. Each of the major religions found in South Africa have affiliated youth organisations, and each of the major political parties have youth wings. The party youth organisations have played significant, though sometimes controversial roles in the political transition process.

University student organisations

The history of the student movement in South Africa is similarly tied to the struggle for universal academic freedom and the need to build an anti-racist university and student body culture. However, universities and the voluntary student bodies within them also reflected the broader social and political environment. Student organisations emerged representing the same prevailing forces and mirrored the divisions in society at large.

The aim of the apartheid regime was to create specific universities for each of the four main racial groups, and then to divide those groups into further language or tribal groups, as happened specifically with White universities (on a language basis) and African universities (on a tribal basis). This legacy is still being felt today by the administrators who struggle to bridge these divides and attempt to build institutions of higher learning free of discrimination.

The National Union of South African Students (NUSAS) was founded in 1924 at a conference in Bloemfontein attended by representatives from seven universities: Pretoria, Natal, Witwatersrand, Rhodes, Free State, Potchefstrom and Cape Town. Membership of NUSAS was open to students of all races and language groups. However, the segmentation of the universities was soon reflected in separate student movements.

Afrikaner nationalism was strong in the early 1930s and resulted in the creation of four universities by that time: Potchefstrom, Stellenbosch, Pretoria and the Free State. Whilst these institutions were autonomous, they had strong informal links, probably through the Afrikaner Broederbond, keeping them effectively tied to a common ideology and direction. The universities were intended to continue the education of Afrikaner children through the medium of the Afrikaans language -- a process which began in kindergarten.

---

[514] Percy Qoboza, in *City Press,* 20 April 1986.
[515] Since then, another guide -- "The Youth Book" -- was produced by the Human Sciences Research Council (HSRC) in 1997.

A strategy of closing Afrikaner ranks occurred in 1933 when three of the four Afrikaans campuses severed their links with the NUSAS -- which represented primarily English-speaking students -- and sought through the vehicle of the Afrikaanse Nationale Studentebond (ASB) to promote a militant nationalism. Stellenbosch, the fourth campus, followed in 1936. Students could now further their own platforms and air their deepest convictions in an organisation founded upon their Protestant-Christian philosophy.

Over the decades, the ASB continued to emphasise the necessity of protecting the Afrikaner identity and supported 'separate development' policies. It almost always took a conservative stance on issues, despite a few individuals and groups who tried to move it forward. Though it did seek contact with some other student groups, it had little interest in pursuing a dialogue with either NUSAS or SASO (and later AZASO / SANSCO) which were deemed to be too radical. In 1978, the ASB's annual conference rejected suggestions that it support the repeal of the Immorality and Mixed Marriages Acts. Two years later, members voted first against and then in favour of a motion "calling on Afrikaans universities not to limit their intake of students of other races unless this was likely to endanger the Afrikaans character of the campuses".[516] The motion was accepted in the second instance on condition that students of other races could only be admitted if the courses they wished to study were not available at their "own" universities. Some concern was expressed at the potential abuse of security laws, and shortcomings were noted with regard to the new constitutional proposals, in particular the failure to consult with Blacks.[517] The views of ASB members were mixed and positions taken by the organisation reflected some very hesitant moves in a more progressive direction.

By 1980, a growing tension was evident between the liberal and conservative members of the ASB. The more liberal ones were increasingly willing to consider alternatives to past policies. That year, a former ASB president, Theuns Eloff, led a breakaway group to form the Political Students' Organisation (POLSTU). Within one year, POLSTU had grown from 18 to 500 members. It acknowledged that all races should be involved in working out a new political dispensation for the country, and it called for the repeal of statutory discrimination on the basis of race, colour or creed. It also called for equal educational and economic opportunities for all races. It condemned the bannings of students, but acquiesced to the need for security legislation.[518] Two years later, POLSTU condemned the "traditional authoritarianism of Afrikaans education" and called for a more democratic approach. Interestingly, at this time, the Inkatha Youth organisation regarded POLSTU as the best student group to work with – the "light at the end of the tunnel".[519]

Divisions persisted within the ranks of the ASB. At its 1983 conference, it decided to focus on being a cultural body, and to avoid partisan politics. It would continue to work towards Afrikaner unity but would encourage open political discussion. In 1985, the ASB held a joint political conference with the Inkatha Youth Brigade, The conference voted to investigate the possibility of engaging with the UDF – quite a turnaround from its past views. The president of the ASB at this time was Marthinus van Schalkwyk. Then, later that year, yet another Afrikaner student group was formed: the Jeug Aksie Suid Afrika was established "to provide a formal structure for young Afrikaners to take up political issues" but not in opposition to the ASB.[520] In 1986, a serious split occurred, with the more moderate members withdrawing and "abandoning the sinking ship" as they felt they had no hope of achieving their objectives from within the ASB.[521] This resulted in the calling of referenda at several universities to

---

[516] SAIRR, *1978 Survey*, p. 454.
[517] Ibid., p. 455.
[518] SAIRR, *1981 Survey*, p. 382.
[519] SAIRR, *1982 Survey*, p. 510.
[520] SAIRR, *1985 Survey*, pp. 402-403.
[521] SAIRR, *1986 Survey*, p. 468.

reconsider their affiliation with the ASB. Reaction was mixed, but by the end of the year the ASB disbanded.

It was not long, however, before a new Afrikaner student organisation surfaced: Jeugkrag. Its aim, according to Marthinus van Schalkwyk, was to "clearly establish ourselves as the major opinion-maker among Afrikaner youth". It was mainly composed of the more liberal ASB members who had earlier broken away. By 1989, the Jeugkrag was well-established at all White Afrikaans-speaking universities except Stellenbosch. The Jeugkrag was also well funded, with support from local and American business. The group was against discriminatory legislation and for universal suffrage, with the caveat that minority rights be protected. Afrikaans language rights were considered non-negotiable.[522] They expressed a willingness to begin a dialogue with other student groups, but said that they would exercise caution as some groups were not wholly transparent about what they stood for.

The English language universities were: Cape Town, Rhodes, Natal and Witwatersrand. Even with full faculties, these universities did not retain their initial Afrikaner students as they were essentially English language institutions with deep roots in British cultural life and academic traditions. The minority leadership and vice-chancellorships were often awarded to unilingual English speakers without a tolerant political orientation toward Afrikaner students. They were often committed also to the enhancement of British imperialism. A majority of the teaching staff were often British born and educated -- in the words of de Kiewert, "a sort of minor British provincialism".[523] NUSAS was the prevalent student organisation on the English campuses.

The University College of Fort Hare was established in 1915 for non-Europeans and Africans, providing the first significant opportunity for higher education within the country and reducing the outflow of Black students to overseas institutions.[524] Fort Hare had an enrolment of three students in 1916, 43 in 1930, and 156 in 1935.[525] In 1930, it was the site of a seminal national inter-racial Students' Conference. Many students who became leading figures in the South African resistance movement as well as leaders in other countries in the region graduated from Fort Hare. For example, in the late 1940s, when senior members of the ANC Youth League took on positions of national responsibility in the ANC proper, recent graduates of Fort Hare formed the new Youth League leadership.[526] The All African Convention (AAC) organised the Society of Young Africa (SOYA) in 1951 as a rival to the ANC Youth League. SOYA opposed the Defiance Campaign. "Three-fourths of the students at Fort Hare may have been members of the Youth League or SOYA in 1952. The Youth League had the support of a majority and dominated the Students' Representative Council (SRC)."[527] Also in 1952, the Fort Hare Student Representative Council (SRC) decided to disaffiliate from NUSAS because it was "realised that they had not been too successful in their attempts to radicalise NUSAS". There was also a perception that Black students had been slighted by the White-dominated NUSAS.[528] Fort Hare became a focal point of African nationalism after the establishment of SASO (see below).

Until the 1950s, NUSAS largely confined its activities to student matters. It did not, however, challenge the social segregation which prevailed even on those campuses where some academic openness existed. The so-called 'open' universities were really a myth as the Black (African, Coloured and Indian) student population never exceeded 5-6% of the total

---

[522] SAIRR, *1989/90 Survey,* pp. 875-876.
[523] de Kiewert, 1956, p. 26.
[524] Walshe, 1987, p.90.
[525] Ibid., p. 152.
[526] Ibid., p. 360.
[527] Karis and Carter, 1973, Vol. 2, p. 435.
[528] Badat, 1999, p. 80.

student body in any of these institutions. Racial interaction at these institutions was limited. Nor were the universities, academics and administration interested in any kind of racial integration. They attempted to espouse academic equality whilst opposing social integration inside these institutions. In a contorted attempt to excuse their policy, this dichotomy was explained by the universities as follows: "Segregation... is only applied at the social or non-academic level...it is applied at the university residences, dances and sports."[529]

However, government's move in 1959 to legislate academic segregation at previously "open" campuses was seen as direct interference in the internal affairs of the universities.[530] Student matters became overtly political and NUSAS as well as some Student Representative Councils (SRCs) became more proactive in demanding an end to all racial discrimination on their campuses. Over the 1960s, NUSAS was more and more willing to openly protest against government policies. NUSAS was particularly a thorn in the side of the government due to its multi-racial membership. Following the banning of the mass political movements in 1960, NUSAS became one of the few avenues for opposition to apartheid. Several NUSAS leaders were detained in 1964, and NUSAS activists were harassed regularly thereafter. NUSAS initiated a programme to assist student detainees to continue their studies whilst incarcerated, and they also launched a Students' Defence Fund to help with legal defence costs. Many White NUSAS leaders left South Africa after their release from detention. Security police tried, sometimes successfully, to infiltrate and undermine the organisation. Both student leaders and professors who supported their aims were banned, leading to a series of major student protests across the country.

Several relatively short-lived student organisations emerged in the early 1960s. In December 1961, students aligned to the ANC formed the African Students' Association (ASA). Similarly, a PAC-aligned group was established – the African Students' Union of South Africa (ASUSA). However, neither organisation was able to build a substantial membership. Other small groups aligned with the Non-European Unity Movement (NEUM) were the Durban Students' Union, the Cape Peninsula Students' Union, and the Society of Young Africa (SOYA). None of these groups lasted past the mid-1960s.[531]

Students at other Black universities besides Fort Hare were less radically inclined and continued to try to send delegations to NUSAS conferences until around 1968. In some cases, they were forbidden by government to do so. "In seeking affiliation, the Black students were demanding the right to associate with organisations of their own choice, and the more intransigent the government showed itself, the more determined the students seemed to become".[532] Affiliation to NUSAS also gave students an opportunity to interact with students from other campuses and to compare experiences. However, "non-whites, as delegates and office holders, did play a role, but were for the most part overshadowed by their White counterparts, and in some instances were callously used and manipulated as symbols of NUSAS' integrated non-racialism".[533]

In 1974, NUSAS was subjected to investigation by the government's Schlebusch Commission, which concluded that the NUSAS leadership training programme aimed to produce "student radicals imbued with left-wing views". It also accused the NUSAS Wages Campaign of stirring up labour unrest.[534] The same year, NUSAS was declared an "affected

---

[529] Open Universities in South Africa, 1957.
[530] Whilst universities such as Cape Town and Witwatersrand had allowed academic integration up to a point, they had continued to insist on social segregation. Thus, their protests against the 1959 legislation were somewhat disingenuous.
[531] Karis and Gerhart, 1997, Vol. 5, pp. 64-65.
[532] Baruch Hirson, cited in Badat, 1999, p. 82.
[533] Legassik and Shingler, cited in Badat, 1999, p. 84.
[534] SAIRR, 1974 Survey, pp. 31-33.

organisation" so that it was forbidden to receive funds from abroad. During 1976, five NUSAS members – Eddie Webster, Charles Nupen, Karel Tip, Glen Moss and Cedric de Beer -- were tried under the Suppression of Communism Act, but all were acquitted.

Toward the late 1970s, NUSAS leadership became more radical and aligned itself with the Congress movement. Detentions and bannings of its leaders became a fairly regular occurrence. NUSAS was continually subjected to infiltration by agents of the security police, aimed at collecting evidence against the organisation and its leaders. In 1981, as part of its theme of "Students for a Democratic Future", NUSAS argued that "by joining the broad democratic front against apartheid, students were showing that the conflict in South Africa was not simply between Black and White, but between those who supported democracy and those who opposed it". They felt that students could make a meaningful contribution to the struggle for democracy, especially if SRCs on campuses could be strengthened. They also felt that students should use their relatively privileged position in society to work towards democracy for all.[535] They recognised the need to "educate themselves about broad political questions as a basis for their active support of struggles and campaigns in the broader community".[536]

In 1986, NUSAS sent a delegation to meet with the ANC leadership in exile in Lusaka to discuss both the education crisis and the role of Whites in a future South Africa.[537] In 1987, to protest against the Whites-only election, NUSAS mounted a "one person-one vote" campaign. In testing student opinion in referenda on several campuses (Rhodes, Cape Town, Natal, Stellenbosch and Wits), 86% of the 13,835 students who voted were in favour of one person-one vote in a unitary state.[538] March 1988 saw NUSAS leading a protest at the Union buildings in Pretoria against government's proposed subsidy changes to universities and against the February 1988 bannings of 17 organisations. The protest was supported by over 200 student organisations in an "unprecedented" show of support.[539] NUSAS also led protests in October that year against the conditions under which municipal elections were being held. They also protested against the banning of SASCO and other issues. In response to the wide range of demands articulated by the protests the NUSAS offices at Wits University were set on fire – another example of state intimidation.

"Since NUSAS adopted consistently radical positions on political and educational issues, it was [eventually] defined [by AZASO/SANSCO] as a progressive formation" and was considered an appropriate partner in a "strategic" though not "principled" alliance with AZASO/SANSCO.[540] By 1991, NUSAS and SANSCO had merged to form the South African Students' Congress (SASCO).

The formation of the University Christian Movement (UCM) by a number of liberal, White clergy, mostly in positions at White universities, occurred in mid-1967. It had the backing of several key Protestant churches as well as the Catholic church. Its innovative multiracial work camps for students offered an excellent opportunity for open discussion amongst students of different races and for debate on current social and political issues. By its second national conference, 60% of the delegates were Black. A significant difference between the UCM and NUSAS was the fact that White students did more listening to Black student views. The clergy who initiated UCM also promoted an interest in Black theology. UCM used "formation schools" to provide leadership training. However, it soon got the government's attention and was one of the groups investigated by the Schlebusch Commission in the early

[535] SAIRR, *1981 Survey*, p. 381.
[536] SAIRR, *1983 Survey*, p. 464.
[537] SAIRR, *1986 Survey*, p. 469.
[538] SAIRR, *1987/88 Survey*, p. 182.
[539] SAIRR, *1988/99 Survey*, p. 301.
[540] Badat, 1999, pp. 317-318.

1970s. It disbanded as a result of the investigation and transferred its assets to SASO.[541] Essentially, its approach offered an incubator for many of the ideas that led to the formation of SASO.

The growing dissatisfaction of some Black student activists with NUSAS led to increasing criticism of multi-racial organisations. In particular, medical students such as Steve Biko at the University of Natal Medical School decided to form a Black student organisation – a move they felt was "long overdue". Biko said "what we want is not Black visibility, but real Black participation".[542] In July 1969, at its inaugural conference, Black students broke from NUSAS and established the South African Student Organisation (SASO) under the leadership of Biko and others. SASO's objective was initially stated as the promotion of contact amongst students at affiliated centres and the representation of students at national level. Later, its objectives were restated in more political terms: to "become involved in the political, economic and social development of the Black people" and "to become a platform for expression of Black opinion",[543] as well as to "foster Black community awareness, capabilities, achievement and pride".[544] This heralded a new emphasis on "self-discovery" and "self-realisation", described by Hirson as "liberation from psychological oppression, the building of a new awareness, the establishment of a new basic dignity, the framing of a new attitude of mind, a rediscovery of the history of the people, and a cultural revival".[545]

In its early days SASO viewed race as the fundamental source of cleavage in South African society (as opposed to class) and it played a major role in developing the concept of Black Consciousness in South Africa.[546] SASO had some contact with NUSAS, but it soon came to the conclusion that it preferred not to co-operate with White organisations even though it also claimed that it was not anti-White. However, the creation of SASO was seen by some as "a defeat for attempts at building a non-racial student culture" or even as a demonstration of the success of apartheid in forcing the creation of racially-segregated student organisations. Later, SASO did liaise with NUSAS out of necessity, and also with the Christian Institute, which provided it with financial and other support.

By the mid-1970s, developments in SASO indicated an ideological shift to greater interest in the impact of class – specifically the emergence of a Black middle class with a vested interest in the status quo – on the anti-apartheid struggle. This led SASO to think more about forming alliances with workers, seen as a significant political force after the Natal strikes of 1973. The Black Workers' Project (BWP) was founded as a result, with full-time organisers, but failed to take off. These issues were a source of contention within SASO, and tensions existed between the traditional Black Consciousness approaches and the evolving ideas.[547] SASO focused in the first instance on building up its membership and organisational structures. Student action was largely localised and it was only in 1972 that SASO began to call for nationwide student protests. The change in tactics was prompted by the expulsion of Onkgopotse Tiro from the University of the North as a result of the graduation speech he gave which attacked government education policies. After initial protests, a further 1,140 students were expelled for refusing to sign a document promising orderly behaviour. Within a few weeks, all of the Black universities and many other Black higher education institutions were involved in the protest. These actions were the first of many instances of student solidarity across ethnic and racial barriers, and reinforced SASO's importance through the demonstration of widespread support.

---

[541] Karis and Gerhart, 1997, Vol. 5, pp. 72-75.
[542] Badat, 1999, p. 85.
[543] Ibid., p. 92.
[544] SAIRR, 1976 Survey, p. 22.
[545] Baruch Hirson, cited in Badat, 1999, p. 89.
[546] See the section on the Black Consciousness Movement in Chapter Five.
[547] Badat, 1999, pp. 102-103.

The Black People's Convention (BPC) was a direct result of SASO interventions.[548] SASO and the BC movement also succeeded in fomenting an explosion of Black cultural activities in the 1970s, including visual art, music, poetry and drama. SASO members helped to establish various cultural organisations, and many became well-known cultural icons who are still active today.

Besides its political role, SASO became involved in community development projects known as the Black Community Programmes (BCPs). These were not particularly successful, aside from the construction of a few dams and school buildings. Nonetheless, they provided useful opportunities to the student participants. Projects instilled notions of self-reliance and community service, and in the words of Dr. Mamphela Ramphele, they were a "valuable educational opportunity". Students were able to see for themselves the "enormity of the economic and social problems of the poor, the extent of poverty of relocated people and put 'paid to the romanticism we as students had about poverty and people's responses to it'".[549] On the negative side, SASO had to admit that there was less enthusiasm amongst its members for these activities than they had hoped, and many projects never came to fruition.

As SASO increased its attacks on apartheid, the Bantustans and segregated education, government responded with its usual repression of opposition organisations. By 1972, some SASO leaders had been served with banning orders, and by 1975/76, every member of the national executive had been detained at some point. Many SASO members were also forced into exile. In addition to government, SASO was under pressure from university administrations. It was banned at Fort Hare in 1973 and at the University of the North in 1975. The detentions, bannings and departures for exile left SASO short of experienced leadership able to develop effective new strategies and to assert discipline amongst its members. Furthermore, SASO was declared an "affected organisation" in 1974, meaning that it could no longer have access to overseas funding. This created major financial pressures, which in turn restricted its ability to print its publications on a regular basis. Badat also argues that SASO "was characterised by a distinct voluntarism and a tendency to underestimate the ruthlessness of the apartheid state".[550] SASO was finally banned completely by the government in October 1977.

Members and leaders of SASO tried to "transform social relations in the education and political spheres". SASO differed from Africanist organisations in that it admitted all Blacks as members, including Indians and Coloureds. SASO's preoccupation with reversing all forms of Black subordination and its emphasis on "Black solidarity and unity in opposition to White power" were defined by the experiences actually lived by its members. SASO made another contribution by refusing to accept the appellation "non-White" and therefore rejecting the notion of Black assimilation into White culture.[551]

The SASO generation developed their own views and ideologies, and though some commentators characterised them as somewhat naïve, the organisation made a major contribution to the engagement of young people in the anti-apartheid struggle. The voluntarism which was so much a part of SASO's ethic stemmed partly from frustration with the seeming apathy of their parents' generation and partly from what they witnessed every day in terms of "White prosperity and Black deprivation". This ethic also demonstrated that government's attempt to disempower and co-opt Black youth through Bantu education had largely failed.[552] Students who were active in SASO and therefore exposed to considerable

---

[548] See section on the Black Consciousness Movement in Chapter Five for more on the BPC.
[549] Badat, 1999, p. 124.
[550] Ibid., pp. 132-137.
[551] Ibid., pp. 140-141.
[552] Ibid., pp. 140-153.

political education played a major role in developing the spirit underpinning the Soweto uprising and in later joining / leading other resistance organisations such as the United Democratic Front and the National Forum.

Despite the banning of SASO, Black university student protests continued. Campus-level Black student organisations maintained the activism previously led by SASO. The initiative for a new national student structure, however, came from AZAPO at its September 1979 conference. Though there was a somewhat limited consultative process, an interim structure was elected by the 100 students at the conference. Then, an inaugural conference of the Azanian Students' Organisation (AZASO) was held in November 1979. The name reflected its initial adherence to the BC philosophy. However, AZASO regarded itself as an independent body, not a wing of AZAPO.

The major education protests in early and mid-1980, and formation of the Committee of 81 with representatives of schools, colleges and universities to co-ordinate the protests, had a considerable impact on the future of student politics. The Committee of 81 took the view that "Black education and conditions within Black schooling were...the outcome of the whole system of racial oppression and capitalist exploitation". They also recognised the potential power of the workers and decided to prioritise building worker support. In addition, they looked to religious and civic organisations for support. Parent-student committees were formed to co-ordinate mass actions of various kinds. This approach resulted in increasing unity amongst different sectors of society. The more strategic thinking made linkages between the short-term goals of education boycotts and the longer-term political goals of replacing the apartheid system with a non-racial, democratic one. This period saw the proliferation of many youth, student, women's and civic groupings as well as the formation of SRCs at universities and COSAS branches at schools. It also saw moves to align the student movement more closely with the ANC.[553]

AZASO lost favour on a number of campuses, especially those where students aligned to the Congress movement prevailed. Its BC ideology was seen as the cause of its failure to successfully mobilise students. It was opposed by those who advocated a non-racial approach to the struggle. Then, the participation of AZASO in the 1981 anti-Republic Day protests alongside NUSAS demonstrated a major shift away from its BC ideology. At the first AZASO National Congress in July 1981, the organisation made a major shift in direction, with a much diminished emphasis on race in its new constitution. Its links with AZAPO and BC declined drastically from this time on. Nonetheless, it remained open only to Black members – a contradiction that it managed to rationalise.

In addition to its protests regarding education issues, AZASO began a proactive process to develop a democratic alternative to apartheid education in the form of its mass campaign for an Education Charter. The concept of "peoples' education" was formulated in the course of this effort, and a related concept was adopted in the mid-1980s by the National Education Co-ordinating Committee (NECC, see Education organisations, above). The Education Charter campaign was implemented in alliance with COSAS, NUSAS, and NEUSA (a teacher's professional organisation, see below).

Between 1981 and 1985, AZASO concentrated its efforts on building membership and establishing branches on campuses around the country. It "spearheaded campaigns for democratic and autonomous SRCs on campuses and engaged in mobilisation to defend and expand the space for student organisation". It also used alternative groups such as academic societies or even drama clubs as fronts and bases for activism on particularly repressive campuses.[554] Its organising efforts paid off, with growing representation at its

---

[553] Ibid., pp. 212-216.
[554] Ibid., p. 249.

annual congresses and a presence at more and more tertiary institutions. Its 1985 congress was attended by more than 600 members from 52 campuses, including universities, colleges and technikons.

On various occasions, AZASO (like SASO) mobilised its members to participate in campaigns in support of township organisations and trade unions – on issues ranging from transport, consumer and rent boycotts to protests against evictions or against local authorities. The relationships amongst these groupings were mutually beneficial and supportive. AZASO contributed to the UDF by building support for it on campuses, including those inside Bantustans and in rural areas. It also helped build the capacity of leadership cadres. Like SASO, it also often mobilised Black parents, professionals and religious groups in support of student actions and to mediate conflict where necessary.[555]

However, AZASO was challenged from time to time by AZAPO supporters on campuses, in some cases leading to violent clashes. In mid-1983, BC students formed the Azanian Students' Movement (AZASM), claiming that they better represented the traditions of SASO. AZASO also suffered as university administrations continued to clamp down on its branches and activities. Regarded increasingly as a front for the ANC, the state engaged in concerted repression of AZASO leadership through detentions, bannings and imprisonment.

The 1985 state of emergency was a constraint on student organisations as with all other sectors of civil society. Relations between branches and national headquarters and amongst local structures were limited. The Education Charter campaign had to be curtailed. University administrators used the state of emergency to crack down on AZASO. Activists were detained or forced into hiding. The 1986 congress inevitably had lower attendance in absolute numbers (190) but 72 branches were represented. [556]

At this congress, AZASO was renamed the South African National Students' Congress (SANSCO). The increasing political tension between the ANC and BC movements led AZASO to feel compelled to make clear its shift of allegiance from BC to the ANC / Congress movement which was increasingly predominant amongst students. The name change also reflected the organisation's self-confidence that it did not need to rely on name recognition.[557] SANSCO continued to operate under the state of emergency, campaigning against repression on campuses and advocating peoples' education. However, in February 1988, along with the UDF, the NECC and 14 other resistance organisations, SANSCO was banned under new regulations. Despite this, SANSCO managed to persist in some of its activities, including mass mobilisation under the guise of ad hoc structures.

SANSCO did not have quite the "vanguard" role that SASO occupied in the earlier struggle, but it did succeed in linking limited educational goals on campuses to broader political goals and thereby developing students' political consciousness. It also helped to bring to the attention of White students the grievances of Black students and the reasons behind their political struggle, particularly through its strong presence on the White English-language university campuses.

Unbanned with other anti-apartheid groups in 1990, SANSCO had become a genuinely non-racial organisation and therefore a direct challenge to NUSAS. Both organisations adopted resolutions to look into a merger, which ultimately took place in 1991. The new organisation was called the South African Students' Congress (SASCO). Since 1994, SASCO has focused largely on issues relevant to higher education policy.

---

[555] Ibid., p. 364.
[556] Ibid., pp. 256-258.
[557] Ibid., p. 260.

As South African Black universities were established (Fort Hare, Durban-Westville, Western Cape, Zululand, Bophutatswana, Venda, North), they all experienced strikingly similar underlying causes of strife on their campuses, including amongst others:

- The dissatisfaction of the student body with the attitudes, practices and laws;
- The frustration which flowed from the backlog in the level of development;
- The use of White (largely Afrikaans-speaking) academics;
- The involvement again of mainly White Afrikaans-speaking persons in the higher levels of the university administrations;
- The dearth of course options;
- The junior degree options were not enhanced with meaningful higher degree opportunities;
- The perception both within the SA 'open' universities and foreign universities that these institutions maintained inferior standards.

These issues formed the basis of the Black student organisations' campaigns on the campuses.

On some campuses, student organisations received support from "small, progressive, non-racial or black academic staff associations", but it was only in the late 1980s that the Union of Democratic University Staff Associations was formed. There was therefore quite limited scope for joint campaigns between students and academics on campuses. Such co-operation was more likely in the context of the wider political struggle off-campus. Liberal academics were reluctant to become involved in campus struggles and conservative academics supported the repression by campus administrations.[558] It is also true that activist members of AZASO/SANSCO constituted a fairly small proportion of the total number of students on campuses.

In both SASO and AZASO/SANSCO, women were seriously under-represented in relation to the composition of student bodies. It has been argued that Black women suffered from a "triple oppression: race, class and sex". Also, some women activists argued that women were "socialised into particular roles" and were "forced to accept their subservient position in society as natural". The educational system was also seen as a factor in perpetuating sexism. AZASO appointed a women's organiser in 1983 and held a women's conference in 1984 with a view to organising women around issues which specifically concerned them, whilst linking these to the struggle for democracy. As was so often the case with a range of organisations, AZASO/SANSCO established special women's sections in its branches. This approach was not very successful, and it was only in the late 1980s that some progress was made. However, male students were less committed than they should have been to women's engagement in these organisations, and branches did not implement their mandates in this regard. Patriarchy persisted as a problem.[559]

Specific types of student associations also reflected the broader racial divisions. For example, in 1981 seven student bodies petitioned the International Federation of Medical Students' Associations to expel the South African Medical Student's Association (SAMSA) from the world organisation. The student organisations – including the Medical Students' Council of the University of the Witwatersrand, the executive of the Wits SRC, NUSAS, Natal University Medical SRC, Wits Black Students' Society, and Wits Medical School Black Students' Society – argued that SAMSA did not accept "the principle that politics and health were inseparable".[560] In 1981/2, student organisations received moral support from the Black Academic Staff Association (BASA) at the University of the North. BASA issued a statement

---

[558] Ibid., pp. 301-302.
[559] Ibid., pp. 268-272.
[560] SAIRR, *1981 Survey,* pp. 407-408.

protesting against detention without trial and the disruption of classes by the security police.[561]

Student organisations played a crucial role in the political education and mobilisation of a generation of anti-apartheid activists of all races, many of whom became major actors in the anti-apartheid movement and later in the post-1994 democratic transition. Perhaps most important, participation in these student groups provided thousands of young people with experience of democratic decision-making and various forms of collective action   both of which have stood them in good stead as they engage in the structures of the new democratic South Africa.

Nonetheless, the pre-existing ethnic and linguistic divisions within and amongst universities and student organisations still manifest themselves in South Africa today. Students at universities, technikons and colleges still find themselves largely socially segregated – even though it could be said to be by choice now rather than by statute. It will take decades and millions of rands to overcome these barriers.

The labour movement

Government's obstinate refusal to allow the registration of African trade unions was probably the single most challenging issue of the post-1948 period for the entire labour movement in South Africa. The protests of African workers became louder and louder, and more and more unions across the racial and political spectrum joined their chorus. Individual unions varied enormously in their views on this matter, and their positions changed over time. Some left their federations due to differences of opinion on this issue.

Inevitably, trade unions became embroiled in politics early on. However, there were unions and federations that tried to stay out of the political fray and to concentrate on the needs of workers. Given the nature of the prevailing labour issues and their direct linkage to the inequalities and discrimination inherent in the political system, it was difficult if not impossible to be apolitical. Those who argued that unions should focus on economics and not politics only demonstrated their naivety. There were many attempts to unify the various union federations, but varying political stances largely prevented these from making much headway.

Up to the 1950s, most unions belonged to the Trades and Labour Council (TLC). These included exclusively White unions and mixed race unions of varying composition. Even though African unions could not legally register, the TLC allowed a small number to affiliate. Most African workers belonged to unions affiliated to the Council of Non-European Trade Unions (CNETU) formed in 1941. By 1945, CNETU claimed a membership of 158,000, organised into 119 affiliates. Baskin argues that having so many unions, rather than a few strong national affiliates, weakened CNETU's chances of surviving.[562] The TLC was losing strength by the mid-1950s and was further damaged by the government order under the Suppression of Communism Act to fifty or so union leaders (non-Communists) to resign and to stay away from union gatherings.

In 1954, the South African Trade Union Council (soon to be renamed the Trade Union Council of South Africa – TUCSA) was established for those unions who did not insist on the admission of Africans. Its members were registered unions, many but not all of which were multi-racial. However, especially its powerful craft union members were anxious to protect their jobs against African entry. White unions were particularly parochial in terms of protecting their specific interests. As a result, TUCSA dithered on the question of accepting

---

[561] SAIRR, *1982 Survey,* p. 515.
[562] Baskin, 1991, p. 11.

unregistered African unions. Nonetheless, TUCSA was the largest union federation at this time, and had quite a few Coloured and Indian members.

In 1956, government passed the amended Industrial Conciliation Act which "prohibited the registration of racially mixed unions and facilitated the splitting of existing unions along racial lines, and for those unions which did not split, insisted on racially separate branches and all-White executive committees". It also gave the Minister the power to reserve jobs according to race.[563] The Act was used to protect semi-skilled White workers from competition from Black (African, Indian and Coloured) workers. This approach inevitably divided workers and consequently reduced their bargaining power across the board.

The TLC disbanded in 1954, and its affiliates joined with most of the CNETU affiliates to establish the South African Congress of Trade Unions (SACTU) in March 1955. SACTU had, at its formation, a membership of 19 unions and about 20,000 individuals. It was part of the Congress alliance and endorsed the adoption of the Freedom Charter. It advocated the right of admission of Africans to all unions. At its first annual conference in 1956, SACTU stated its position on the need for political unionism:

> "SACTU is conscious of the fact that the organising of the mass of workers for higher wages, better conditions of life and labour is inextricably bound up with a determined struggle for political rights and liberation from all oppressive laws and practices. It follows that a mere struggle for the economic rights of all workers without participation in the general struggle for political emancipation would condemn the trade union movement to uselessness and to a betrayal of the interests of the workers".[564]

SACTU launched a number of mass campaigns which helped to promote its organising efforts. The most important of these was the "pound-a-day" campaign. SACTU, with ANC support, called for a one day stay-away on 26 June 1957, and 70-80% of workers in Johannesburg, Vereeniging and Port Elizabeth participated. Partly as a result of this action, government and employers offered the first real wage increases in years. Then, angry at the prospect of the upcoming all-White election of 1958, the ANC and SACTU and other groups in the Congress alliance organised a second "National Workers' Conference" in 1958 which decided to call a stay-away for three days in protest. When the first day had mixed results, the ANC called off the protest without consulting SACTU. This caused strains in the Congress alliance, but the two organisations continued to work closely together.[565]

SACTU grew to a membership of 35 affiliates and 46,000 members by 1959 as a result of active grassroots organisation and the building of structures starting at factory level. Not surprisingly, it never made an effort to organise White workers despite its non-racial stance. After Sharpeville and the banning of the ANC and PAC in 1960, along with the ANC / SACP initiation of the armed struggle in 1961, most of the SACTU leadership joined Umkhonto we Sizwe (MK). "The combination of crippling discrimination at the level of the industrial relations system, the deployment of wide-ranging security legislation, and the deep-seated, indeed intractable, divisions in the union movement, ensured that by the mid-1960s SACTU had all but ceased to exist".[566] Remnants of its leadership continued to operate in exile. Its major contribution was "planting the roots of non-racial trade unionism in the soil of apartheid South Africa".[567]

---

[563] Karis, Carter and Gerhart, 1977, Vol. 3, p. 54. The legislation was debated starting in 1954 and the unions were all too aware of its potential consequences.
[564] Cited in Baskin, 1991, p. 13.
[565] Baskin, 1991, p. 14.
[566] Karis and Gerhart, 1997, Vol. 5, p. 193.
[567] Baskin, 1991, p. 16.

After 1973, SACTU activists outside the country campaigned for recognition and support under the wing of the ANC and the SACP. SACTU's position on the internal trade union movement was at best ambivalent. On the one hand, they claimed to influence and lead events inside the country and yet argued that they were the authentic leaders of the workers' movement. As late as June 1982, in "SACTU's Present Role", a Lusaka 1982 mimeo, the organisation spoke on the one hand of the "open trade union movement becoming a powerful force" yet it reiterated the view that repression would win: "SACTU was forced underground. And there is nothing to suggest that the apartheid regime will ever tolerate a strong, progressive and open trade union movement for very long. It would be a mistake to act on this basis". This defeatist attitude probably stemmed from SACTU's distance from union mobilisation efforts within the country.

Some CNETU affiliates refused to join SACTU and maintained an unofficial link with TUCSA for several years. In 1959 they joined the Federation of Free African Trade Unions of South Africa (FOFATUSA). FOFATUSA leaders were not comfortable with the closeness of SACTU with the Congress alliance. They argued that SACTU had lost its autonomy and had become a "political tool of the Congress alliance 'multi-racialists'". It is therefore a little ironic that they proceeded to align themselves instead with the Pan Africanist Congress (PAC) which was keen to develop links with African unions.[568] FOFATUSA, despite its claim of 17,000 members, was unable to attract international support (and thus, funding) and it proved largely ineffective in mobilising African unions. The banning of the PAC in 1960 and the arrest of its leaders also hampered the progress of FOFATUSA.

The number of strikes dropped significantly in the early 1960s, due not least to the increased government repression of any group deemed to be "in opposition" to it or to apartheid. "Whereas between 1955 and 1960 there had been an average of 76 strikes a year, in 1962 and 1963 this dropped to 16 and 17 respectively. Although the numbers increased somewhat over the rest of the decade, they remained considerably below the average for the latter half of the 1950s."[569] Whilst the South African economy was growing at a substantial rate and corporate profits soared, the Black working class did not benefit.

TUCSA continued to maintain its apolitical position, but because of its large number of Coloured and Indian affiliates it had to begin to engage at least in a small way in opposing some of the worst aspects of apartheid as it affected the workplace. Finally, in 1965, it took a mild stand against job reservation on the basis that there was no longer a need for it as there were not enough Whites to fill all the reserved jobs. Their new position, therefore, had nothing to do with the inherent injustice of job reservation. Some TUCSA member unions were more outspoken, but they failed to push the federation to take a stronger stand. TUCSA's view on the admission of unregistered African unions was "both pragmatic and paternalistic" – they tried to maintain credibility with the broader labour movement (local and international) by "keeping the issue of African union affiliation alive" but made few concrete moves in this direction.[570] Its centrist positioning failed to satisfy any of the role players – government, affiliate unions, African workers, etc. But, in the absence of SACTU, unions had few choices. In light of the continuing government repression of the labour movement, unions aimed simply to stay alive and to maintain their membership during the 1960s.

By the early 1970s, government had not changed its view about permitting African workers to form and register trade unions. Nonetheless, new opportunities presented themselves for African workers in the early 1970s. Other civil society organisations were pressing for a policy change and for a newly strengthened union movement, e.g. the BCM, radical

---

[568] Karis, Carter and Gerhart, 1977, Vol. 3, pp. 55-56.
[569] Karis and Gerhart, 1997, Vol. 5, p. 193.
[570] Karis and Gerhart, 1997, Vol. 5, pp. 194-195.

university student groups such as SASO, former SACTU activists, and dissident members of TUCSA. The emergence of the Black Allied Workers Union (BAWU), a general union open to all Black workers, emerged out of SASO's Black Workers' Project and the Black People's Convention (BPC).[571] BAWU issued a "call to organise and form Black trade unions" which strongly criticised TUCSA for being deceitful, misleading Black workers about the opportunities to form multi-racial unions, trying to pull the wool over the eyes of international labour, and suppressing Black initiative through its patronising approach. BAWU called for Black workers to form their own trade unions and to be given legal recognition. They also recognised that:

> "Black worker interests extend beyond the factory: they extend to the ghetto where Black workers stay together in hostels under squalid conditions; to the crowded trains and buses – to the absence of amenities – to the stringent, irksome and humiliating application of influx control laws – to the lack of proper channels whereby people could equip themselves with basic skills."[572]

BAWU also demanded the right to collective bargaining, a living wage for all Black workers, the removal of job reservation, and training facilities for Black workers in industry and commerce. It had little success though, reaching only about 1,000 paid-up members by 1977 out of a claimed 6,000 members. Repeated splits and the banning of its leader, Drake Koka, led to its demise.[573]

White students also became involved in Black worker issues through NUSAS' Wages Commissions on its affiliated campuses. These commissions conducted research into wages and working conditions and conducted advocacy on behalf of Black workers. NUSAS also opened advice offices for workers who had legal problems and helped others form works committees which "offered a halfway house to unorganised workers trying to draw themselves into closer forms of co-operation".[574]

TUCSA's inconsistent attitude towards African unions led it to lose affiliates from both sides of the issue. In 1976, the Boilermakers' Society quit TUCSA because it opposed the movement of African workers into skilled jobs. They said they could not protect their Coloured and Indian members' jobs "at the same time as putting Africans into their union as proposed by TUCSA. We cannot allow Africans to move into their jobs". The National Union of Furniture and Allied Workers disaffiliated from TUCSA for the same reason. In contrast, other unions such as the National Union of Motor Assembly Rubber Workers threatened to disaffiliate as TUCSA was not doing enough for Africans. At the same time, White workers in the right-wing South African Confederation of Labour feared losing their jobs to Blacks, and were also unhappy about the lack of retraining opportunities.[575]

TUCSA's negative attitude to the affiliation of African unions led a number of unions with African members to disaffiliate. It also led a number of officials and members to leave the federation, e.g. the head of TUCSA's African Affairs Bureau, Eric Tyacke, left and was instrumental in the creation of the Urban Training Project (UTP) based in Johannesburg in 1970, a group which focused on training and providing advice to workers, including members of unions which had been former TUCSA affiliates. The UTP later became the educational arm of the Consultative Committee of Black Trade Unions (CCOBTU) in 1973, which in turn

---

[571] Ibid., p. 198.
[572] See Document 80, "Call to Organise and Form Black Trade Unions in South Africa", Statement by the Black Allied Workers' Union, Johannesburg, 1973?, in Karis and Gerhart, 1997, Vol. 5, pp. 607-610.
[573] Baskin, 1991, p. 19.
[574] Karis and Gerhart, 1997, Vol. 5, p. 199.
[575] SAIRR, 1976 Survey, pp. 315-316.

was the precursor of the Council of Unions of South Africa (CUSA), formed in 1979. The CCOBTU unions claimed a paid-up membership of 19,000 by 1976.[576]

In Durban, the General Factory Workers' Benefit Fund was established in 1972 to represent Black workers. It was overtaken by the Trade Union Advisory and Co-ordinating Council (TUACC) in 1973 as an umbrella group comprised of some parallel African unions formed by TUCSA affiliates as well as some independent unions. TUACC claimed to represent over 45,000 workers in Natal. In 1975 it called on TUCSA to consult with the unregistered union movement as to how more progress could be made especially with regard to African trade unionisation.[577] The Industrial Aid Society (IAS) was established in 1974 to assist the TUACC unions to set up Transvaal branches. These unions in turn formed the Council of Industrial Workers of the Witwatersrand (CIWW) in 1975.[578] In the Cape, the Western Province Workers' Advice Bureau (WPWAB) was established with the help of the local NUSAS Wages Commission. By 1976, it had a membership of 5,000. The WPWAB later changed its name to the Western Province General Workers Union (WPGWU), the forerunner of the General Workers Union (GWU).[579] These and other groups represented the large portion of the progressive trade union movement which was extremely frustrated with the constraints they faced in organising and assisting Black workers.

In August 1972, at the annual congress of the Trade Union Council of South Africa (TUCSA) 50 affiliated unions representing more than 190,000 White, Coloured and Indian workers adopted a resolution calling for individual affiliates to establish parallel unions for African workers. They did this on the assumption that government was not likely to permit the registration of African unions.[580] In March 1973, the Students' Representative Council's Wages Commission at the University of Cape Town issued a *Charter of Workers' Rights* which called, *inter alia*, for all workers to "have the right to free association and the right to organise", and insisted that "every worker, regardless of race, colour or creed, should have equality of opportunity in respect of training and employment".[581]

The Durban strikes of 1973 marked a turning point in labour struggles. Between January and March of that year, more than 146 firms faced strikes by over 61,000 workers. These were the largest actions taken by workers since the 1946 Black miners' strike in 1946 and the White miners' strike of 1922. They differed from earlier strikes in that there were no visible leaders – the strikes seemingly emanated from the mass of workers themselves. Furthermore, many of the strikes were successful, resulting in wage increases for the workers. Many Whites in Durban seemed to sympathise with the workers, and the government's response was relatively mild in comparison to past actions. Even Prime Minister Vorster said that employers should "recognise [workers] as human beings with souls", not just as "a unit producing for them so many hours of service a day".[582] The Minister of Labour, however, was not impressed and continued his attacks on the unions.

Nonetheless, these strikes initiated a resurgence of worker activism. Ncube argued that:

> "It was precisely this racial separation and the 1973 strike waves which prepared the ground for the unprecedented growth of a new brand of trade unionism in this country. The emergent unions were predominantly organised along the lines of

[576] Baskin, 1991, p. 19.
[577] See Document 81, "Memorandum for the 21st Annual General Conference of TUCSA, by the affiliates of TUACC, 23 September 1975, in Karis and Gerhart, 1997, Vol. 5, pp. 610-612.
[578] Baskin, 1991, p. 19.
[579] Ibid., p. 19.
[580] SAIRR, *1973 Survey*, p. 269.
[581] Ibid., pp. 267-268.
[582] Karis and Gerhart, 1997, Vol. 5, pp. 202-203.

existing industries and were imbued with the spirit of forming independent and legitimate worker organisations. In the main these unions were underpinned by two dominant ideological schools, namely non-racialism and Black Consciousness".[583]

Thus, to some extent at least, the divisions in the union movement corresponded to those in the broader political tendencies at the time. Some White unions tried to argue that unions should remain apolitical and focus solely on economic issues. Whilst this may have worked to some extent amongst exclusively White unions, it was totally untenable for Black workers and their unions. Hostility from employers and the government meant that even attempts to use official channels to air their grievances pushed the Black unions into more radical action.

Police harassment grew in tandem with this increasing activism and defiance. Eleven Black miners were shot in 1973 in Carletonville, and in 1974, several key White unionists in Durban were banned. African unionists were detained.[584] In 1976, government served five-year banning orders on 22 trade unionists (mostly White) who had been involved in helping to organise African trade unions or in conducting research on Black labour. The banned individuals were members of various organisations, including the Urban Training Project, the Industrial Aid Society, the Institute for Industrial Education, the Institute of Industrial Relations, the Trade Union Advisory and Co-ordinating Council, Students' Wages Commissions, or the Western Province Advice Bureau.[585]

In the second half of the 1970s, some of the most important employers in the country were beginning to realise that the legitimisation of African unions was inevitable. International pressure on multinational companies was rapidly increasing and calls for sanctions and disinvestment were becoming louder. Stronger shop-floor organisation was also a factor. That the unions in the 1970s were more focused on specific labour issues and less on broader political ones (unlike SACTU of the 1960s) may have also increased the changing response. The student uprisings in 1976 fuelled the growth of unions. Nonetheless, when 18 civil society organisations were banned in 1977, the unions were not. By 1978, even government was offering more hints that trade union rights might be accorded to African workers.

The appointment of the Wiehahn Commission in 1977 instigated an examination of required changes to the industrial relations system. The government thought that by giving African unions legal status and bringing them under existing labour law, they would be better able to control them. They expected that such a situation would give African unions a greater stake in the status quo and would thus moderate their actions. The Commission included representatives of the state, employers, TUCSA and right-wing unions, but no progressive unions. Its report in 1979 recommended that "African workers be incorporated in the definition of 'employee' and be permitted to form and join registered entities". The reasons cited for this recommendation included:

- The need to "insulate the unions from the political world of the townships";
- The need to "insulate the state from industrial relations lest the state become a target of worker activism".[586]

Government was not inclined to risk adoption of this recommendation without further restrictions, e.g. that trade union rights should not include migrant workers. But the strong protests against this proposal forced government to retract it and to accept the Wiehahn recommendation.

---

[583] Ncube, 1985, p. 114.
[584] Karis and Gerhart, 1997, Vol. 5, p. 205.
[585] SAIRR, *1976 Survey*, p. 315.
[586] Karis and Gerhart, 1997, Vol. 5, p. 212.

Webster wrote that "the Wiehahn solution was clearly contradictory. The intention was to control the emerging unions by drawing them into the established industrial relations structures, in particular the industrial councils, thus pre-empting the unions' attempts to establish a shop-floor presence. However, this required giving these unions official recognition, enabling them to gain more space in their attempt to move beyond the struggle for recognition to direct negotiations at shop-floor level."[587] Friedman summarised the main conclusions of the Wiehahn report as follows: "The unions' potential strength meant that they must be controlled – their present weakness... meant that this should be done soon... It would... be 'far healthier' to allow the unions to register at an 'early stage'... This would counter 'polarisation', ensure 'a more orderly process of bargaining', and expose African unions 'more directly to South Africa's trade union traditions, and the existing institutions thus inculcating a sense of responsibility for a free market'."[588] Such cynical viewpoints did not, however, deny the reality that recognition was now possible for Black unions.

Registered Trade Unions in South Africa

	1972	1978	1982	1988	1991
Racially exclusive unions					
White	88	83	71	40	37
Asian / Coloured	48	50	46	26	11
African	-	-	26	28	17
Mixed unions					127
White, Coloured & Asian	42	41	16	6	n/a
Coloured, Asian & African	-	-	10	19	n/a
African and White	-	-	-	6	n/a
All population groups	-	-	30	62	n/a
Unspecified	-	-	-	22	n/a
TOTAL	178	174	199	209	192
Total membership	637,480	692,102	1,226,454	2,000,000	2,700,000
No. of union federations	11	10	13	10	7

Source: SAIRR, *1983 Survey*, p. 177; SAIRR, *1992/3 Survey*, p. 321.

Once the government had accepted the Wiehahn policy changes, vigorous debate began within the union movement itself as to whether to register or not. Some feared that the existing industrial relations system would constrain both the internal democracy favoured by their members and their advocacy activity if they registered. It should also be noted that registration implied regular financial accounting to government as well as regular reporting on membership. Some unions were not sure they wanted government to have such a window onto their internal operations. Others saw advantages in using the existing mechanisms of the industrial relations system for their benefit. All of the unions agreed on one point – that the prevailing system still needed much reform.

Major changes took place in 1979 and 1980 with the formation of two new trade union federations. The Federation of South African Trade Unions (FOSATU) was established in April 1979 with a total paid-up membership of about 20,000 workers amongst 12 unions.[589] It was open to all unions and all races. The founding affiliates included three former TUCSA unions, six unions from the TUACC group, and three from CCOBTU/UTP. A fourth union from the latter group joined soon thereafter. Alec Erwin was FOSATU's first general secretary. Baskin described FOSATU as "a tight federation with strongly centralised decision-making, and policies binding on affiliates. It pioneered the principle of direct worker control in South Africa, with worker delegates constituting a majority in all structures of the

---

[587] Webster, 1988, p. 180.

[588] Friedman, 1987, p. 6.

[589] Baskin, 1991, p. 25. A frequently cited figure of 45,000 members did not refer to paid-up members.

federation. It also developed the system of union branch executive committees composed of delegates from every factory, rather than a branch executive which was elected at an annual general meeting. Other key FOSATU principles involved non-racialism, shop-floor organisation, a stress on developing shop stewards, and worker independence from political organisations. It favoured intensive organising, based on the targeting of key plants".[590]

FOSATU decided that its affiliates would apply for registration, but only if they were granted "non-racial" status. By the end of 1981, FOSATU was the largest union grouping with 95,000 members in 387 organised factories.[591] It adopted some of the mobilising methods of the "community unions", e.g. engaging in local community issues such as housing, but also learned from their failures, e.g. organisational weaknesses. It focused on developing local shop steward councils as the foundation of the federation structures and developed an emphasis on worker control, mandates and report backs. It also maintained a distance from the UDF, arguing for the importance of working class autonomy.[592]

The Council of Unions of South Africa (CUSA) was founded in September 1980, with most of the CCOBTU group joining. Initially, CUSA had 9 affiliates with 30,000 members. It differed from FOSATU in its rejection of "'non-racialism' in favour of 'black leadership', charging, with some justification, that there were too many Whites in influential positions within FOSATU". It was organised as a looser federation, giving its affiliates more flexibility and autonomy in determining their positions on issues and actions to be taken.[593] Phiroshaw Camay was elected as the first general secretary of CUSA.

One of the most important contributions made by CUSA was its initiative to establish the National Union of Mineworkers (NUM) in 1982. CUSA appointed Cyril Ramaphosa to lead the initiative, and within two years, NUM claimed 110,000 members – drastically increasing CUSA's total membership. For various reasons, however, NUM disaffiliated from CUSA and joined COSATU in 1985.

Another contribution was its decision to build women's participation in the union movement, way ahead of FOSATU and other federations. CUSA adopted a Women's Charter early in 1983. It also began promoting Health and Safety Charters for various unions.

FOSATU and CUSA formed the core of a growing independent and democratic labour movement within the country. Both federations were respected and listened to in local quarters as well as regional and international forums. They and all their member affiliates as well as Black unions independent of these two federations such as the General and Allied Workers Union (GAWU), the South African Allied Workers Union (SAAWU), the African Food and Canning Workers Union (AFCWU), all agreed that they had a political role: it was the nature and context of their involvement which eluded the debate.

Huge growth in African union membership occurred over only two years in the early 1980s. The International Labour Organisation (ILO) Report on South Africa presented to the ILO Conference under the Declaration against Apartheid in 1984, noted the following union membership figures:

Union membership	1981	1983
Africans	360 000	545 000
Whites	468 000	488 000
Coloureds & Indians	327 000	343 000

---

[590] Ibid., pp. 25-26.
[591] Ibid., p. 29.
[592] Ibid., p. 31.
[593] Ibid., p. 30.

The ILO also reported on the membership of the trade union federations in South Africa, reflecting the rapid growth of FOSATU and CUSA relative to the established White-led federations:

Trade union federation membership in 1984			
Federation	Acronym	Member-ship base	Number
1. Federation of South African Unions	FOSATU	non-racial	106 000
2. Council of Unions of South Africa	CUSA	anti-racist	248 000
3. Trade Union Council of South Africa	TUCSA	mixed	446 000
4. South Africa Confederation of Labour	SACOL	white	126 000
5. Various unaffiliated unions		various	550 000

In 1981, the Mine Surface Officials Association (MSOA) opened its ranks to African membership with the Minister's approval. However, it accused the Chamber of Mines of refusing to acknowledge that Africans were acting as officials on the mines. The MSOA argued that Africans recruited for these jobs should be employed under the same conditions as Whites. In contrast, the all-White Mine Workers' Union threatened to go on strike if African miners were given blasting certificates – a highly skilled aspect of the job. They rationalised their threat by denying that there was a shortage of White skilled workers in the mining industry.[594] Thus, job reservation for Whites continued to be a contentious issue, especially on the mines. In other industries, labour shortages had been recognised and African workers were being trained as artisans, skilled production line workers and managers, e.g. in the automobile and building industries.

Progress also came in other forms. In 1981, the AHI and the FCI resolved to recognise African trade unions, both registered and unregistered. They did, however, encourage unregistered unions to join the "official" labour relations system. By 1982, the Chamber of Mines, which had previously refused to negotiate with unregistered unions, had changed its policy and agreed to recognise unions which refused to register with the government. The Chamber also acknowledged the need to speed up the abolition of job reservation on the mines.[595] These changing positions were no doubt partly a result of the Wiehahn Commission's report. As noted above, it had recommended that all workers should be entitled to freedom of association and trade union autonomy, and that registration of unions should remain voluntary rather than compulsory.[596]

In 1982, Reverend Denis Hurley of the Catholic Church added the moral weight of the Church in support of the Black trade union movement. He urged management to make good use of the opportunities offered by the new trade unions and stressed their importance in achieving transformation in labour relations.[597]

When the United Democratic Front (UDF) and its precursor, the National Forum Committee (NFC) were established, the internal union movement split once again on how to be engaged in these movements. FOSATU leadership's position, echoed by the General Workers Union (GWU) and the African Food and Canning Workers Union (AFCWU), was that workers must first establish their own perspective and organisational capacity. The alternate view was taken by CUSA which argued that both the UDF and the NFC deserved the support of the workers as members had a diversity of political views. CUSA pledged to

---

[594] SAIRR, *1981 Survey*, pp. 151-153.
[595] SAIRR, *1982 Survey*, p. 116.
[596] SAIRR, *1981 Survey*, pp. 200-201.
[597] SAIRR, *1982 Survey*, p. 577.

support all forces and all efforts to work towards a common citizenship in an undivided, democratic and just society. Some general workers unions such as the General and Allied Workers Union (GAWU) and the South African Allied Workers Union (SAAWU) joined only the UDF.

FOSATU did not rule out the possibility of supporting some of the campaigns of the UDF. The position to affiliate only to the UDF taken by GAWU, SAAWU, etc. was based on the code word 'non-racial' which at that time signified support for the Freedom Charter and hence the ANC. The CUSA position was based on supporting all organisations which opposed the tricameral parliament. CUSA was willing to work with such organisations on a principled basis for the achievement of a just society.

Whilst the new non-racial unions were building strong democratic industrial unions, they were also building a workers' culture through song and dance, newspapers and biographies. They concentrated on building leadership and on health and safety issues as well as other worker rights. These issues were easy to deal with compared to their need to identify with the social and mass movements of the time.

Meanwhile, FOSATU and CUSA and some of the unaffiliated unions had begun informal discussions about federation unity with a view to achieving strength through a unified worker movement. In August 1981, the first major formal consultation on this issue was held in Langa, convened by the GWU and attended by all the major emerging unions and representatives of both FOSATU and CUSA. "The Langa summit aimed to develop a united response to the newly introduced labour laws which had emerged from the Wiehahn report. The emerging unions were conscious that these provisions aimed to divide and control them while at the same time extending rights previously denied to Black unions".[598] The conference did manage to put unity on the agenda, but little concrete emerged other than agreement to create joint solidarity committees.

The death in police custody of Neil Aggett, an organiser for FCWU/AFCWU, in early 1982 was another turning point. It resulted in a call for a 30-minute work stoppage in factories less than a week later. Over 40,000 workers responded. This success was a major confidence boost as the first labour initiative attempting to mobilise workers nationally at their workplaces, over an issue that went beyond the factory floor.

More talk of unity and the creation of a new federation continued throughout 1982-84, but not without problems. The unrest of 1984 and campaigning by student, community and union groupings against the elections for the tricameral racially-based parliament led to changes within the union movement. UDF unions were excluded from the talks due to their lack of autonomy, especially as perceived by FOSATU leaders. Disagreement over the plans for unity led NUM in mid-1984 to decide to join the new federation even if CUSA decided not to.[599] SACTU was pushing for unity from its base in exile. Then, the formation of the Azanian Confederation of Trade Unions (AZACTU) in 1984, grouping unions adhering to the Black Consciousness tradition, also created a new factor in the prospects for unity.

When COSAS called for union support of the student struggles in October 1984, the November Transvaal-specific stay-away was organised jointly by FOSATU, the Soweto Youth Congress, the Release Mandela Committee (RMC) and UDF-affiliated unions. This time, 800,000 workers from the Witwatersrand and the Vaal Triangle participated. This led to the re-inclusion of UDF unions in the unity talks. Then on 8-9 June 1985, unity talks reopened, with the participation of a wide range of unions. Delegates were asked to pronounce themselves on the draft constitution of a new federation and on five unifying

---

[598] Baskin, 1991, p. 35.
[599] Ibid., p. 43.

principles: non-racialism, one union--one industry, worker control, representation on the basis of paid-up membership, and co-operation at national level. Many CUSA and AZACTU affiliates were not willing to endorse the constitution or the principles for various reasons. It was at this point that it became clearer which unions would be likely to join a new federation and which would not.[600]

The Congress of South African Trade Unions (COSATU) was finally launched in November 1985 at a conference of 760 delegates from 33 unions, representing about 460,000 organised workers.[601] In opening the conference, Cyril Ramaphosa, general secretary of NUM, argued that the "struggle of workers on the shop floor cannot be separated from the wider political struggle for liberation in this country". But he added that "if we are to get into alliances with other progressive organisations, it must be on terms that are favourable to us as workers".[602] The conference resolutions called for "the lifting of the state of emergency, withdrawal of troops from the townships, release of political prisoners and unbanning of all restricted individuals and organisations. Delegates also agreed, in defiance of the law, that all forms of international pressure, 'including disinvestment or the threat of disinvestment', were essential and should be supported". They also called for the right to strike and picket, and for a national minimum living wage. The Bantustans and the resultant migrant labour system were also condemned.[603] Elected officials included Elijah Barayi as president, Chris Dlamini as vice-president, and Jay Naidoo as general secretary and Sidney Mufamadi as assistant general secretary. Both the UDF and SACTU welcomed the launch of COSATU, and the ANC from exile encouraged COSATU to become more involved in UDF activities.

Inkatha president and Chief Minister of KwaZulu, Mangosuthu Buthelezi, quickly expressed his concerns about COSATU. This was partly a result of unwise remarks by Elijah Barayi directly attacking Buthelezi. Buthelezi responded by accusing COSATU of being a front for the ANC and of "declaring war on Inkatha". He also disapproved of COSATU's stand in support of disinvestment. His solution was to launch Inkatha's own union federation – the United Workers Union of South Africa (UWUSA). The result was open confrontation and violence between the two federations in the Natal region. Workers and shop stewards were ultimately the victims of pressure from both sides. Some employers were also wary of potential conflict in their factories.[604]

COSATU tried to defuse the tension by downplaying the conflict, arguing that "if political differences between COSATU and any other organisation exist then we do not see this as 'a state of war'".[605] However, these political differences were fundamental and the war of words continued. The conflict escalated and attacks on officials on both sides occurred throughout 1986. But UWUSA never gained much support at factory level, and many who had initially joined its ranks returned to COSATU. Baskin concluded that "UWUSA was a major political error by Buthelezi. While it placed COSATU on the defensive to some extent, it alienated Buthelezi totally and irreversibly from the organised labour movement". UWUSA's membership went from 85,000 at its launch to 150,000 in 1987, but it fell to less than 50,000 by mid-1988.[606]

COSATU's arrival on the scene also led to the final dissolution of TUCSA in December 1986. TUCSA had been unable to offer valuable services to its affiliates despite its high affiliation fees. Its continued domination by Whites and its political conservatism were fatal.

---

[600] Ibid., pp. 45-50.
[601] Ibid., p. 53.
[602] Cited in Ibid., p. 54.
[603] Ibid., pp. 58-59.
[604] Ibid., pp. 71-72.
[605] Ibid., p. 131.
[606] Ibid., pp. 133-134.

Nonetheless, COSATU was unable to attract many of TUCSA's former affiliates for some time.[607]

Further changes to the federation landscape occurred in October 1986 when CUSA merged with AZACTU and changed its name to the National Council of Trade Unions (NACTU). Together they claimed 23 affiliated unions (12 from CUSA and 11 from AZACTU). The new federation elected James Mndaweni as president, with Phiroshaw Camay (formerly general secretary of CUSA) as general secretary, and Mahlomola Skhosana and Pandelani Nefolovhodwe (formerly general secretary of AZACTU) as assistant general secretaries. Similar to CUSA, NACTU adopted principles of "worker control based on anti-racism/non-racialism; black working-class leadership; political non-affiliation; financial accountability within unions; and independent internal actions by unions within federation policy".[608]

Much debate has surrounded the differences between COSATU and NACTU. The political differences were perhaps easier to define than any other principle distinctions. COSATU, through the influence of the general workers unions, adopted a closer position to the ANC, whilst NACTU remained independent of political organisations. Some leaders within NACTU, however, overtly supported the Black Consciousness Movement and others the PAC, whilst others supported the ANC. However, there was never the type of conflict between these two federations as had transpired between COSATU and UWUSA.[609]

Despite the growth in membership, the lack of unity amongst the Black trade union federations undermined union leverage. Emphasising this issue of union unity and mutual assistance, the general secretary of NACTU, Phiroshaw Camay, noted in June 1987:

> "We foresee over the short- to medium-term that government will hammer various worker bodies. This requires a concerted response on the part of the union movement and we are trying to lay the ground in anticipation. If the unions are united, our response will be more coherent and logical... In the long term, we would want to see all workers united in one federation".[610]

Camay said of the political positioning by NACTU and unions in general:

> "Among our members there would be adherence to all those ideological groups [BC, Africanist, Charterist]. But NACTU itself is independent of all these movements and will decide on its own path. Trade unions are by their nature democratic bodies; that means there is a plurality of views. But it does not mean that ideological differences override the collective ideas of the workers... In fact it is the needs of the workers which override the narrowness of those positions. It is time that people got away from the naïve belief that the Freedom Charter belongs to one political group. It belongs to us all. It is a basic historical document and has to be respected. But there are other documents like the National Forum Manifesto which should be respected and these things should be the basis of a new society".[611]

The Labour Relations Act

The union campaigns against the government's and employers' proposed changes to the Labour Relations Act proved this sentiment that the needs of workers should be paramount. In 1987, moves were made to amend the labour law such that it would restrict the right to strike, reduce job security, impose punitive damages for illegal strike action, and reduce the

---

[607] Ibid., pp. 161-162.
[608] Ibid., p. 158.
[609] COSATU's goal of "one country, one federation" has yet to be realised in 2006.
[610] SAIRR, *1987/88 Survey*, p. 614.
[611] Ibid., p. 615.

powers of the industrial court by including in the law a schedule of 'unfair labour practices'. The proposals also threatened to reverse the principle of majoritarianism – that a union should have more than 50% support in a particular factory or company in order to call a strike – now that the majority was Black.[612]

Unions and federations had not been consulted on any of these proposals, and they quickly mobilised to oppose them. COSATU rejected the new bill in its entirety and embarked on a campaign of demonstrations and other means of spreading their message, e.g. on trains and buses, to avoid bans on meetings. COSATU also tried to build international pressure and to hold discussions with employer bodies.

The COSATU campaign was hugely affected by restrictions imposed on its political activities (it was not banned outright) at the same time that 17 anti-apartheid organisations were banned in February 1988. COSATU fought back, saying that:

> "The state is attempting to restrict COSATU to what they see as legitimate trade union functions. We reject this because there is no democracy in South Africa and COSATU and other organisations are part of the extra-parliamentary opposition that are legitimately putting forward the demands and interests of our members both on the shop-floor and in the broader society".[613]

COSATU resolved to ignore the new restrictions. It also called a special congress in May 1988 to consider the way forward. This congress was also attended by delegates from UDF affiliates who were given full speaking rights. Given the major differences of opinion regarding strategy and the risks of various actions expressed at the conference, it resolved to hold a broader conference of anti-apartheid groups and in particular, to co-operate more closely with NACTU. The conference also called for "three days of action" and "a national peaceful protest" on 6-8 June 1988 – euphemisms for a 'stay-away' which was not permitted under the state of emergency.

Regarding the bill, NACTU initially took the position that "neither business nor government would reject a bill so obviously favouring their interests". It opted to focus on "amending existing recognition agreements to protect its relationship with management, and protect its structures from the anti-union provisions of the bill". It also refused to make representations to the parliamentary sub-committee considering the bill as it did not wish to "co-operate with [apartheid] state structures".[614] However, immediately after the COSATU special congress, NACTU decided to call a five-day stay-away on 6-10 June. A meeting was held with COSATU, and NACTU agreed to support the three-day stay-away instead. This was a first step towards co-operation between the two federations.

In response, SACCOLA – the employers' umbrella association – tried to discredit the union leadership. They met with COSATU leaders to persuade them to call off the action, but the federation refused. Then the employers' tried to claim that "the revised version of the bill deals with most of the objections raised by COSATU". The Chamber of Mines joined the attack on COSATU, saying that it was "either unwilling or unable to back up its allegations that the bill was a repressive measure aimed at curbing trade union activity". The Chamber argued that the union protest must be politically motivated.[615] These statements tried to distract attention from the genuine grievances of the unions with regard to the legislation.

---

[612] Baskin, 1991, pp. 261-264.
[613] Quoted in Ibid., p. 269.
[614] Ibid., pp. 266-267.
[615] Ibid., pp. 285-286.

Between 2.5 and 3 million people stayed away from work on the first day, June 6th. These numbers decreased somewhat on the second and third days due to threats from employers and government that participating workers would be dismissed. Participation varied from region to region, with the strongest being in the Witwatersrand and Natal, and the weakest in the Western Cape. Mineworker participation was particularly low (between 9,000 and 35,000 depending on whose estimate was believed – the Chamber of Mines or NUM respectively). NUM had apparently not recovered from its strike the previous year.[616] Despite the inconsistent turnout, the stay-away was deemed a major success.

SACCOLA was persuaded that it needed to begin negotiations with COSATU and NACTU on the content of the bill. Whilst the three parties agreed on six "offensive clauses" to be suspended and subject to further negotiation, the government went ahead and promulgated the Labour Relations Amendment Act (LRA), ignoring the unions' agreement with SACCOLA. Naturally, the unions felt betrayed. They learned that mass protests should not cease whilst negotiations took place as this weakened the unions' position. Talks should not be an alternative but a complementary action. Nonetheless, the LRA was now on the agenda and the campaign and its outcome demonstrated just how undemocratic legislative processes were. Workers were also much more aware of labour law and its impact, and this experience increased their defiance and determination.

Following the failure of the Anti-Apartheid Conference initiated by COSATU and meant to include the widest possible spectrum of anti-apartheid groups, COSATU moved to consolidate its internal unity and build its strength. In contrast, at its national congress, there were indications that NACTU was losing membership. Its Africanist members and leaders were gaining support, particularly those aligned with the PAC, though the federation retained its stance of political non-alignment. Amongst its leaders, only Phiroshaw Camay and Mahlomola Skhosana were not part of the Africanist camp. They were re-elected in 1988 "more on the strength of their experience as unionists than their political affiliations".[617] NACTU did, however, agree at a meeting with the ANC in Harare in May 1988 that "it was imperative for the labour movement inside the country to strive toward unity with the eventual objective of a single labour federation".[618] At this point, NACTU appeared to be more willing to engage in unity negotiations than did COSATU.

In late 1988, the two federations met to discuss future action in response to the LRA. A worker summit was planned for March 1989, to be attended by worker delegates without union officials (the latter were seen as the cause of divisions). Negotiations between COSATU and NACTU leadership on the summit agenda made some progress and a principle agreement was reached. However, when the NACTU leadership went back to the federation structures to confirm the agreement, its national council requested a postponement of the summit so as to have more time to develop its position on unity. COSATU, however, decided to proceed with the summit. Subsequently, 11 NACTU affiliates (representing one-third of total membership) broke with the council and decided to attend the summit. NACTU general secretary Phiroshaw Camay expressed his frustration with the national council's decision, saying:

> "Despite the fact that congresses and national councils had taken decisions on building working-class unity, we found that representatives to a national council decided to ask for a postponement of the workers' summit when they actually knew that arrangements had progressed beyond a cancellation of the summit… To pull out of conferences or summits at the last minute for some small short-term political gains

---

[616] Ibid., pp. 287-288.
[617] Ibid., p. 311.
[618] Ibid., p. 312.

does not benefit unity of the working people nor does it benefit the unity of the liberation struggle as a whole".[619]

The summit went ahead, with all 14 COSATU affiliates in attendance, and 10 NACTU affiliates as well as individuals from some other NACTU unions and 16 unaffiliated unions. Though there was extensive debate and considerable disagreement on certain issues, the summit took a decision to relaunch the campaign against the LRA and to submit six major demands to employers. Initially, Cunningham Ngcukana of NACTU expressed dissatisfaction with the summit conclusions and the strategy adopted. But eventually, NACTU joined the anti-LRA campaign.

A second workers' summit was held near Soweto on 26 August 1989. It was attended by 750 worker delegates. However, its proceedings were constrained by the fact that "scores of police wearing riot-blue outfits and armed with R1 rifles, gas grenades and sten guns arrived at the summit venue in the early hours of the morning".[620] The police informed Chris Dlamini that the meeting had been restricted under emergency regulations and imposed certain conditions on the manner in which the summit could be conducted: no flags, banners or stickers; no speeches on issues other than the LRA; no singing or talking after 5 pm. This restriction was resisted in an urgent Superior Court petition led by Phiroshaw Camay. However, the state's advocate prolonged witness evidence such that at 5 pm the court action was abandoned as any decision by the Court then would be of academic interest only. To avoid some of the restrictions, delegates were broken up into small groups which the police could not adequately monitor. Thus, the summit was still able to adopt an action plan.

Another stay-away was planned for early September. On 5th September, about 39% of Black workers in the PWV area stayed away from work, and the next day this rose to 72%. In the Eastern Cape, over 80% of Black workers stayed home, and in the Durban area, 68% supported the action.[621] As with earlier actions, the response varied from region to region. The relatively successful stay-away was followed by other actions, with workers ignoring court interdicts, restrictions and bannings. The view that these repressive measures were the actions of an illegitimate government reinforced their defiance.

The National Defiance Campaign was launched by the Mass Democratic Movement, COSATU and the UDF. Many banned organisations openly participated. The de Klerk government began to make small concessions in repealing some apartheid laws such as the Separate Amenities Act so as to defuse the campaign. However, huge marches were organised in major urban areas. The Cape Town march of 50,000 people led by Archbishop Tutu and Jay Naidoo (COSATU general secretary) was followed by massive gatherings in smaller cities and towns. The fact that these gatherings were allowed at all showed the de Klerk government's more open approach, as opposed to that of P.W. Botha.

COSATU's frustration was compounded by the NACTU council's refusal to participate in the Conference for a Democratic Future (CDF) in December 1989. The CDF was an attempt to revive the 1988 Anti-Apartheid Conference which had been banned by government, and NACTU had sat on the convening committee. NACTU again withdrew at the last minute, this time due to unhappiness with the proposed presence of some Bantustan leaders. Again, some of the non-Africanist NACTU leaders decided to attend the CDF, despite the

---

[619] Interview cited in Ibid., p. 322.
[620] Ibid., pp. 388-389.
[621] Ibid., p. 390.

federation's decision. The most important issue at the CDF was whether or not the democratic movement should begin negotiations with the government.[622]

Negotiations with SACCOLA proceeded in an on-off fashion, with the employers refusing to yield much ground. By March 1990, however, SACCOLA and the National Manpower Commission indicated their willingness rethink the labour law. On 11 May 1990, COSATU, NACTU and SACCOLA signed an accord which "endorsed basic labour rights for all workers and agreed to reverse the most offensive provisions of the 1988 amendments".[623] Government agreed to further consultations, but learning from past mistakes, the unions maintained pressure through ongoing demonstrations. Then, on 13 September 1990, the LRA Minute was signed, signalling the government's acceptance of the basic right of workers to join unions and bargain collectively. Government also agreed to consult with labour and business prior to making any future changes to labour law. The LRA Minute was a major victory for the unions. It led to the formulation of a new LRA, finally passed in 1997.

The union response to the LRA and the eventual success of the Defiance Campaign led directly to the de Klerk government's decisions regarding the release of political prisoners, the unbanning of the ANC and other anti-apartheid groups, and the advent of negotiations involving all key stakeholders. The government saw that it could no longer contain the power of the mass democratic movement.

Women workers

Attitudes of both employers and male workers toward women workers militated against "full and equal integration of Black women workers into the industrial labour force". Male workers opposed equal wages for women, resisted female job advancement and women in positions of authority.[624] Generally speaking, until the mid-1980s, women's issues fell at the bottom of trade unions' priority list. In the second half of the 1980s, women became more involved in trade unions, as members but also as organisers and shop stewards. However, they continued to be marginalised in the decision-making structures, and remained "under-trained, under-educated and under-paid". Black women were "even more exploitable than Black men", and they were kept inferior through a combination of race and patriarchy.[625]

A study for the Institute for Black Research in the mid-1980s, led by Fatima Meer, noted that "since 80% of African women are employed in agriculture and domestic work, they remain excluded both from the right to unionise, and from the protection of labour laws. Wages in these two sectors remain lowest of all and hours of work depend on the whim of the employers." [626] A 1984 study of nearly 1,000 women in the Durban-Pinetown region revealed that the women who were gainfully employed were grouped several occupational categories: 39% in social and personal service; 27% in manufacture; 22% in commerce and industry. African women were concentrated in personal service (70%), Indian women in manufacture (59%) and Coloured women in manufacture (29%) or commerce (31%). White women – whether in agriculture or manufacture – were in clerical or secretarial jobs.[627]

Several unions for domestic workers – an occupation in which workers were traditionally highly exploited -- had been created over the years. The SAIRR instituted the Domestic

---

[622] Ibid., p. 419. By the end of 1989, Phiroshaw Camay had resigned from his position as general secretary of NACTU partly out of exasperation with the inconsistent and vacillating attitude of his colleagues with regard to worker unity.

[623] Ibid., p. 437.

[624] Meer et al., 1990, p. 268. See this study for a comprehensive overview of issues affecting women workers in the 1980s.

[625] Ibid., 1990, p. 271.

[626] Ibid., 1990, p. 76.

[627] Ibid., p. 84.

Workers' and Employers' Project to make recommendations on working conditions, wages, etc. Out of this project grew the South African Domestic Workers' Association (SADWA) to protect domestic workers from exploitation, to speak on their behalf, to negotiate with employers' associations, to handle complaints and take appropriate action. The same year, 1981, other groups were formed, including the Domestic Workers' and Salesladies' Association in Port Elizabeth (under the auspices of Roots, a black cultural movement) and the National Union of Domestic Workers. Legislation which slightly improved their working lives followed a government inquiry.[628] In November 1986, six domestic worker organisations joined together to form the South African Domestic Workers' Union (SADWU), claiming 50,000 members.[629]

Women faced many hurdles in trying to become leaders in their unions. One female office bearer said that "It is our tradition... that a man is the head of the family. This means men don't accept women telling them what to do. This attitude is very tough to crack". Women were also seen as "unreliable" union members, e.g. when they were unable to attend union meetings due to childcare problems, housework or the dangers of transport at night. In 1989, COSATU called for "breaking down of all practical barriers to the full participation of women" but little progress was made in implementing this resolution.[630]

Trade unions which included both male and female workers have traditionally been very patriarchal institutions. Meer et al. wrote that "even when women constitute the bulk of the membership, it is men who control them. Made to feel inadequate and out of place in a male preserve, they submit to the authority of their male 'colleagues'. If bosses and supervisors take sexual advantage of young women workers, so too do authoritative males in the trade union. Women contribute to the trade union mass, the power of members on which male leaders stake their claim to power".[631] Thus, women were (and are) essentially a subordinate class within the working class. Gender divides were therefore used to divide workers as a class. Positive change only occurs if women challenge this patriarchal system and alter their perceptions of themselves, demanding their just place in the socio-economic sphere.

Various unions and union federations put in place campaigns to assist women to participate more effectively and to protect their rights in the workplace. Issues such as paid maternity leave, childcare (e.g. workplace-based crèches), the fight against strip searching and sexual harassment, and wage inequalities were addressed. Some unions also became involved in strengthening of community-based women's organisations, and COSATU advocated the revival of FEDSAW. However, the issue of separate women's structures within unions or federations as opposed to promoting women's leadership within mainstream structures was the subject of ongoing debate. Women's forums and committees were established to ensure that women's issues were attended to. However, women soon realised that they wanted and needed to make inputs on all labour issues in the union-wide structures so as to avoid marginalisation. Women participated in the Living Wage campaign and in the campaign against the Labour Relations Act.[632]

Women's position in the workplace has changed since 1994, but evidence shows that glass-ceilings still exist. At its most recent annual congress, COSATU once again noted their lack of success in integrating women into leadership structures and senior official positions. Thus, this struggle certainly continues.

---

[628] SAIRR, *1981 Survey*, pp. 158-160.
[629] SAIRR, *1986 Survey*, p. 735.
[630] Baskin, 1990, p. 375.
[631] Meer et al., 1990, p. 273.
[632] Baskin, 1990, pp. 375-383.

International trade union support

International pressure also played a role. During a visit by a Trades Union Congress (TUC) delegation from the UK in 1972, meetings were held with African trade unionists representing ten unions with 20,000 members. They criticised TUCSA for not doing enough to assist African unions, and also criticised White mining unions for not helping to organise their African counterparts.[633] Several individuals were encouraged to establish unions for African workers.

Service organisations such as the Trade Union Advisory and Co-ordinating Council (TUACC) and the Urban Training Project (UTP) were established to help with organising and training African workers. The UTP started in 1971. Its *Workers' Calendars* were published in English, Zulu and Sotho, and provided important information on Workers' Committees, legal rights and the basics of organisation. The UTP also provided legal advice and assistance to workers in disputes with employers or other situations. It helped in forming some unions and benefit funds and held courses for African trade unionists around the country.[634] Through the assistance of foreign donors, mainly trade union federations, including the International Confederation of Free Trade Unions (ICFTU), union organising activities, education, support for detainees and their families, legal fees, manuals, etc. were supported and encouraged.

This trade union support is probably one of the best examples of North-South co-operation in South Africa's recent history, for several reasons related to the establishment by the ICFTU of a co-ordinating committee of donor members and South African recipients of funds:

- Co-ordination was achieved between donors, supporters and the recipients and other members.
- The process was transparent and accountable as reports were tabled and all parties reported back to their principals.
- The process was an open one and not closed. New entrants were able to motivate their proposals and find favour and support.
- Shifts were possible. Meetings were held on a six-monthly basis so shifts in views, strategies and responses could be made. In emergency situations, co-ordination was possible through the ICFTU Secretariat and its Africa Desk.
- At different times different priorities were accommodated for relief funding, legal fees, funding service organisations, organising or educational activities.
- The donor base was open to members as well as non-members and funds could be accessed through other agencies/donors as well. Similarly, the recipient base was not curtailed by ideological or other conditions imposed by the ICFTU or the donors.
- The ICFTU Secretariat acted as a link. It received funds and reports, and channelled them appropriately. A fairly smooth accounting and reporting structure was therefore in place.

Lessons for the trade union movement

The history of the trade union movement in South Africa shows that:

- It is possible to unite workers across the artificial colour barriers.
- Strong independent industrial unions can be established.
- Democracy, accountability and transparency can be practiced and achieved in unions.
- Co-ordinated and directed international support can be of benefit to both the donors and the recipients.
- Political affiliation comes with its own costs and has to be experienced before lessons can be drawn from such affiliation, e.g. the AFL-CIO and the Democratic

---

[633] SAIRR, *1973 Survey*, pp. 272-273.
[634] SAIRR, *1974 Survey*, p. 323-324.

Party in the USA, or the TUC and the Labour Party in the UK, or the DGB and the SPD in Germany.

- The most salutary achievement is that over a quarter of a century's practice of democracy on the shop floor, the farms and the mines has encouraged, enhanced and institutionalised the practice and understanding of democracy.
- Bilateral relationships were established on the one hand to assist South African unionists, and, on the other, to develop trade union capacity in the region (SATUCC), on the continent (OATU), and internationally (ICFTU).

The leadership provided by the trade union movement illustrates both the potential as well as the principles which civil society can emulate to enhance its influence in communities, with government, and with donors.

Worker producer co-operatives

As a consequence of strike action, retrenchments and unfair dismissals by management, unions began to challenge workers to fend for themselves instead of looking to their unions for support. An early experiment occurred following the dismissal of some AECI workers who established themselves as a co-operative to produce soap, household cleaning detergents, etc. Their union, the South African Chemical Workers Union (SACWU), was not able to maintain the required discipline and support. The co-operative survives today as a commercial operation in Alexandra.[635]

The restructuring of the South African industrial scene also resulted in a need to respond by creating alternative jobs. The following is a list of some worker co-operatives:

Examples of Worker Producer Co-operatives in South Africa in the 1980s

Date	Union origin	Name	No. of workers	Location	Product
1984	SACWU	SACWU co-op	30	Alexandra	Household detergents, soap, etc.
1985	NUMSA	SAWCO	20	Howick	T-shirts
1987	Church	Laurisma Group	50	Cape Town	Sewing
1987	NUM	Transkei Mineworkers	60	Umtata	Brickmaking
1987	NUM	Transkei Mineworkers	60	Flagstaff	Brickmaking
1988	NUM	Mineworkers Co-operative	Unknown	Lesotho	Various
1988	FAWU	--	56	Stanger	T-shirts
1988	NUM	PAWCO	50	Phalaborwa	T-shirts
1989	SACTU	Zenzeleni	300	Durban	Workwear

Source: Camay, unpublished.

---

[635] Camay, *Izwilethu, NACTU Newsletter,* 1988.

Business and employer organisations

Business or employer organisations have long been a feature of South African civil society.[636] Some represented particular interests, such as the mining, textile or automobile industries. For example, the Chamber of Mines and other groups have been discussed earlier. Other organisations created early on aimed to speak on behalf of a broader business constituency. The Association of Chambers of Commerce (ASSOCOM) was formed in 1892 to represent retail commercial interests. The Federated Chamber of Industries (FCI) was established In 1918 to represent organised industry in South Africa. By 1972, there were 239 employer organisations with a total membership of 22,223 firms, and by 1982, these had increased to 262 employer organisations with 31,424 members.[637]

The *Afrikaanse Handelsinstitut* (AHI) was established in 1942, "in the midst of World War II, with a view to bringing Afrikaner-owned business together so as to uplift the economically impoverished Afrikaners at the time".[638] For more than four decades, the AHI "worked closely with a succession of apartheid governments and other Afrikaner cultural and political formations to protect the interests of Afrikaners to the exclusion of other racially defined groups".[639] In the early 1980s, the AHI changed its constitution to encourage people of other language and population groups to join as members. Then in the 1990s, it "broadened its vision and its commitment to economic growth for the benefit of all sectors of the population".[640]

The National African Federated Chamber of Commerce and Industry (NAFCOC) was created in 1969 to represent the interests of small and medium-sized black-owned business, with the objective to "promote and encourage the development of business in South Africa, and thereby draw the majority of South Africans into economic activity and the decision-making process. It aims to promote a spirit of co-operation and unity amongst all business people, to encourage self-help in all communities and full participation in the economy of the country".[641] It was constituted as a federation of provincial Chambers of Commerce and Industry, as well as sectoral chambers. The latter have included the African Council of Hawkers and Informal Business (ACHIB), the National African Federated Building Industry (NAFBI), the National African Farmers' Union (NAFU), the National African Federated Transport Organisation (NAFTO), the South African Liquor Traders' Association (NAFTA), and others.

As noted above, employer organisations were divided along racial and language lines as well as by the sector they represented. For example, by 1969, Indian industrialists in Durban had formed a "division" of the Natal Chamber of Industries. NAFCOC and the FCI reflected the divergent viewpoints respectively of the Black and White commercial interests in South Africa. The AHI and the FCI represented the views of Afrikaans and English owned capital interests, respectively. The Association of Chambers of Commerce (ASSOCOM) represented the interests of the provincially-based commercial interests, whilst the FCI represented large industrialists. These divisions split employers, often resulting in one group contradicting the other, or the government seeking to ally itself with the group whose view they favoured for that moment.

---

[636] Various groups of migrating workers from Europe to the mines, new industries, commerce and the professions brought to South Africa the tradition of unions, professional societies, as well as employer organisations.
[637] SAIRR, *1983 Survey*, p. 177.
[638] Camay and Gordon, 2004, p. 392. See this source also for more discussion of the recent development of South African business organisations and other sectors of civil society.
[639] *Enterprise*, March 2003, p. 46.
[640] Camay and Gordon, 1004, p. 394.
[641] SAIRR, Information Service, 5 December 2003.

During the 1970s and 1980s, these organisations sent representatives abroad to counter the increasing call for economic sanctions and attempted to persuade foreign governments and international organisations that sanctions should not be applied against the White government. This effort failed in the face of more effective lobbying by South African and international anti-apartheid groups.

NAFCOC was consistent in its demands for independent African business ventures and in its opposition to White businesses being allowed to trade freely in Black areas. The latter was felt to be "altogether unfair and morally unsound", even where White businessmen undertook to employ and train Africans. NAFCOC also opposed government participation in business through shareholding by development organisations (e.g. the Small Business Development Corporation (SBDC)), and argued that the roles of such parastatals should be limited to the provision of finance and advice. NAFCOC lobbied persistently for the removal of trading restrictions for African businesses, with some limited success.[642] By the early 1980s, NAFCOC was getting some support from ASSOCOM and the Chambers of Commerce in major metropolitan areas on issues such as allowing Black business into city and town shopping centres and appointing African, Indian and Coloured managers in White-owned businesses in White areas.[643] However, African businessmen continued to confront difficulties in obtaining capital and premises to assist in expanding their outreach.

Other black business organisations also became involved in the struggle over the "invasion" of Soweto by White businessmen using Africans as fronts. These included leaders of the Soweto Chamber of Commerce and Industry (SCCI) and the Southern Transvaal Chamber of Commerce (STCC). They protested against some of the "partnerships" that had been formed and some members of the STCC were expelled for participating in such arrangements (e.g. Metro Cash and Carry's initiative called Afrimet Ltd).[644]

In 1985, 40 prominent Muslim members of the Natal Indian business community joined NAFCOC, adding to the 30 Indian members in the Transvaal.[645] This indicated a new willingness for African and Indian business people to work together within the same organisation.

Whilst business leaders did not wish to get personally involved in speaking out against the arrests and detentions of workers and shop stewards, often strategies were adopted by the unionists to take matters to the individual decision-makers. For example, in the Transport and Allied Workers Union strike in 1981, the union approached directly the Carleo brothers, owners of the PUTCO bus company, resulting in a dawn meeting which attempted to settle the strike. In the Fatti and Moni's strike, on a Sunday morning a group of workers barricaded a Catholic Church where the owners were known to worship.

During the 1984 and 1986 detentions, certain individual business leaders, often acting in their own capacity but sometimes with backing from their company or employer organisation, made representations to the State or met with government officials or ministers urging them to "charge or release" detainees. The AHI, ASSOCOM and FCI joined in a telex protesting against the 1984 detentions of trade unionists, saying that it "had put at risk the harmonious

---

[642] SAIRR, *1978 Survey*, pp. 223-226. NAFCOC also warned of the dangers of Blacks "fronting" for White owners – a problem which has become quite serious as a result of the post-1994 "Black Economic Empowerment" policy.
[643] SAIRR, *1981 Survey*, p. 163.
[644] SAIRR, *1983 Survey*, pp. 291-292.
[645] SAIRR, *1985 Survey*, p. 104.

relationship between employers and a large section of their workforce", but the unions felt that such gestures were insufficient.[646]

Business and employer associations also belatedly began to take a stronger public stand on the need for change. In early 1985, six employer bodies – AHI, ASSOCOM, FCI, NAFCOC, the Chamber of Mines, and the Steel and Engineering Industries Federation of South Africa (SEIFSA) – released a joint statement "pledging support for economic and political reform and calling on the government to give visible expression to its reform statements". In June 1985, ASSOCOM released a report on "The Removal of Discrimination against Blacks in the Political Economy of the Republic of South Africa". This report was prepared in response to the government's request for help in bringing about peaceful change,[647] but also stemmed from an increasing realisation on the part of business leaders that unless Blacks became full citizens and equal participants in the economy, the country's economic prospects were not good. A year later, the South African Sugar Association, representing about 25,000 sugar growers in KwaZulu / Natal, articulated its opposition to apartheid and indicated its intention to develop an affirmative action programme in the near future. Such statements showed that business associations were increasingly jumping on the reform bandwagon.

As the tension increased within the country, Gavin Reilly, Chief Executive of Anglo American Corporation, led a grouping of senior business leaders to meet with the leadership of the ANC in exile in Zambia in September 1985. Shortly thereafter, major business associations called on multinational companies operating in South Africa to help them in pressing for political change. Then, in 1986 and 1987, Johan van Zyl and Marius Wiechers of the FCI developed a Charter of Human Rights for Business in South Africa. Whilst the Charter did not gain much popularity, the initiative created a framework within which business could motivate a stronger socio-political stance.

In 1988, a new black business organisation called the Foundation for African Business and Consumer Services (FABCOS) emerged. It "self-consciously identified itself as an organisation committed to assisting the struggle against apartheid. It was informed by a particular understanding of democracy: the (Black) political freedom 'could be achieved only if it was underpinned by economic power'".[648] "FABCOS was formed with 13 member associations representing sectors such as builders, hairdressing, travel agents, stokvels, cottage industries, tuckshops, taxis, taverners and consumers"[649]. One of the founders, Joas Mogale, said that FABCOS was conceived as "essentially a developmental organisation that would mobilise the informal sector, with consumers, to break into the formal sector".[650]

The membership sectors represented in both NAFCOC and FABCOS show the substantial diversity of economic interest organisations that had emerged within the Black community.

When FCI and ASSOCOM merged to establish the South African Chamber of Business (SACOB) in 1990, a coherent and united approach to the political situation still did not emerge and a small group of business leaders were frustrated at the lack of progress.

The Consultative Business Movement (CBM)
Finally, towards the end of the 1980s, several key business leaders decided to become more proactive in bringing an end to the political violence and moving towards a negotiated settlement. In February 1988, Prof. Van Zyl Slabbert and Dr. Alex Boraine of IDASA led a

---

[646] SAIRR, *1984 Survey,* p. 765.
[647] SAIRR, *1985 Survey*, p. 563.
[648] Hlophe, Mathoho and Reitzes, 2001, p. 6.
[649] Camay and Gordon, 2004, p. 395.
[650] Hlophe et al., 2001, p. 7.

group of Afrikaners to meet with the ANC in Dakar, Senegal. Disarmed by Thabo Mbeki's opening remark, "I too am an Afrikaner!", the real possibility of accelerated dialogue and established relationships was put in place. Further meetings were held within and outside South Africa with the ANC and other liberation organisations. Within South Africa, meetings were held to determine whether business leaders would commit themselves to actively creating relationships with recognised Black political leaders of established mass socio-political movements.

This process was led by a few committed business personalities and unselfish supporters who put their personal interests aside and attempted to reach out and have a dialogue with Black community leaders, civic organisations and unions. Often these meetings were illegal because they violated some or other state of emergency regulations.

This dialogue eventually led to the Broederstrom Encounter in August 1988 at which approximately 40 business leaders and academics met with a similar number of black activists. At the meeting, a new initiative was formally launched with the establishment of the Consultative Business Movement (CBM). It is probably the first time in the history of South Africa (or elsewhere for that matter) that a business-led initiative was created through consultation with the leadership of mass-based peoples' organisations.

The CBM adopted the following mission statement:

> "To participate in and initiate processes geared towards bridging the polarisation in South Africa as the means to restoring economic strength, by consulting across the broader spectrum of interest groups to help create a prosperous, non-racial democratic South Africa".

Whilst the CBM established a formal structure and had a nucleus of some 40 business leaders, they found it extremely difficult to extend membership or have a visible impact on the rulers of the day. The CBM focused on a macro approach but failed in its micro initiatives. Individual business initiatives in some townships had greater success at the micro level.

When President F.W. de Klerk announced the unbanning of political organisations and the release of political leaders in February 1990, the CBM began to find a new relevance and set in motion an accelerated network of contacts and meetings. In May 1990, these contacts culminated in a meeting in Johannesburg between 300 business leaders and the senior leadership of the ANC. As a result, the CBM was invited to play a vital role as the Secretariat during the CODESA negotiations. It fulfilled this task to the satisfaction of all the political parties involved.

The CBM later merged with the Urban Foundation to form the National Business Initiative (NBI) which played the role of advocate and facilitator for business.

Organisations representing small business and consumers

Taxi associations
The history of associations in the taxi industry is interwoven with the response of the government of the day to the taxi industry.

The taxi industry remained divided along racial lines. The Black taxi industry emerged out of the anger against apartheid: defiantly aggressive and incontrollable, attributes which still manifest themselves today. In the apartheid era, following the principle of "one man, one business", the entrepreneurs in the townships could not diversify their interests. To provide a safe, clean and speedy transportation system between town and townships, a number of operators began to emerge from the early 1930s.

The first organisation of the taxi associations was established in Johannesburg by Jimmy Sojane in 1960, called the Johannesburg Non-European Taxi Association. Attempts to forge unity amongst taxi operators only bore fruit in the 1970s when, in response to the oil crisis, taxi operators established the United Soweto Taxi Owners Association (USTOA). Taxis in this period were not allowed to carry more than five passengers. Operators were limited in the number of vehicle licenses they could hold, and they could operate on specifically designated routes only.

With the passage of the Road Transportation Act 1977, the situation developed into one of limited tolerance. Taxi operators were now able to acquire minivans seating 8+1, i.e. eight passengers and a driver. However, they still had to contend with the South African Bus Owners' Association (SABOA) which was a powerful lobby with access to government. In the mid-1980s, regulations were further relaxed so that taxi operators could carry 16 passengers. So the industry moved from strict regulation to nearly complete deregulation through the influence of the taxi associations. By 1984, it was estimated that around 500,000 Africans were using approximately 82,000 kombi-taxis to travel between the townships and their workplaces.[651]

From local taxi associations, regional associations were formed. In October 1980 at the DOCC Hall in Orlando, Soweto, the South African Black Taxi Association (SABTA) was established. This association was seen to cover short-distance taxi operators. The Southern African Long Distance Transport Association (SALDTA) was established in June 1987 with 300 drivers to represent taxi drivers transporting passengers between the cities and rural areas. By late 1988, SALDTA claimed a membership of over 10,000 with 48 affiliated taxi associations. They provided a cheaper, cleaner, more flexible and timesaving service than the trains or buses between the major centres of South Africa.

Short-haul taxis (usually sedans as opposed to minibuses) in the cities by law provided a source of transportation only to the White inhabitants. Many of these taxis and their associations are fighting for survival as their territories are being encroached upon by both legal and illegal taxi operators engaged in short hauls.

The taxi industry enjoys substantial support from various quarters: the financial institutions which see it as a lucrative loan market, White operators who see it as a rewarding enterprise, minibus manufacturers who have a number of models on the market with various options, the insurance industry which provides coverage, and the petrol companies which have taken to franchising petrol stations to the industry. More recently, the advertising sector has used minibus taxis to advertise on. In addition, music tapes, TV as well as video tape showings occur on many taxis, especially on the longer hauls.

However, the industry has been plagued with acrimony and conflict caused by jealousy, rivalry, opposition and personality differences, often leading to death and mayhem with passengers as innocent victims. Taxi wars commonly occur between competing regional or local affiliates of the umbrella bodies. Since the early 1990s, strong arguments have been made for more effective regulation of the industry. This is an ongoing issue of concern for both the associations and government.

---

[651] SAIRR, *1984 Survey*, p. 431.

Organisations representing the informal sector

Kirsten[652] concluded that nearly 2 million Black people were involved in the informal economy in 1985. Estimates by the Institute for Futures Research indicate that nearly 4.7 million may have become involved in the sector by the year 2000. Whilst the informal sector has been romanticised by many including some economists, it does offer a number of stimulants to a developing economy like South Africa. These cannot be underestimated: creating employment, reducing crime, generating income, stimulating entrepreneurial development, increasing purchasing power, and contributing to the GDP.

The sector saw a growth in associations, represented by the African Council of Hawkers and Informal Businesses (ACHIB). In October 1988 it was reported that ACHIB had 14,000 members in the Pretoria/Witwatersrand/Vaal Triangle area, most of whom were spaza shop owners. ACHIB negotiated with local authorities on behalf of its members, as well as with wholesalers who were interested in selling to hawkers. It also made other representations to protect the interests of its members. For example, it launched a national campaign to persuade government to remove restrictions on hawkers' rights to trade freely. This campaign had little impact on the number of cases against hawkers. ACHIB encouraged township residents to shop at spaza shops and informal businesses. [653] In 1992, ACHIB joined with Fedlife, First National Bank and Investec in launching a new micro-loan scheme for hawkers and spaza-shop owners, guaranteed by the Development Bank of Southern Africa. At this time, it was estimated that there were about 900,000 informal businesses involved in street trading and spaza shops, employing around 3 million people.[654] However, ACHIB only had limited success in providing services to its members, despite access to donor funding.

A number of smaller, more regional organisations have emerged and have had greater success in supporting their members, e.g. the Self-Employed Women's Association (SEWA) operating in Durban. Also, Siphamandla Hawkers and Vendors Association (formed in 1987) tried to make representations to the city council on their conditions of trade and regarding harassment by local council officials in Pietermaritzburg. Other associations elsewhere in the country have played similar roles.

Spaza ('camouflaged') shop associations

These are a manifestation of home-based retail stores providing basic commodities to the neighbourhood. They are found mainly in the urban areas. The concept of the corner grocery store has been replaced by these spaza shops. However, a looming danger for the spaza shops is the development of retail stores located at petrol stations. All the major petrol companies are now venturing into enlarging their stations to accommodate these stores.

The spaza shop associations are at a big disadvantage vis-a-vis the six major multinational petrol companies, their buying power, their advertising potential, and the convenience of their locations. As a result, no effective lobby has been launched by any of the existing spaza shop associations.

Consumer unions

The Black Consumer Union (BCU) was created in Johannesburg in 1984 as the first national Black consumer body. It aimed to educate Black consumers regarding their rights and to represent them vis-à-vis other stakeholders. The first president was Ellen Kuzwayo. The increased levels of African retail spending gave these consumers more market power, and

---

[652] Kirsten, 1991.
[653] SAIRR, *1988/89 Survey*, pp. 363, 382
[654] SAIRR, *1992/93 Survey*, p. 111.

boycotts of various products or retailers became an effective political tool used, for example, in labour disputes or in protests against high prices.[655]

Mutual fund associations or stokvels

Stokvels or credit associations are known by many other terms in South Africa: *gooi-goois*, pooling clubs, *umgalalos*, *mohodisano* ('we pay each other back'), *kubolisana* (cause to grow or draw wages), *mtshaolo, matshido* or *masibanbane* ('hold hands together') are all in use. The term *stokvel* is said to stem from a contraction of "stockfair" where money is pooled to buy cattle.[656]

Hellman[657] wrote of stokvels in her research on a slumyard in Johannesburg. There she found the activity confined mainly to women. She discounted it as an institution which could be abused and would therefore not survive. Kuper and Kaplan,[658] in a study of voluntary associations in a Witwatersrand township, found that 20% of their sample were members of a stokvel. Thus, their socio-economic importance cannot be dismissed. The sharing of resources – to provide moral, social and financial support -- within stokvel groups began as and continues to be a key aspect of Black families' culture of survival. They help enormously in stretching low wages much further.

Stokvels have always fulfilled a social gathering function in African and Coloured communities across age, background, urban or rural origin, residence, occupation, gender or even tribal affiliation. Their size is often determined by the members. Stokvels also often have a loan bank function where money is loaned and interest charged until both interest and capital are repaid.

A typology of organisations which have emerged includes: small saving clubs, small loan clubs, specific goal-oriented savings clubs (e.g. to purchase sewing machines or a taxi), investment clubs (where money is pooled and invested in shebeens, liquour outlets, shares), or high budget rotating credits where large sums of money are collected from a large membership and loaned at interest or rotated to the members (e.g. to purchase vehicles or houses or make investments). Women also used stokvels to pool small amounts of money so as to buy food and other goods more cheaply in bulk (e.g. as in co-operative societies). Funds might also be used to pay for funerals, birthday celebrations or weddings.

In 1988, the National Stokvels' Association of South Africa (NASASA) was launched. Though membership initially was limited to the Transvaal, it now operates as a national organisation. In 1989, it was estimated that the number of existing stokvels in South Africa was approximately 800,000, with a turnover of approximately R200 million per month.[659] In 1991, a Markinor survey estimated that 28% of Africans in major metropolitan areas (Cape Town, Johannesburg and Durban, and informal settlements in these areas) were stockvel members.[660] Stokvels have made use of the banking institutions, seeking out their best offers. They are therefore not a substitute for formal banking, but a financial resource to their members which offers benefits far superior to those of the formal banking sector. They continue to be extremely popular.

---

[655] SAIRR, *1984 Survey*, pp. 228-230.
[656] See Callinicos, 1987, p. 200; Barrett et al., 1985, pp. 215-217.
[657] Hellman, 1948.
[658] Kuper and Kaplan, 1944.
[659] *Weekly Mail*, 2 June 1989.
[660] SAIRR, *1992/93 Survey*, p. 112.

Professional societies and associations

Most key professions have been represented by associations which were divided on a racial basis. These excluded Black colleagues by design and established separate branches with voting rights to ensure overall control by the usually White minority branch. The constitution of the Nursing Association of South Africa was a case in point. Some of these associations have focused primarily on the direct interests of the members of their profession and on networking amongst them.

Other associations have been more engaged in broader issues of socio-political and economic transformation. This is historically particularly true of those representing Black professionals. To address the needs of Black accountants and their lack of opportunity in the mainstream of the profession, the Association of Black Accountants of South Africa (ABASA) was established. Similarly, the Black Lawyers Association (BLA) and the National Association of Democratic Lawyers (NADEL) were formed. In the mid-1980s, the BLA argued on behalf of its members, *inter alia*, that African lawyers were subjected to discrimination in the courts and to restrictions on where they could establish their practices, making it difficult for them to provide proper service to their clients. At that time, out of 8,000 lawyers in the country, only about 600 were African. The Transvaal Law Society claimed that it was lobbying government to have African lawyers exempted from restrictive legislation regarding freedom of movement.[661]

Teachers

In 1953 the Bantu Education Act was passed, directly transferring control of education from each provincial authority to the Department of Native Affairs. Teachers' opposition to Bantu education came from the Cape and Transvaal Teachers' Associations (CATA and TTA respectively). The multi-racial South African Federation of Teachers' Associations emerged in the 1970s and was joined by the South African Teachers' Association (SATA) based in the Cape, the TTA (White), the South African Indian Teachers' Association (SAITA), and the Union of Teachers' Associations of South Africa (UTASA)(Coloured). However, these individual associations largely remained racially-based.

Organised opposition to Bantu education from Natal teachers developed later, partly because in Natal direct state control of education was common before the passage of the 1953 Act and there was a dearth of political organisations prepared to involve themselves in education affairs. In the 1970s, the Natal African Teachers' Union (NATU) was affiliated to Inkatha. The Natal Teachers Association (NATA), however, was a strong teacher's union contributing a sizeable active membership when it merged with other unions to create the South African Democratic Teachers' Union (SADTU) in 1990.

Attempts to unify the teachers' groupings began in earnest in the 1980s. The National Education Union of South Africa (NEUSA) was established in 1980, and saw itself as "a non-racial, open teachers' body that saw the struggle for educational change as part of the struggle against apartheid". It supported only organisations "striving for a non-racial society". In 1983, NEUSA affiliated to the UDF. NEUSA's Black membership grew quite rapidly, especially because it acknowledged the need to play both an educational and political role. It also made an effort to organise rural teachers. For example, its Sekhukhuneland branch was established in 1986.[662]

The Joint Council of Teachers' Associations of South Africa (JOCTASA), representing 80.000 teachers around the country, held its first conference in 1981. JOCTASA was made

---

[661] SAIRR, *1985 Survey*, p. 103.
[662] Mathabatha, 2005, p. 80.

up of Coloured organisations in the Union of Teachers' Associations of South Africa (UTASA) and organisational members of the African Teachers' Association of South Africa (ATASA). The Joint Council was established with a view to co-ordinating action in support of "a free and open educational system in a non-racial society". JOCTASA was also seen as a step towards a fully non-racial teachers' association. A proposed charter prepared by JOCTASA in 1984 which called on teachers' organisations to campaign for a unitary educational system was discussed. The Afrikaans-speaking teachers' groups did not support this, and in February 1985, they formed their own umbrella body called the Federasie van Afrikaanse Onderwysvereninginge.[663] Later that year, teachers in the Western Cape formed a non-racial body – the Western Cape Teachers' Union -- to give guidance and support to "progressive" teachers. A unitary system, including equality of pay for teachers of all races, was still far from being a reality.

Around the same time, the Council for Black Education and Research was created, led by Professor Eskia Mphahlele, with the objective of moving away from the usual protest rhetoric to developing strategies on the basis of sound educational research.[664] There was general consensus (except on the part of some of the remaining Whites-only teachers' unions) that education was "the handmaiden of apartheid" and that apartheid was the root cause of the shortages of qualified teachers in Coloured and African schools.[665]

Some of the professional associations engaged with government on key policy issues and offered inputs in the course of government inquiries or after the release of the reports. For example, when the De Lange Committee on Education reported back in 1981, the public were invited to comment. Education professional associations such as ATASA criticised the recommendations, saying that the progressive recommendations of the De Lange Report would be unable to ensure equal education until all socio-economic and political problems were attended to. NEUSA also argued that the Report focused on education to meet the needs of industry, instead of the real need – how "to prepare people for full participation in a democratic society". NEUSA Teachers' Advice Bureau also began a study of the employment conditions of teachers in the racially-divided departments of education. In contrast, Afrikaner groups took the position that education for Whites must remain in the hands of Whites. Franklin Sonn, president of the Cape Teachers' Association and a member of the De Lange Committee, said that the Afrikaners' response undermined attempts to peacefully reform education.[666] Government accepted some of the recommendations of the De Lange Report but refused to place education under a single ministry.

Out of frustration with the lack of progress towards a unitary education system, ATASA decided to withdraw from all government committees and councils on education and training until there was "genuine power sharing" – that is, power sharing negotiated with genuine Black leaders. Shortly thereafter, UTASA did much the same. The situation was not improved by the formation of a new Whites-only teachers' group in 1986 – the Federal Teachers' Council – comprised of the Federal Council of Teachers' Associations in South Africa and the South African Teachers' Council for Whites. The Natal Teachers' Society and the Transvaal Teachers' Association refused to join a new racially exclusive group.[667]

1988 saw more progress towards teacher unity, though there were still a few racially exclusive groups holding out. ATASA indicated that it wished to establish greater solidarity with other teachers' associations with a view to forming a national umbrella body. The only major groups which did not attend were NEUSA and the Transvaalse Onderwysers

---

[663] SAIRR, *1984 Survey*, p. 655.
[664] SAIRR, *1981 Survey*, pp. 335-337.
[665] SAIRR, *1983 Survey*, p. 432.
[666] SAIRR, *1982 Survey*, pp. 467-469.
[667] SAIRR, *1986 Survey*, pp. 423-424.

Vereniging. At the annual congress of the Cape Teachers' Professional Association (CTPA), after an education campaign to familiarise teachers with the Freedom Charter, 2,000 members voted to adopt the Charter. Two Black teachers' groups in the Cape – the Democratic Teachers' Union (DETU) and the Peninsula African Teachers' Association (PENATA) decided to work together as they both supported the Charter and the NECC's 'people's education' programme. They also were facing similar problems with new DET regulations. The Indian Teachers' Association of South Africa (ITASA) stated its opposition to political interference in education, to the DET's lack of consultation, and a number of other issues related to working conditions. The Coloured Union of Teachers' Associations of South Africa (UTASA) threatened to sanction any teachers participating in the municipal elections. Several other associations joined this campaign. The same year, NEUSA was banned, not least for arguing that "the crisis in apartheid education was unresolved". They listed a host of specific reasons for drawing this conclusion. A new organisation was formed after the banning of NEUSA and the NECC – the Progressive Teachers' Congress (PROTECO) – which was also committed to the formation of a single national union.[668]

Teachers' groups also proliferated in some rural areas. As a result of the student revolt in Sekhukuneland in 1986, major teachers' organisations met to form the Northern Transvaal Teachers' Unity Forum (NTTUF) to co-ordinate teachers' activities. One of its aims was to "reduce the proliferation of new organisations by persuading the teachers 'to affiliate to the progressive associations that were already in existence". In May 1990, more than 6,000 teachers from the Lowveld marched to the circuit offices in protest against the non-payment of recently appointed teachers.[669] Teacher activism was spreading.

COSATU became involved in trying to form a national teachers' union, in line with its "one union per industry" policy. In August 1989, 11 teachers' associations, representing about 150,000 teachers, voted to support the Mass Democratic Movement and its campaign of non-violent mass action against apartheid laws. In 1990, the South African Democratic Teachers' Union (SADTU) was established bringing together all the progressive teachers' associations into a single multi-racial union. SADTU "offered teachers a voice in the new political order, in a context where they had been marginalised by the youth who viewed them as part of the problem. Teachers and the youth now found a common enemy in the apartheid regime and its surrogate Bantustans".[670]

Whilst younger teachers joined SADTU in large numbers, many of the older teachers were uncomfortable with the politicised trade unions and preferred the pre-existing professional associations. In 1991, a new loose federation of "ethnically-constituted" teachers' associations was established by these established groups: the National Professional Teachers' Organisation of South Africa (NAPTOSA). Their emphasis on "professionalism" was seen by their younger colleagues in SADTU as "conservatism". NAPTOSA was also seen to be protecting their own interests because they entered into collective bargaining with the educational authorities. However, the alternative view was that NAPTOSA and its member groups were eschewing politics and putting the interests of the children first. These different viewpoints amongst teachers in the Northern Transvaal reflected a considerable gap in approach, and even disturbed teaching in schools due to the need for constant conflict resolution.[671]

After two years of discussions between the 50,000 member SADTU and the education authorities, and sizeable marches and strikes, SADTU was finally given official recognition for collective bargaining purposes in September 1992. This was, of course, complicated by

---

[668] SAIRR, *1988/89 Survey*, pp. 252-255.
[669] Mathabatha, 2005, p. 83.
[670] Ibid., p. 83.
[671] Ibid., pp. 83-85.

the continued existence of different departments of education for each racial group and each homeland. For example, the Lebowa government did not agree with the national government's recognition of SADTU, and many SADTU members in Lebowa schools were dismissed, suspended, and/or harassed by the authorities. SADTU did not help its situation by intimidating teachers to encourage them to join SADTU, including teachers at Catholic schools in the Northern Transvaal. In response, Catholic teachers formed their own union (CSTA) in 1994, whilst conceding that CSTA members could also join SADTU. Before long, however, the CSTA was considered to be too closely aligned with the management of the Catholic schools, and it ceased to exist.[672] SADTU has remained the pre-eminent teachers' union in post-democratic South Africa.

Medical professions

African nurses and doctors were subjected to repeated humiliations and inequalities, despite the burning need for their services around the country. For example, in December 1957, the National Council of Nurses endorsed a requirement that all African nurses be required to produce identity numbers before they could register for a midwifery course. This effectively made it necessary for all African nurses to obtain pass books.[673]

In 1976, it was suggested that African nurses who belonged to the South African Nursing Association (SANA) – then a multi-racial body – should leave that body and form separate nursing councils based in each of the homelands. The African nurses rejected this proposal for ethnically-based associations, and instead opted for the establishment of a single African nurses' association.[674] In 1978, Parliament passed the Nursing Act which provided for the Nursing Council to become non-racial. However, again, African nurses in the independent homelands were excluded as members of the Council had to be South African citizens. As a result, many Black nurses were unemployed as the majority of vacancies were reserved for White South Africans. As a result of further discriminatory legislation regarding the registration of nurses in 1982, and deprived of the opportunity to belong to SANA, African nurses based in most of the homelands (except Lebowa and KwaZulu) formed the League of Nursing Associations of South Africa (LONASA).

SANA acknowledged the shortage of nursing staff in 1983 when it recommended to the Minister of Health that training facilities should be extended, especially to African nurses. Despite the official policy that each population group should be nursed by members of the same group, the shortage had already resulted in Coloured nurses being employed in Free State hospitals. White nurses in the province, however, still held racist attitudes toward their Coloured colleagues, leading some to resign.[675]

In the case of doctors, the Medical Association of South Africa (MASA) was uninterested in meeting the needs of the Black population. It failed to condemn and expel the doctors involved in treating Steve Biko before he died from injuries inflicted by the police and was unwilling to deal with broader issues of treatment of detainees. Some international medical associations rejected MASA as a result, but it was allowed to rejoin the World Medical Association in 1982. Influential Black doctors such as Dr. Jerry Coovadia criticised MASA for failing to address "the social, political and economic basis of ill health". Progressive medical professionals, including doctors, nurses, radiographers, hospital administrators and others formed other organisations, such as the Transvaal Medical Society, the Natal Health Workers' Association and the National Medical and Dental Association (NAMDA).[676] Representatives of medical students from various South African universities opposed the

---

[672] Ibid., pp. 89-92.
[673] Walker, 1991, p. 269.
[674] SAIRR, *1976 Survey,* p. 387.
[675] SAIRR, *1983 Survey,* p. 489.
[676] SAIRR, *1982 Survey,* pp. 542-543.

readmission of the South African Medical Students' Association (SAMSA) to the International Federation of Medical Students' Associations (IFMSA). They said that SAMSA refused to condemn apartheid and represented mainly students from Afrikaans universities. SAMSA was disbanded shortly thereafter.[677]

At its first annual conference in 1983, NAMDA asserted that "while MASA acted primarily in the interests of its members, NAMDA focused more on the needs of the community, questioned the role of the medical profession in maintaining the status quo, was committed to the belief that health was a basic human right which should be available to all, and sought to create the conditions for optimum health, which could only exist in a free and democratic society".[678] NAMDA also spoke out on behalf of people with bullet wounds who were arrested when they went to seek help at hospitals. Their wounds were often not treated in time, and amputations became necessary.[679]

In 1986, the Health Workers' Association (HWA) said that health facilities for the different race groups were far from equal. A meeting of the HWA, NAMDA, the Transvaal Indian Congress, the Coronation Hospital Crisis Committee, the Wits University Black Students' Society, the Lenasia Federation of Residents' Associations, the Riverlea Youth Congress and the Anti-President's Council Committee called for "the establishment of a "just and equitable health service for all South Africans".[680] The HWA then prepared a health charter making the same demand and also calling for more dialogue on health issues to take place in the townships instead of at universities, and for imbalances in the health budget to be rectified. They also criticised government proposals to privatise health services, saying that "health is a government responsibility".[681]

The following year, NAMDA also expressed concern about the health implications of the conditions under which detainees were held in prison. They said that 72% of detainees seen by their members in 1987 had been assaulted in detention and 97% showed signs of abuse. The earlier recommendations of MASA regarding treatment of detainees had never been implemented.[682]

In 1992, the South African Health and Social Services Organisation (SAHSSO) was created, joining several progressive / left-wing health and welfare organisations, including the Health Workers' Society, NAMDA, the Organisation for Appropriate Social Services in South Africa, the Overseas Medical Graduates' Society, and the South African Health Workers' Congress. Its initial 5,000 members included doctors, dentists, nurses, psychologists, social workers and community workers. SAHSSO's aims were to "address the urgent task of democratising health and welfare, and undoing the disastrous effects of apartheid on these services" and to "empower our communities in the health and social service sector through the establishment of a non-racial, non-sexist, and democratic national health service in the country".[683]

MASA continued to exist, and -- changing with the times -- by 1992 had begun to work towards the establishment of a unitary health system with equitable access for all. It called for the desegregation of hospitals as well as other reforms, and generally became more proactive in trying to influence health policy. MASA membership of 12,700 at this time

---

[677] Ibid., p. 546.
[678] SAIRR, *1983 Survey*, p. 487.
[679] SAIRR, *1985 Survey*, p. 494.
[680] SAIRR, *1986 Survey*, p. 790.
[681] SAIRR, *1987/88 Survey*, p. 793.
[682] Ibid., p. 796.
[683] SAIRR, *1992/93 Survey*, p. 297.

constituted 60% of doctors practising in the country. It also advocated on behalf of 47 special interest groups from various medical disciplines – a complex task for a single organisation!

Herbalists
This is an example of a professional association based in traditional practice. Traditional medicine, a vital but often neglected part of health care services, has always been an important source of employment, especially in the African communities. It has also encouraged and maintained faith and trust in culture, tradition and healing, both physical and spiritual.

As early as the 1930s, traditional African herbalists attempted to secure their interests and obtain recognition from the authorities. In 1938, the South African Black Dingaka Midwives and Sangomas Society was formed in Sophiatown. It was established to harbour and preserve native custom, to gain the authorities' recognition of traditional healers and to provide certificates for healers. Their petitions met with little success. Instead, they were threatened that their activities were illegal and they would be prosecuted.

This saga is similar to that experienced by other organisations which emerged later:
- The Natal Native Medical Association (1930)
- The African National Native Herb Association (Johannesburg, late 1940s)
- The South African Bantu Herbal Co. (Pretoria, 1960s)
- The Republic of South Africa Herbalist Association (East London, 1960s)

These organisations attempted to pursue their goals separate from the broader liberation struggle so as to avoid a stereotypical response from the state. However, they failed because they did not have a legal framework within which to operate. Consequently, they could not achieve the status of a national organisation or recognition as a profession of traditional medicine. Their representation was not marketable within the larger and general Black political effort. National legislation also covertly textured the environment within which the herbalists operated. The Witchcraft Suppression Act was passed in 1957 and undermined traditional medicine.[684] Nonetheless, an association which pursued a largely progressive agenda and survived for about 30 years from 1930 to the late 1960s was the African Dingaka Association.

Regardless of size, state support and access, traditional medicine has co-existed with modern medicine primarily because it attempts to treat and provide holistic healing through a cosmology which modern medicine reduces to mere physical or mechanical dysfunction.

Social workers
In 1976, social workers formed a new non-racial association in the Transvaal. Efforts from within the White Social Workers' Association to transform it into a multi-racial association failed. At that time there was no professional association for Coloured and Indian social workers. The Black Social Workers' Association had an informal relationship with the White grouping.[685] Other social welfare groups were racially specific. For example, African social workers in Johannesburg formed the Council for Voluntary Social Service in Black Communities, and Indian social workers operated through the Johannesburg Indian Social Welfare Association (JISWA). The JISWA Training Centre for Mentally Handicapped Children was registered around that time and continues to operate today.[686] By 1981, social workers' associations were demanding a single government department for all race groups.

---

[684] Last and Chavunduka, 1986, p. 96.
[685] SAIRR, *1976 Survey*, p. 393.
[686] Ibid., p. 393.

Towards the end of the 1970s, some professional associations began to allow Blacks to join. These included the Master Builders Association of the Witwatersrand and the SA Library Association. However, many continued in their racial exclusivity. For example, the Pretoria Bar Council continued to refuse admission to Black advocates.[687] Progress in deracialising professional associations was generally slow. Exclusively White associations, in particular, behaved shamefully in continuing to restrict their membership and in not speaking up in support of equal rights and working conditions for their Black professional colleagues.

The media

Since its stormy beginnings in the 19th century, press freedom in South Africa has been threatened by successive governments. Many scholars, editors and journalists have recorded these ongoing struggles for press freedom.

In the period of British dominance between 1910 and 1948, the English press dominated the country. There was a healthy exchange of typesetters, printers, and journalists who emigrated from Britain to work in South Africa. The ownership of the newspapers was local in the main and therefore little British control was exercised. Recently, however, the first incursion into the ownership of the press occurred when the Argus was bought out by the Irish magnate, Tony Reilly. The media companies SA Associated Newspapers and the Argus dominated the control of the English newspapers.

Afrikaans newspapers also took root, championing the cause of Afrikaners. With the electoral triumph in 1948, the Afrikaans press came into its own. The newspapers, however, reflected a *verkampt* (conservative) to *verlig* (enlightened) view of events. After 1994, a changing market has resulted in the demise of the conservative newspapers, with only the more liberal ones surviving.

White-owned and managed media paid little attention to events and issues within the non-White communities. Through the establishment of community and political newspapers, information on political developments and other important topics was provided. This was particularly important as these communities were unable to make inputs regarding decisions on issues affecting them. Officials did not consider it necessary to inform the people until those decisions were a *fait accompli*.

Opposition to the apartheid government led several independent or English-owned newspapers (e.g. *Drum, Black World, The World* – the sequel to *Bantu World,* and later *The Sowetan*) to emerge to lead the Black cause. Cautiously at first, but more boldly and vigorously later, they espoused the cause of the Black people. They exposed conditions on the farms, in the factories and the mines. They reported on strikes and Black living conditions. They reported on civic life, police brutality, and political funerals. During 1976 most White papers lifted news from *The World* as they had few political reporters. English language newspapers reported only marginally on Black affairs, briefly on sport, and marginally on Black political activism. They "editionalised" news. This legacy still obtains today with the *Sunday Times* publishing an African and an Indian edition of its newspapers alongside a "White" edition.

Alternative media

In the 1970s and 1980s, a wide array of alternative media emerged to cater particularly to those involved in the cultural and political resistance to apartheid. Some of these were linked to a particular organisation, whilst others were aimed at a wider audience. They all tried to

---

[687] SAIRR, *1978 Survey,* p. 375.

give voice to marginalised communities and/or marginalised ideas.[688] They were particularly significant due to government's domination of most of the print and electronic media. Whilst these alternative media could not always be strictly considered part of civil society themselves, in the main they had strong links to particular organisations or movements within civil society.

Some of these publications were directly linked to the Black Consciousness Movement. *Black Review,* put out by the Black Community Programmes from 1972, was one example of a journal dedicated to drawing attention to new prose and poetry, *inter alia,* written by authors aligned with the BCM. The SACC and the Christian Institute helped to support the wider publishing programme of the Black Community Programmes in the 1970s.

Several publishing houses emerged in this period to publish fiction and poetry as well as history and social commentary. Ravan Press was originally established to publish the reports of the Spro-Cas Commission (the joint research initiative of the SACC and the Christian Institute). Some of Ravan's titles were banned outright by the government, as was its first director in 1977. Buchu Books was founded in the late 1980s by a group of people who were all "engaged in writing or producing political, cultural or educational materials" and "were drawn together by the shared struggle to have their material published and distributed".[689]

Magazines such as *Contrast* and *Staffrider* were founded by Whites but had Black colleagues who took leadership roles and developed linkages with Black writers. *Staffrider* worked closely with community arts groups who distributed it, and sponsored cultural workshops. In 1990, *Staffrider* was taken over by the Congress of South African Writers (COSAW) who produced it until 1994.

In the early 1980s, some Black writers grew impatient with their White colleagues. They left PEN, the international writers' association, and founded the African Writers' Association (AWA). AWA then set up Skotaville Publishers in 1982, as a means of controlling their own output and creating their own standards. Skotaville aimed to establish "a truly independent Black printing and publishing house based in Soweto". It received support from both international churches and, interestingly, local corporates. It "pioneered the publication of affordable books aimed at the mass market", also publishing educational and children's books. Like Ravan Press, Skotaville was harassed by the government and subjected to bannings. By the early 1990s, Skotaville no longer existed due to financial difficulties and internal tensions.[690]

The South African Council for Higher Education (SACHED) was formed in the late 1960s to support higher education amongst Black students. It developed learning materials for students studying English as a second language and other educational materials as alternatives to government approved ones. In 1975, workbooks produced for its Turret College for secondary school students and teachers were incorporated into the Peoples' College supplement in the Saturday edition of *The World*. In 1977, after the banning of *The World*, SACHED produced its own supplement called *Catch Up*. Then in the early 1980s, *Learning Post* was disseminated as a supplement to *The Post*. All of these materials encouraged young people to improve their reading and writing skills, and also involved more critical thinking skills than the typical school curriculum. Unfortunately, SACHED closed in 1999.[691]

---

[688] Cloete, 2000, p. 44.
[689] Ibid., p. 52.
[690] Ibid., pp. 49-52.
[691] Ibid., pp. 52-53.

Some other journals started by civil society organisations included the *South African Labour Bulletin* (SALB) which was well established by the 1980s (despite being banned in 1976); *LINK*, from the Environmental Development Agency (EDA); and *Speak*, published by people working with women's organisations in the Durban area. The *SALB*, unlike many of the other journals, is still running. It has successfully raised issues emerging from the labour movement, and has targeted union members and shop stewards as well as other activists. *The Shop Steward* was another magazine that moved from Umanyano to COSATU's in-house publishing operation. *LINK* offered a platform for White activists working in the Black rural areas as well as Black activists emerging from community organisations. *Speak* was published in both English and Zulu, and took a feminist / socialist perspective on women's issues. Its focus became national when it moved to Johannesburg in the mid-1980s due to the violence in Natal. The Zulu edition ceased publication in 1989. *Speak* closed completely when the editor moved into government (as did many other CSO staff).[692]

Work in Progress, a magazine launched in 1972, took a marxist / socialist perspective. Founded by development studies honours students at the University of the Witwatersrand, it started life as an academic journal but later evolved into a leftist news magazine. "Throughout its existence, it played a major role in defining approaches to analysis and engagement amongst left intellectual activists".[693] It focused on a range of development issues, including rural issues which were neglected by others, and developed an increasing trade union audience by the late 1980s. By the mid-1980s, its circulation was between 25,000-30,000 copies, with multiple readers per copy. This is extraordinary for this type of publication. It had become an invaluable resource for anti-apartheid activists. As with other such publications, its raison d'etre disappeared in the early 1990s. It collapsed due to lack of funds.

Overtly political publications, linked e.g. to the ANC or the South African Communist Party, appeared in the late 1970s. These included *Sechaba* and *African Communist*. Later, the ANC introduced *Mayibuye*. The ANC's radio station, Radio Freedom, was also an important means of communicating to people within South Africa.

A number of independent weekly papers emerged in the late 1980s. These included the *Weekly Mail, Vrye Weekblad, New Nation, Cosatu News, Al Qalam, Izwe LaseRhini, Umafrika, South, Die Suid Afrikaan*. These papers broke some huge stories despite the threats from government – on police hit squads, KwaZulu warlords, murders of political activists, and many others. The creation of the Independent Media Development Trust (IMDT) and the Independent Magazine Group (IMG) in the early 1990s was intended to help some of these alternative media survive. The IMDT tried to stall the closure of two newspapers, *New Nation* and *Vrye Weekbald*, but this effort did not last long.

In the Cape, *Grassroots* was founded as a fortnightly community newspaper run largely by Coloured activists with BC leanings. *Grassroots*' content focused on "fomenting dissatisfaction with apartheid living conditions, popularising community organisations and leaders, and mobilising readers into supporting campaigns". Edited by Laila Patel, it represented a range of different constituency-based organisations including council tenants, school pupils, unions and others.[694] Its rationale was the "tremendous need for community organisations in the Western Cape" and the fact that "civil and community news [were] increasingly kept out of the major newspapers".[695] Its slogan, "We speak for ourselves", reflected giving voice to the voiceless. *Grassroots* closed down in 1989, having been banned, bombed and subjected to all sorts of government harassment. Other community

---

[692] Ibid., pp. 58-61.
[693] Ibid., p. 56.
[694] Berger, 2000, p. 77.
[695] *Grassroots* cited in Ibid., p. 77.

papers modelled on *Grassroots* included *The Eye* (Pretoria), *Speak* (Lenasia), *Umthonyama* (Port Elizabeth), *Ukusa* (Durban), and *Saamstaan* (Oudtshoorn). These papers played a vital role in uniting the 400 civil society organisations that eventually made up the United Democratic Front (UDF) in August 1983.[696]

A variety of student publications emerged around the country, including *SASPU National, SASPU Focus,* and *State of the Nation* issued by the South African Students' Press Union. Student newspapers issues on campuses included *Varsity, Wits Student, Dome, Rhodeo, The Spike, and So Where To.* Trade union publications other than those already alluded to above included *Fosatu News* (FOSATU) and *Izwi Lethu* (National Council of Trade Unions), as well as *Clothesline (*Garment Workers' Union).

The vast majority of these publications had disappeared by the mid-1990s. Many had suffered enormously under the series of states of emergency despite valiant efforts on the part of staff and supporters to keep them going. Finances were depleted and staff were exhausted. Funding from foreign donors such as the Dutch and Nordic countries also dried up. It was estimated that R8 million went into the alternative press between 1986 and 1991.[697] With the motivation of the struggle gone, and the exodus of staff to other roles in the negotiations and preparations for democracy, the role of the alternative media declined. Berger concludes that "a press that is linked to a social movement is dependent on the health and direction of that movement", but also says that without the alternative press in the 1970s and 1980s, "there may not have been that democracy".[698]

Media unions

As with ownership and readership, the media unions were also split along the lines of class and race. The SA Typographical Union was long associated with its British counterpart representing the print media workers in the typographical industry. Due to the changes in the industry, the Typographical Union has seen significant decline in membership in the newspapers, but still has membership in small printing works throughout the country. It is sustained mainly by the fact that it has large medical and pension benefit funds.

The South African Society of Journalists (SASJ) represented the White workers. In the mid-1970s, the SASJ protested against the "conspiracy of silence" with regard to military censorship of news of the Angolan war. They said that the "government has subverted the Press and its role as watchdog of the public interest, and the honesty and integrity of the Press has been brought into question". They also complained that the government was abusing the Press by only releasing certain information and that only to "accredited" journalists. They also argued that the SABC and foreign journalists were often given preferential treatment.[699]

Many Black journalists were employed by the White-owned media. They were often assaulted or detained by police when trying to cover protests in the townships, including well-known figures such as photographer Peter Magubane and editor of the *World*, Percy Qoboza. Even the SASJ protested about this, saying that this indicated "a concerted campaign by the government to reduce the effectiveness of the press as Black journalists have a greater capacity to report what is happening in Black townships".[700] Black journalists established the Union of Black Journalists (UBJ) to protect their interests as employees of the White media. When the UBJ was banned by the apartheid government in October 1977, the Writers' Association of South Africa (WASA) replaced it, and became the Media Workers'

---

[696] Ibid., pp. 78-79.
[697] *South,* 16-22 January 1992.
[698] Berger, 2000, pp. 98-99.
[699] SAIRR, *1976 Survey,* p. 150.
[700] Ibid., p. 151.

Association of South Africa (MWASA) in 1981. MWASA catered for journalists and other types of media workers. In 1983 when government created the South African Media Council, both the SASJ and MWASA refused to participate. The Council was also attacked by the South African Students' Press Union (SASPU) as a threat to freedom of the press which was likely to ban progressive publications. More recently, a third grouping -- the Democratic Journalists of South Africa -- emerged in 1989. They positioned themselves to the left of the SASJ and drew on both Black and White media workers as their members.

Sports organisations

Government continued to actively discourage mixed race sporting events. Legislation such as the Group Areas Act and the Separate Amenities Act largely sufficed to keep the different races apart, without the need for sport-specific laws. Government nonetheless took "stringent action to prevent multi-racial sport from being conducted at club level".[701] From the early 1900s to the 1960s, sport was almost totally segregated. Even attempts at non-racial sport activity across the Black races was discouraged and virtually wiped out.[702] However, some clubs persisted in their determination to promote multi-racial sport at local, provincial and national levels. Nauright has emphasised how "sport has served to both unify and divide groups" and "it has been closely interwoven with the broader fabric of South African society and has been at the forefront of social and political change".[703]

Non-White sporting clubs often operated under difficult conditions, with uneven and poorly maintained sports grounds with inadequate surfaces, few resources, few coaching or training facilities, and little press coverage. "Despite these adversities, sport was played with great enthusiasm, attracted huge followings, and produced quality sportspersons who would have excelled in the international arena, if given half a chance. Unfortunately, the apartheid policies... meant that no 'non-white', no matter how good they were, would ever be able to represent their country because they had the 'wrong skin colour'". As a result, many persons of colour went overseas to pursue their sports careers and gain the recognition they deserved.[704] This was, of course, in direct contrast to the excellent facilities provided for Whites by the government. Whites-only sports stadiums, in fact, became symbols of White political power in communities around the country.

The formation in 1952 of the first association grouping all of the Black groups – the South African Soccer Federation (SASF) – constituted a major event in the development of Black sports organisations. It brought under one roof the South African African Football Association, the South African Coloured Football Association and the South African Indian Football Association. The SASF became non-racial in 1963 with a membership of 46,000 players. The Whites-only Football Association of South Africa (FASA) had only 20,000 members. FIFA (the world soccer body) suspended FASA's membership in 1961 but did not accept the SASF in its stead. In the 1960s, professional soccer began to emerge for Blacks with the establishment of the SASF-PL and the FASA-sponsored National Professional Soccer League (NPSL). The latter predominated in the 1970s, with teams such as the Pirates and Swallows within its ranks. Then in 1985, a split led to the creation of the National Soccer League (NSL).[705]

---

[701] SAIRR, *1973 Survey*, p. 365.
[702] Booley, 1998, p. 15, notes that between 1950 and 1967 there were 11 inter-race test matches played between Coloured and African rugby teams. This was an exception, but one which helped to increase the mutual respect between players of different races.
[703] Nauright, 1997, p. 2.
[704] Agherdien, et al., 1997, p.4.
[705] Nauright, 1997, pp. 118-119.

In 1970, an attempt was made to establish a non-racial rugby association that would have merged the South African Rugby Football Board, the South African Rugby Board, the South African Rugby Football Federation, and the South African Rugby Union. However, issues regarding a potential tour to Britain and widely differing views about how to proceed towards a truly non-racial sport scuppered the potential merger. Some progress was made in 1977 when the associations agreed in principle to forming a single controlling body for rugby and that all provincial clubs should affiliate to one provincial association. However, this attempt also failed. In 1978, the White-dominated South African Rugby Board dissolved itself and reformed under the same name as a multi-racial body, with the South African Rugby Federation (Coloured) and the South African Rugby Association (African) as affiliated members. Then the 1985 state of emergency had a huge impact on sport, putting a possible merger again on the back burner. Rugby continued to be mired in conflict rooted in the broader political environment, and only in 1990 did the sport succeed in creating a single unified national rugby body, the South African Rugby Football Union (SARFU).[706]

Participation in international sporting competitions continued to be an issue. Sport was closely intertwined with broader racial politics. The South African Sports Association (SASA) was formed in 1958 to promote non-racial sport. Initially, it had little impact on the views of White-controlled national sporting organisations such as the South African Olympic and Commonwealth Games Association. This was despite the fact that South Africa was forced to leave the International Cricket Council (ICC) when it left the Commonwealth in 1961 and was suspended from FIFA in the same year.[707] However, SASA soon garnered support from various ANC-allied groups, including the Youth League, SACTU, and others. Soon, SASA formed the South African Non-Racial Olympic Committee (SANROC) with the goal of eliminating racially-based sport and forcing all racially-based organisations out of international competitions. SANROC's leader, Dennis Brutus, was forced into exile, and the organisation was reconstituted in exile. Other leaders were banned and otherwise harassed.[708] Finally, in 1964, the International Olympic Committee (IOC) barred South Africa from the Tokyo Games when the government refused to include Black athletes in the national team. In 1970, South Africa was "expelled from the Olympic movement for violating the Olympic Charter" and only rejoined in time for the 1992 games in Barcelona.[709]

In 1973, the call for international sports sanctions was reinforced by the creation of the South African Council of Sport (SACOS). SACOS' position was defined by its motto: "No normal sport in an abnormal society". Whilst SACOS' success in promoting non-racial sport internally was limited and it did not succeed in getting non-racial sport associations accepted by international bodies, it did provide an effective internal voice for sanctions.[710] SACOS developed a "charter of normal sport" which demanded that every code of sport should have only one non-racial national body, every provincial body should consist of open clubs, all racially-exclusive clubs should be abolished, any overseas teams should only play against non-racial South African teams, and no visiting team in any sport should be invited to South Africa until totally non-racial sport was achieved.[711] A more opportunistic approach was taken by the South African Olympic and National Games Association (SAONGA) which wanted to retain international links whilst trying to eliminate discrimination at home. It was accused by SACOS of only wanting to end discrimination so as to gain international acceptance.

---

[706] See Booley, 1998, Chapter 1.
[707] Nauright, 1997, p. 37.
[708] Ibid., p. 129.
[709] Ibid., p. 137.
[710] Ibid., p. 140.
[711] SAIRR, *1978 Survey*, p. 492.

In 1977, the Commonwealth Heads of Government issued the Gleneagles Declaration on Apartheid and Sport" calling on member governments to discourage all sporting contact with South Africa.[712] It was international action such as that of the IOC and the Commonwealth (very belated, of course) that finally exerted real pressure for political change on the South African government. The international sanctions against Whites-only sport provided a significant push towards political negotiations in the late 1980s.

Over the years, many civil society organisations participated in boycotts and protests against visits by touring overseas sports teams. For example, in 1982, more than 70 sports bodies, community organisations, trade unions and student bodies in Durban, Pietermaritzburg, Johannesburg and Cape Town opposed the tour of a Sri Lankan cricket team and called for a boycott of its matches. Of interest is the fact that not just sports organisations were involved in promoting such boycotts, as deracialisation of sport had become a key part of the anti-apartheid struggle.[713] Events such as this also demonstrated the increasing willingness of different racial groups and different sectors of community life to co-operate with each other in the interest of wider impact. This was just one of many such campaigns.

Also in 1982, a government-sponsored Human Sciences Research Council report called for the establishment of a council of sport to co-ordinate administration of sport, and the removal of any discriminatory measures affecting sport. It confirmed that White people had infinitely better sports facilities than other racial groups. It called for freedom of association and choice, including free access to amenities, as well as equal opportunity in sport and equal financing of sports facilities. It also said that sport should be "depoliticised as far as possible and various obnoxious and humiliating pieces of legislation should be amended".[714]

A significant aspect of Black participation in sports clubs, especially in senior administrative positions, was the high profile thus provided to Black political leaders which in turn helped in their political mobilisation efforts. Even in the 1970s and 1980s, United Democratic Front and Black Consciousness Movement leaders "used soccer matches to make speeches to large crowds where they could also escape police detection".[715]

Whilst sport was one of the most segregated activities under apartheid, it was seen by the first ANC government led by Nelson Mandela as "one of the key areas of reconciliation in the New South Africa" and "perhaps the best cultural activity through which to promote or generate a new national identity".[716] However, the power structures of sport associations are being transformed only slowly. It is proving difficult to overcome the entrenched legacy of fragmented community identities in national sport.

Concluding Remarks

It is not possible or desirable to even attempt to summarise each section of this extremely lengthy chapter. This was the period in which race, repression and resistance were most pronounced as features of the prevailing socio-political environment and of civil society. The interests of White people were protected by the apartheid system, and they were favoured in

---

[712] Nauright, 1997, p. 149.
[713] SAIRR, *1982 Survey*, p. 41.The diverse organisations involved in this boycott included the South African Council of Sport, AZAPO, the Anti-SAIC Committee, the Lenasia-based Federation of Ratepayers' Associations, Actstop, the General and Allied Workers' Union, the Media Workers' Association of South Africa, Wits University SRC and Black Students' Society, the Natal Indian Congress, and the Soweto Committee of Ten.
[714] SAIRR, *1982 Survey*, p. 586-587.
[715] Nauright, 1997, p. 57.
[716] Ibid., p. 1.

all aspects of their life: health, education, sport, property ownership, freedom of movement, access to employment and workers' rights, etc. They constituted a privileged racial group and a class of people who voted repeatedly in favour of the apartheid system so as to protect these privileges. In contrast, the interests and rights of Black South Africans were severely limited and diabolically prescribed by government. The implications of the policy of segregated development or apartheid, and its resultant legislation, were discussed. Disempowerment of and discrimination against all Black people resulted in a highly unequal and unjust society. Black people were deprived of their political rights, and extensively restricted in their access to the benefits of the formal economy. Limitations on their freedom of movement and gross differentials in government funding were particularly heinous, causing the vast majority of Black communities to live in abject poverty with poor housing, education, health and other services.

This was also the period in which civil society blossomed, with organisations emerging in all sectors of life and in all South African communities. They were funded mainly by foreign donors, who sought to support the disadvantaged and dispossessed. However, the government found numerous means to hamper the growth and impact of those it regarded as being opposed to the apartheid system. Racial exclusivity was the order of the day. Afrikaner organisations were formed to help entrench apartheid and to protect their political, economic, religious and cultural interests. English-speakers did much the same. The 1950s saw a resurgence of Black political resistance, e.g. the ANC-led Congress of the People and its Freedom Charter, the Defiance Campaign, women's protests against the pass laws, and economic boycotts in the townships. Indian and Coloured communities also revived organisations and formed new ones to resist government oppression and lobby for their rights.

The 1960s brought an economic boom which caused some of the more middle class Blacks to again adopt a relatively conservative approach so that they could continue to reap benefits from their (limited) participation in the economic expansion. Racial groups were divided by class – the African township economic elite, the Indian merchant elite, and Coloureds who sought acceptance as equals by Afrikaners were all less willing to engage in protest for fear of compromising their positions. The creation of the homelands on a tribal basis, excluded African people from the metropolitan centres of commerce and industry. They were forced to live in remote areas with few job opportunities, minimal infrastructure, and lacking in water, sanitation and electricity. The homelands were totally dependent on Pretoria and its machinations.

The Sharpeville massacre and the bannings in 1960 of key political organisations (ANC, PAC) constituted a huge blow to resistance organisations. Opinion was divided on how best to respond to this severe repression. In a major turn-around, the ANC leadership abandoned its commitment to non-violence and went into exile to continue the struggle. Other groups began to develop the ideology which became the Black Consciousness Movement and the many organisations formed to promote it. Thus Black communities became sites of conflict themselves, allowing the government's divide and rule tactics to succeed for some time.

The Soweto uprising of 1976 was a major turning point. At this time, the role of young people – school children, university students and unemployed youth – came to the fore. They challenged the older generation to overcome their passivity and become more involved in resistance activity. The young people's struggles led to the creation of various student and parent organisations to address the education crisis. Separate organisations were formed for school and university students and for non-student youth. They soon moved beyond protest action regarding the educational system to become involved in the wider socio-political protests against apartheid. Some youth organisations were affiliated to particular political organisations or adhered to specific ideological orientations. The youth emerged as a vibrant political force, having sacrificed their childhood and their education for the liberation struggle.

They persisted despite detentions, bannings and departure for exile. These organisations also played a significant role in analysing the sources of division in South African society: race and class. In the 1980s, many so-called "graduates" of the 1976 uprisings became civil society leaders in the broader struggle. Participation in these organisations also provided thousands of people with experience in democratic decision-making and collective action.

Township unrest, election and economic boycotts helped to politicise the wider community. The 1970s also saw a rapid emergence of Black trade unions and civic organisations. Coloured and Indian organisations became more strident in their resistance and began to co-operate with African organisations despite government attempts to further divide them via the introduction of the tricameral parliament. Instead, the latter helped to create more solidarity amongst all the disenfranchised groups. Resistance against forced removals politicised those directly affected as well as those who sympathised with their plight. But at the same time, the forced removals destroyed vibrant communities, family ties, economic connections, livelihoods and social networks. Government's repressive tactics and violations of human rights led to the creation of martyrs, and new leaders constantly stepped in to take their place. A panoply of human rights organisations were established to deal with specific violations by government – mistreatment of political prisoners, racial discrimination, exploitation of farm workers, forced removals, etc. Though they were unable to stop government's systematic human rights abuses, they provided at least some relief and protection for some victims, and were able on certain occasions to hold government and its officials to account.

In the main, religious organisations played a significant role in provision of services to communities, especially in education and welfare services, as well as addressing their spiritual needs. However, they generally established faith-based schools on racial grounds – their schools were largely segregated until as late as 1988. In this and other ways, many churches condoned apartheid policies, even if they did not actively support them. Nonetheless, Christian churches spawned individuals and organisations to provide leadership in the struggle against apartheid. As Christians increasingly began to see apartheid as "anti-Christian" and as contrary to the Gospel, various churches took stronger public stances against the government's policies, couching their opposition in a reinterpretation of the Gospel. An emphasis on individual conscience also emerged in calls for conscientious objection to military service, especially due to the army's hated role in subduing township unrest and in suppressing the Angolan independence movement. The desire of Black independent churches for greater autonomy from their "parent" churches and frustration amongst Black clerics regarding the continuing church hypocrisy regarding racial issues led to their formulation of Black theology. The churches – individually and in groups – issued a series of liturgically-based documents calling for an end to the injustices of apartheid. Some churches also began to admit responsibility for their support of or acquiescence to the system of separate development. Other statements offered justification for the just struggle, including even violent resistance where all other means had failed. It became clear that religious organisations needed to be more aware of the social forces affecting their communities, to engage with these forces, and to contest their actions where appropriate. Religious thought needed to be reinterpreted such that it was more relevant to changing circumstances.

As tensions rose, and politicisation increased country-wide, civil society organisations found that they had to choose between supporting apartheid or opposing it. In the 1970s and 1980s, new organisations were formed in communities to contest apartheid. It was more difficult organising in some homelands due to the dependence of homeland leadership on the apartheid government and the conflicted views of the homeland leaders regarding the anti-apartheid struggle.

Whilst women's organisations performed many important functions both at community and national levels, women's rights and equality tended to be subordinated to the liberation struggle. Some broad-based coalitions of women's organisations did help to put women's issues on the table, and took a strong stance against patriarchy and oppression of women by supposedly progressive political structures. But other women's groups were quite conservative and did not challenge power relations. Women found it difficult to rise to positions of influence and authority in most types of organisations, e.g. political, youth, trade unions, professional associations, etc. In the unions, women were essentially a subordinate class. In the early 1980s this began to change as women realised the need to confront this patriarchy and to alter their self-perceptions. They also increasingly recognised that their need to make inputs on all labour issues was compromised by their relegation to separate women's structures. The unions were foremost in promoting integrated leadership of women.

The refusal of government to allow registration of African trade unions was the most challenging issue for the entire labour movement in this period. The relatively high number of strikes in the 1950s fell dramatically in the 1960s due to government repression and the constraints on Black worker mobilisation into unions. White workers continued to be protected from competition by Black workers through various laws and policies, including job reservation, influx control and others. A hierarchy even existed within the Black working class, with Coloured and Indian workers in some sectors also trying to protect their jobs against incursion by Africans. Thus, a divided labour movement reduced its overall bargaining power, allowing the status quo to persist.

Although some unions and federations – both White and multi-racial – tried to remain apolitical, it became clear to most that labour issues and politics inevitably overlapped. The Durban strikes of 1973, many of which succeeded in improving worker conditions, led to a resurgence of worker activism. This activism was not restricted to the workplace, but rather spilled out into society at large. The creation of SACTU planted the seeds of non-racial unionism, but its closeness to the ANC alliance and consequent lack of autonomy was a problem for some unions. The Wiehahn Commission's recommendations to government in the late 1970s were received with caution by the unions, because the integration of non-registered Black unions into the existing unfavourable industrial relations system was seen as a tactic to facilitate government control of labour. The early 1980s saw huge growth of a new, independent and democratic labour movement, spurred on by the formation of FOSATU and CUSA. Subsequent draft labour law amendments were opposed by a large section of the labour movement, and the campaigns against the Labour Relations Act created a focal point for unified action and increased union clout. The needs of the workers became paramount and led to co-operation amongst federations such as COSATU and NACTU. A series of effective stayaways eventually convinced employer organisations such as SACCOLA to commence negotiations with these federations on future labour policy. Despite slow progress, agreement was eventually reached. With business on board, government could no longer resist the union challenge and the rights of workers of all races were reinforced. Worker struggles therefore played an essential role in creating the necessary space for the political transition.

Business / employer organisations were divided along racial and language lines as well as by the sector they represented. Thus, they were often split on issues. Attempts by Black business associations to lobby for greater access to White areas and to limit the entry of White business into Black areas had little success. It was only in the early 1980s that Black business federations began to get some support from ASSOCOM and the Chambers of Commerce in metropolitan areas regarding permission for Black business to operate in town and city shopping centres and for Black managers to work in White businesses in White areas. By the mid-1980s, a few White business leaders began to speak out against the detentions of political prisoners, but little action followed their statements. Some of these leaders finally recognised that the need for reform was becoming urgent if South African business and the economy as a whole were to prosper. A small delegation met with the ANC in exile in 1985. A few high level business leaders also began discussions with the mass-based resistance organisations within the country. As greater mutual understanding was achieved, pressure increased on the government to agree to negotiations leading to a democratic political transition. The full range of business organisations later played a crucial role in the CODESA talks, both as participants and in providing financial and logistical support.

Most professional associations excluded Black people or were divided on a racial basis. Those few which allowed the admission of Blacks relegated them to separate branches so that Whites retained overall control. The existence of the homelands further complicated the situation, as professionals restricted to these areas were encouraged or compelled to form ethnically-based associations. This chapter related the experience of several professions – teachers, medical professionals, social workers and others.

Some of the non-racial teachers' organisations acknowledged the link between education and politics. However, the plethora of teachers' unions also made co-ordinated action difficult. It was only in the late 1980s that attempts were made to get all teachers to join existing progressive organisations rather than creating new ones. The formation of SADTU in 1990 was the culmination of this effort, though older, more conservative teachers retained their non-politicised professional associations.

Media professionals also had racially separate unions. Whilst White journalists, members of the SASJ, protested against censorship as early as the 1970s, this was largely related to government control of the information flow regarding the Angolan war. These journalists had little concern for the repression of Black journalists, even those working for the White-owned media. The efforts by many Black journalists to cover events in the townships and homelands were often repressed. The Union of Black Journalists was banned, and MWASA replaced it, eventually becoming a non-racial union for media workers. The alternative media, described at length in this chapter, also struggled in the face of constant government harassment, but managed to play a significant role in consciousness-raising and dissemination of information regarding the struggle, political, cultural and community issues. There was some useful cross-fertilisation and mutual support amongst the various alternative media publications, their organisations, owners, editors and writers. Few of these publications, however, survived the democratic transition.

Many unsuccessful attempts were made to create non-racial sports organisations and to promote non-racial sport. Government consistently opposed non-racial sport at all levels and in all sports. Leaders of such groups were harassed and banned. Though these organisations had little impact on the sports scene within the country, they did succeed in persuading international sporting federations to boycott South African teams and events and to expel White South African sports federations from international bodies. This trend increased in the early 1970s due to the creation of SACOS, but it too had limited success in promoting non-racial sports associations. Its aim of one national non-racial sports body for each sport proved difficult to achieve mainly due to a lack of funds and lack of sponsorship from corporates. Nonetheless, deracialisation of sport became a key goal of the anti-apartheid struggle and international sanctions against Whites-only sport helped to push government towards ameliorating apartheid in sport.

The apartheid government exploited race, class and ethnic differences in every sector to achieve its own political and economic ends. In response, communities, political groups, workers, business, professionals, sporting bodies and a huge range of others mobilised to protect their particular group interests. Many of these organisations also became involved in the anti-apartheid movement, joining together in federations and coalitions to promote their goals. They saw clearly that they would never be able to achieve their particular aims without bringing about the abolition of apartheid and the creation of a non-racial society. Despite appalling repression over this period and the consequent struggles faced by anti-apartheid organisations, they gradually mobilised enough support across South African society to achieve their hard-fought goals of freedom and democracy.

Chapter Five

Social Movements

Throughout the history of resistance to apartheid and racial segregation, various urban as well as rural social movements emerged in South Africa. Some directly resisted the racist policies, some opposed land usage, some opposed mineral exploitation, and some sought to protect their informal income generation against government regulation. In the rural areas these movements were populist, not necessarily supported by the tribal hierarchies. In the urban areas, these movements manifested themselves as networks, alliances, fronts, associations, committees. They often relied on the support of existing organisations to espouse their cause. Some movements transformed themselves into formal organisations --- either civil society or political parties -- in the longer term, whilst others disbanded once their initial objectives were achieved.

After discussing some general points with regard to processes of mass mobilisation, six social movements which played important roles during the anti-apartheid struggle are discussed below:

1. *Rural community resistance:* In various rural communities, spontaneous revolts occurred against apartheid government policies. Some of these were led by tribal authorities, but many emerged from communities themselves in situations where tribal leaders had been co-opted by the government. Some of the protests were led by women who had been left behind in rural areas whilst their husbands migrated to work in urban areas.
2. *Inkatha*: The Zulu-based political organisation led by Dr. Mangosuthu Buthelezi which played ambiguous roles vis-à-vis the apartheid government and the ANC.
3. *Black Consciousness Movement* (BCM): A movement based on a broad social philosophy which responded to the socio-cultural as well as political effects of apartheid and whose ideology was later espoused by political parties such as AZAPO.
4. *United Democratic Front* (UDF): The internal arm of the ANC, created when the ANC was banned, which aimed to unite all organisations opposed to apartheid.
5. *Civic associations*: Township-based community organisations which used various forms of protest to undermine the Black Local Authorities and the apartheid system as a whole.
6. *Associations in informal settlements*: Associations formed to improve the quality of life of the most disadvantaged people, many of whom had been moved off their land in rural areas due to apartheid laws or who moved to the cities in search of jobs and were living in shanties, hostels, and other areas adjacent to existing communities.

Mass mobilisation

Mobilisation for peaceful mass action is an area in which South Africa has unique experience. From the days of Gandhi in the early 1900s to the end of the century in the early 1990s, mass mobilisation was an integral part of the search for human dignity and for a democratic state. In the context of the struggle, mobilisation represented the demands of the people at the grassroots. It was about creating and filling space for struggle, an expression against successive repressive racist governments. It was also about demonstrating critical dissent, targeting specific conditions, and seeking redress.

An examination of the phenomenon of organising for mass mobilisation shows that independent organisations with certain capabilities need to exist. They should be able to build a critical mass and, in a planned organic way, gather support for a cause. With agreed (often limited) objectives, such organisations can attack a specific issue or apply pressure to attain a specific goal or sectoral interests. These interests may coincide with those of other stakeholders or interest groups, or may be particular to that movement/organisation alone.

The elements which shaped mobilisation, especially in South Africa, are:
- The historical racist processes, including all the elements of colonialism and economic deprivation;
- The nascent and overt ideological factors;
- The economic, social, political, technological environments; and
- The systems, institutions and structural frameworks which underpinned them.

Mass mobilisation usually involves the following processes (not necessarily in this order):
- Understanding the historical basis of the problem;
- Identifying specific goals or objectives;
- Communicating the problem in an emotional and personal tone;
- Mobilising human and financial resources;
- Gathering local, national and even international attention and support;
- Understanding the constituencies / stakeholders and their respective needs;
- Providing leadership and direction;
- Building solidarity;
- Developing campaign materials; and
- Promoting a counter-culture.

Some of these processes and movements in South Africa are examined here. However, space and time preclude the examination of each in detail to fully understand the nuances of their particular experience and their medium- and long-term historical political significance.

It was Albert Luthuli who, in accepting the Nobel Peace Prize on 11 December 1961, said that the prize recognised "the role played by the African people during the last fifty years to establish, peacefully, a society in which merit and not race would fix the position of the individual in the life of the nation".[717] It is with this acknowledgement in mind that the following movements are described.

Rural community resistance

Localised resistance provided evidence to the government that many rural communities were angry at being further disempowered and disadvantaged due to apartheid laws and regulations. The following are four examples of the types of rural uprising which occurred:

1. Marico Reserve: The Lehurutshe area of Bophutatswana was so poorly endowed that half the men worked outside the area. The proposal of pass laws for women as well as men would have meant further impoverishment of the community, by limiting their opportunities to find work. In March 1957, a mobile pass unit arrived in the community. Chief Moiloa was ordered to make all the women attend a *legotla* to obtain passes. The community refused... This created growing tension between the Chief and the government. Only a few teachers and wives of civil servants registered. Chief Moiloa was stripped of his office.

---

[717] Karis, Carter and Gerhart, 1977, Vol. 3, p. 706.

Women from the Johannesburg area arrived and proposed a boycott of the local trader and the school in protest. The school was shut by the authorities. Men from the Reef arrived and put the complainants against Moiloa on trial. They were sentenced to death. Police intervened, but revenge attacks continued, leading to a series of trials. Due to the expenses related to the trials, the community's savings were drained. In June and July, women burned their passes and took passive resistance actions against the police. Action followed action, and retribution was rife. Police brutally raided villages seeking ANC agitators. Two thousand people fled into what is now Botswana. In August 1959, Lucas Mangope was installed by the Pretoria government as Chief.

2. Sekhukhuneland: In 1958-59, several events led to a confrontation in the Sekhukhuneland area of Lebowa. New local taxes, stock restrictions, interference with traditional polygamous marital arrangements, the deterioration of Bantu education, and finally, the deposing of the Bapedi Paramount Chief combined to create serious tension in this community. The final trigger was the attempted arrest of a minor chief. This resulted in a violent confrontation between the community and the police in which two people were killed. Subsequently, pro-Bantu Affairs chiefs, teachers and traders were attacked. The spiral of violence increased when the area was sealed off and police reinforcements, including a special mobile unit, were brought it.

3. Mpondoland: In 1960 in the Transkei, resistance to the Bantu Authorities coalesced with the establishment of *Intaba* (the Mountain). This group spread its influence over 4,000 square kilometres and involved 180,000 people. This resistance movement insisted that the chiefs and headmen should denounce the authorities. When 17 chiefs and headmen refused to do so, they were killed. Five suspected police informers were also killed.

The tension escalated. A meeting was called in Flagstaff by Botha Sigcau. The meeting was attacked by police and 11 Mpondo were killed. The following week, 29 *kraal* of government supporters were destroyed in revenge. As *Intaba*'s resources were drained, they coerced local teachers -- black and white -- to pay a five pound license. Boycotts of White-owned stores were initiated.

No ANC influence or assistance was discernible in these activities. Appeals were made by the Mpondo to the United Nations to no avail. A commission of inquiry was established, but their findings entrenched government policy. On 1 November 1960, 3,000 Mpondo watched the arrest of their chief. Over 5,000 people were interned. By February the next year, the Bizana revolt had collapsed.

These revolts set the stage for the establishment of the Transkei Territorial Assembly and the subsequent creation of a homeland under Chief Mantanzima.

4. Tembu District: Whilst they were initially compliant, the General Council (*Bungu*) of the Tembu in Western Transkei was increasingly opposed to the rehabilitation schemes proposed by the Bantu Authorities. The authorities intended to consolidate farming units and began removing people from their land. Interference in land tenure as well as in the allocation of land led to growing violent reactions.

The disturbances were sporadic and uncoordinated. Opposition to the Bantu Authorities was also affected by rivalry between Paramount Chief Sabata and Mantanzima. These disturbances led to killings and arrests, burning of huts and killing of cattle and sheep.

In late 1962, three abortive attempts on Mantanzima's life were made by POQO (the PAC armed wing). Peasant resistance peaked in this area in 1963. The Bantu Authorities were intimidated, leading to the arrest of large numbers of people. However, the lack of coherence, unity and strategy in the resistance limited its effect. In 1964, Mantanzima was given enhanced powers.

The drought, which began in 1965 and lasted for five years, forced many people to leave the area to seek work elsewhere. One-fifth of the cattle were lost in this period.

Impact of the rural uprisings

The development of a local organisation in the Witzieshoek incident   the Lingangele -- brought direction and coherence under local leadership. This appeared to be the best solution for effective resistance. The experience of the Mpondo, who used *Intaba* to express their dissatisfaction, supports this view.

The two incidents in the Tembu district can be linked directly to Poqo activities in the Western Cape. When messages were received by then migrant workers that their land was being taken away, meetings were held, resistance was planned and plotted, and funds were raised. Workers travelled back to the rural areas to redress the situation and find justice. Police preparedness (possibly through informers) stymied their efforts, leading to arrests, detention and trials -- no justice was found. These actions also hastened the creation of self-governing independent homelands, regardless of how economically unviable they were.

In other instances, direct links can be traced to organisations created by migrant workers in the urban areas. For example, the Batarutshe Association was linked to the urban-based Witzieshoek Vigilance Association which was revived in Johannesburg. Originally established in 1914, it emerged again in the 1940s. These organisations, however, were limited in membership and were akin to clan organisations found elsewhere. They aimed to support, enhance and often protect their members' interests in an often hostile and competitive urban industrial setting.

Neither Poqo nor the clan organisations succeeded in their plans. The influence of national political organisations such as the ANC and later the PAC was limited. These movements failed primarily because they lacked leadership, organisation, structure, strategy, specific objectives and coherent massed power. The political power of government was coherent and enforceable. It was able to sow dissension, and divide communities. It applied its power ruthlessly and brutally when required. It provided patronage and created chiefs and leaders to support its heinous aim of apartheid hegemony.

Rural women's protests

Rural women were the most affected by the social, economic and political impact of industrialisation on the one hand and inflexible racist policies on the other. The dislocation forced upon them by colonialism and the migrant labour system disrupted their family life and undermined their rights and status in patriarchal rural societies. Marital instability, early widowhood, domestic conflicts with in-laws, the humiliation and subservience of most men's urban work experiences, daily poverty and economic struggles for survival -- all these factors influenced women to become more assertive and politicised.

The indignation women expressed in urban areas (1956-57) came somewhat later to the rural areas. By 1959, women in the rural areas of Natal, faced with their particular problems, rebelled in several districts and towns. Their rebellion was caused by an increasing pressure on available land. They faced stringent influx control measures accompanied by the reparation to rural areas of illegal residents in the towns and cities. Cattle stock controls were being imposed and enforced. Linked to the onerous process of dipping the cattle, women were no longer guaranteed fields to plough. An additional increased tax on wines was imposed in 1959.

The rebellion started in Harding on 21 July 1959 following the arrest of 30 protesting women. Men marched on the jail and demanded the release of their wives. When this failed, they set alight nearby sugar plantations and attempted to block the railway lines. This incident in Harding was the only one involving men.[718]

Other incidents reported occurred in Umzinto, Idutywa, Port Shepstone, Hibberdene, Ixopo and other reserved areas. A meeting at St. Faith's in mid-August 1959 attracted 1,000 women. They demanded a reply from the Native Commissioner, but were told instead to return home and channel their requests through their husbands and headmen. In response, the women knelt and prayed, refusing to move. Then, 366 of them were arrested and sentenced to four months imprisonment with the option of a 35 pound fine.

It is necessary to point out that this was not a feminist movement. Their sentiment was matriarchal. It is captured best and most vividly in Lilian Ngoyi's statement: "My womb is shaken when they speak of Bantu education".[719] Women in this period were not seeking an alteration to their domestic relationships and responsibilities. Nor were they seeking an extension of their economic or political role. Rather, they were expressing gender solidarity and possibly scorn for the more acquiescent men.

Why a broad-based rural revolt did not occur

Due to a lack of capacity, infrastructure and funds, only a few organisations played a role in rural areas. Many of these associated themselves with local churches and used their premises and facilities. They concerned themselves with issues related to forced removals, land, detention, education, health services, water provision, etc.

Leadership in rural communities emanated primarily from the ranks of African teachers and nurses. Their opposition to racist and apartheid authority in the rural areas emerged for several reasons:

- They were the only educated group in these societies which placed a high premium on education.
- They were often without formal power in their communities.
- They were poorly paid and badly treated by their (often) White supervisors.
- There was little to set them apart from the rest of the community: they suffered the same indignities and lack of services.
- The authorities often threatened their job security and status.

However, much of life in the rural areas was dominated by traditional leaders and structures which they controlled. Whilst some did have a genuine interest in promoting the welfare of their people, they had few resources. Many were co-opted by the apartheid government and persuaded to accept the homelands and other racist policies.

Giliomee and Schlemmer[720] discounted the view that South Africa in the late 1970s and 1980s was experiencing the same conditions as elsewhere which led to rural revolts. They advanced the following views:

- The population density does not permit such revolts.
- Colonial and racial exploitation and domination by colonial and neo-colonial governments were cushioned through the social systems extant in African societies, with the strong emphasis on sharing, and by their political system.
- The relatively recent history of the peasantry and the process of proletarianisation were not conducive to rural revolt.

---

[718] Yawitch, 1977.
[719] *Bantu World*, Johannesburg, 8 October 1955.
[720] Giliomee and Schlemmer, 1985.

- The particular difficulties surrounding organisation and the high incidence of migrant labour made a homeland / rural revolt unlikely.
- The rare combination of misery and tyranny required for a rural revolt was not enough. Outside leadership was required.
- The multiple divisions and cleavages within the rural population itself prevented a unified revolt.
- The rural elites (homeland leaders, civil servants, Black businessmen) themselves exploited the apartheid situation in their own interests.
- The conditions which existed in the period 1940-1960 for the mass rural revolts were eliminated by the imposition of National Party regulations covering all aspects of rural life, including ownership of land, cattle, property, business, education, health, transport, etc.

Inkatha

Founded in 1928 as a Zulu cultural organisation by the royal house, *Inkatha ka Zulu* (Zulu national movement) was an "attempt to generate mass support for the Zulu monarchy faced with the disintegration of pre-capitalist social relations".[721] It was revived in the early 1970s by Dr. Mangosuthu Buthelezi, the uncle of King Goodwill Zwelithini. The name of the organisation was changed in 1975 to *Inkatha ye Nkululeke ye Sizwe* (Freedom of the Nation) when it began to structure itself as a national mass organisation, a political base within the KwaZulu homeland, and a political platform for Buthelezi.

Buthelezi was a contemporary of many of South Africa's political leaders who studied at Fort Hare, where he was a member of the ANC Youth League. He was later expelled from the university. Buthelezi rose to political influence as chief advisor to the King as a hereditary function in 1970. He was appointed as Chief Executive Councillor of the Kwa Zulu Legislative Assembly in 1972. In 1973, following the industrial disputes in Durban, Buthelezi dispatched Barney Dladla, the Community Affairs Councillor, to intervene. Dladla succeeded in his efforts, but was later dismissed from this position as Buthelezi is alleged to have feared his popularity.

Whilst it was opposed to apartheid, Inkatha worked within the framework of the apartheid political machinery for leverage. It was increasingly seen as an ally of Pretoria rather than of the liberation movement. Inkatha espoused an economic policy which in the Cold War era was manifestly pro-West and capitalist. For example, though in 1978 Buthelezi visited major companies in the US, he urged them to pressure the South African government to call a national convention, but did not support disinvestment. Inkatha also made contact with a range of organisations in South Africa with the aim of achieving more co-ordination within the anti-apartheid movement. However, Buthelezi antagonised various groups, not least with his inconsistency – sometimes trying to move closer to the movement and at others being quite critical of key players in the movement. In the Soweto student uprisings, Buthelezi backed the Zulu hostel-dwellers against the youth. At the funeral of Robert Sobukwe in March 1978, large groups of militant BC youth present insisted that Buthelezi leave. He was stoned as he was leaving.[722]

By 1978, the Inkatha organisation had expanded to over 300 branches in Natal, Transvaal and the Orange Free State. Buthelezi claimed that there were 150,000 paid-up members, and that for every paid-up member there were about 30 to 50 sympathisers.[723] Inkatha also had a Women's Brigade with a similar number of branches, and a Youth Brigade.

---

[721] Davies et al., 1984, p. 388.
[722] SAIRR, *1978 Survey*, p. 30.
[723] Ibid., p. 28. We have no independent verification of these figures.

Furthermore, in Kwa Zulu schools, pupils had a weekly hour of "instruction" regarding the aims of Inkatha, and schoolteachers who were not members of Inkatha faced disapproval and suspicion.[724] "The KwaZulu Legislative Assembly decreed in 1978 that a civil servant's standing within Inkatha would be a key factor in decisions about promotion". In some cases, traditional Zulu leaders insisted that their subjects pay annual subscriptions to Inkatha. These practices provide a clear indication of the level of "heavy-handed persuasion and coercion" within Inkatha.[725] This lack of freedom of association was never commented on or Buthelezi chastised for it in the capitals of London or Washington.

The vast majority of Inkatha members and Buthelezi's political constituency were Zulu, though he did have some Indian and White supporters. Inkatha power was entrenched in Kwa Zulu. It influenced every sphere of life in the homeland. It is of note that due to the large number of labour migrants who had left the homeland in search of urban jobs, women played a significant role in the day-to-day running of the organisation. Inkatha was represented in the Transvaal first by John Mavuso and later by Gibson Thula.

Whilst Inkatha membership continued to grow, tensions between Inkatha and the ANC-SACP alliance began to seriously deteriorate from the early 1980s. Though Buthelezi emphasised that Inkatha was committed to the ideals espoused by the founders of the ANC in the early 20th century, it became clear that the positions of the two groups on key issues had since diverged. For example, Buthelezi opposed the emerging labour movement and campaigned against sanctions and the withdrawal of foreign investment. To the chagrin of the South African labour movement, he accepted the first George Meany Award from the U.S. labour federation -- the AFL-CIO -- with the parents of Neil Aggett. In 1980, when a student boycott erupted at universities in KwaZulu and Natal, Buthelezi mobilised armed men to attack the students, claiming that the student actions were "part and parcel of a total onslaught against Inkatha". This view was rather an indication of Buthelezi's increasing political vulnerability even within Inkatha due to internal divisions regarding his co-operation with the apartheid state.[726]

Inkatha was part of the South African Black Alliance (SABA), also comprising the like-minded Labour Party (Coloured) and the Reform Party (Indian). SABA was chaired by Buthelezi, who therefore exerted considerable influence. Like Inkatha, SABA rejected the idea that the ANC and PAC were the only real representatives of Black South Africans. However, SABA agreed with the view that the government's constitutional proposals were unacceptable on the grounds that all racial and ethnic groups should participate directly in government.[727] Inkatha campaigned against the constitutional proposals saying that they would lead to permanent White domination. The Labour Party was suspended from SABA in 1983 when it decided to participate in the constitutional proposals, and Buthelezi warned that such moves would lead Africans to see Coloureds as their enemies. He urged Coloureds and Indians to maintain their unity with Africans within SABA.[728]

By 1983, Inkatha claimed membership of 750,000, organised in 2,000 branches. Buthelezi sent out mixed messages about his support for a unitary state, also indicating a willingness to consider a "federal formula... based on geographically determined units". Yet, he said that Inkatha opposed ethnic politics (despite Inkatha's clear reliance on its Zulu base) and divisions and would not accept homeland independence as an option. His attitude shifted back and forth, from accusing the ANC of being jealous of Inkatha and of therefore trying to

---

[724] Ibid., p. 292.
[725] Davies et al., 1984, p. 390.
[726] Ibid., p. 393.
[727] SAIRR, *1982 Survey*, p. 41.
[728] SAIRR, *1983 Survey*, p. 56.

destroy it, to proposing greater unity with the ANC and PAC. Tensions increased on the ground between Inkatha and UDF supporters, often erupting in violence. [729]

In the mid-1980s, Inkatha established the Buthelezi Commission to investigate and report on a separate Kingdom of Zululand and to propose a blueprint for the constitutional development of South Africa as a whole. The Commission comprised Inkatha members but was dominated by representatives of White-owned corporates, professional bodies, conservative academics and the Progressive Federal and New Republic political parties. The composition and conclusions of the Commission were vehemently opposed in extra-parliamentary circles, and the independent report which emerged was quickly discounted by Pretoria. However, other events did not have such a peaceful outcome.

The first was the blistering attack launched on Inkatha and Buthelezi by Elijah Barayi, the newly elected President of COSATU, at the launch rally. The reaction was immediate. Within months, Buthelezi launched the United Workers Union of South Africa (UWUSA) and began, not very successfully, appealing to Inkatha members to join this rather than any other union or federation.

The second was the release of some ANC political leaders by the national government. In their recruitment drive to organise members under the UDF banner, almost daily skirmishes occurred to win the hearts and minds of the African people of KwaZulu and Natal. The White, Coloured and Indian communities on both sides found the emerging conflict a matter they could no longer influence, and they disengaged. It is now clear that both sides (ANC and Inkatha) were infiltrated by the forces of the Pretoria government in an attempt to worsen the conflict and thereby weaken the parties. This war flowed over into other provinces, mainly Gauteng. Increasing violence was witnessed in the urban centres of Thokoza, Katlehong, Tembisa, Kagiso, Vereeniging and elsewhere. In 1993, the Boipatong massacre of men, women and children took place in the Vereeniging district. Whilst initially attributed to Inkatha, even the Goldstone Commission initially and the Truth and Reconciliation Commission later have not been able to arrive at a conclusion as to who was formally responsible for the massacre.

In 1990, Buthelezi announced that Inkatha would become a political party – the Inkatha Freedom Party (IFP). Serious attempts were made by the ANC to strengthen links with Buthelezi and the IFP and to reduce the violent tensions between them through an accord. Whilst Buthelezi did sign the National Peace Accord in 1991, he was severely embarrassed the same year when "Inkathagate" revealed that Inkatha had been covertly receiving funds from the South African government. He was angered in 1992 when the de Klerk government signed the Record of Understanding with the ANC, part of which benned IFP members from carrying their traditional weapons in public and ordered the fencing in of the mainly Inkatha-aligned migrant worker hostels. As a result, Buthelezi threw himself and the IFP into the arms of the right-wing Concerned South Africans Group (COSAG) and then refused to participate in the CODESA (Convention for a Democratic South Africa) negotiations at Kempton Park because a federal system had been rejected.[730] Buthelezi also snubbed the Kissinger delegation which had arrived in South Africa to broker an agreement by refusing to meet them at the Carlton Centre in Johannesburg. Further negotiations with Buthelezi regarding the IFP's participation in the forthcoming 1994 first democratic elections succeeded only at the very last minute, literally days beforehand. Special IFP stickers had to be added to the election ballot to accommodate the IFP's entry in the elections.

Following the outcome of the 1994 democratic elections in which the IFP won 10% of the vote, Inkatha joined with the ANC and the National Party to establish a Government of

---

[729] Ibid., pp. 51-53.
[730] Saunders and Southey, 1998, p. 91.

National Unity. Buthelezi served as Minister of Home Affairs and had the honour of being Acting President of South Africa on several occasions during the absence of both the President and the Deputy President. First the National Party exited the Government of National Unity, followed later by the IFP.

The Black Consciousness Movement (BCM)

Several factors led to the emergence within South Africa of what became the Black Consciousness Movement (BCM):
- The suppression of the nationalist movement;
- The leadership of such movements being banned, imprisoned or in exile;
- The police recruitment of informers which paralysed political initiatives;
- The mainly White and increasingly compliant student movement;
- The establishment of ethnic universities;
- The creation of the homelands;
- The reduction of the urban African population and the forced consolidation of rural Africans into homelands;
- Increasing poverty amongst African people in urban areas through low wages and in rural areas through culling of cattle and the effects of drought;
- The international climate on the African continent and in the USA;
- The emergence of Black theology which permeated the University Christian Movement; and
- The development philosophy and thinking in the Third World.[731]

Out of these conditions emerged the South African Student Organisation (SASO)[732] at Turfloop University in 1969. In several respects, this organisation differed from the Africanist philosophy:
- It defined all politically disadvantaged groups as Blacks and included Indians and Coloureds in its ranks.
- It conceded differences and divisions within the Black community based on ethnicity, class, etc.
- It required that a dependency mentality be eradicated.
- It maintained that Whites needed to continue the struggle in their own areas and spaces without African integration into a western capitalist society.
- It argued that Black people should draw on indigenous values and mores and reject externally conceived ideological systems and cultures.
- It rejected the notion of Black inferiority and recognised that the immediate problem of mobilising Black resistance was mainly psychological.

SASO played a huge role in the mobilisation of grassroots support – especially university students – for the BCM.

In 1972, the Black Peoples Convention (BPC) was created on the principle that Black people should determine their own future and solve their own problems. The first national congress in Hammanskraal was attended by about 200 African, Indian and Coloured delegates and observers. The BPC aimed to counter economic oppression through Black communalism, building economic co-operatives, health projects, and literacy campaigns. It also decided to oppose foreign investment in South Africa as it support the White-dominated economy and exploited Black workers.[733]

---

[731] For example, that of African post-independence leaders such as Julius Nyerere and Kwame Nkrumah, and development thinkers such as Frantz Fanon and Paolo Freire.
[732] See section In Chapter Four on University and Student Organisations for more on SASO.
[733] SAIRR, *1976 Survey,* p. 23. The BPC sent letters in 1973 to 31 foreign companies urging them to disinvest. See p. 184.

The BPC was quickly subjected to government harassment. Banning orders were almost immediately served on all of the leadership except one. In 1975/76, nine BPC/SASO leaders were tried under the Terrorism Act despite the fact that none of the charges related to physical acts of terrorism. Ironically for the government, the trial provided the defendants and witnesses with an opportunity to present a detailed explanation of the Black Consciousness philosophy and BPC policy – essentially making the trial an effective political forum. After 16 months in court, the defendants were all found guilty and sentenced to jail terms of five or six years each.

BCM activists became increasingly aware of the role played by the White media in reinforcing negative stereotypes of Africans. Government completely controlled the broadcast media, but not the print media. In order to provide a more positive influence in the Black community through the media, Black journalists in the Transvaal established the Union of Black Journalists (UBJ). Many of its members were detained and imprisoned, including well-known and respected journalists such as Joe Thloloe, Aggrey Klaaste, Percy Qoboza, Juby Mayet, Mike Mzileni, Thenjiwe Mtintso, and Enoch Duma.[734] After the UBJ was banned in 1977, it was reincarnated as the Writers Association of South Africa (WASA). In the late 1970s, WASA played an important role in expounding BC rhetoric and opposition to White control of the media. For example, in 1979 at its annual conference, Zwelakhe Sisulu, president of WASA, noted the attacks by the government on the freedom of the press as well as on Black culture in general. He said that the government was trying to create class divisions amongst Blacks, and that therefore Black Consciousness and solidarity was essential. Others spoke about the growing distance between Black workers and the Black middle-class and argued for greater class consciousness as well as race consciousness. As a result, WASA voted to widen its membership to include other newspaper workers, and changed its name to the Media Workers' Association of South Africa (MWASA) – thus becoming a real industrial union with more political and economic clout.[735]

The Black and Allied Workers Union (BAWU) was established by the BCM to build an organisational base amongst Black workers. BAWU opposed the attempt to encourage Black workers to join White trade unions, seeing it as a blatant attempt to dilute Black's potential political and economic power. Instead, they encouraged the formation of Black trade unions, and suggested that Whites should facilitate this process. They also argued that "Black workers' interests extend beyond the factory; they extend to the ghetto where black workers stay together in hostels under squalid conditions, to the crowded trains and buses – to the absence of amenities – to the stringent irksome and humiliating application of influx control laws – to the lack of proper channels whereby people could equip themselves with basic skills". BAWU intended to mobilise unorganised workers, implement a workers' education programme, to engage in collective bargaining for better wages and working conditions, to demand legal recognition for Black unions, and to consult with existing Black unions.[736] BAWU was not included in the organisational bannings of 1977, largely because of the international attention and condemnation in response to government repression of Black trade unions. However, union leaders continued to be harassed. By 1984, BAWU remained unregistered but claimed 86,000 signed-up members in the 19 unions affiliated to it. It declined to join the UDF and reaffirmed its allegiance to the BC philosophy.[737][738]

---

[734] Karis and Gerhart, 1997, Vol. 5, p. 322.
[735] Ibid., pp. 322-323. For the full text of Sisulu's speech, see pp. 758-760.
[736] BAWU, "Call to Organise and Form Black Trade Unions in South Africa", Johanneburg, 1973(?). For abridged text, see Karis and Carter, 1997, Vol. 5, pp. 607-610.
[737] SAIRR, *1984 Survey*, p. 313.
[738] When the Council of Unions of South Africa (CUSA) was established in 1980, this federation was unfairly and incorrectly lumped by state security agencies and White intellectuals into the Black

In the early 1970s, the Study Project on Christianity in Apartheid Society (SPROCAS), led by Dr. Beyers Naude of the Christian Institute and Bennie Khoapa, launched the Black Community Programmes (BCP). It was closely linked to the BCM, e.g. Steve Biko also joined the paid staff of the BCP in 1972. It promoted the Black self-reliance message through the creation of clinics and home industry projects. BPC conducted a national survey of Black organisations and published a directory of about 70 of them, ranging from local burial societies and drama clubs to national organisations. It also encouraged Black professionals to become more involved in providing leadership in Black society, but was more successful in its efforts to develop leadership amongst the youth through training seminars and the creation of a national network of regional youth organisations – the National Youth Organisation (NAYO) – in 1973. High school students were also beginning to organise, e.g. through the South African Students' Movement (SASM), by 1974.[739]

Other Black Consciousness organisations were formed around this time. In December 1975, the Black Women's Federation (BWF) was established "to work for solidarity and co-operation among Black women and their organisations". Its members were African, Indian and Coloured women and the elected president was Fatima Meer. They took the view that before affiliating with any White women's organisations, they should build up their own independence and self-reliance.[740]

The Institute of Black Studies was an initiative of Black academics in the Transvaal to discuss the role of Blacks in the present and future. Also in 1976, in the Durban area, the Institute of Black Research was formed for similar purposes. Both organisations aimed to promote Black pride, to realise Black people's potential, and to ensure that Black people's voices were heard.[741]

However, not all efforts to develop links with organisations across Black society were successful. Attempts to involve two national organisations of Black clergy, the African Independent Churches Association (AICA) and the Interdenominational African Ministers' Association (IDAMASA), were relatively stillborn. AICA's members were relatively conservative in political terms. IDAMASA, though initially sympathetic to SASO and willing to convene a meeting of other Black organisations to discuss the formation of a non-student Black Consciousness grouping, pulled back once it realised that the new organisation was going to be overtly political. Similarly, the Association for the Educational and Cultural Advancement of the African People (ASSECA), which was opposed to Bantu education, was too conservative due to its middle-class membership and reliance on corporate contributions to join the BPC.[742]

Three significant instances of repression interfered with the growth of the BCM:
1. The 1974 Viva Frelimo rallies held to celebrate the independence of Mozambique from Portugal were planned by the BCM. Police moved in to suppress the rallies, arrested and detained the leaders, and eventually brought them to trial. The leaders were sentenced to imprisonment and joined the ANC leaders on Robben Island, bringing with them to the liberation struggle a new impatience, philosophy and strategic view.
2. The arrest and subsequent death in detention of Steve Biko on the 12th September 1977. Biko was the leader of the Movement who had been banned

---

Consciousness camp as the federation espoused the principle of Black leadership of the working people.
[739] See section on Youth Organisations in Chapter Four for more on SASM.
[740] SAIRR, *1976 Survey*, p. 24.
[741] Ibid., p. 24.
[742] Karis and Gerhart, 1997, Vol. 5, pp. 120-121.

and restricted to the township of King William's Town. His funeral was attended by about 20,000 BCM supporters.

3. The banning of 18 organisations on 19 October 1977, most of which were allied to the BCM.[743] Three publications were also banned: *The World, Weekend World,* and *Pro Veritate;* and journalists and other activists were detained.

Nonetheless, within months of the bannings, spearheaded by the Soweto Action Committee, the idea of a new BC organisation was mooted. The Azanian Peoples Organisation (AZAPO) was launched in 1979. Its leaders espoused a socialist philosophy intertwined with Black Consciousness. AZAPO wanted to work towards a society with a common education system for all and one parliament for a unitary state. The "independence" of the Bantustans and the creation of ethnically-based organisations of all kinds were opposed as means of "balkanisation" of the country to undermine Black unity. AZAPO also supported Black theology, and aimed to empower Black workers.[744] In the early 1980s, AZAPO was active in opposing the government's constitutional proposals as well as in sports and cultural boycotts against visiting teams and entertainers. It campaigned against the elections for Black Local Authorities ("a sham reform") and also embarked upon a health education campaign to prevent the spread of contagious diseases amongst the Black community.

Outside South Africa, BC leaders who had gone into exile united into a single organisation called the Black Consciousness Movement of Azania (BCMA). They began a battle for recognition as liberation organisations by the Organisation of African Unity (OAU) and the United Nations. These efforts were jointly stymied by the ANC and the PAC, both of which opposed to the racial exclusivism of the BCMA.

Conflicts between those who supported Black Consciousness and those who opposed its Black exclusivism created divisions within the anti-apartheid movement. Debates amongst BC adherents also emerged in the early 1980s, not least related to whether the struggle in South Africa was based on race or on class. Some argued that race was a determinant of class. Others promoted the need to politicise the Black working class along with the idea, for example, of a BC-oriented trade union federation.

Whilst AZAPO established a university student and later a high school student organisation, it began to be overtaken by events both inside and outside the country when it steadfastly refused to engage in dialogue or strategic alliances with other emerging mass movements such as the United Democratic Front (UDF). It did, however, participate in the establishment in the mid-1980s of the National Forum which was an attempt to unite the strategy and explore methods of challenging the increasingly brutal and covert efforts of the South African state to eliminate opposition.

The BCMA refused to apply for amnesty as part of the de Klerk plan to normalise internal arrangements before a negotiated settlement. AZAPO declined to participate in the 1994 elections claiming that the Constitution was a negotiated one and did not reflect the view of the majority of South Africans. By 1999, when AZAPO agreed to participate in the elections, it found that it was only able to obtain 0.17 % of the vote, gaining one seat in the National Assembly. The breakaway faction, the Socialist Party of Azania (SOPA), won 0.06% of the

---

[743] The banned organisations included the Black People's Convention, South African Student's Organisation (SASO), Black Community Programmes (BCP), Black Parents' Association (BPA), Black Women's Federation (BWF), National Association of Youth Organisations (NAYO), and all its provincial structures, Medupe Writers' Association, South African Students Movement (SASM), Union of Black Journalists (UBJ), Soweto Teachers' Action Committee (TAC), Zimele Trust Fund, the Christian Institute (CI), the Association for the Educational and Cultural Advancement of African People (ASSECA), and the Soweto Students Representative Council (SSRC).

[744] See www.azapo.org.za and SAIRR, *1978 Survey,* pp. 33-34.

vote and did not obtain any seats at all. This disunity and eventual disintegration will doubtless be the subject of much interrogation by future political scientists and historians.

The philosophy AZAPO -- in a disguised form -- has found new currency with the ANC. This has been mooted as the African Renaissance. It is also expressed in terms of employment legislation as the Employment Equity Act which aims to advance the cause of Black workers in workplaces throughout South Africa, and in other policy approaches such as Black economic empowerment (BEE).

The emotional power of Black Consciousness permeated the 1970s and 1980s. The BCM student activists became teachers, priests, health workers and legal professionals. BC themes were taken up in the daily Black newspapers and township cultural events. Through the organisations and measures discussed above, Black Consciousness took hold in all aspects of life and became a broader social philosophy rather than one promulgated only by African intellectuals.

The United Democratic Front (UDF)

The United Democratic Front, launched in Cape Town in August 1983, was brought into being as a broad front of organisations willing to work together to end apartheid, to unban banned organisations, to support the release of all political prisoners, and to achieve a negotiated political settlement in South Africa. It served as the internal arm of the ANC which was banned and forced into exile. The founding conference was attended by 575 organisations.[745]

Police harassment of UDF officials and activists and interference in their activities was a matter of course. UDF informational pamphlets and other publications (*UDF News and UDF Declaration*) were confiscated by police even though they had not been declared undesirable. They were eventually handed back after the UDF took legal advice. A later booklet providing legal advice about detention was banned in November 1983.[746] Not all of the UDF campaigns were successful as they did not capture the imagination of the people. For example, in January 1984, the UDF planned a one million signature campaign rejecting the new constitution, demanding a non-racial democratic country, and demanding the release of all political prisoners. The campaign did not elicit the desired response and by late October had only obtained about 400,000 signatures. Later the organisers claimed that the target of one million signatures was a symbolic figure.

In the months leading up to the tricameral parliamentary elections in 1984, the UDF mounted a successful and brazen effort to cause the failure of the elections by ensuring an insignificant turnout. Many rallies were held and a number of joint efforts were made to urge the boycott of the elections. On the eve of the elections, 14 leading figures in the UDF were detained. Six UDF leaders sought refuge in the British Consulate in Durban. In a three-month period, charges were dropped, detention orders were withdrawn and yet, when three of the leaders left the Consulate, they were immediately arrested. The three remaining leaders were also arrested and later charged with treason when they left the Consulate after 90 days.

In November 1984, the UDF resolved with their member organisations to call for a two-day stay-away. The police raided several offices and detained activists country-wide. The UDF then called for a "Black Christmas" – a boycott of White-owned stores – which resulted in many individuals being physically harmed when re-entering townships if they were found

---

[745] For a complete list of the participating organizations, see SAIRR, *1983 Survey*, pp. 68-69.
[746] Ibid., pp. 209-210.

with their Christmas shopping. Thus, some UDF members were also guilty of intimidating those who did not agree with them.

The UDF was involved in establishing new organisations such as the Huhudi Youth Organisation and the Vaal Residents' Organisation as mechanisms for further popular mobilisation. It campaigned with trade unions to assist political detainees and protested against various forms of repression around the country, including in the homelands. The UDF also launched a programme to organise supporters in the rural areas as its initial base was primarily urban.

However, several factors militated against the growth of the UDF. A number of pamphlets surfaced aimed at sowing discontent and slandering leaders of various organisations. This was manifestly the work of government agents, and intended to create disunity and suspicion. Some homeland leaders were wary of the UDF. It was banned in the Transkei and its leadership in the Ciskei was harassed. Relations between the UDF and Inkatha remained tense and frequent clashes occurred in various areas of KwaZulu Natal, as well as in the East and West Rand.

Initially, FOSATU was unwilling to join the UDF. Similarly, MWASA split along regional lines during a vote to affiliate to the UDF. Splits occurred in other organisations with regard to UDF affiliation, including the Muslim Judicial Council and the Islamic Council of South Africa. Many in the opposition movement were against the involvement of Whites in the UDF, the way the UDF organisational structures made decisions, and the heterogeneity of the UDF. Some unionists argued that the class struggle would be eroded in joining with the multi-class UDF. The Cape Action League was one such organisation. Racial tensions occurred within the UDF at time, for example, when Archie Gumede, UDF president, said in an interview that Indians thought "in terms of pecuniary gain" and did not "appreciate the value of concepts such as democracy".[747] Class tensions also emerged, for example when the Cape Western Youth League and the Cape Action League said that because the UDF was organised across classes it could not adequately defend the interests of the working class. The UDF did not gain as much trade union support as it had hoped due to union fears that UDF structures would not sufficiently reflect the strength of the union movement and concerns that not all UDF affiliates were adequately accountable to their constituencies through democratic processes. Such issues were never completely resolved, but the overarching aims of the UDF were compelling enough to hold the front together in the face of many challenges from various quarters.

By 1985, the UDF claimed to have 650 affiliates and 2.5 million members. The movement rejected any suggestion by government of a fourth chamber of parliament for Africans. They also rejected the proposition that a national convention of leaders of all political groupings should be held to negotiate the political future of the country. They insisted, in the words of Murphy Morobe, that "any negotiation must be a product of a democratic process which involves the masses" and that "a climate favourable to mass participation needs to be created". The UDF also insisted that any political solution should include provision for the redistribution of wealth and conditions of equality in all spheres of life.[748]

The UDF's first annual conference, held in April 1985, had the theme of "From Protest to Challenge...Mobilisation to Organisation". This reflected its acknowledgement of the need to increase the "effectiveness and democratic content" of the UDF itself, as well as the urgency of nurturing more quality leaders and activists to maintain the struggle's momentum. The conference also called for an end to forced removals, the dissolution of the homelands and the end of the migrant labour system, the scrapping of the tricameral parliament and all

---

[747] Ibid., p. 61.
[748] Cited in SAIRR, *1985 Survey*, p. 39.

bodies created under the Black Local Authorities Act of 1982, the establishment of a unified and democratic educational system, the repeal of the pass laws and all other restrictions on freedom of movement. They also called for the right of workers to organise freely in trade unions, to bargain collectively and to strike without being penalised. They insisted on security of employment, housing, social welfare, pensions and maternity benefits. The UDF also demanded the release of all political prisoners, the lifting of bans on individuals and organisations, the return of exiles, and the lifting of all restrictions on freedom of speech and assembly. Finally, they said the SADF (army) and SAP (police) should be disbanded along with all other repressive state apparatus, and insisted that all security laws be scrapped.[749]

Also in 1985, UDF affiliates participated in various consumer boycotts around the country to reinforce its demands. They also held several meetings to celebrate the 30th anniversary of the Freedom Charter. In May 1985, 16 UDF leaders were detained and accused of being part of a "revolutionary alliance" to overthrow the government. Charges were withdrawn against 12 of them in December, and the other four stood trial. By August 1985, 45 of the 80 executive members of the UDF (national and regional) were either in detention, awaiting trial or had been assassinated. During the whole year, at least 136 UDF activists were detained. This government repression continued unabated for the next five years.

The cause of unity in the anti-apartheid struggle was not served by the violence that occurred between members of the UDF and AZAPO and the UDF/ANC and Inkatha. Violence also stemmed from conflict within each of these organisations. Whilst truces did occur, for example in response to the declaration of the second state of emergency on 12 June 1986, they did not last long. Violence erupted between competing affiliates representing particular constituencies, such as youth organisations: e.g. the Soweto Students' Congress (SOSCO), a UDF affiliate, and AZASM, an AZAPO affiliate. In KwaZulu and Natal, the rivalry between the UDF and Inkatha became more and more intense and violent. The war of words between the ANC in exile and Buthelezi continued, and many deaths on both sides occurred. Meetings of UDF affiliates such as the NECC were attacked by Inkatha *impis* (armed warriors) and many delegates were injured. These rivalries were exploited and fanned by the government security forces, as became very clear in testimony at the Truth and Reconciliation Commission. They were also exploited by vigilantes and criminal gangs in various communities, who settled personal scores through violence claiming to be motivated by "legitimate" political concerns. In addition, the state security apparatus was responsible for many assassinations of members of the ANC in exile, as well as members of other opposition groups inside and outside the country.

When the ANC was unbanned, the UDF was dissolved. The lessons from the organisation and campaigns of the UDF are obvious:
1. Clear overarching goals have to be set.
2. Organisations have to solicit support for their goals.
3. A simple structure has to be established.
4. A cohesive determined leadership must exist.
5. Foreign and local funds must support their efforts.
6. Brazenly challenging tactics have to be engaged in.
7. The overall goal should always be used to unite organisations.
8. Leadership has to be willing to accept the consequences of their actions.
9. Divisive tactics will be employed by the opposition.
10. Not all organisations, even if they respect its goals and sentiments, will join.
11. Violence, intimidation and coercion should be avoided.
12. Youth and other volatile personalities and groups have to be held in check.
13. The cause should not be tarnished by scandal.
14. When goals set are not achieved, a pragmatic retreat may be desirable.

---

[749] Ibid., p. 40.

15. Foreign support, especially at the grassroots level in other countries, is essential and supportive actions (sit-ins, demonstrations, interviews) help to popularise the cause.

Civic associations

The form of community organisation known as civic associations or civics first emerged in South Africa during the Soweto conflicts in 1976. Monty Narsoo[750] provided this definition:

"Civics are usually located within a specific geographical area; they represent a wide variety of interests -- business, workers, informal traders, residents, tenants, the homeless, squatters, different political movements, etc. By and large, civic structures were created to mobilise their constituencies behind specific demands, usually made to state authorities and business. They seek to press these through negotiations with these actors on policy, boycotts and other mass action activities to achieve demands, and by informing communities of developments."

Thozamile Botha[751] described them further:

"A civic association is not only a collection of individuals; it also has within its fold (and liaises with) professional bodies, traders' associations, cultural clubs, schools, hospitals, clinics and old age homes. Furthermore, it liaises with trade unions and parent/teacher/student associations on major campaigns for their localities. Although these sectoral associations are not structurally accountable to civic associations, they are expected to consult with them on public projects. Similarly, where an initiative is taken by civic associations, they have to consult with specific interest groups before major decisions are taken."

During the election of township community councillors in 1976 a boycott of these elections was called by many organisations, religious groups and others. In Soweto, the campaign against the elections and the subsequent resignation of certain councillors led to a meeting convened by the Black Lawyers' Convention. The meeting was held on 26 June 1977 at the offices of The World newspaper, chaired by its editor, Percy Qoboza. It was attended by nearly 60 Soweto leaders. They agreed to the establishment of a properly representative civic organisation reflecting popular aspirations of the residents. The meeting elected a Committee of Ten which in later months and years became the voice of the people in Soweto.

The Committee of Ten drew up a blueprint for Soweto's municipal autonomy and viability. It argued for freehold land tenure, expansion of retail and industrial activity, and the creation of a viable rates base. Whilst the model itself was one which could fit in with the apartheid government's plans and philosophy, the government reacted in a hostile fashion. It banned meetings and rallies of the Committee and imprisoned its leaders. When, after their release, the individual members of the Committee were called upon by the apartheid government to participate in various advisory committees or meetings, they steadfastly refused on the basis of the BC non-collaborationist stance.

In June 1979, a residents' association in Zwide township was launched. Within months, an umbrella body called the Port Elizabeth Black Civic Organisation (PEBCO) was formed. Rent boycotts followed. When the PEBCO leader, Thozamile Botha, was fired by Ford Motor Company, two weeks of strikes and rallies demanding his reinstatement followed. Botha was detained and banned and subsequently fled into exile. In 1982, PEBCO and other

[750] Narsoo, 1993, p. 15.
[751] Botha, 1992, pp. 58-59.

community organisations in Port Elizabeth were heavily involved in protests against rent increases, the housing shortage, and bus fare increases.

First steps to build the Soweto Civic Association (which evolved from the Committee of Ten) occurred in September 1979. By 1980, it had established 33 branches and was spearheading an effective rent and rates boycott. By 1982, the local council elections had also been successfully scuppered. However, a new tension emerged between members of the Committee. One faction promoted the cause of Black capitalism and its survival, whilst the other espoused socialism. Nonetheless, many townships across the country modelled themselves on the Soweto example and began to establish civic associations.

Civic associations were key players in the resistance movement advocating mainly the Charterist position.[752] As such, their strategic thrust was to seize power from the apartheid government and its structures at local level. "A central element of this strategy was the need to delegitimise the state at all levels, to undermine state attempts to either co-opt or win kudos from the disenfranchised through limited political reform and patronage". The strategy aimed "to make the townships ungovernable" and to establish "alternative organs of people's power". [753]

This strategy was implemented on a number of fronts. Civics mobilised people against the state. They attempted to force the resignation of Black local government councillors as a means of forcing the collapse of illegitimate Black Local Authorities. They challenged the laws which underpinned the apartheid system such as those which separated Black townships from White municipalities. They "champion[ed] their constituencies' needs", using tactics such as rent boycotts which denied the Black Local Authorities their main source of income and led to their financial collapse, as well as consumer boycotts of White businesses to persuade White owners to distance themselves from apartheid policies. As part of the democratic movement, civics allied themselves with the trade unions' struggle on behalf of workers, for example by supporting strike actions. They also articulated the political programme of the United Democratic Front (UDF) and the ANC.

In 1992, civics formed the South African National Civic Organisation (SANCO) to co-ordinate and represent civic associations at the national level. Whilst SANCO claimed to be non-partisan, its office-bearers and branches often publicly and privately reflected the views of the ANC. SANCO also acted as a gatekeeper in many communities: SANCO approval and participation was deemed to be vital for any local or national development project. The organisation threw its weight behind the Tripartite Alliance (of the ANC, SACP and COSATU) in November 1993, and was informally co-opted into the Alliance. SANCO was also represented on several forums and a range of development discussion groups in the pre-1994 period.

SANCO's linkage to a specific political organisation (the ANC) raised difficult questions for the civic movement regarding the roles which civics could or should play in a post-transition civil society. By the early 1990s when the political transition began, civics had crippled the running of the townships in some parts of the country. However, as with other CSOs, their resistance roles and the structures and skills they had developed were not necessarily compatible with the new roles they were expected to play in the transformation. Moving from a resistance strategy to one of engagement, with all its complexities, was far from simple.

The work needed to achieve local development is more mundane, lower profile, and aimed at achieving incremental on-the-ground progress through negotiation, facilitation and even tender processes, rather than making dramatic political points. In the new democratic

---

[752] Charterist refers to the espousal of the Freedom Charter and its principles.
[753] Narsoo, 1993, p. 2.

dispensation, community organisations need to advocate with their communities and share skills with them rather than always trying to be out in front.

Post-1994, civics had to face questions such as should they operate independently of political organisations and serve as the "popular" voice of civil society in development? Or, should they maintain their alliance with the ANC in order to enjoy influence in civil society and in the new democratic government?

Further, the lack of capacity on the part of the leadership to discipline and control their members is manifested by the fact that many of the inner city areas were beginning to collapse due to the rent boycotts, culture of non-payment, and lack of respect for authority of landlords, police, the courts, etc. This collapse in turn led many to flee these areas to 'greener' suburbs. Lack of revenue from the inner cities has negatively impacted on their budgets thus making it difficult for local authorities to implement much-needed maintenance of essential services and infrastructure. As a result, national government had had to step in to provide large amounts of grant funding to cover many of these costs.

The option of "recognising the importance of autonomous and vigorous grassroots organisations within civil society" and of giving civil society an effective voice in development[754] would require major changes in the way civics were managed and how they related to communities and stakeholders. Narsoo rightly cited the negative impact that politically aligned projects in communities had in terms of creating conflict and even violence. He noted that development resources always have the potential to be used as a political weapon, and therefore development in general is a political terrain contested by competing interests. In a democracy, those interests would include both pro-transformation as well as the formerly predominant ones. Even within the anti-apartheid movement, the pre-transition unity of purpose was likely to unravel (as it has in fact) when its various role-players began to compete amongst themselves for power and influence in development. Post-1994, civics largely failed to position themselves to mediate such interests and play a constructive role in democratic development processes.

Narsoo[755] explained why civics faced problems in recasting the role of the civic movement after the political transition. He wrote particularly about the difference between skills required for mobilisation during the period of resistance and the organisational skills needed for reconstruction and development. Because the civics had a comparative advantage in mobilisation, Narsoo suggested that they should play a "programme" rather than a "project" role. They could "lobby, pressure, negotiate and form alliances to press for the programmes they want, and then, with other interests and institutions, state and private, monitor the implementation of those which are agreed". However, this proposal did not take into account the other skills (e.g. facilitation, management, etc.) needed even for a programme role. Other types of CSOs turned out to be better equipped to play such roles.

Three key reasons explain the civics' decline:
1. Civics mainly operated in the townships and did not seek support from other sections of local government. When, in terms of local government restructuring, White towns were merged with Black townships, civics lost their captive support.
2. An ongoing tension arose between the South African National Civic Organisation, as a key part of the ANC's political alliance at the national level, and the attempt by some civics to become more non-partisan or politically non-aligned at the local level. The alliance issue also played out at the local level in terms of rivalries between civics and local ANC branches for control of local agendas and power. This was clearly manifested in the local government elections in 1995/6. SANCO members

---

[754] Ibid., p. 4.
[755] Ibid., pp. 17-18

often embarrassed the ANC during these elections when they attempted to dislodge and stand against ANC-nominated candidates. Only strong, national level intervention dissuaded many of these aspiring leaders from drawing votes away from the ANC.

3. A related tension existed between the civics, which had been in some cases essentially in control of the townships in the absence of any legitimate local authorities, and the emergence of legitimate, democratically-elected local government structures. Whilst SANCO played a central role in the negotiated reform of local government during 1992-93, and contributed to debates about financing development,[756] its profile has declined sharply since 1994.

Seekings cited several other reasons for the civics' decline:[757]

- **Institutional environment:** Since local government elections took place in 1995/6, "many of the representative roles performed by civics at the local level hitherto have been ceded to political parties and elected councillors".

- **Popular discontent:** Interests in Black communities became more diversified and it was therefore "more difficult for a single organisation to provide collective representation for the whole 'community'". Also, the types of grievances changed, and civics were less well-equipped or positioned to deal with them.

- **Strategies and tactics:** The earlier struggle tactics of resistance were no longer appropriate or effective in a democratic context. Also, some civic leaders were increasingly perceived as self-serving, thus alienating ordinary people. Civics' coercive tactics were received poorly in communities which had gained alternative mechanisms for making their voices heard.[758]

- **Resources:** Civics had declining access to both financing and experienced leadership. In this, they were victims of the same trends which faced CSOs as a whole. But they also failed to develop the necessary expertise to make useful inputs on a regular basis to key local development issues.

A number of other reasons can be added to this list, such as poor organisation, leadership struggles, a Gauteng urban leadership bias, and financial impropriety. Overall, the "civic movement has become fragmented, and lacks coherence and a sense of direction and purpose".[759] The future role of the civics in civil society is therefore very much in question.

Informal settlements and their organisational voices

Urbanisation increased as the influx control legislation fell into disuse and was challenged regularly in the courts. Rural poverty increased as source of income disappeared. Land which rural people inhabited had been reduced progressively over the decades. Rural and homeland leaders, bought off by patronage, became the lackeys of the Pretoria government.

However, it is important to note the emergence of organisations located in the informal settlements to address special needs as rural people migrated to the cities in search of jobs. In moving to the urban areas, rural people first found support and accommodation with friends and relatives in urban homes and hostels. Later they moved into backyards and shanties or occupied domestic quarters in the suburbs, or cleaners' accommodation on rooftops in the inner cities. They also occupied areas on the dunes left by mine waste, dotted

---

[756] See SANCO, 1994.
[757] Ibid., pp. 1-2.
[758] Comment: Whilst this criticism might well be valid for civics, a fundamental of civil society advocacy work is to apply different strategies and methods in the appropriate situations. Boycotts, demonstrations, petitions, representations, meetings all have their specific roles for protagonists to apply as and when they desire.
[759] Seekings, 1997, pp. 4-5.

around the Witwatersrand. Then, more boldly and sometimes with support from urban organisations, they occupied land contiguous to existing Black settlements and industrial areas.

The poorest households, especially women and squatters, were largely left out of the development interventions of the male-dominated civics.[760] These under-represented groups found that in order to protect their interests and enhance the quality of their lives, they needed voices to alert others regarding their concerns. They initially formed loose associations which, especially in the 1980s and 1990s, became cohesive organisations with dues-paying members, structure, organisation and clear objectives.

Homeless People's Federation

Perhaps the best example was the Homeless People's Federation, initiated by an intervention of Catholic Welfare and Development (CWD)[761] which organised a conference of 150 informal settlement leaders plus Asian NGOs and CBOs at Broederstrom in March 1991. The conference was entitled "A People's Dialogue on Land and Shelter". About 50 of the leaders agreed to strengthen ties amongst their communities, and exchange visits took place to India to learn from their experience. In 1992, they created an NGO called People's Dialogue on Land and Shelter and also began to establish Housing Savings Schemes in their communities. Members of these schemes were mostly poor women in informal settlements, backyard shacks and hostels. People's Dialogue also continued to bring people from poor settlements together to share ideas and experiences and to encourage the homeless to develop informal settlements themselves by organising women in particular. "After three years of sustained community-level networking a point had been reached where a people's housing movement had rooted itself in the poor settlements in South Africa".[762] In 1994, these savings schemes were formalised in the SA Homeless People's Federation. The purpose of the Federation "was definitely not to put an organisation ahead of everyday process. Rather it was to signal to the formal world that homeless people had woken up and were now actively organising around their specific interests. It was also a signal to homeless people that there are an ever growing number of collectives in informal settlements that are ideal mechanisms for people-centred development".[763]

People's Dialogue and the Homeless People's Federation engaged with communities on the basis of three linked change processes: organisation for empowerment; community-based problem-solving; and learning to negotiate. Every area that had five or more savings schemes was permitted to set itself up as a federation and elect convenors to provide voluntary support. It was created as an autonomous organisation of the poor based on the principle that "democratic rights are often given best effect through conscious organisation and action based on the needs of a specific interest group". This conclusion was reached partly as a result of the experience of homeless groups in India who had decided to wait for their newly democratic government[764] to meet their needs, only to find that 40 years later this had not happened.[765] It is also significant to note that the concentration on women played a major role in empowering these women to play leadership roles in their communities as well as to manage the assets owned and controlled by their communities. Women were also better able to negotiate their relationships with traditional leaders and to speak for their

---

[760] Khan and Pieterse, 2004, p. 6. This study also provides analysis of the role of the Federation and its partners in the Homeless People's Alliance post-1994.
[761] CWD was a branch of the Southern African Catholic Bishop's Conference (SACBC).
[762] "Wat Ons Wil He!" The Story of the People's Dialogue Housing Policy Conference and the Launch of the SA Homeless People's Federation, 21-25 March 1994", www.utshani.org.za., p. 1.
[763] Ibid., p. 6.
[764] India gained its independence in 1947 and became the first Republic in the Commonwealth in 1950.
[765] Khan and Pieterse, 2004, p. 11.

communities in relation to outside stakeholders. By 2002, the Federation comprised a network of 1,100 savings schemes and 100,000 members, of whom 85% were women.[766]

This homeless people's movement thus varied dramatically from the civics movement in that it was totally independent of the ANC and other political parties. It also retained an emphasis on collective effort and a more loosely connected federal network of autonomous member groups, with a flat leadership structure as opposed to the unitary structure adopted by SANCO. Decision-making in the HPF was based on equal participation of all members whereas SANCO was governed more by elected committees with extensive powers.[767] The Homeless People's Federation focused exclusively on the poor in implementing its pro-poor agenda, rather than building political elites who became distanced from their communities as occurred in the civics.

Obstacles to organisation in informal settlements
Many other localised informal settlement groupings worked in concert or affiliation with some or other accepted urban organisation, including church organisations, the UDF or Inkatha, or even taxi associations. However, violent confrontations amongst these organisations or internal disputes and leadership battles often led to dissension. This weakened their support and rendered them ineffective. Sometimes these organisations were misled and used as cannon fodder for the hidden objectives of other groups purporting to represent urban settlements. They also became nesting grounds for crime, drug and hijacking syndicates. The fragility of their own insecurity forced organisations to turn a blind eye to these misdeeds.

The obstacles to effective participation and organisation within these communities have continued to flourish despite a new political era. The gross power imbalances established or entrenched by apartheid have not been significantly challenged or changed. The key obstacles faced by these communities all relate to power and the relationships that lack of such power creates. These obstacles are obvious:

- *Location*: relating to economic circumstances;
- *Attitude*: relating to the absence of a sense of personal worth;
- *Resources*: relating to their lack of participation in processes;
- *Organisation*: relating to the inability to build and sustain structures.

Social movements in deprived and disempowered communities have continued to emerge as the people maintain their struggle for access to economic and political power / resources. Individuals seeking personal gain have continued to act as gatekeepers and to sow division in communities. Organised, coherent and independent voices may diminish under the force of new elites unless democratic processes, leadership and decentralised local organisations are enhanced.

Concluding Remarks

This chapter has shown how, in addition to individual civil society organisations, the 20th century saw the creation of social movements comprising both informal and formal groups. Throughout this volume, the role of mass mobilisation has been highlighted as a means by which people searched for dignity and expressed their demands. The six social movements described in this chapter were each shaped by their economic, social, political and technological environments as well as by history, ideology and institutions.

---

[766] Ibid., p. 13.
[767] Ibid., pp. 15-16.

Localised rural community actions emerged in resistance to apartheid policies such as influx control, forced removals, restrictions on land and cattle ownership, and oppressive taxes. These government measures combined with the economic forces of industrialisation tore at the hearts of rural communities, promoting labour migration and with it the destruction of family and traditional lifestyles. Whilst clan-based organisations formed by migrant workers in urban areas provided some access for rural dwellers to information and politicisation, the lack of education, capacity and resources in rural areas proved to be a vital constraint, especially in the face of brutal government repression of any attempts to speak out. Patriarchal society and traditional leaders co-opted by the government also limited the ability of rural communities to protest. Women in some areas became so infuriated with the impact of policies that made it impossible to provide a living for their families whilst their husbands were in the cities that they mounted passive resistance but largely to no avail. Very few formal organisations emerged, links to urban-based groups were difficult, and government succeeded in regulating all aspects of rural life. Consequently, despite occasional limited resistance, a unified rural revolt was never possible.

The Inkatha movement began as a Zulu cultural organisation but was revived in 1970s by Dr. Mangosuthu Buthelezi with a view to making it a political force and a vehicle for his personal political ambitions. The Inkatha power base was primarily in KwaZulu but also included migrant Zulu workers in the Transvaal and the Free State. Buthelezi issued mixed messages about whether he advocated a unitary or federal state, changing his public positions regularly. Similarly, his relations with the ANC and the UDF fluctuated wildly back and forth, and he was unpopular with the BC groups. Inkatha was not subjected to the levels of government repression experienced by other anti-apartheid groups. By the 1980s, tensions between Inkatha and many elements of the anti-apartheid movement erupted into ongoing violence. Suspicions of government infiltration of Inkatha also increased conflict. Many thousands of people died as a result, and it was only in the early 1990s that Inkatha began to participate (however half-heartedly) in the peace processes (e.g. the National Peace Accord) and eventually, after much negotiation, in the first democratic elections and government in 1994. Inkatha's role in the anti-apartheid movement overall was therefore complex and fraught with inconsistencies.

The Black Consciousness Movement was singularly instrumental in encouraging Black people (including African, Indian, Coloured and other exploited and oppressed people under apartheid) to determine their own future and to solve their own problems. It countered negative stereotypes in the White media and fostered a positive self-image amongst Blacks. The BCM engaged in the labour movement as part of its efforts to counter economic oppression, and encouraged the formation of Black trade unions. It had a major influence on the youth and university students through SASO, NAYO and SASM. It also inspired Black clergy and academics to develop BC organisations. In doing so, it garnered support from certain segments of White civil society. However, further growth of the BCM was hampered by constant government repression, arrests and bannings. Nonetheless, like other sectors of civil society, when one BC organisation was banned, another was formed to replace it, e.g. AZAPO. Conflict between BC and other Black political ideologies diminished its influence and created divisions within the anti-apartheid movement as a whole. The BC movement was also not helped by European and American donors who were wary of the BC philosophy and more prone to fund ANC front organisations due to their overt non-racial stance. Despite all its challenges, the BCM continued to exert emotional power and played out in all aspects of life, becoming a broader social philosophy owned by the wider community. It continues to influence many individuals and organisations in the socio-political sphere.

Both the BC movement and Inkatha spawned a wide range of affiliated cultural, social and economic organisations. This contrasted with the UDF which was formed as a broad front of mostly pre-existing anti-apartheid organisations, though the UDF did create some new groups to assist in the mobilisation of specific communities. The United Democratic Front had mixed success in its many specific campaigns against a wide range of apartheid policies and government actions, but it provided a hugely important vehicle for co-ordination of the anti-apartheid movement. White participants played key dominating roles in UDF formations and found a natural home in their structures as opposed to starting at the grassroots as required by BC organisations. The UDF was instrumental in nurturing many new leaders to maintain the momentum of the movement – as many leaders were detained, others emerged to take their place. It too faced serious challenges, including infiltration and disinformation by government agents and difficult relations with homeland leaders. Some UDF-affiliated organisations engaged in violent confrontations with other Black organisations as part of rivalries that were exploited by government. Not all civil society organistions opposed to apartheid were willing to join the UDF, and in some cases, the issue of UDF membership caused splits within organisations. Issues regarding the accountability of UDF affiliates to their own constituencies also arose. As a broad front, the UDF inevitably suffered from internal divisions, not the least of which ran along race and class lines. Whilst these issues persisted, the UDF managed to achieve an amazing degree of unity, laying the groundwork for the unbanning of the ANC, the release-of ·political prisoners, and the advent of democracy. Many UDF leaders have gone on to become major public figures in the new South Africa.

Civic associations emerged in the mid-1970s, as community leaders were inspired to challenge the apartheid state by mobilising residents in support of specific demands. They became a powerful force in established townships – almost an alternative local government – as the Black Local Authorities lost credibility and councillors resigned out of fear of retribution. Rent, rates and consumer boycotts led by civics severely undermined the ability of the state to control townships. Civics joined the UDF and supported the trade unions in their struggle for workers' rights. These struggles overlapped considerably as the workers were also residents of the townships and they had many interests in common. The formation of the SA National Civic Organisation (SANCO) was intended to give the civics movement a greater say in the political negotiations preceding the 1994 elections. However, through its support of the ANC, it was rapidly co-opted into the ANC Alliance with the SACP and COSATU. This political affiliation limited its roles in post-apartheid communities. The civics' politicisation of development processes and their ongoing attempts to control resource allocation in their communities made it impossible for them to play a constructive role in the new democratic local government institutions. Furthermore, their lack of support in other communities and amongst other races compromised their leverage when townships were merged into much broader municipalities. As organisations and as a movement, they have lost their direction and failed to carve out new and effective roles in a democratic society.

Somewhat ironically, in contrast, organisations based in informal settlements (as opposed to the civics in established townships) which emerged largely in the 1980s and 1990s have come to the fore in the post-apartheid era. These groups focused their activities on rural people who had recently moved to urban areas who constituted a different class from those township residents who had migrated many years before and formed part of the formal working and professional classes. The new migrants tended to live in shacks, domestic quarters or other undesirable vacant areas. They had no power and were victimised by local gatekeepers, used and abused by other groups claiming to represent them. As they began to create their own groups to defend their own particular interests, some of these evolved as democratically-governed grassroots organisations with a strong constituency and an effective voice. The Homeless Peoples' Federation is one such group. Many challenges remain for these organisations, especially in terms of the issues they take up, how realistic and viable their goals are, and the extent to which they manage to avoid the pitfalls of other grassroots groups – leaders distancing themselves from their constituencies' actual interests, leaders seeking personal profiles and economic gain, and very importantly, the extent to which the democratic government decides to address the needs of these poorest of the poor.

Conclusion

Interpreting the Evolution of Civil Society: Key Analytical Themes

"Our history has been a bitter one dominated by colonialism, racism, apartheid, sexism and repressive labour policies. The result is that poverty and degradation exist side by side with modern cities and a developed mining, industrial and commercial infrastructure. Our income distribution is racially distorted and ranks as one of the most unequal in the world -- lavish wealth and abject poverty characterise our society."[768]

Colonial occupation began a racial division of South Africa which ultimately manifested itself in the apartheid era when the National Party came to power in 1948. Before 1948, a number of barriers existed by custom or law which prevented Coloured, Indian and African people from free involvement in the political, social and economic life of the country. The implications of this have been clearly demonstrated.

Two key factors which emerged out of this colonial and apartheid history of separate development have been largely responsible for the manner in which civil society evolved in South Africa: race and class. Three other factors have also played a highly significant role: reliance on euro-centric models of non-profit organisations and their emphasis on welfare; the focus of traditional organisations on survival and community solidarity in coping with poverty; and the anti-apartheid struggle. These are factors which merit far more analytical attention than is possible in this volume. We are only able to deal with each of them briefly here.

Race

The concept of racial discrimination and segregation has figured throughout South African history and its impact has been seen since the 17th century, in society as a whole and in the evolution of civil society organisations.[769] It has divided communities and affected their relative economic, political and social power and influence, as well as their respective ability to address community development issues. It has led to extreme disadvantage and suffering for the South African peoples of colour -- a consequence which will take generations to be remedied. Not only was racial discrimination applied by successive governments as a means of maintaining political control and economic exploitation, but it also led to huge disparities in the availability of financial and human resources which could be put to use by communities through their civil society organisations. It has therefore accentuated their differential access to services such as education, health, and other aspects of human welfare.

The creation by the apartheid government of the African homelands (Bantustans) was a further diabolical attempt to rid themselves of responsibility for large sections of the poorer

---

[768] ANC, 1994, p. 2.
[769] The view that racial discrimination and segregation were institutionalised by the Afrikaner government after 1948 is patently untrue. This process began long before under British rule.

African population. The homelands also reinforced ethnic divisions. Forced removals affected many Black communities, causing major upheavals and disruptions to family and community life. Such policies also had long-term effects on the level of infrastructure and development in different parts of the country. Furthermore, by strengthening the hand of traditional leaders who did not always have the best interests of their people at heart, and giving opportunities to despots, the homelands further disadvantaged the African people and limited their ability to organise and develop their civil society. It also kept other minority communities out of the homelands, its civil services, its universities as well as the private sector. The lack of development in these areas – particularly rural ones -- can be directly attributed to the lack of space for civil society organisations to operate.

Overall, the poor quality of services available to Black communities today – under-skilled teachers, inadequate facilities, lack of water and hygiene, etc. -- are all a result of the apartheid system. Thus, the needs faced today are being dealt with by a mix of agencies and departments of the democratic government and by continuously under-resourced civil society organisations.

We have shown how, from the earliest colonial days, through the missionary churches, civil society was largely divided along racial lines. Each racial group formed organisations to serve their own people. Organisations formed and run by Whites were better resourced than those run by Blacks. It was only when the movement towards self-identification gained ground in the mid-20th century that more organisations began to emerge to bring racial groups together. Older racially-based groups began to serve the wider community. This is still a work in progress.

Debates regarding racialism, multi-racialism, non-racialism and anti-racialism were carried on throughout South African political and civil society organisations. Differences around the implications of these terms played out in welfare, youth, sports and other organisations, as well as in trade unions. Reflecting these tensions, on the 30th anniversary of the Freedom Charter, Neville Alexander of the Cape Action League wrote: "If in practice (and in theory) we believe that South Africa is inhabited by four races, we are still trapped in multi-racialism and thus in racialism. Non-racialism, meaning the denial of the existence of races, leads to anti-racism, which goes beyond it, because the term not only involves the denial of 'race', but also opposition to the capitalist structures for the perpetuation of which the ideology and theory of 'race' exist".[770] The challenge of present day South Africa is to overcome all of these "isms", to create a society in which race is no longer a factor in political ideology, economic opportunity, access to services, and so on. Rather, such a society would treat all citizens equally – in accordance with the South African Constitution. Many civil society organisations have been in the vanguard of achieving this.

Class

Class has been a factor in many aspects of South African life, between and within groups of people. Along with race, it has served to differentiate access to economic, political and social power. Racial discrimination resulted in people of colour being treated as second-class citizens who were used primarily as a source of cheap labour to benefit the Whites. This began with the subjugation and exploitation of indigenous peoples and the importation of slaves. White business reinforced class divisions through support for racialist policies such as job reservation and influx control. The apartheid system created a more complex hierarchy of classes through its racial categorisation of Whites, Indians, Coloureds and Africans. For many years this tactic of divide and rule served the apartheid government's

---

[770] Cited in SAIRR, *1985 Survey*, p. 13.

purposes in limiting the coherent, joint action of all the suppressed peoples in an effort to regain their rights.

Economically also, class divisions were apparent. This began with the appropriation of land from indigenous peoples, creating a class of farm tenants, workers and servants. It was further reinforced with the arrival of slaves and indentured workers. Whilst the British eventually freed the slaves, they did little if anything to improve the access of Blacks to economic advancement and social welfare. Many Afrikaners (e.g., Trekboers) felt forced to migrate further inland in order to escape the British colonial masters. Some Afrikaners were forced off the land altogether, becoming a class of 'poor whites' who were also exploited. As the country became more industrialised, the class divisions continued to play a role -- on the mines, in the factories, etc. Black and White workers were deprived of their rights, with Blacks consistently being paid lower wages, working under harsher conditions and having less protection from labour legislation. With economic and technological development, the class divisions between the employers and the employees grew, and income disparities between the 'haves' and the 'have-nots' multiplied. Political power became increasingly linked with economic power, and the franchise (or lack thereof) became a further tool of oppression.

Differential access to resources -- both public and private -- led to a proliferation of organisations and wastage of resources as organisations emerged in a fashion which duplicated structures and effort. It also led to a welfare-oriented and patronising mentality amongst those with access to wealth and power, aimed at maintaining the dependence of the disadvantaged. Where philanthropy or attempts at upliftment did occur, e.g. via religious organisations, there were either legislated or tacit limits placed on people of colour in terms of human rights, employment, accommodation and so on.

Class identity also played itself out in the early Black political organisations, with significant divisions between those representing the largely professional, Christian elite and those representing working class or rural people. The strategies and tactics adopted by these different groups – e.g. the conciliatory approach of the early ANC and APO versus the more radical activism of the ICU -- were generally a direct result of the education, experience and class of the respective leadership of those organisations. Later, divisions between the class interests of university students as opposed to trade unionists played out in evolving political strategies of the anti-apartheid movement.

Many CSOs emerged to represent the interests of particular economic classes. The most obvious are the business and professional organisations and the trade unions. These CSOs were either quite specific or more general in their aims, but their primary motivating factor was protecting their class or group interests. This approach continues in the current economic dispensation.

Colonialism and euro-centric models

The character of much of the non-profit sector -- especially its early emphasis on welfare – was a result of colonialism and White dominance. A tendency to adopt euro-centric, hierarchical models of civil society organisation, with top-down approaches to development and a "we-they" mentality, dictated the style and working methods of many welfare and service-oriented organisations. Much of this phenomenon also stemmed from the proselytising and conversion mission of the Christian churches which was part and parcel of the British colonial era.

The emergence of African independent churches was a direct reaction against the colonial mentality of the European-based mission churches. It represented a reaffirmation of African culture in the face of an onslaught to destroy traditional life and spirituality, and an attempt to combine what were regarded as the constructive aspects of European religion with the basic elements of Africanness. The independent churches also provided an avenue for African leadership and meaningful participation which was denied by the European religious hierarchies.

The impact of missionary education on the African elite was also hugely significant in the development of opposition to the colonial and then the apartheid governments. Whilst offering some opportunities for further education in South Africa and overseas, missionary education also instilled in some early African leaders a reluctance to be confrontational or radical in their efforts to protect the rights of their people. It could be argued that this delayed to some degree the development of an effective resistance movement.

In a different fashion, British colonialism and attempts at anglicisation led to the reactive formation of an extensive network of Afrikaner civil society organisations which were largely aimed at cultural preservation and cohesion, maintenance of a particular lifestyle, and resistance against control by colonialists. These organisations played and still play an important role.

Survival and solidarity: coping with poverty

Black (African, Coloured and Indian) communities' primary interest in creating civil society organisations was in providing for their basic survival (material and spiritual) and in maintaining solidarity and cohesion. They were faced on a daily basis with the need to cope with their poverty and other forms of deprivation imposed by the colonial and apartheid systems. Africans drew on their tradition of *ubuntu* to create community-based self-help initiatives. In areas such as District Six, residents drew on "the spirit of *kanala,* of looking out for one's neighbour, [which] ran deep in these communities".[771] Some argue that poverty, forced removals, and "the overall desperation induced by apartheid did not extinguish the humanity of the people in the township". The "ordinariness" of *ubuntu* and *kanala* and other deep-seated community norms of mutual support inspired community members to participate in local activities for the common good without need for recognition.[772] Because of political repression and controls, many traditional Black organisations maintained their more informal character in order to avoid the long tentacles of the state.

Afrikaner civil society organisations emerged in response to their need for solidarity initially against the perceived threat of the British, and later against the growing economic strength of the various Black communities. Their economic struggles in the early 20th century led to a variety of organisations aimed specifically at ensuring the economic protection and promotion of their own people, especially the impoverished.

Black community protest organisations focused primarily on tangible issues such as housing or food prices to mobilise support. However, their leadership often took it upon themselves to engage in the wider political issues, creating a less than democratic organisational environment and a failure to deliver on the tangible issues. This lack of accountability led to some of these leaders and organisations being discredited especially since 1994. Some, on the other hand, provided important experience in democratic decision-making. The conduct of democratic elections and the existence of legitimate government have also led the people to demand that their leaders demonstrate more accountability to the constituencies. Civil society organisations are now expected to operate in a quite different and democratic manner.

---

[771] Craig Soudien, in Willemse, ed., 2000, p. 25.
[772] Soudien cites the work of sociologist Elaine Salo in Manenberg as evidence. See Willemse, ed., 2000, p. 37.

The isolation which stemmed from marginalisation has also meant that Black communities have not had access to information and other resources which could benefit them. This is particularly true of rural communities where people have continued to rely on their traditional forms of organisation and leadership. Traditional leaders have protected their own power and interests by limiting the development of alternative organisations and/or the entry into their communities of outside groups. Communities were unable to assert themselves directly vis-a-vis outside authorities such as local government. This resulted in a dearth of development activity and of grassroots-based organisations. Those organisations that did emerge to advocate on rural poverty and land issues were largely urban-based. With a government now committed to public participation and democratic practice, as people in those rural areas are being informed of their new rights, more democratic and proactive organisations are emerging in rural areas.

The anti-apartheid struggle

The anti-apartheid struggle and the resulting resistance organisations were essential to the emergence of civil society as it appears now. Organisations which grew out of Black communities as part of the resistance played a major role in the social and political mobilisation of the majority Black population and served to augment their ability to organise themselves and to win back their rights. Other organisations were started by liberal Whites to assist in the struggle. Some were multi- or non-racial. The ideological and strategic positions taken by various organisations with regard to the struggle affected the level of support they received, their access to resources within and outside the country, and therefore, their ability to make an impact and to grow.

Apartheid and the growing struggle against it led many religious communities -- whether Christian, Muslim, Hindu, Jewish, etc. – to establish organisations which promoted their own communities' interests and protected those communities as best they could from the various forms of repression and control. In numerous cases, they were also a source of education and mobilisation, leading to the intensification of the struggle. They contributed significant leadership to the struggle and to post-apartheid government and civil society.

Some of the resistance roles played by CSOs, whilst appropriate and important at the time, have had long-lasting effects on community attitudes and behaviour which in the present context are not necessarily constructive. For example, the role played civics in promoting rent and service payment boycotts – whilst an effective political tool at the time – created a culture of non-payment and entitlement which now hinders development processes. It has, in turn, led to new civil society initiatives, e.g. democracy education and community development, which put more emphasis on rights **and** responsibilities.

The necessity for secrecy and subterfuge experienced by many organisations during the struggle so as to avoid government's repressive measures had some ongoing negative effects on the CSO community. These included inadequate and ineffective governance structures, a lack of internal and external accountability (to boards, members, constituencies, donors, etc.), and a reluctance in some cases to co-operate and share information with other organisations working in the same sector and/or geographical area. It will take some time before CSOs can progress completely beyond these unfortunate legacies.

The role of youth organisations in the struggle, especially in terms of protests in the schools and universities, was essential in giving momentum to the resistance movement and mobilising parents to engage as well. However, the unintended result of an inadequately educated and skilled labour force led directly to the need for new types of organisations in the post-apartheid era. Thus, South Africa has seen a proliferation of organisations dealing with adult basic education, life skills, vocational and small business skills, career guidance, and others related to job creation. In the present context, youth need to show more respect for the knowledge and experience of their elders. The courageous belligerence, impatience and 'instant gratification' of the past must be replaced by a willingness to work hard over the long term for the achievement of the rewards and satisfaction they desire.

The promotion within CSOs of all kinds of a culture of human and civil rights -- though perhaps viewed through different lenses -- emerged also through the years of conflict and struggle. This culture is reflected in the 1996 Constitution and in the considerable spirit of tolerance and reconciliation within the country post-1994. It is also reflected in the relative ease with which people of different races, classes and cultures have been able to work together in the new democratic South Africa. Again, this is a work in progress.

Multiple identities: fragmentation and cohesion

In conclusion, this study has shown how some civil society organisations reflect the fragmentation of society and others reflect social cohesion.

The history of many segments of civil society has been characterised by division and fragmentation rather than unity. These divides have occurred between and within races and classes – for example, the divides within a White identity, between English and Afrikaners; within the Indian community, between successful small businessmen and indentured labourers; within the Coloured community, between those who aspired to be welcomed into the Afrikaner community and those who wanted to strengthen a particular Coloured identity and to fight for Coloured rights on their own merits; and within the African community, between different ethnic groups or between those who achieved a certain level of education and economic prosperity versus those who continued to live in dire poverty. Such divides are a natural reflection of the broader society we live in – a heterogeneous society – but never again should they be a result of state-imposed legislative and policy discrimination and human rights violations.

This history has also shown that individuals have multiple identities and join a range of organisations to pursue those. For example, a township resident might be an amalgam of several identities – a Zulu liquor seller, businessman and property owner who is also a political organiser.[773] Each of these identities might involve membership in a civil society organisation: a Zulu cultural group, an African independent church, a liquor retailer's association, a small business organisation, a resident's association, and a political organisation. Another example is the author of the only major study of Black rugby, Abdurahman Booley, who was said to have served, by the age of 39, "at various times in more than twenty social, religious, sporting and cultural organisations".[774]

Such varied identities and memberships can allow for a great deal of cross-fertilisation of ideas and contacts across classes, races, professions, and so on. They also hugely enrich individual lives. They show how racial and class identities overlap with each other – even though under apartheid they were artificially separated. In democratic non-racial South Africa, these activities are amongst the best means of fostering a broad-based social cohesion with regard to generally accepted norms and standards of behaviour.

---

[773] Bozzoli, cited in Nauright, 1997, p. 16.
[774] See Preface to Booley, 1998.

REFERENCES

Adhikari, Mohamed, 2005, *Not White Enough, Not Black Enough: Racial Identity in the South African Coloured Community,* Cape Town, Double Storey Books, and Athens, Ohio University Press.

African National Congress (ANC), 1994, *The Reconstruction and Development Programme: A Policy Framework,* Johannesburg, Umanyano Publications.

Agherdien, Yusuf, Ambrose C. George, and Shaheed Hendricks, 1997, (edited by Roy H. du Pre), *South End: [As We Knew It],* Port Elizabeth, Western Research Group.

Alexander, Neville, 2002, *An Ordinary Country: Issues in the Transition from Apartheid to Democracy in South Africa,* Pietermaritzburg, University of Natal Press.

Alexander, Neville, 1994, "The National Forum", in Liebenberg et al., 1994, pp. 199-204.

Badat, Saleem, 1999, *Black Student Politics: Higher Education and Apartheid from SASO to SANSCO, 1968-1990,* Pretoria, Human Sciences Research Council.

Barnard, David, ed., 1998/9 and 2000, *Prodder, The South African Development Directory,* Johannesburg, Programme for Development Research (PRODDER), Human Sciences Research Council.

Barrett, Jane, Aneene Dawber, Barbara Klugman, Ingrid Obery, Jennifer Shindler, and Joanne Yawitch, 1985, *Vukani Makhosikazi: South African Women Speak,* London, Catholic Institute for International Relations.

Baskin, Jeremy, 1991, *Striking Back: A History of COSATU,* Johannesburg, Ravan Press.

Berger, Guy, 2000, "Publishing for the People: The Alternative Press, 1980-1999", in Evans and Seeber, eds., 2000, pp. 73-103.

Bhana, Surendra, 1997, *Gandhi's Legacy: The Natal Indian Congress, 1894-1994,* Pietermaritzburg, University of Natal Press.

Biko, Steve, 1978, *I Write What I Like (The Church as Seen by a Young Layman),* in A. Stubbs, ed., *I Write What I Like,* London, Bowerdean Press.

Bloch, Graeme, 1993, "Let's Have Some Action! Action for Change -- Revisiting Civil Society", *Work in Progress,* No. 89, June, pp. 24-25.

Booley, Abdurahman (Manie), 1998, *Forgotten Heroes: History of Black Rugby, 1882-1992,* Cape Town, Manie Booley Publications (sponsored by Independent Newspapers Holdings Ltd.).

Botha, Thozamile, 1992, "Civil Associations as Autonomous Organs of Grassroots' Participation", CPS Special Issue, *Theoria,* No. 79, May, pp. 57-74.

Bozzoli, Belinda, 2004, *Theatres of Struggle and the End of Apartheid,* Johannesburg, Wits University Press.

Bozzoli, Belinda, with Mmantho Nkotsoe, 1991, *Women of Phokeng: Consciousness, Life Strategy, and Migrancy in South Africa, 1900-1983,* Johannesburg, Ravan Press.

Bradlow, E., 1991, "The Oldest Charitable Society in South Africa: One Hundred Years and More of the Ladies' Benevolent Society at the Cape of Good Hope", *South African Historical Journal,* No. 25, November, pp. 77-104.

Brain, J.B., 1983, *Christian Indians in Natal, 1860-1911: An Historical and Statistical Study,* Cape Town, Oxford University Press.

Brookes, Edgar, and C. de B. Webb, 1965, *History of Natal,* University of Natal Press.

Bundy, Colin and William Beinart, 1980, "State Intervention and Rural Resistance", in Martin Klein (ed.), *Peasants in Africa,* California, Sage Publications.

Callinicos, Luli, 1987, *Working Life: Factories, Townships and Popular Culture on the Rand, 1886-1940, A People's History of South Africa, Vol. 2,* Johannesburg, Ravan Press.

Camay, Phiroshaw, and Anne J. Gordon, 2004, *Evolving Democratic Governance in South Africa,* Johannesburg, CORE.

Cameron, Trewhella, ed., 1987, *An Illustrated History of South Africa,* Johannesburg, Jonathan Ball Publishers.

Choonoo, A.G., 1967, "Indentured Indian Immigration into Natal", Unpublished MA Thesis, University of Natal.

Clarke, Bob, 1989, "Confronting the Crisis: Church-State Relations", in England and Paterson, 1989, pp. 130-158.

Cloete, Dick, 2000, "Alternative Publishing in South Africa in the 1970s and 1980s", in Evans and Seeber, eds., 2000, pp. 43-72.

Cobbett, William and Robin Cohen, eds., 1988, *Popular Struggles in South Africa,* Africa World Press and James Currey, for the *Review of African Political Economy.*

Cochrane, J.R., 1987, *Servants of Power: The Role of English-speaking Churches, 1903-1930. Towards a Critical Theology via an Historical Analysis of the Anglican and Methodist Churches,* Johannesburg, Ravan Press.

Cole, Josette, 1987, *Crossroads: The Politics of Reform and Repression, 1976-1986,* Johannesburg, Ravan Press.

Comaroff, John L., and Jean Comaroff, 1999, "Cultivation, Christianity and Colonialism: Towards a New African Genesis", in de Gruchy, ed., 1999, pp. 55-81.

Constitution of the Republic of South Africa 1996, No. 108 of 1996, Government Gazette, Cape Town, 18 December 1996.

Copelyn, J., 1975, *Mpondo Revolt,* Johannesburg, University of the Witwatersrand.

Davids, Achmat, 1985, *The History of the Tana Baru,* Cape Town, Committee for the Preservation of Tana Baru.

Davies, Rob, Dan O'Meara, and Sipho Dlamini, 1984, *The Struggle for South Africa: A Reference Guide to Movements, Organizations and Institutions,* Vols. One and Two, London, Zed Books Ltd.

de Gruchy, John W., ed., 1999, *The London Missionary Society in Southern Africa: Historical Essays in Celebration of the Bicentenary of the LMS in Southern Africa, 1799-1999,* Cape Town, David Philip.

de Gruchy, John W., 1995, "Settler Christianity", in Prozesky and de Gruchy, eds., pp. 28-44.

de Gruchy, John W., 1986a, *The Church Struggle in South Africa,* Cape Town, David Philip, and Grand Rapids, MI, Wm. B. Eerdmanns Publishing Co., and London, Wm. Collins & Sons.

de Gruchy, John W., 1986b, "The Church and the Struggle for South Africa", in Tlhagale and Mosala, eds., 1986.

de Kiewert, C.W., 1956, *The Anatomy of South African Misery,* London, Oxford University Press.

Dowson, Thomas A., 1995, "Hunter-Gatherers, Traders and Slaves: The Mfecane Impact on Bushmen, their Ritual and their Art", in Hamilton, ed., 1995, pp. 51-70.

Draper, Jonathan, and Gerry West, 1989, "Anglicans and Scripture in South Africa", in England and Paterson, eds., 1989, pp. 30-52.

Elbourne, Elizabeth, 1999, "Whose Gospel? Conflict in the LMS in the Early 1840s", in de Gruchy, ed., 1999, pp. 132-155.

England, Frank, 1989, "Tracing Southern African Anglicanism", in England and Paterson, eds., 1989, pp. 14-29.

England, Frank, and Torquil Paterson, eds., 1989, *Bounty in Bondage: The Anglican Church in Southern Africa, Essays in Honour of Edward King, Dean of Cape Town,* Johannesburg, Ravan Press.

Evans, Nicholas, and Monica Seeber, eds., 2000, *The Politics of Publishing in South Africa,* Scottsville, University of Natal Press, and London, Holger Ehling Publishing.

Everatt, David, Grace Rapholo, Hein Marais, and Sarah Davies, 1997, "Civil Society and Local Governance in the Johannesburg 'Mega-city'", study prepared by Community Agency for Society Enquiry (CASE), Johannesburg, for the United Nations Research Institute for Social Development (UNRISD), Geneva, November.

Everatt, David, and Elinor Sisulu, eds., 1992, *Black Youth in Crisis: Facing the Future,* Johannesburg, Ravan Press and the Joint Enrichment Project.

Feinstein, Charles, 2005, *An Economic History of South Africa: Conquest, Discrimination and Development,* Cambridge University Press.

Frankel, Philip, Noam Pines, and Mark Swilling, eds., 1988, *State, Resistance and Change in South Africa,* UK, Croom Helm.

Friedman, Steven, 1987, *Building Tomorrow Today: African Workers in Trade Unions, 1970-1985,* Johannesburg.

Freund, Bill, 1995, *Insiders and Outsiders: The Indian Working Class of Durban, 1910-1990,* Pietermaritzburg, University of Natal Press.

Gerhart, Gail M., 1979, *Black Power in South Africa: The Evolution of an Ideology,* Berkeley, Los Angeles and London, University of California Press, Perspectives on Southern Africa, No. 19.

Giliomee, H. and L. Schlemmer, eds., 1985, *Up Against the Fences: Poverty, Passes and Privilege in South Africa,* Cape Town, David Philip.

Goba, B., 1986, "The Use of Scripture in the Kairos Document", *Journal of Theology for Southern Africa,* No. 56, pp. 61-66.

Goba, B., 1988, *An Agenda for Black Theology,* Braamfontein, Skotaville.

Goedhals, Mandy, 1989, "From Paternalism to Partnership? The Church of the Province of Southern Africa and Mission 1848-1988", in England and Paterson, eds., 1989, pp. 104-129.

Gottschalk, Keith, 1994, "United Democratic Front, 1983-1991: Rise, Impact and Consequences", in Liebenberg, et al., 1994, pp. 187-198.

Gouws, Amanda, and Rhoda Kadalie, 1994, "Women in the Struggle: The Past and the Future", in Liebenberg et al., 1994, pp. 213-226.

Greenberg, Stanley, 1980, *Race & State in Capitalist Development: Comparative Perspectives,* New Haven and London, Yale University Press.

Guy, J.J., 1983, *The Heretic: A Study of the Life of John William Colenso, 1814-1883,* Johannesburg, Ravan Press.

Hamilton, Carolyn, ed., 1995, *The Mfecane Aftermath: Reconstructive Debates in Southern African History,* Johannesburg, University of Witwatersrand Press, and Scottsville, University of Natal Press.

Hammond-Tooke, David, 1993, *The Roots of Black South Africa: An Introduction to the Traditional Culture of the Black People of South Africa,* Johannesburg, Jonathan Ball Publishers.

Haron, Muhammed, 1997, *Muslims in South Africa: An Annotated Bibliography,* Grey Bibliography Series, No. 21, South African Library and Centre for Contemporary Islam, University of Cape Town, 1997.

Hassim, Shireen, 1991, "Gender, Social Location and Feminist Politics in South Africa", *Transformation,* Vol. 15.

Hastings, A., 1979, *A History of African Christianity 1950-1975,* Cambridge University Press.

Hellig, Jocelyn, 1995, "The Jewish Community in South Africa", in Prozesky and de Gruchy, eds., pp. 155-176.

Hellman, E., 1948, *Rooiyard: A Sociological Survey of an Urban Native Slumyard,* Cape Town, Oxford University Press.

Hendrie, D., A. Kooy, et al. (eds.), 1977, *Farm Labour in South Africa,* Cape Town, David Philip.

Hirson, B., 1976, *Rural Revolts in South Africa,* University of London.

Hlophe, Dumisani, Malachia Mathoho, and Maxine Reitzes, 2001, "The Business of Blackness: The Foundation of African Business and Consumer Services, Democracy and Donor Funding", *Research Report No. 83*, Johannesburg, Centre for Policy Studies, June.

Humphries, Richard, and Maxine Reitzes (eds.), 1995, *Civil Society after Apartheid*, Proceedings of a Conference convened by the Centre for Policy Studies on the role and status of civil society in post-apartheid South Africa, Johannesburg, Centre for Policy Studies, December.

Hyslop, Jonathan, 1988, "School Student Movements and State Education Policy, 1972-87", in Cobbett and Cohen, eds., pp. 183-209.

Joint Enrichment Project (JEP), 1993, *Directory of Youth Organisations in South Africa*, compiled by Mokheti Moshoeshoe, Johannesburg.

Kairos, 1986, *The Kairos Document*, 2nd ed., Johannesburg, Skotaville.

Karis, Thomas, and Gwendolen M. Carter, eds., 1972, *From Protest to Challenge, A Documentary History of African Politics in South Africa, 1882-1964*, Vol. 1, Protest and Hope, 1882-1934, Stanford, California, Hoover Institution Press, Stanford University.

Karis, Thomas, and Gwendolen M. Carter, eds., 1973, *From Protest to Challenge, A Documentary History of African Politics in South Africa, 1882-1964*, Vol. 2, Hope and Challenge, 1935-1952, Stanford, California, Hoover Institution Press, Stanford University.

Karis, Thomas, Gwendolen M. Carter, and Gail M. Gerhart, eds., 1977, *From Protest to Challenge, A Documentary History of African Politics in South Africa, 1882-1964*, Vol. 3, Challenge and Violence, 1953-1964, Stanford, California, Hoover Institution Press, Stanford University.

Karis, Thomas, Gwendolen M. Carter, and Gail M. Gerhart, eds., 1977, *From Protest to Challenge, A Documentary History of African Politics in South Africa, 1882-1964*, Vol. 4, Political Profiles, 1882-1964, Stanford, California, Hoover Institution Press, Stanford University.

Karis, Thomas and Gail M. Gerhart, 1997, *From Protest to Challenge, A Documentary History of African Politics in South Africa, 1882-1990*, Vol. 5, Nadir and Resistance, 1964-1979, Pretoria, UNISA Press.

Khan, Firoz and Edgar Pieterse, 2004, "The Homeless People's Alliance: Purposive Creation and Ambiguated Realities", School of Development Studies, University of KwaZulu-Natal, see www.ukzn.ac.za/ccs/.

Kiernan, Jim, 1995, "The African Independent Churches", in Prozesky and de Gruchy, eds., 1995, pp. 116-128.

Kinghorn, Johan, 1994, "The Churches against Apartheid", in Liebenberg, et al., 1994, pp. 149-153.

Kinsman, Margaret, 1995, "The Impact of Violence on Rolong Life, 1823-1836", in Hamilton, ed., 1995, pp. 363-394.

Kirsten, Marie, 1991, "A Quantitative Assessment of the Informal Sector", in E. Preston-Whyte and C. Rogerson, eds., *South Africa's Informal Economy,* Cape Town, Oxford University Press.

Kruger, D.W., 1969, *The Making of a Nation: A History of the Union of South Africa, 1910-1961,* Macmillan, Johannesburg.

Kuper, Hilda, 1960, *Indian People in South Africa,* Pietermaritzburg, Natal University Press.

Kuper, H. and S. Kaplan, 1944, "Voluntary Associations in an Urban Township", *African Studies,* 3, pp. 178-186.

Kynoch, Gary, 2005, *We Are Fighting the World: A History of the Marashea Gangs in South Africa, 1947-1999,* Scottsville, University of KwaZulu Natal Press, and Athens, Ohio University Press.

Lamola, John, 1986, "Debate on Violence", in Tlhagale and Mosala, 1986.

Last, M. and G.L. Chavunduka, eds., 1986, *The Professionalism of African Medicine,* Manchester University Press for International African Institute.

Lawrence, Patrick, 1976, *The Transkei,* Johannesburg, Ravan Press.

Liebenberg, Ian, and Fiona Lortan, 1994, "The Role of the Labour Movement in the Struggle for Liberation", in Liebenberg, et al., 1994, pp. 227-240.

Liebenberg, Ian, Fiona Lortan, Bobby Nel and Gert van der Westhuizen, eds., 1994, *The Long March: The Story of the Struggle for Liberation in South Africa,* Pretoria, HAUM.

Luckhardt, K. and B. Wall, 1980, *Organise or Starve... ,* London, Laurence & Wishart.

Ludlow, Helen, 1999, "'Working at the Heart': The London Missionary Society in Cape Town, 1819-1844", in de Gruchy, ed., 1999, pp. 99-119.

Maimela, S.S., 1991, "Religion and Culture: Blessings or Curses?", *Journal of Black Theology of South Africa,* Vol. 5, No. 1.

Maimela, S.S., 1987, *Proclaim Freedom to My People,* Braamfontein, Skotaville.

Mangena, M., 1989, *On Your Own: Evolution of Black Consciousness in South Africa/Azania.*

Maphai, Vincent, 1994, "The Role of Black Consciousness in the Liberation Struggle", in Liebenberg, et al., 1994, pp. 125-137.

Mathabatha, Ngoanamadima Johannes Sello, 2005, *The Struggle over Education in the Northern Transvaal: The Case of Catholic Mission Schools, 1948 to 1994,* Amsterdam, The Netherlands, Savusa-NiZa Student Publication Series, Rozenberg Publishers.

Maxwell, Patrick, Alleyn Diesel, and Thillay Naidoo, 1995, "Hinduism in South Africa", in Prozesky and de Gruchy, eds., 1995, pp. 177-202.

Mayende, Peter, "What Role Exists for Civil Society Formations in the Development Process?", in Humphries and Reitzes, eds., 1995, pp. 168-171.

Mayer, P. and I., 1974, *Townsman and Tribesman,* Cape Town, Oxford University Press.

McCaul, Colleen, 1988, "The Wild Card: Inkatha and Contemporary Black Politics", in Frankel, et al., 1988, pp. 146-174.

Meer, Fatima, et al., 1990, *Black Woman Worker: A Study in Patriarchy and Women Production Workers in South Africa,* Durban, Institute for Black Research.

Meer, Fatima, 1969, *Portrait of Indian South Africans,* Durban, Avon House.

Meyer, Rudolph, and Beyers Naude, 1994, "The Christian Institute of South Africa: A Short History of a Quest for Christian Liberation", in Liebenberg, et al., 1994, pp. 164-172.

Mkhatshwa, Smangaliso, 1994, "The Churches, Liberation and the Future", in Liebenberg, et al., 1994, pp. 154-163.

Mofokeng, T., 1988, "Black Christians, the Bible and Liberation", *Journal of Black Theology in South Africa,* Vol. 2, pp. 234-239.

Molema, M., 1920, *The Bantu Past and Present,* Edinburgh.

Moore, Basil (ed.), 1974, *The Challenge of Black Theology in South Africa,* Atlanta, John Knox Press.

Moosa, Ebrahim, 1995, "Islam in South Africa", in Prozesky and de Gruchy, eds., 1995, pp. 129-154.

Motlhabi, M., 1985, *The Theory and Practice of Black Resistance to Apartheid: A Social-Ethical Analysis,* Johannesburg, Skotaville.

Mpe, Phaswane, and Monica Seeber, 2000, "The Politics of Book Publishing in South Africa", in Evans and Seeber, eds., 2000, pp. 15-42.

Naidoo, Thillayvel, 1992, *The Arya Samaj Movement in South Africa,* Delhi, Motilal Banarsidass Publishers Private Limited.

Narsoo, Monty, 1991, "Civil Society: A Contested Terrain", *Work in Progress,* No. 76, pp. 24-27.

Narsoo, Monty, 1993, "Doing What Comes Naturally: A Development Role for the Civic Movement", Johannesburg, Centre for Policy Studies, *Policy: Issues and Actors,* Vol. 6, No. 2, June.

Nauright, John, 1997, *Sport, Cultures and Identities in South Africa,* Cape Town, David Philip, and London, Leicester University Press.

Ncube, D., 1985, *The Influence of Apartheid and Capitalism on the Development of Black Trade Unions in South Africa,* Johannesburg, Skotaville.

Nel, Bobby, 1994, "The Story of Black Theology of Liberation in South Africa", in Liebenberg, et al., 1994, pp. 138-148.

Nkondo, G.M., ed., 1976, *Turfloop Testimony: The Dilemma of a Black University in South Africa,* Johannesburg, Ravan Press.

Nzimande, Blade, 1995, "How Should Civil Society Formations Relate to Structures of Representative Government?", in Humphries and Reitzes, eds., 1995, pp. 105-110.

Oliphant, Andries, 2000, "From Colonialism to Democracy: Writers and Publishing in South Africa", in Evans and Seeber, eds., 2000, pp. 107-126.

Omer-Coopor, J.D., 1988, *History of Southern Africa,* Cape Town, David Philip.

Pachai, B., ed., 1979, *South African Indians,* Washington University Press of America.

Pato, Luke, 1989, "Becoming an African Church", in England and Paterson, 1989, pp. 159-176.

Pieterse, Edgar A., and Abdul Maliq Simone, eds., 1994, *Governance & Development: A Critical Analysis of Community Based Organisations in the Western Cape,* Cape Town, Foundation for Contemporary Research.

Pityana, B., M. Ramphele, M. Mpumlwana and L. Wilson, eds., 1991, *Bounds of Possibility: The Legacy of Steve Biko and Black Consciousness,* Cape Town, David Philip.

Polak, H.S.L., 1909, *Indians of South Africa,* Madras, G.A. Natesan.

Prozesky, Martin and John de Gruchy (eds.), 1995, *Living Faiths in South Africa,* Cape Town and Johannesburg, David Philip.

Ramphele, Mamphela, 1989, "On Being Anglican: The Pain and the Privilege", in England and Paterson, eds., 1989, pp. 177-190.

Raynard, J.H., 2002, *Dr. Abdurahman, A Biographical Memoir* (edited by Mohamed Adhikari), Cape Town, Friends of the National Library of South Africa and the District Six Museum, Voices of Black South Africans Series, No. 3.

Reitzes, Maxine, 1995, "How Should Civil Society Formations Relate to Structures of Representative Government?", in Humphries and Reitzes, eds., 1995, pp. 99-104.

Rogers, Mirabel, 1956, *The Black Sash: The Story of the South African Women's Defence of the Constitution League,* Johannesburg, Rotonews (Pty) Ltd.

Ross, Robert, 1999, "Congregations, Missionaries and the Grahamstown Schism of 1842-43", in de Gruchy, ed., 1999, pp. 120-131.

Saunders, Christopher, 1999, "Looking Back: 170 Years of Historical Writing on the LMS in South Africa", in de Gruchy, ed., 1999, pp. 7-16.

Saunders, Christopher, and Nicholas Southey, 1998, *A Dictionary of South African History,* Johannesburg and Cape Town, David Philip.

Schlemmer, Lawrence, 1967, "The Resettlement of Indian Communities in Durban and Some Economic, Social and Cultural Effects on the Indian Community", in South African Institute of Race Relations (SAIRR), *The Indian South African,* Papers presented at a conference of the SAIRR Natal Region, 14 October 1966, pp. 12-22.

Seekings, Jeremy, 1988, "Political Mobilisation in the Black Townships of the Transvaal", in Frankel, et al., 1988, pp. 197-228.

Seekings, Jeremy, 1993, *Heroes or Villains? Youth Politics in the 1980s,* Johannesburg, Ravan Press.

Seekings, Jeremy, 1997, "SANCO: Strategic Dilemmas in a Democratic South Africa", *Transformation,* Vol. 34, pp. 1-30.

Setilonae, G.M., 1986, *African Theology: An Introduction,* Johannesburg, Skotaville.

Shrire, B., 1993, "Women and Welfare: Early 20th Century Cape Town", *Jewish Affairs,* Vol. 48, No. 2, Winter, pp. 85-126.

Shubane, Kehla, and Pumla Madiba, 1994, "Civic Associations in the Transition", in Liebenberg, et al., 1994, pp. 241-259.

Sindane, Jabu, n.d., "Democracy in African Societies and Ubuntu", Pretoria, Centre for Constitutional Analysis, Human Sciences Research Council.

South African Council of Churches (SACC) and South African Catholic Bishops' Conference (SACBC), 1984, "Relocations: The Churches' Report on Forced Removals", Johannesburg, SACC and SACBC.

South African Friends of Beth Hatefutsoth, 2002, *Jewish Life in the South African Country Communities, Vol. I [Northern Great Escarpment, Lowveld, Northern Highveld, Bushveld],* Johannesburg.

South African Friends of Beth Hatefutsoth, 2004, *Jewish Life in the South African Country Communities, Vol. II [Boland, Bushmanland, Central Karoo, Fairest Cape, Griqualand West, Kalahari, Koup, Namaqualand, Swartland, West Coast],* Johannesburg.

South African Institute of Race Relations (SAIRR), various issues, *South Africa Survey [formerly Race Relations Survey],* Johannesburg.

South African National Civic Organisation (SANCO), 1994, *Making People-Driven Development Work,* Report of the Commission on Development Finance, 11 April.

Stephen, David, 1982, "The San of the Kalahari", London, Minority Rights Group.

Suggit, John, 1989, "Bishops: Legacy from the Past or Hope for the Future?" in England and Paterson, eds., 1989, pp. 75-103.

Swilling, Mark, and Bev Russell, 2002, *The Size and Scope of the Non-profit Sector in South Africa,* Graduate School of Public and Development Management, University of the Witwatersrand, and Centre for Civil Society, University of Natal, April.

Taylor, Stephen, 1994, *Shaka's Children: A History of the Zulu People,* London, Harper Collins Publishers.

Thompson, L.M. 1938, "Indian Immigration into Natal, 1860-1872", Unpublished MA Thesis, University of South Africa.

Tlhagale, B., and L. Mosala, eds., 1986, *Hammering Swords into Ploughshares,* Johannesburg, Skotaville.

Transvaal Rural Action Committee (TRAC), n.d., "The Myth of Voluntary Removals", TRAC, A Black Sash Project, Johannesburg.

van der Ross, R.E., 1979, *Myths and Attitudes: An Inside Look at the Coloured People,* Cape Town, Tafelberg Publishers.

van Loon, Louis, 1995, "Buddhism in South Africa", in Prozesky and de Gruchy, eds., 1995, pp. 209-216.

van Onselen, Charles, 1982, *Studies in the Social and Economic History of the Witwatersrand, 1886-1914, 1. New Babylon,* Johannesburg, Ravan Press.

van Onselen, Charles, 1982, *Studies in the Social and Economic History of the Witwatersrand, 1886-1914, 2. New Nineveh,* Johannesburg, Ravan Press.

Walker, Cheryl, 1991, *Women and Resistance in South Africa,* Cape Town, David Philip (first published 1982), London, Onyx Press.

Walker, Ivan L. and Ben Weinbren, 1961, *2000 Casualties,* Johannesburg, South African Trade Union Council.

Walshe, Peter, 1987, *The Rise of African Nationalism in South Africa,* Johannesburg, AD. Donker Publisher.

Webster, Eddie, 1988, "The Rise of Social-movement Unionism: The Two Faces of the Black Trade Union Movement in South Africa", in Frankel, et al., 1988, pp. 174-196.

Wells, J.C., 1993, *We Now Demand!,* Witwatersrand University Press, Johannesburg.

Wentzel, Jill, 1995, *The Liberal Slideaway,* Johannesburg, South African Institute of Race Relations.

Western, John, 1981, *Outcast Cape Town,* Cape Town, Human and Rousseau.

Willemse, Hein, ed., 2000, *More than Brothers: Peter Clarke and James Matthews at 70,* Cape Town, Kwela Books.

Wilson, M., and L.M. Thompson, 1969, *Oxford History of South Africa,* Oxford University Press.

Yawich, Joanne, 1977, "Natal 1959: The Women's Riots", *African Perspectives,* No. 5, pp. 1-16.

Yawitch, Joanne, 1980, 'Black Women in South Africa', *Africa Perspective,* Dissertation No. 2, Johannesburg, June.

ABBREVIATIONS

AAC	All Africa Convention
ABASA	Association of Black Accountants of South Africa
ABRESCA	Alliance of Black Reformed Christians in South Africa
ACHIB	African Council of Hawkers and Informal Business
AFCWU	African Food and Canning Workers' Union
AFRA	Association for Rural Advancement
AHI	Afrikaanse Handelsinstitut
AICA	African Independent Churches' Association
AMWU	African Mineworkers' Union
ANB	Afrikaanse Nationale Bond
ANC	African National Congress
ANCWL	ANC Women's League
ANCYL	ANC Youth League
APO	African Political Organisation (later changed to African Peoples' Organisation)
ARM	African Resistance Movement
ASA	African Students' Association
ASB	Afrikaanse Nationale Studentebond
ASSECA	Association for Educational and Cultural Advancement of Africans
ASSOCOM	Association of Chambers of Commerce
ASUSA	African Students' Association of South Africa
AWA	African Writers' Association
AZACTU	Azanian Confederation of Trade Unions
AZAPO	Azanian People's Organisation
AZASM	Azanian Students' Movement
AZASO	Azanian Students' Organisation
AYCO	Alexandra Youth Congress
BAWU	Black Allied Workers' Union
BCM	Black Consciousness Movement
BCP	Black Community Programmes
BCU	Black Consumer Union
BK	Belydende Kring
BLA	Black Lawyers' Association
BMC	Black Methodist Consultation
BMSC	Bantu Men's Social Centre
BPC	Black Peoples' Convention
BSSA	Bible Society of South Africa
BWF	Black Women's Federation
BWP	Black Workers' Project
CAHAC	Cape Housing Action Committee
CATA	Cape Teachers' Association
CAYCO	Cape Youth Congress
CBM	Consultative Business Movement
CBSIA	Colonial Born and Settler Indian Association
CCOBTU	Consultative Committee of Black Trade Unions
CI	Christian Institute
CIWW	Council of Industrial Workers of the Witwatersrand
CMA	Cape Malay Association
CNETU	Council of Non-European Trade Unions
CNVA	Cape Native Voters Association
COD	Congress of Democrats
CODESA	Convention for a Democratic South Africa
COI	Call of Islam
COM	Chamber of Mines
COP	Congress of the People
COSAG	Concerned South Africans Group
COSATU	Congress of South African Trade Unions
COSAS	Congress of South African Students
COSAW	Congress of South African Writers

CP	Conservative Party
CPNU	Coloured Peoples' National Union
CPSA	Church of the Province of South Africa
CSO	Civil society organisation
CSRU	City and Suburban Rugby Union
CTPA	Cape Teachers' Professional Association
CUSA	Council of Unions of South Africa
DDAFA	Durban and District African Football Association
DHAC	Durban Housing Action Committee
DLA	Democratic Lawyers' Association
DPSA	Disabled People of South Africa
DPSC	Detainees' Parents Support Committee
DRC	Dutch Reformed Church
DRCA	Dutch Reformed Church in Africa
DRMC	Dutch Reformed Mission Church
DTU	Democratic Teachers' Union
ECC	End Conscription Campaign
FABCOS	Foundation for African Business and Consumer Services
FAK	Federasie van Afrikaanse Kulturverenigings
FASA	Football Association of South Africa
FCI	Federated Chamber of Industries
FCWU	Food and Canning Workers Union
FEDSAW	Federation of South African Women
FEDTRAW	Federation of Transvaal Women
FIOSA	First International Organisation of South Africa
FOFATUSA	Federation of Free African Trade Unions of South Africa
FOSATU	Federation of South African Trade Unions
FRA	Federation of Civic Associations
GAWU	General and Allied Workers' Union
GRC	Grahamstown Rural Action Committee
GWCRFU	Griqualand West Colonial Rugby Football Union
GWU	General Workers' Union
HNP	Herstigte Nasionale Party (HNP)
HWA	Health Workers' Association
IAC	Industrial Aid Society
ICT	Institute for Contextual Theology
ICU	Industrial and Commercial Workers' Union
ICSA	Islamic Council of South Africa
IDAMASA	Interdenominational African Ministers' Association of South Africa
IEC	Indian Education Committee
IFP	Inkatha Freedom Party
IMA	Islamic Medical Association
IMDT	Independent Media Development Trust
ISRA	Islamic Relief Agency
ITASA	Indian Teachers' Association of South Africa
IYCC	Inter-denominational Youth Christian Club
JBFA	Johannesburg Bantu Football Association
JCWS	Johannesburg Child Welfare Society
JEP	Joint Enrichment Project
JISWA	Johannesburg Indian Social Welfare Association
JOCTASA	Joint Council of Teachers' Associations of South Africa
JRC	Johannesburg Relief Committee
LHR	Lawyers for Human Rights
LMS	London Missionary Society
LONASA	League of Nursing Associations of South Africa
LP	Labour Party
LRC	Legal Resources Centre
MASA	Medical Association of South Africa
MAWU	Metal and Allied Workers' Union
MAYO	Mamelodi Youth Congress

MDM	Mass Democratic Movement
MJC	Muslim Judicial Council
MYMSA	Muslim Youth Movement of South Africa
MSA	Muslim Students' Association
MSOA	Mine Surface Officials' Association
MWASA	Media Workers' Association of South Africa
NACTU	National Council of Trade Unions
NADEL	National Association of Democratic Lawyers
NAFBI	National African Federated Building Industry
NAFCOC	National African Federated Chamber of Commerce and Industry
NAFU	National African Farmers' Union
NAFTO	National African Federated Transport Organisation
NAMDA	National Medical and Dental Association
NAPTOSA	National Professional Teachers' Organisation of South Africa
NASASA	National Stokvels' Association of South Africa
NATA	Natal Teachers' Association
NATU	Natal African Teachers' Union
NAYO	National Youth Organisation
NB	Nationalist Bloc
NCAR	National Committee Against Removals
NCAW	National Council of African Women
NCWSA	National Council of Women of South Africa
NEA	Native Electoral Association
NECC	National Education Crisis Committee (later changed to National Education Co-ordinating Committee)
NEUM	Non-European Unity Movement
NEUSA	National Education Union of South Africa
NF	National Front
NG	Nationalist Group
NGK	Nederduitse Gereformeerde Kerk (Dutch Reformed Church)
NHK	Nederduitsch Hervormde Kerk
NIA	Natal Indian Association
NIC	Natal Indian Congress
NICRO	National Institute for Crime Prevention and the Rehabilitation of Offenders
NIVA	Natal Indian Vigilance Association
NLC	National Liberation Committee
NLL	National Liberation League
NP	National Party
NPO	Non-profit organisation
NPSL	National Professional Soccer League
NSL	National Soccer League
NTTUF	Northern Transvaal Teachers' Unity Forum
NUM	National Union of Mineworkers
NUSAS	National Union of South African Students
PAC	Pan Africanist Congress
PASO	Pan Africanist Students' Organisation
PBPSG	Permanent Black Priests' Solidarity Group
PEBCO	Port Elizabeth Black Civic Association
PENATA	Peninsula African Teachers' Association
PEYCO	Port Elizabeth Youth Congress
POLSTU	Political Students' Organisation
PROTECO	Progressive Teachers' Congress
PTSA	Parent – Teacher – Student Association
RMC	Release Mandela Committee
SAAFA	South African African Football Association
SAAWU	South African Allied Workers' Union
SAAYC	South African Association of Youth Clubs
SABA	South African Black Alliance
SABFA	South African Bantu Football Association
SABOA	South African Bus Owners' Association

SABTA	South African Black Taxi Association
SACBC	Southern African Catholic Bishops' Conference
SACC	South African Council of Churches
SACFA	South African Coloured Football Association
SACHED	South African Council for Higher Education
SACOB	South African Chamber of Business
SACOL	South African Confederation of Labour
SACOS	South African Council of Sport
SACP	South African Communist Party
SACPC	South African Coloured People's Congress
SACPO	South African Coloured People's Organisation
SACRFB	South African Coloured Rugby Football Board
SACTU	South African Congress of Trade Unions
SADTU	South African Democratic Teachers' Union
SADWA	South African Domestic Workers' Association
SADWU	South African Domestic Workers' Union
SAHSSO	South African Health and Social Services Organisation
SAIC	South African Indian Congress
SAIF	South African Industrial Federation
SAIFA	South African Indian Football Association
SAIRR	South African Institute of Race Relations
SAITA	South African Indian Teachers' Association
SAJBD	South African Jewish Board of Deputies
SALDTA	South African Long Distance Taxi Association
SAMSA	South African Medical Students' Association
SANA	South African Nursing Association
SANCO	South African National Civic Organisation
SANNC	South African Native National Congress
SANROC	South African Non-Racial Olympic Committee
SANSCO	South African National Students' Congress
SANZAF	South African National Zakaat Fund
SARA	South African Rugby Association
SARB	South African Rugby Board
SARF	South African Rugby Federation
SARFB	South African Rugby Football Board
SARFF	South African Rugby Football Federation
SARFU	South African Rugby Football Union
SARU	South African Rugby Union
SASA	South African Sports Association
SASCO	South African Students' Congress
SASF	South African Soccer Federation
SASJ	South African Society of Journalists
SASM	South African Students' Movement
SASO	South African Students' Organisation
SASPU	South African Students' Press Union
SATA	South African Teachers' Association
SATUC	South African Trade Union Council
SAYCO	South African Youth Congress
SCA	Soweto Civic Association
SCA	Students' Christian Association
SCCI	Soweto Chamber of Commerce and Industry
SEYO	Sekhukhuneland Youth Organisation
SOSCO	Soweto Students' Congress
SOYA	Society of Young Africa
SOYCO	Soweto Youth Congress
SPCC	Soweto Parents' Crisis Committee
SPOBA	St. Peter's Old Boys Association
SPP	Surplus People Project
SRC	Students' Representative Council
STCC	Southern Transvaal Chamber of Commerce

STEYCO	Steelport Youth Congress
TASC	Transvaal Anti-SAIC Committee
TIC	Transvaal Indian Congress
TIYC	Transvaal Indian Youth Congress
TLC	Trades and Labour Council
TLSA	Teachers' League of South Africa
TRAC	Transvaal Rural Action Committee
TRAYO	Transvaal Youth Organisation
TTA	Transvaal Teachers' Association
TUACC	Trade Union Advisory and Co-ordinating Council
TUCSA	Trade Union Council of South Africa
UBJ	Union of Black Journalists
UCM	United Christian Movement
UDF	United Democratic Front
UO	Unemployed Organisation
USTOA	United Soweto Taxi Owners' Association
UTASA	Union of Teachers' Associations of South Africa
UTP	Urban Training Project
UWUSA	United Workers Union of South Africa
WASA	Writers' Association of South Africa
WCTU	Women's Christian Temperence Union
WDNFA	Witwatersrand District Native Football Association
WEAU	Women's Enfranchisement Association of the Union
WEL	Women's Enfranchisement League
WLSC	Women's Legal Status Committee
WLVA	Witwatersrand Licensed Victuallers' Association
WPCRU	Western Province Coloured Rugby Union
WPCN	Women for Peaceful Change Now
WPGWU	Western Province General Workers' Union
WPWAB	Western Province Workers' Advice Bureau
YCS	Young Christian Students
YCW	Young Christian Workers
YMCA	Young Men's Christian Association
YWCA	Young Women's Christian Association
ZCC	Zion Christian Church